M… Girls

5

by Nami Akimoto

TOKYOPOP®

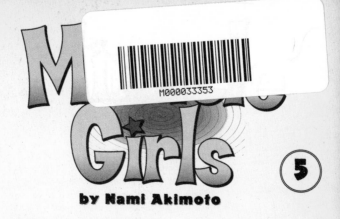

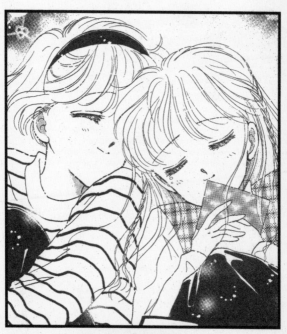

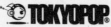

TOKYOPOP® Presents
Miracle Girls 5 by Nami Akimoto
TOKYOPOP® is a registered trademark and
TOKYOPOP® Manga is a trademark of Mixx Entertainment, Inc.
ISBN: 1-892213-83-4
First Printing July 2002

10   9   8   7   6   5   4   3   2   1

Translator - Ray Yoshimoto
Retouch Artists - Pat Rungratanasunthorn and Gary Shun
Cover Design - Rod Sampson
Graphic Designer - Anna Kernbaum
Senior Editor -Julie Taylor
Production Manager - Joaquin Reyes
Art Director - Matt Alford
VP of Production - Ron Klamert
Publisher - Stu Levy

Email: editor@Press.TOKYOPOP.com
Come visit us at www.TOKYOPOP.com.

TOKYOPOP®
Los Angeles - Tokyo

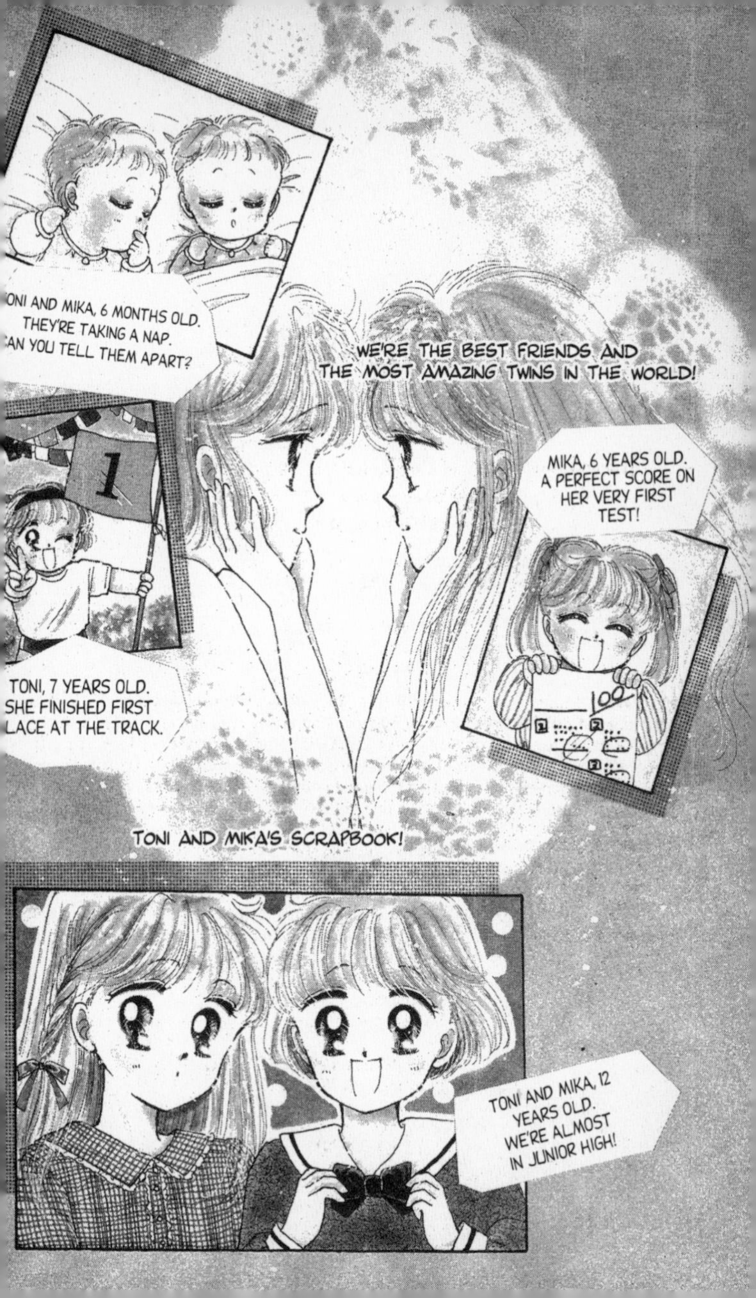
ONI AND MIKA, 6 MONTHS OLD. THEY'RE TAKING A NAP. AN YOU TELL THEM APART?
WE'RE THE BEST FRIENDS AND THE MOST AMAZING TWINS IN THE WORLD!
TONI, 7 YEARS OLD. SHE FINISHED FIRST LACE AT THE TRACK.
MIKA, 6 YEARS OLD. A PERFECT SCORE ON HER VERY FIRST TEST!
100
TONI AND MIKA'S SCRAPBOOK!
TONI AND MIKA, 12 YEARS OLD. WE'RE ALMOST IN JUNIOR HIGH!

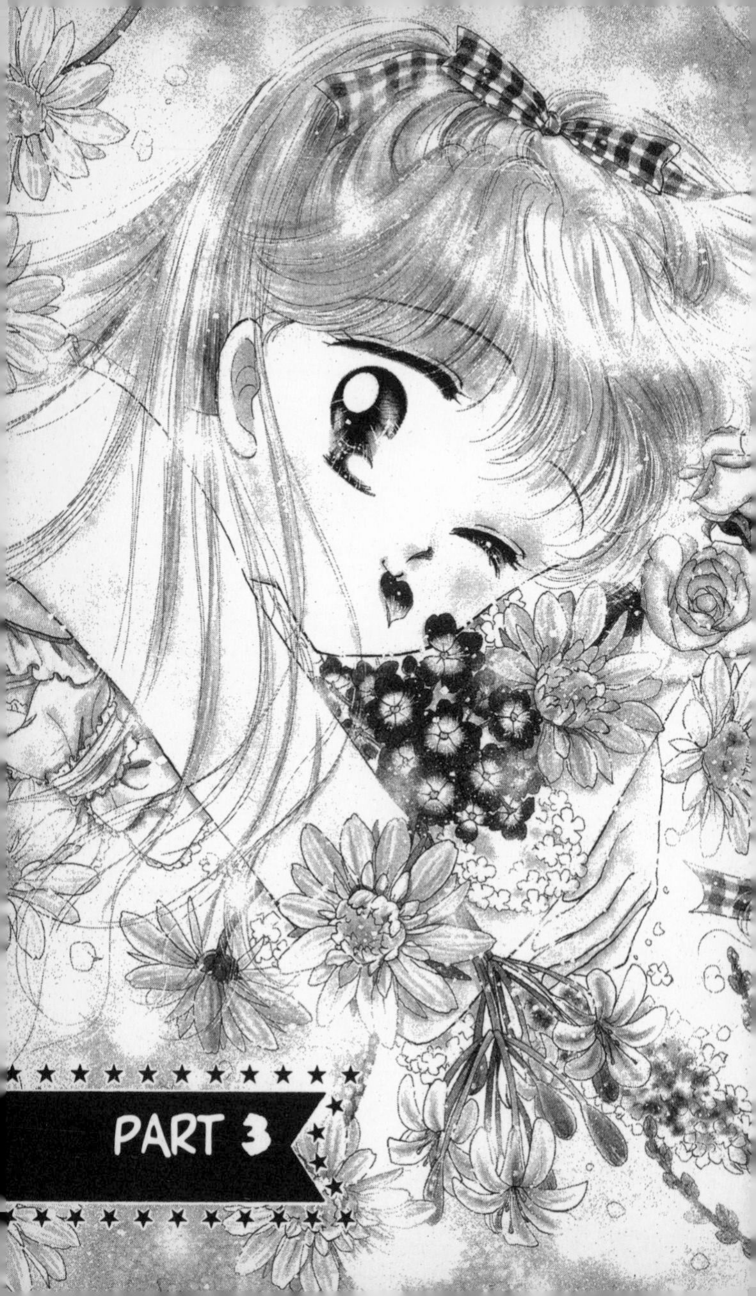
PART 3

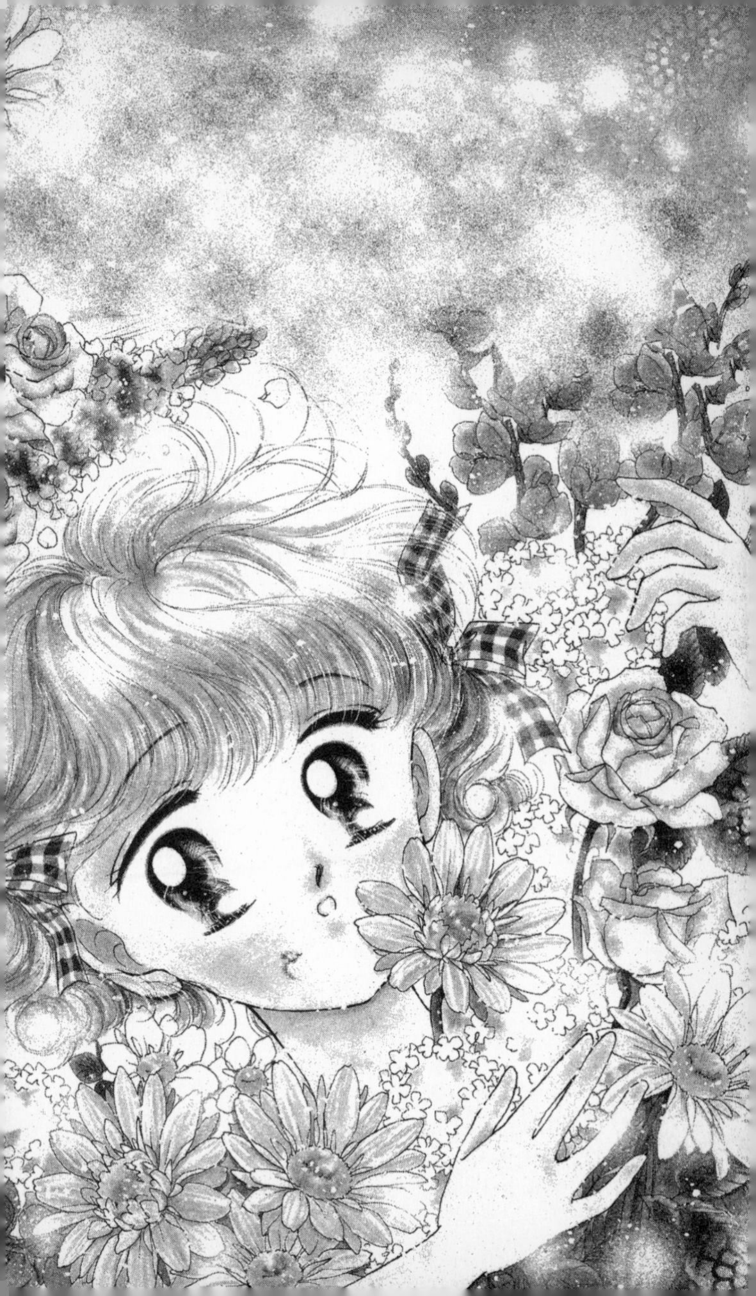

CAST OF CHARACTERS

A FRESHMAN AT UNIVERSITY HIGH. A SUPERB ATHLETE WITH A WONDERFUL PERSONALITY. BUT SHE'S NOT TOO FOND OF SCHOOLWORK.

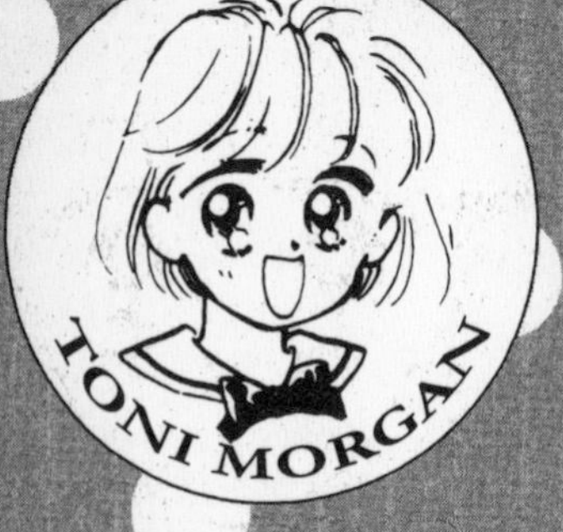
TONI MORGAN

ALSO A FRESHMAN AT UNIVERSITY HIGH. A GIFTED STUDENT AND CRAFTY INVENTOR. A TOTAL KLUTZ WHEN IT COMES TO ATHLETICS. ALSO A BIT SHORT-TEMPERED.

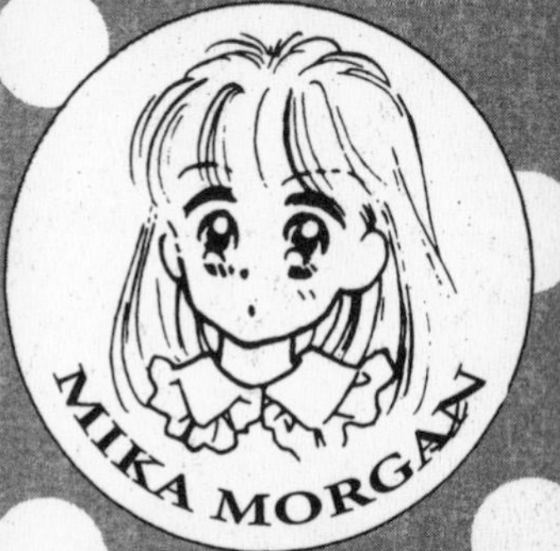
MIKA MORGAN

WHEN THEY WORK TOGETHER, THEY HAVE THE ABILITY TO TELEPORT AND COMMUNICATE TELEPATHICALLY. AND NOW THEY ARE ON THE VERGE OF REALIZING ANOTHER NEW UNDISCOVERED POWER WITHIN THEMSELVES!

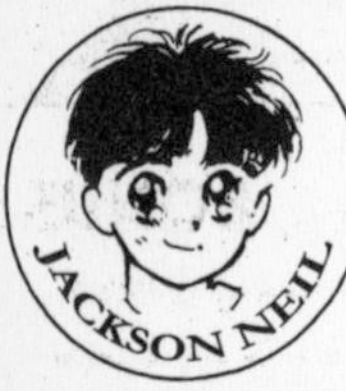
JACKSON NEIL

THE SCHOOL TRACK STAR AND A CLASSMATE OF TONI'S.

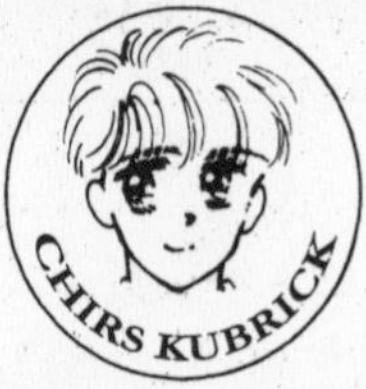
CHIRS KUBRICK

ONE GRADE AHEAD OF MIKA. A MEMBER OF THE TRACK TEAM AND CHEMISTRY CLUB.

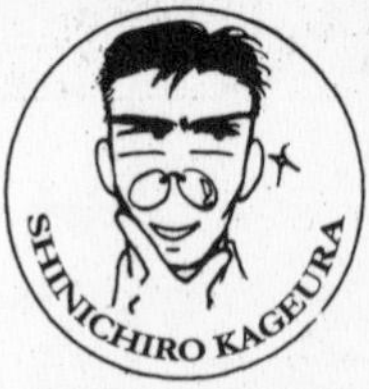
SHINICHIRO KAGEURA

THE NUTTY SCIENCE TEACHER. CRAZY FOR PSYCHIC RESEARCH.

THE STORY TIL NOW:

TONI AND MIKA ARE IDENTICAL TWINS WITH PSYCHIC POWERS. THEY ARE ABLE TO TELEPORT AND COMMUNICATE TELEPATHICALLY, BUT THEIR POWERS WORK ONLY WHEN THEY'RE TOGETHER. LED BY THE MYSTERIOUS PROF. X, THE PSYCHIC POWER ORGANIZATION TRIED TO CAPTURE THE TWINS AND STEAL A SPECIAL PSYCHIC SERUM INVENTED BY MIKA. PROF. X DISPATCHED A POWERFUL PSYCHIC NAMED MASON TEMPLAR TO RECRUIT THE TWINS AND BRING THEM INTO HIS FOLD. HOWEVER, MASON BECAME FRIENDS WITH THE TWINS AND FAILED HIS MISSION. PROF. X'S LAB WAS DESTROYED, AND TONI AND MIKA RETURNED TO A NORMAL, PEACEFUL LIFE.

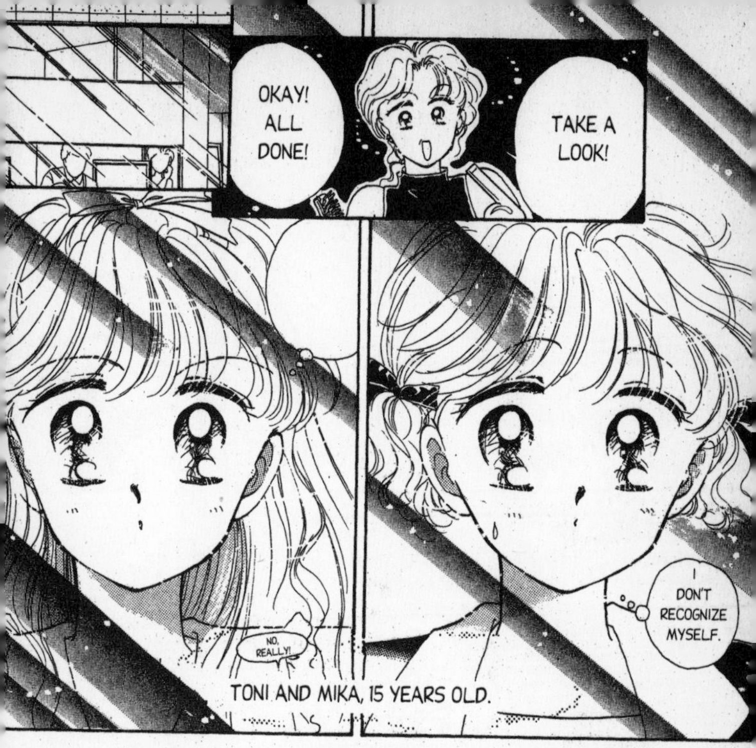

OKAY! ALL DONE!
TAKE A LOOK!
NO, REALLY!
I DON'T RECOGNIZE MYSELF.
TONI AND MIKA, 15 YEARS OLD.

BONUS

Hello everyone! Well, we're into book 5 of Miracle Girls and the beginning of Part 3. Even I'm surprised we've made it this far! Thanks for all your support! In appreciation, today we present...

SECRETS BEHIND THE MAKING OF
MIRACLE GIRLS

(Well, that's the idea, anyway.)

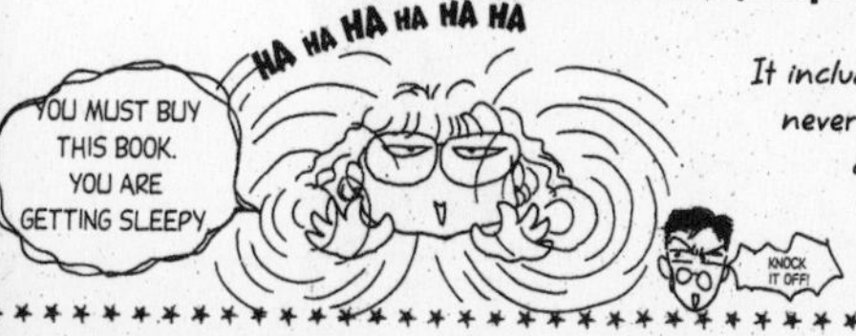

HA HA HA HA HA HA
YOU MUST BUY THIS BOOK. YOU ARE GETTING SLEEPY
KNOCK IT OFF!

It includes all the juicy secrets you'll never get from just reading the comics. Coming soon!

(WARNING: YOU MAY NEVER LOOK AT THINGS THE SAME WAY AGAIN! HA HA HA!)

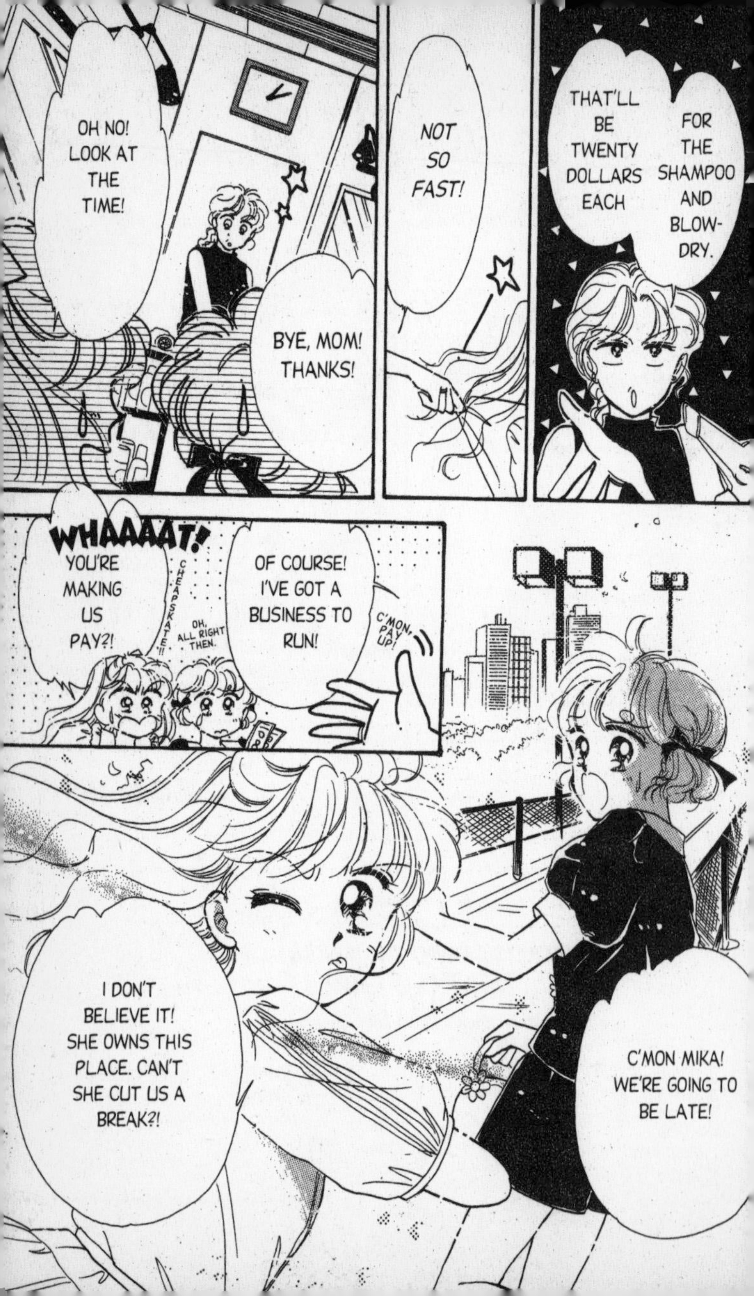
OH NO! LOOK AT THE TIME!
BYE, MOM! THANKS!
NOT SO FAST!
THAT'LL BE TWENTY DOLLARS EACH
FOR THE SHAMPOO AND BLOW-DRY.
WHAAAAT!
YOU'RE MAKING US PAY?!
CHEAPSKATE!!
OH, ALL RIGHT THEN.
OF COURSE! I'VE GOT A BUSINESS TO RUN!
C'MON, PAY UP!
I DON'T BELIEVE IT! SHE OWNS THIS PLACE. CAN'T SHE CUT US A BREAK?!
C'MON MIKA! WE'RE GOING TO BE LATE!

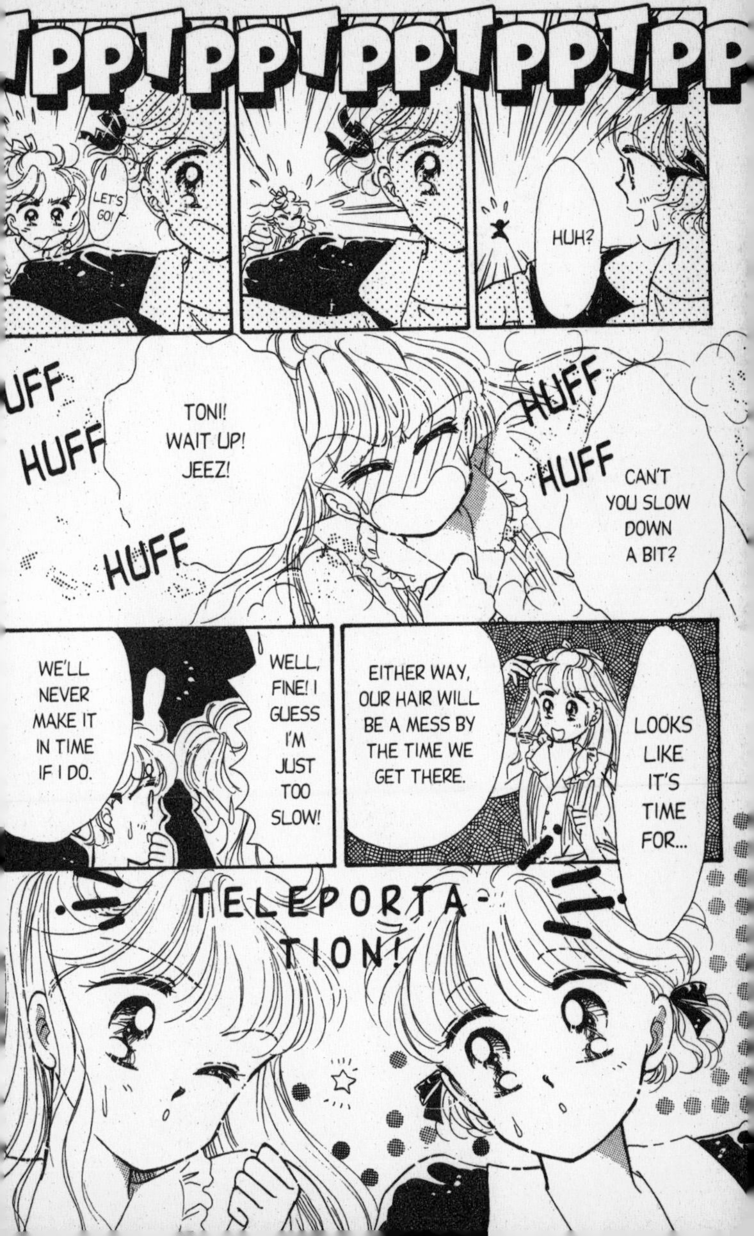
TPPTPPTPPTPPTPP
LET'S GO!
HUH?
HUFF
HUFF
HUFF
TONI! WAIT UP! JEEZ!
HUFF
HUFF
CAN'T YOU SLOW DOWN A BIT?
WE'LL NEVER MAKE IT IN TIME IF I DO.
WELL, FINE! I GUESS I'M JUST TOO SLOW!
EITHER WAY, OUR HAIR WILL BE A MESS BY THE TIME WE GET THERE.
LOOKS LIKE IT'S TIME FOR...
TELEPORTA-TION!

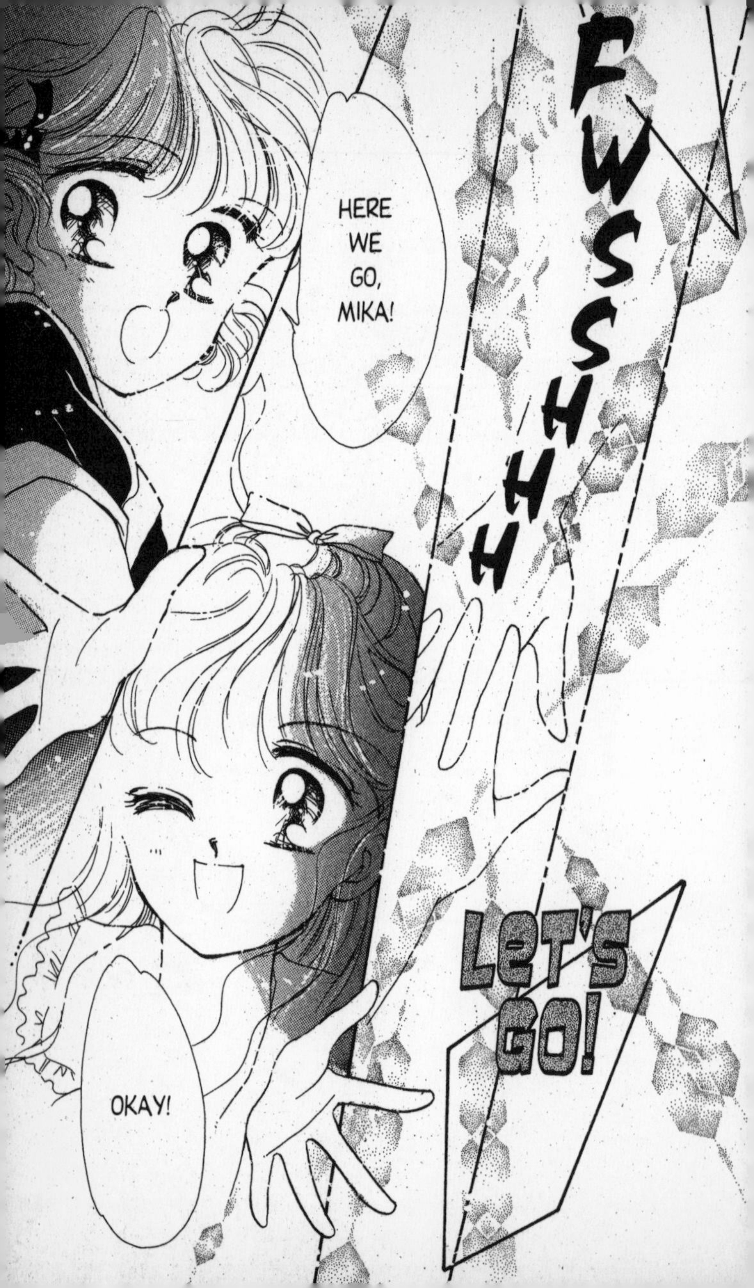
HERE WE GO, MIKA!
FWSSHHHHH
OKAY!
LET'S GO!

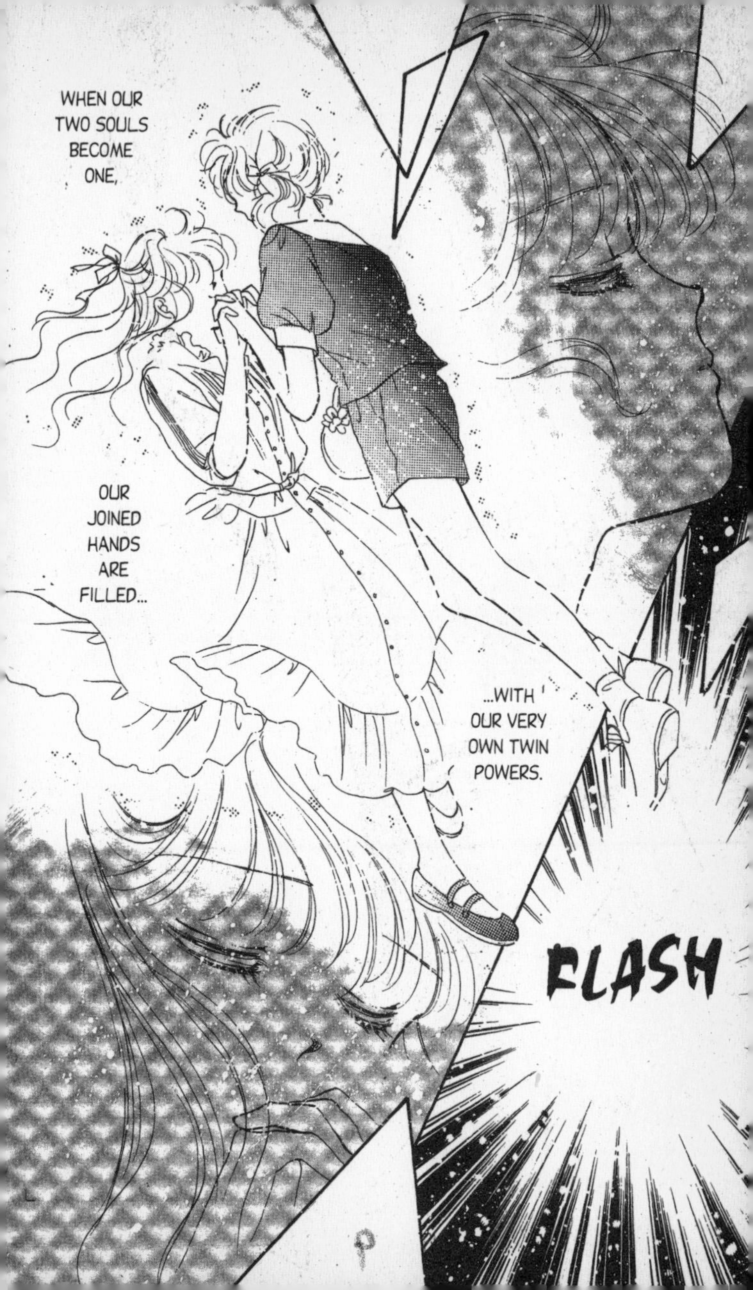
WHEN OUR TWO SOULS BECOME ONE,
OUR JOINED HANDS ARE FILLED...
...WITH OUR VERY OWN TWIN POWERS.
FLASH

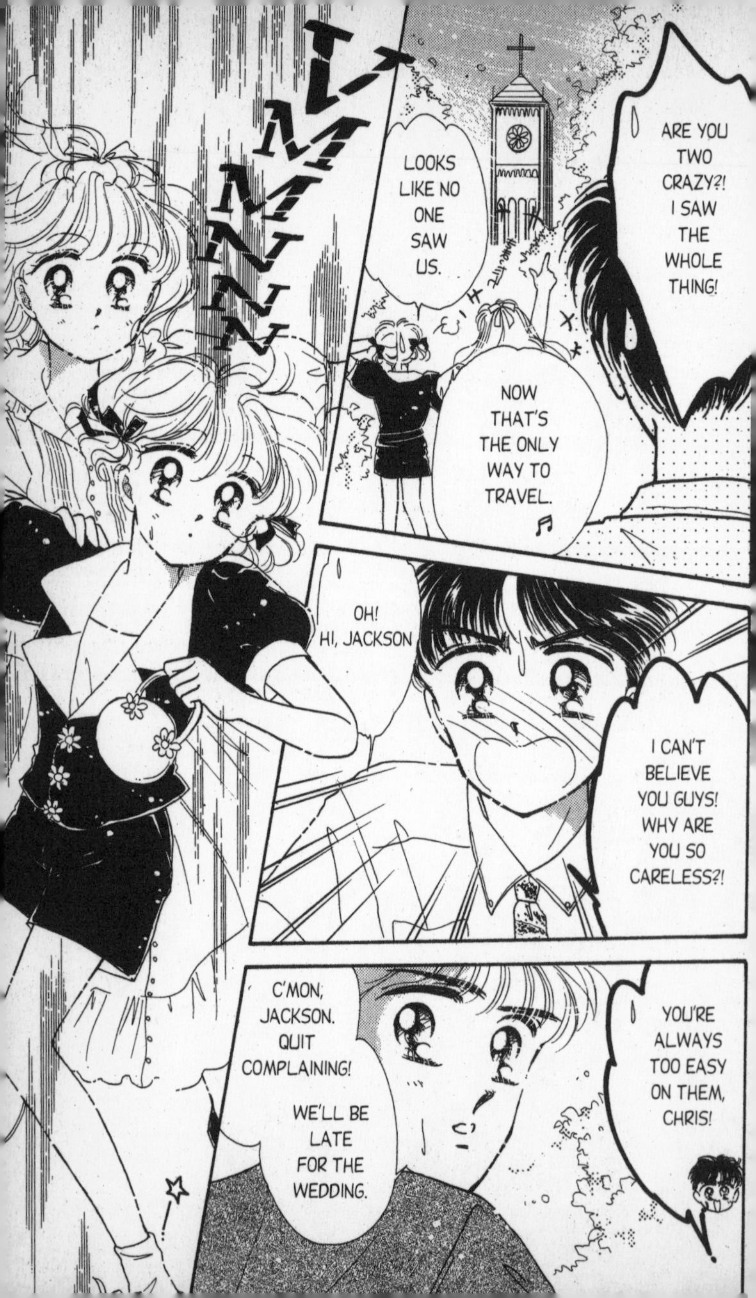
MMMNNN
LOOKS LIKE NO ONE SAW US.
NOW THAT'S THE ONLY WAY TO TRAVEL. ♫
ARE YOU TWO CRAZY?! I SAW THE WHOLE THING!
OH! HI, JACKSON
I CAN'T BELIEVE YOU GUYS! WHY ARE YOU SO CARELESS?!
C'MON, JACKSON. QUIT COMPLAINING!
WE'LL BE LATE FOR THE WEDDING.
YOU'RE ALWAYS TOO EASY ON THEM, CHRIS!

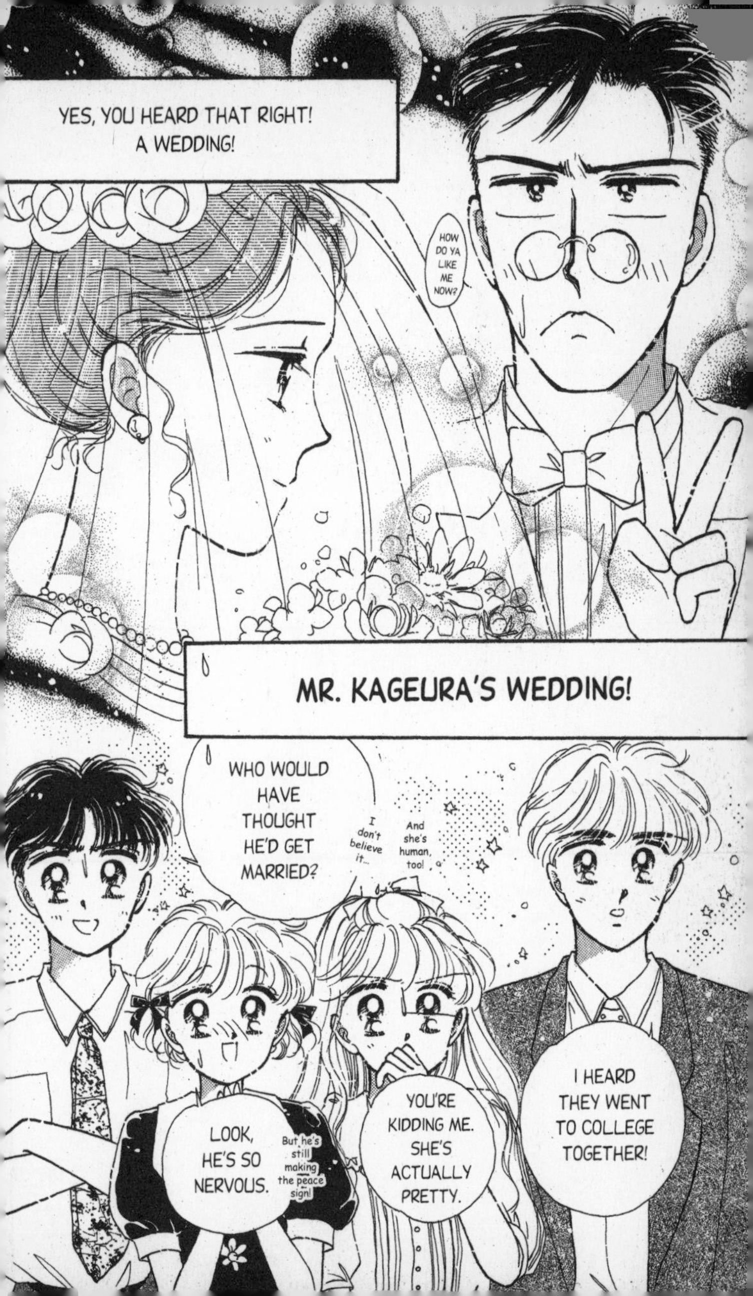
YES, YOU HEARD THAT RIGHT! A WEDDING!
HOW DO YA LIKE ME NOW?
MR. KAGEURA'S WEDDING!
WHO WOULD HAVE THOUGHT HE'D GET MARRIED?
I don't believe it...
And she's human, too!
LOOK, HE'S SO NERVOUS.
But he's still making the peace sign!
YOU'RE KIDDING ME. SHE'S ACTUALLY PRETTY.
I HEARD THEY WENT TO COLLEGE TOGETHER!

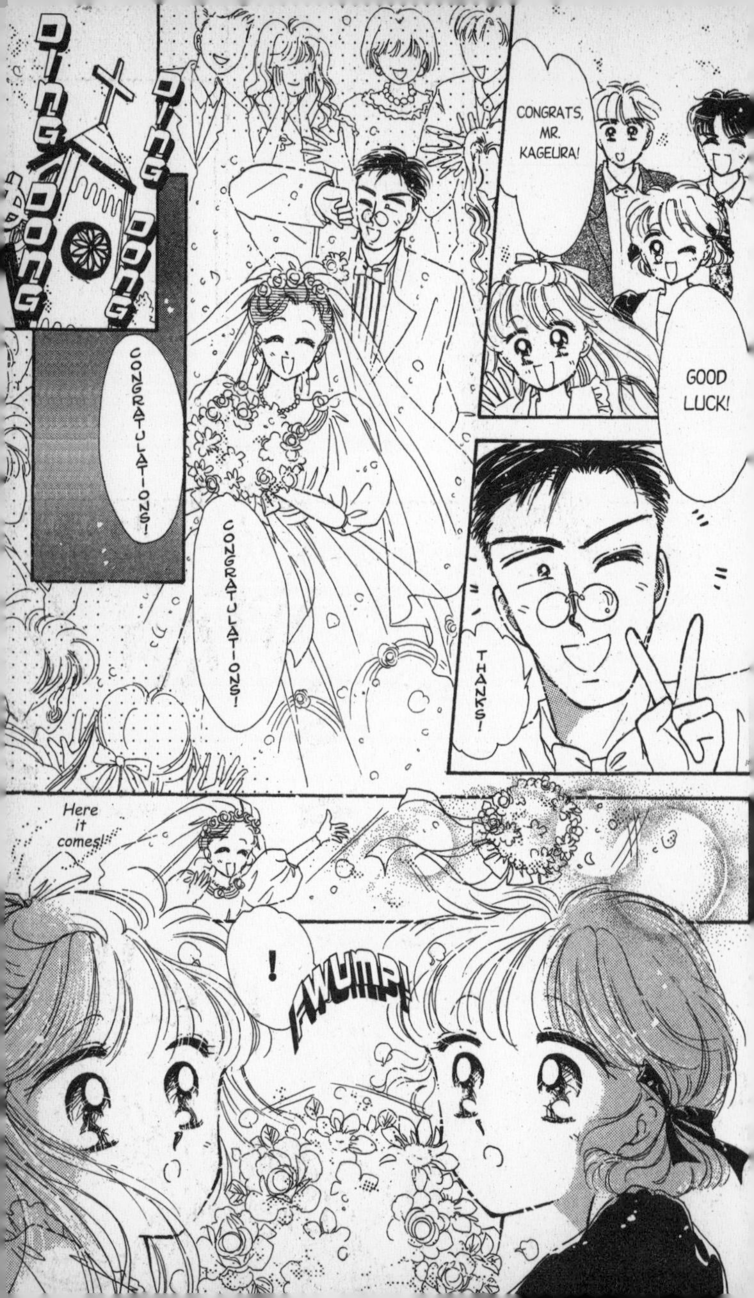
DING DONG
DING DONG
CONGRATULATIONS!
CONGRATULATIONS!
CONGRATS, MR. KAGEURA!
GOOD LUCK!
THANKS!
Here it comes!
!
FWUMP!

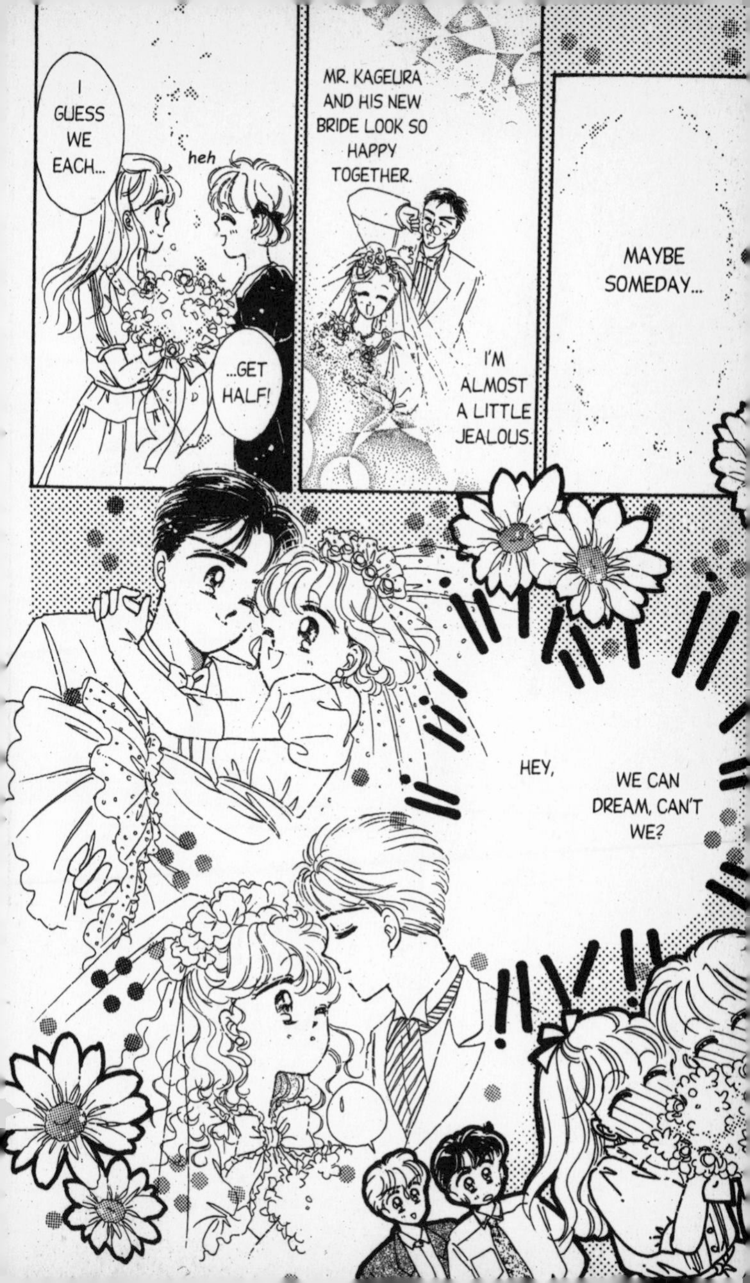
I GUESS WE EACH...
heh
...GET HALF!
MR. KAGEURA AND HIS NEW BRIDE LOOK SO HAPPY TOGETHER.
I'M ALMOST A LITTLE JEALOUS.
MAYBE SOMEDAY...
HEY,
WE CAN DREAM, CAN'T WE?

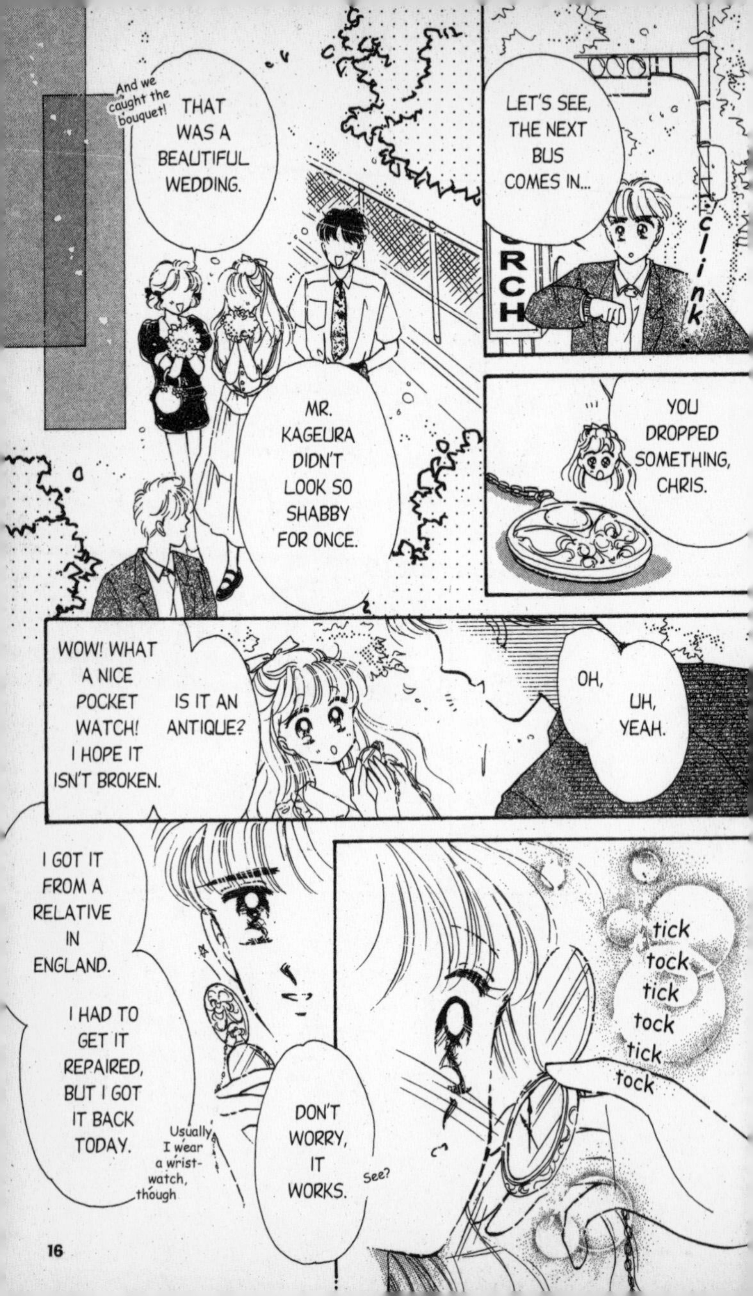

And we caught the bouquet!
THAT WAS A BEAUTIFUL WEDDING.
MR. KAGEURA DIDN'T LOOK SO SHABBY FOR ONCE.
LET'S SEE, THE NEXT BUS COMES IN...
RCH
clink
...
YOU DROPPED SOMETHING, CHRIS.
WOW! WHAT A NICE POCKET WATCH! I HOPE IT ISN'T BROKEN.
IS IT AN ANTIQUE?
OH,
UH, YEAH.
I GOT IT FROM A RELATIVE IN ENGLAND.
I HAD TO GET IT REPAIRED, BUT I GOT IT BACK TODAY.
Usually I wear a wrist-watch, though
DON'T WORRY, IT WORKS.
See?
tick tock tick tock tick tock

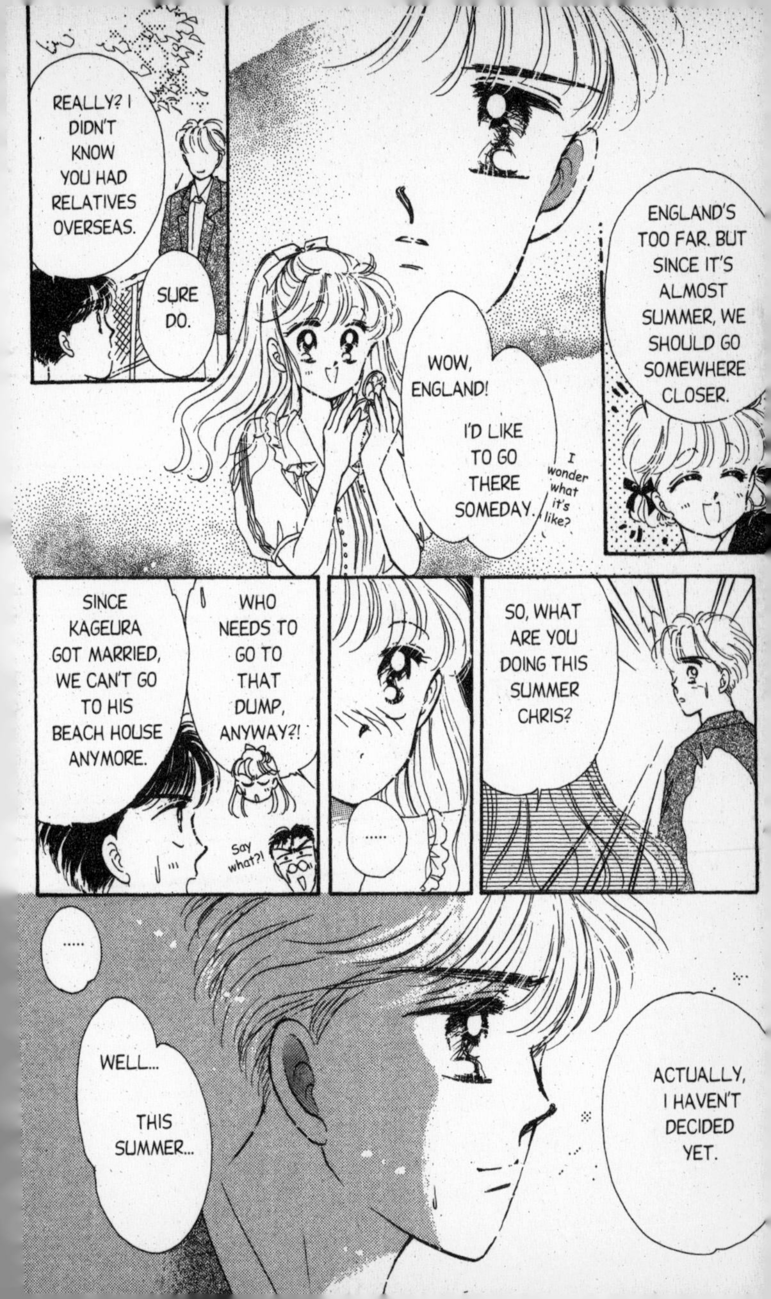

REALLY? I DIDN'T KNOW YOU HAD RELATIVES OVERSEAS.
SURE DO.
WOW, ENGLAND!
I'D LIKE TO GO THERE SOMEDAY.
I wonder what it's like?
ENGLAND'S TOO FAR. BUT SINCE IT'S ALMOST SUMMER, WE SHOULD GO SOMEWHERE CLOSER.
SINCE KAGEURA GOT MARRIED, WE CAN'T GO TO HIS BEACH HOUSE ANYMORE.
WHO NEEDS TO GO TO THAT DUMP, ANYWAY?!
Say what?!
.....
SO, WHAT ARE YOU DOING THIS SUMMER CHRIS?
.....
WELL...
THIS SUMMER...
ACTUALLY, I HAVEN'T DECIDED YET.

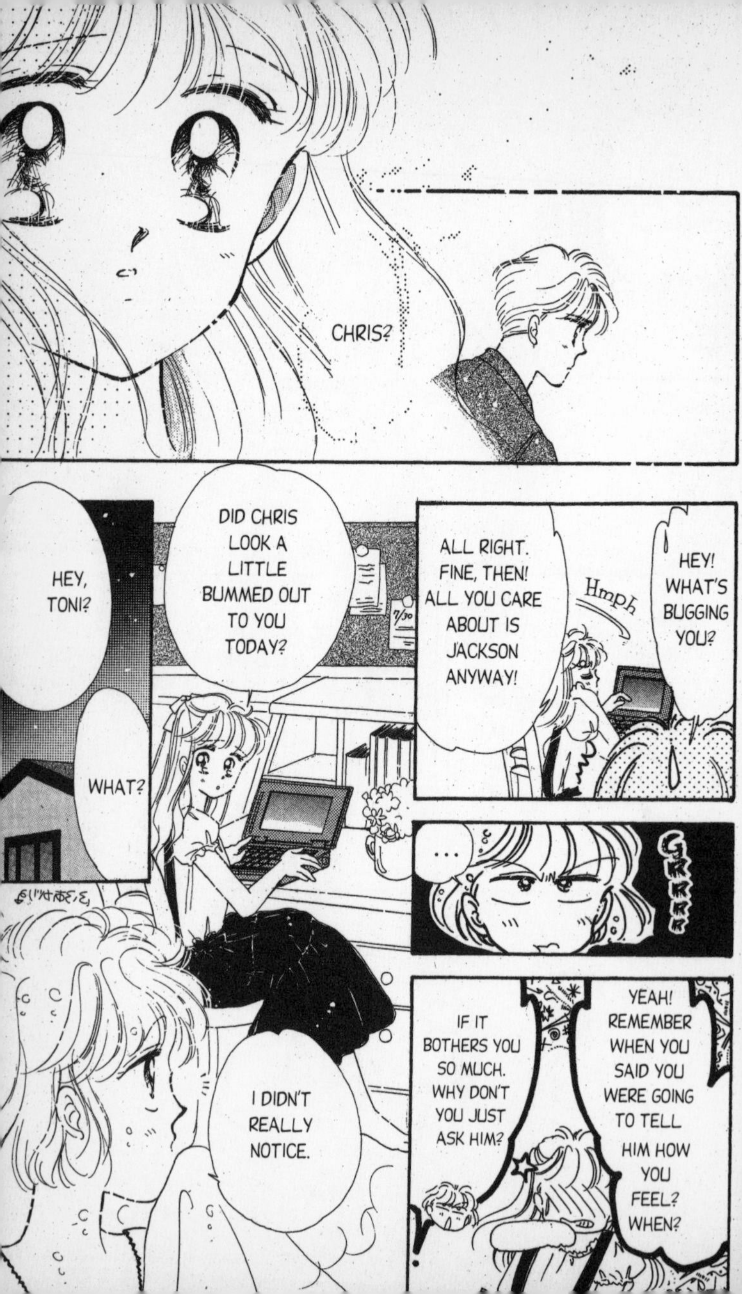
CHRIS?
HEY, TONI?
WHAT?
DID CHRIS LOOK A LITTLE BUMMED OUT TO YOU TODAY?
I DIDN'T REALLY NOTICE.
ALL RIGHT. FINE, THEN! ALL YOU CARE ABOUT IS JACKSON ANYWAY!
Hmph
HEY! WHAT'S BUGGING YOU?
...
GRRRR
IF IT BOTHERS YOU SO MUCH. WHY DON'T YOU JUST ASK HIM?
YEAH! REMEMBER WHEN YOU SAID YOU WERE GOING TO TELL HIM HOW YOU FEEL? WHEN?

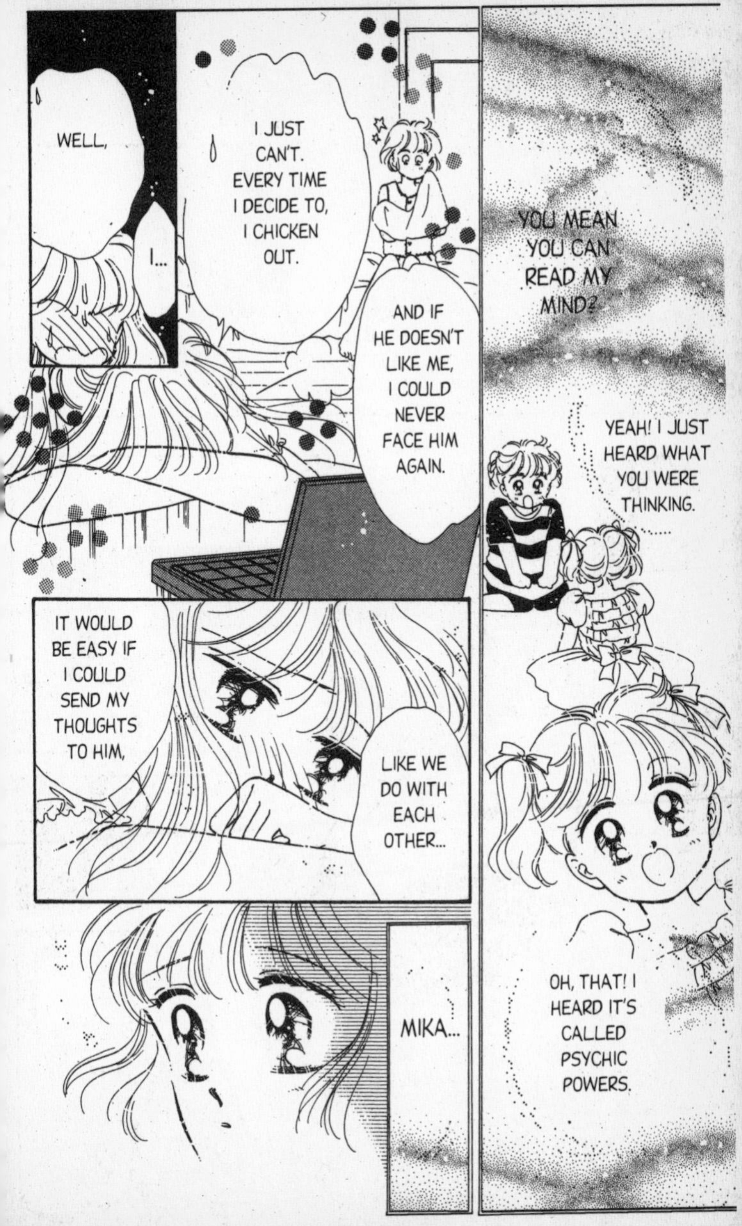
WELL,
I...
I JUST CAN'T. EVERY TIME I DECIDE TO, I CHICKEN OUT.
AND IF HE DOESN'T LIKE ME, I COULD NEVER FACE HIM AGAIN.
IT WOULD BE EASY IF I COULD SEND MY THOUGHTS TO HIM,
LIKE WE DO WITH EACH OTHER...
MIKA...
YOU MEAN YOU CAN READ MY MIND?
YEAH! I JUST HEARD WHAT YOU WERE THINKING.
OH, THAT! I HEARD IT'S CALLED PSYCHIC POWERS.

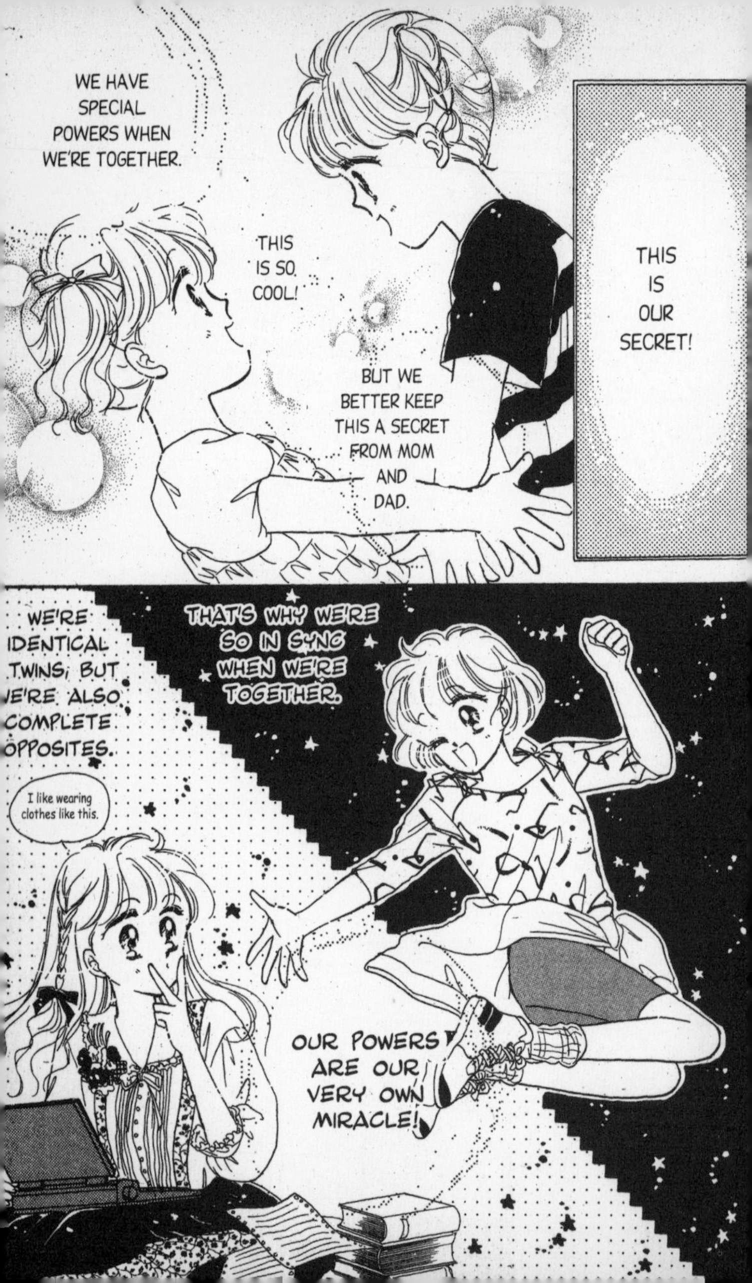
WE HAVE SPECIAL POWERS WHEN WE'RE TOGETHER.
THIS IS SO COOL!
BUT WE BETTER KEEP THIS A SECRET FROM MOM AND DAD.
THIS IS OUR SECRET!
WE'RE IDENTICAL TWINS, BUT E'RE ALSO COMPLETE OPPOSITES.
THAT'S WHY WE'RE SO IN SYNC WHEN WE'RE TOGETHER.
I like wearing clothes like this.
OUR POWERS ARE OUR VERY OWN MIRACLE!

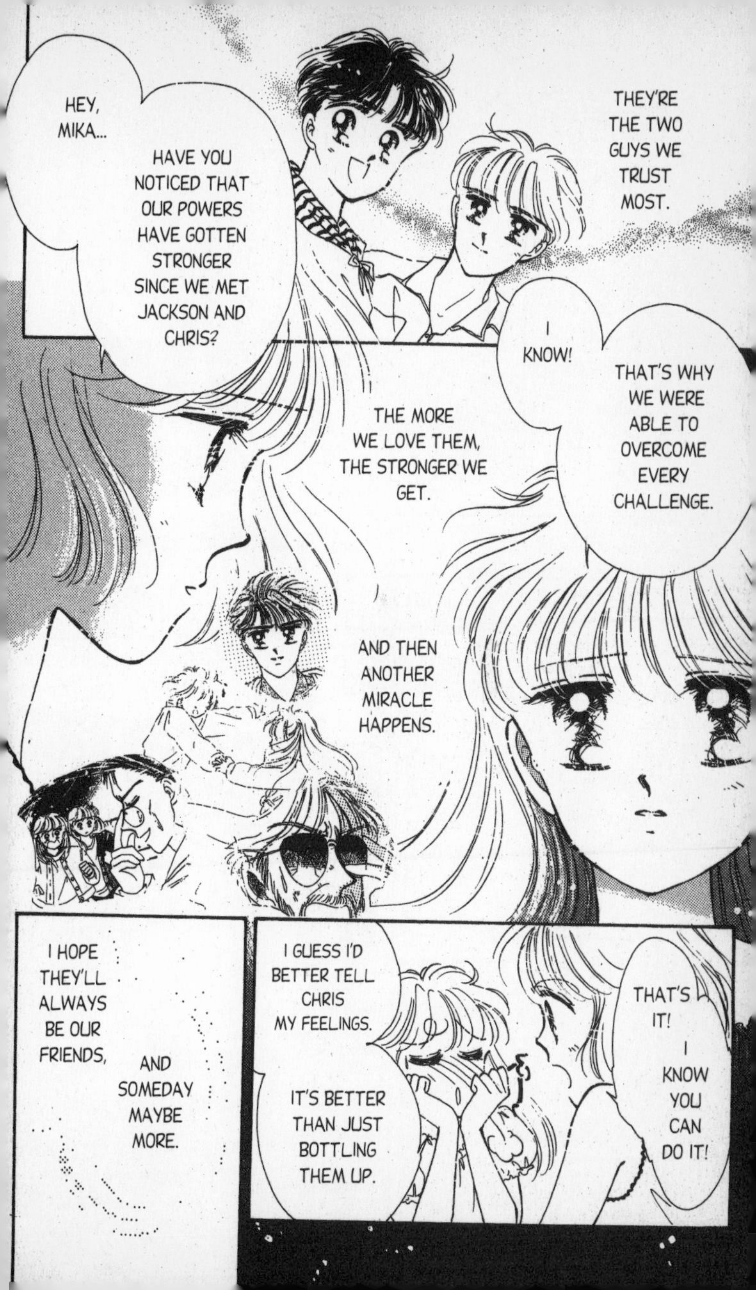
HEY, MIKA...
HAVE YOU NOTICED THAT OUR POWERS HAVE GOTTEN STRONGER SINCE WE MET JACKSON AND CHRIS?
THEY'RE THE TWO GUYS WE TRUST MOST.
I KNOW!
THAT'S WHY WE WERE ABLE TO OVERCOME EVERY CHALLENGE.
THE MORE WE LOVE THEM, THE STRONGER WE GET.
AND THEN ANOTHER MIRACLE HAPPENS.
I HOPE THEY'LL ALWAYS BE OUR FRIENDS,
AND SOMEDAY MAYBE MORE.
I GUESS I'D BETTER TELL CHRIS MY FEELINGS.
IT'S BETTER THAN JUST BOTTLING THEM UP.
THAT'S IT!
I KNOW YOU CAN DO IT!

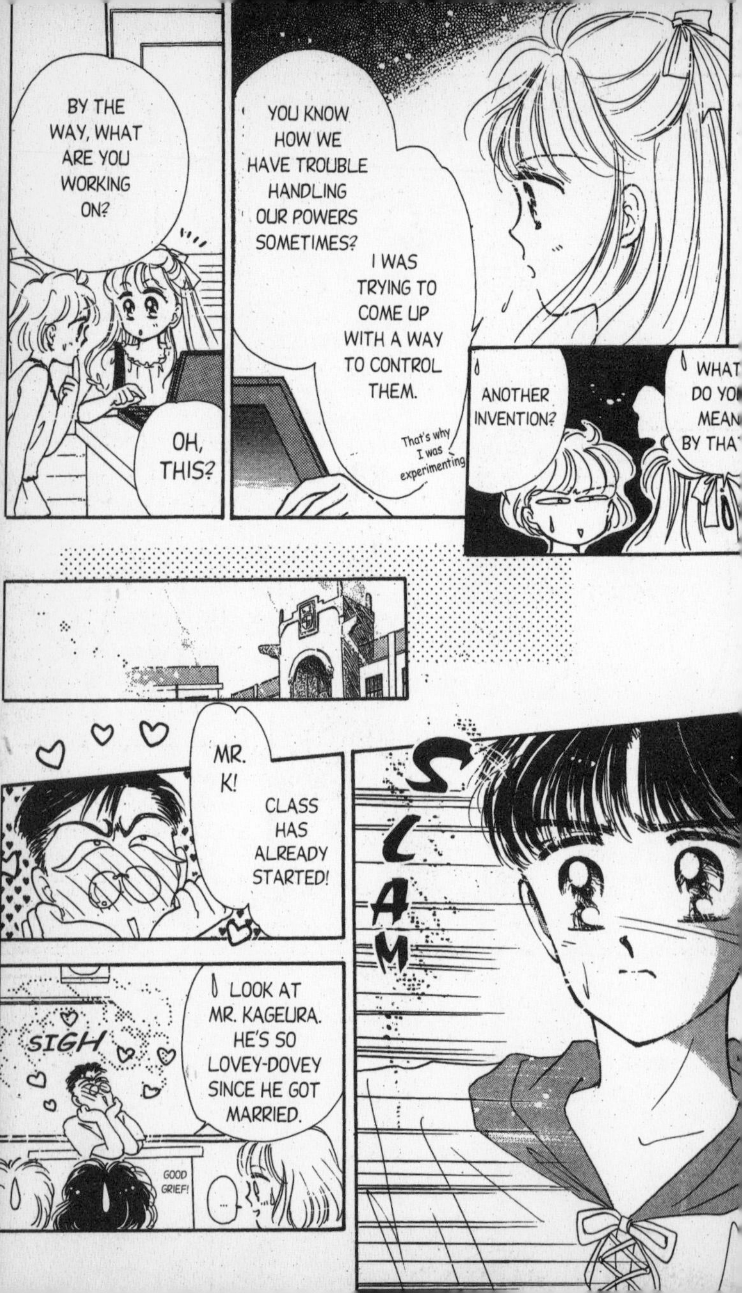
BY THE WAY, WHAT ARE YOU WORKING ON?
OH, THIS?
YOU KNOW HOW WE HAVE TROUBLE HANDLING OUR POWERS SOMETIMES?
I WAS TRYING TO COME UP WITH A WAY TO CONTROL THEM.
That's why I was experimenting
ANOTHER INVENTION?
WHAT DO YO MEAN BY THA
MR. K!
CLASS HAS ALREADY STARTED!
SIGH
LOOK AT MR. KAGEURA. HE'S SO LOVEY-DOVEY SINCE HE GOT MARRIED.
GOOD GRIEF!
...
SLAM

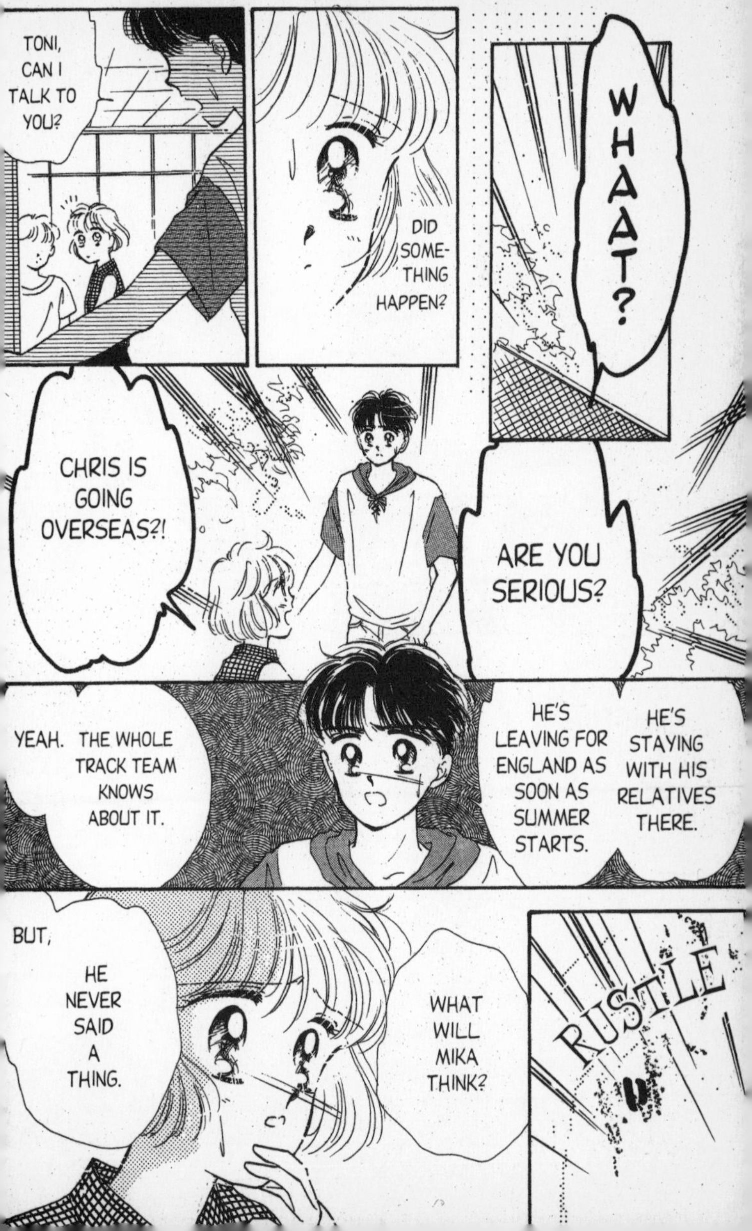
TONI, CAN I TALK TO YOU?
DID SOMETHING HAPPEN?
WHAAT?
CHRIS IS GOING OVERSEAS?!
ARE YOU SERIOUS?
YEAH.
THE WHOLE TRACK TEAM KNOWS ABOUT IT.
HE'S LEAVING FOR ENGLAND AS SOON AS SUMMER STARTS.
HE'S STAYING WITH HIS RELATIVES THERE.
BUT,
HE NEVER SAID A THING.
WHAT WILL MIKA THINK?
RUSTLE

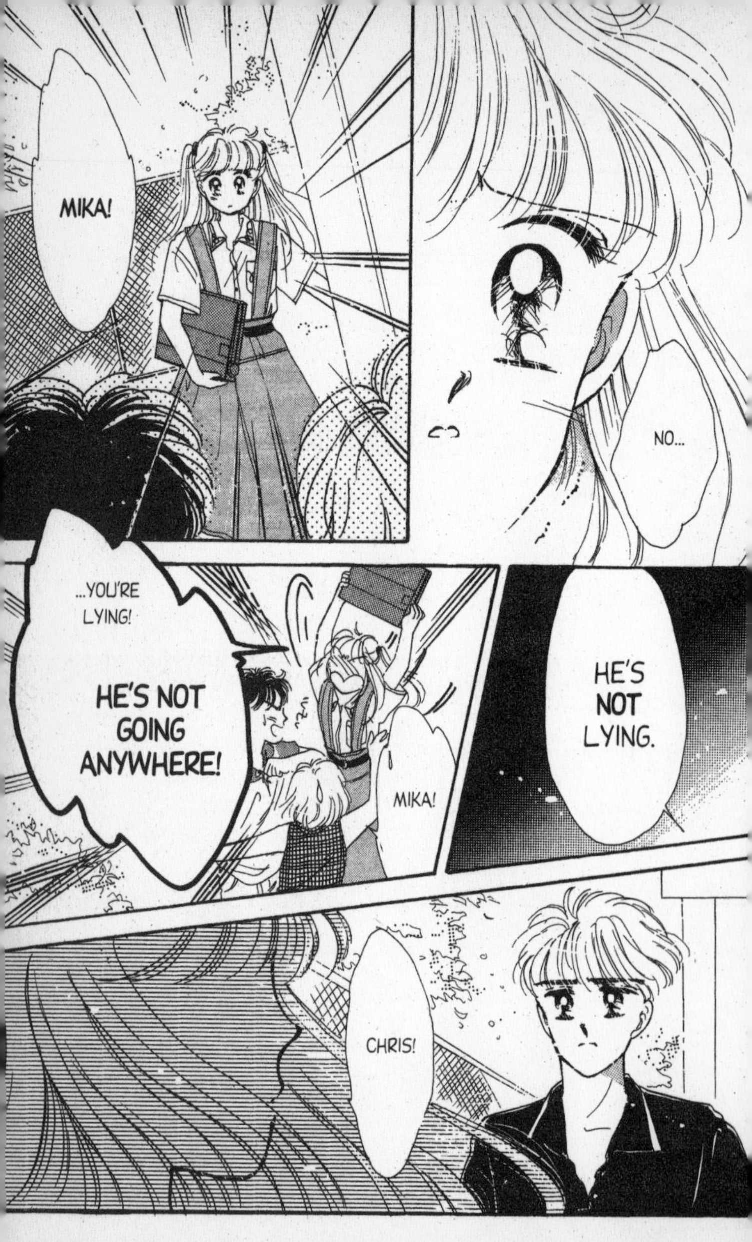
MIKA!
NO...
...YOU'RE LYING!
HE'S NOT GOING ANYWHERE!
MIKA!
HE'S NOT LYING.
CHRIS!

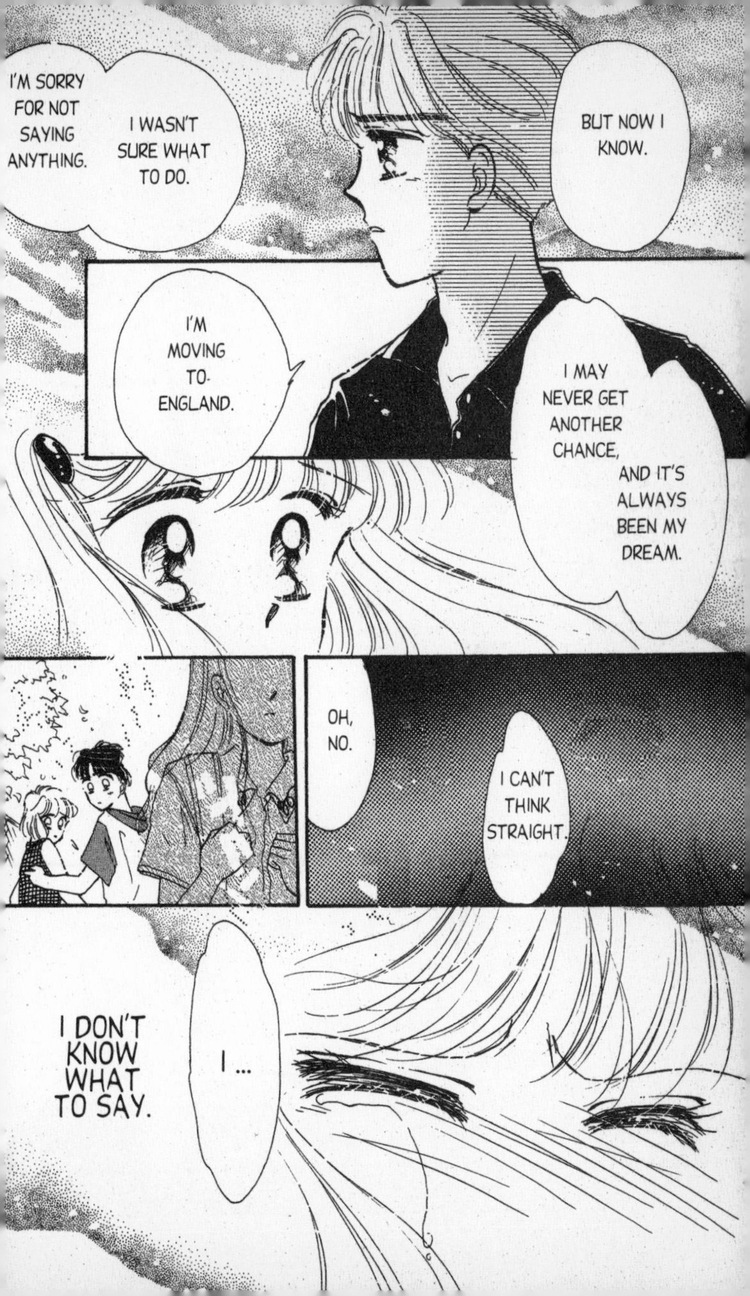
I'M SORRY FOR NOT SAYING ANYTHING.
I WASN'T SURE WHAT TO DO.
BUT NOW I KNOW.
I'M MOVING TO ENGLAND.
I MAY NEVER GET ANOTHER CHANCE,
AND IT'S ALWAYS BEEN MY DREAM.
OH, NO.
I CAN'T THINK STRAIGHT.
I DON'T KNOW WHAT TO SAY.
I ...

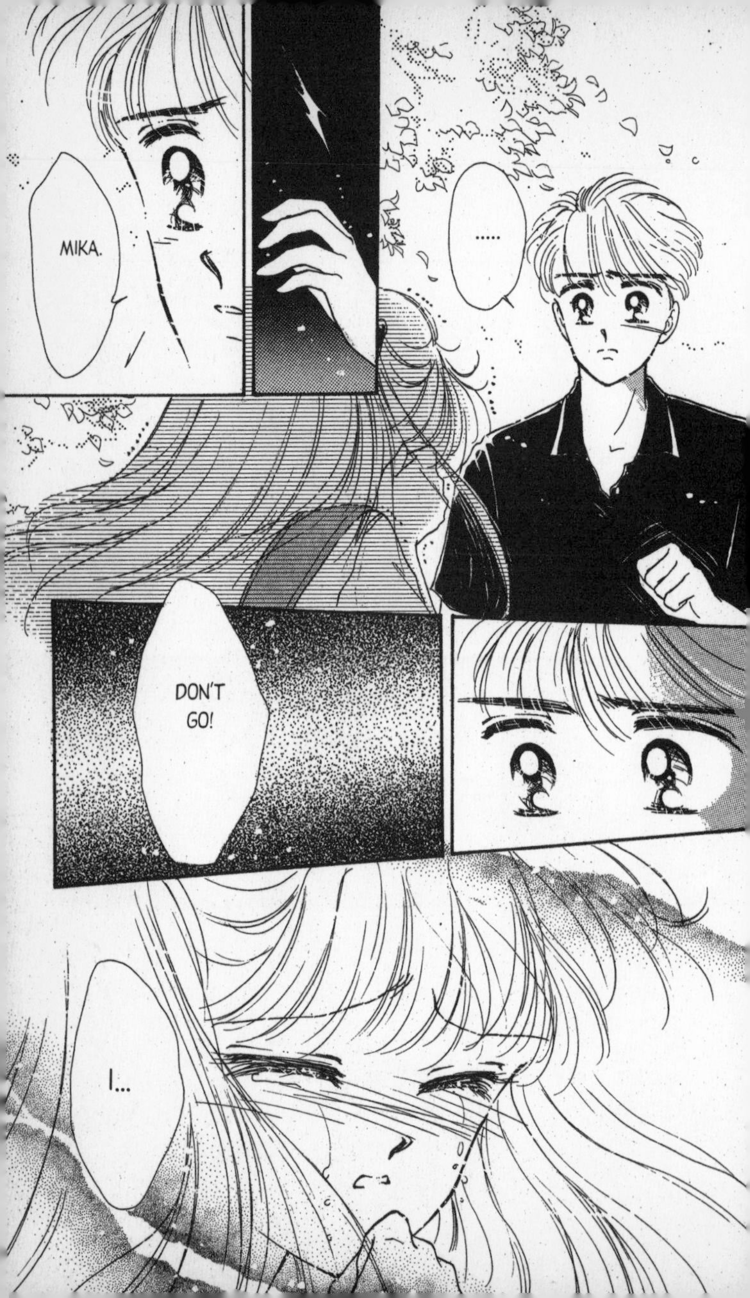
MIKA.
.....
DON'T GO!
I...

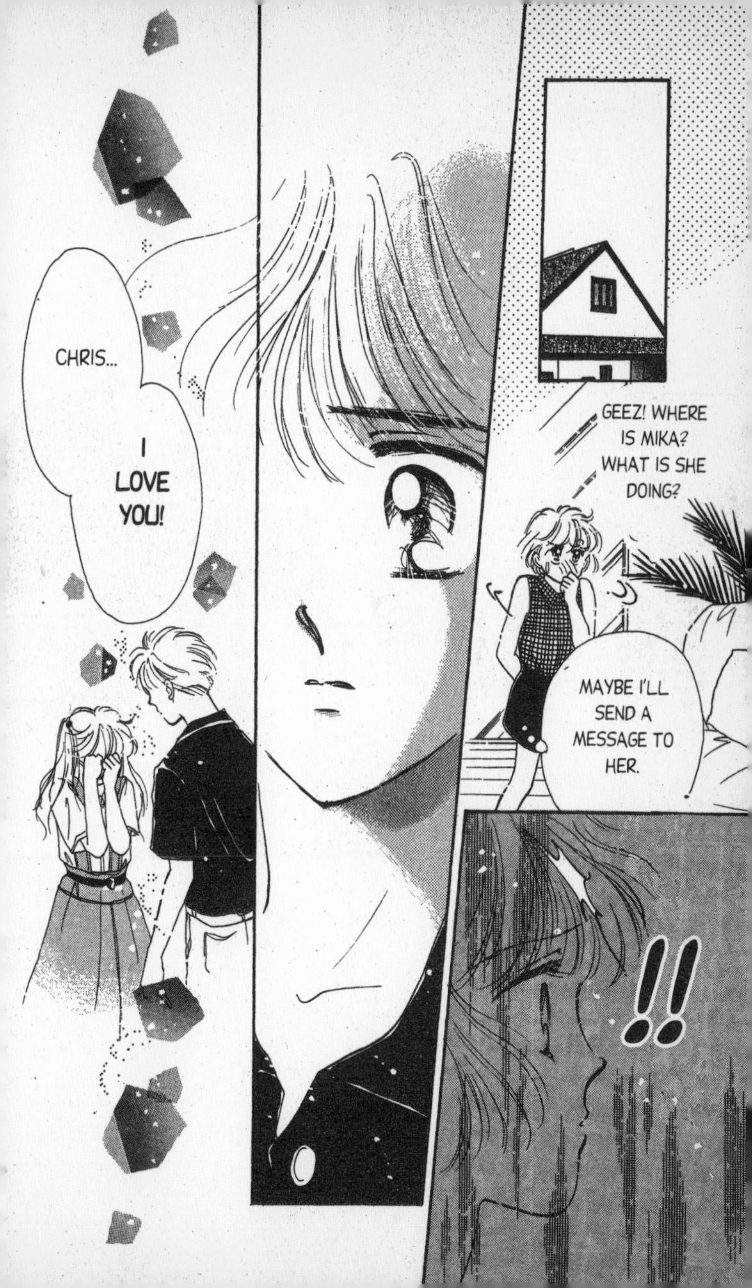
CHRIS...
I LOVE YOU!
GEEZ! WHERE IS MIKA? WHAT IS SHE DOING?
MAYBE I'LL SEND A MESSAGE TO HER.
!!

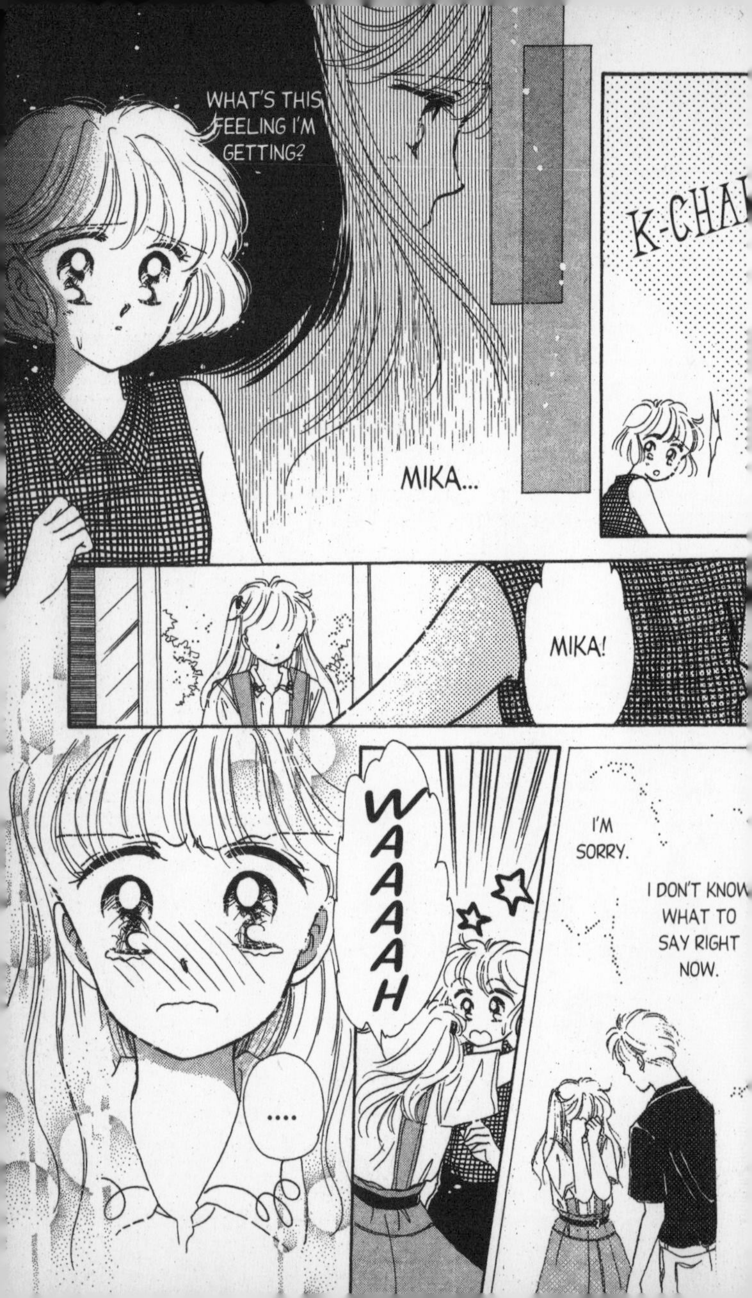
WHAT'S THIS FEELING I'M GETTING?
MIKA...
K-CHA
MIKA!
....
WAAAAAH
I'M SORRY.
I DON'T KNOW WHAT TO SAY RIGHT NOW.

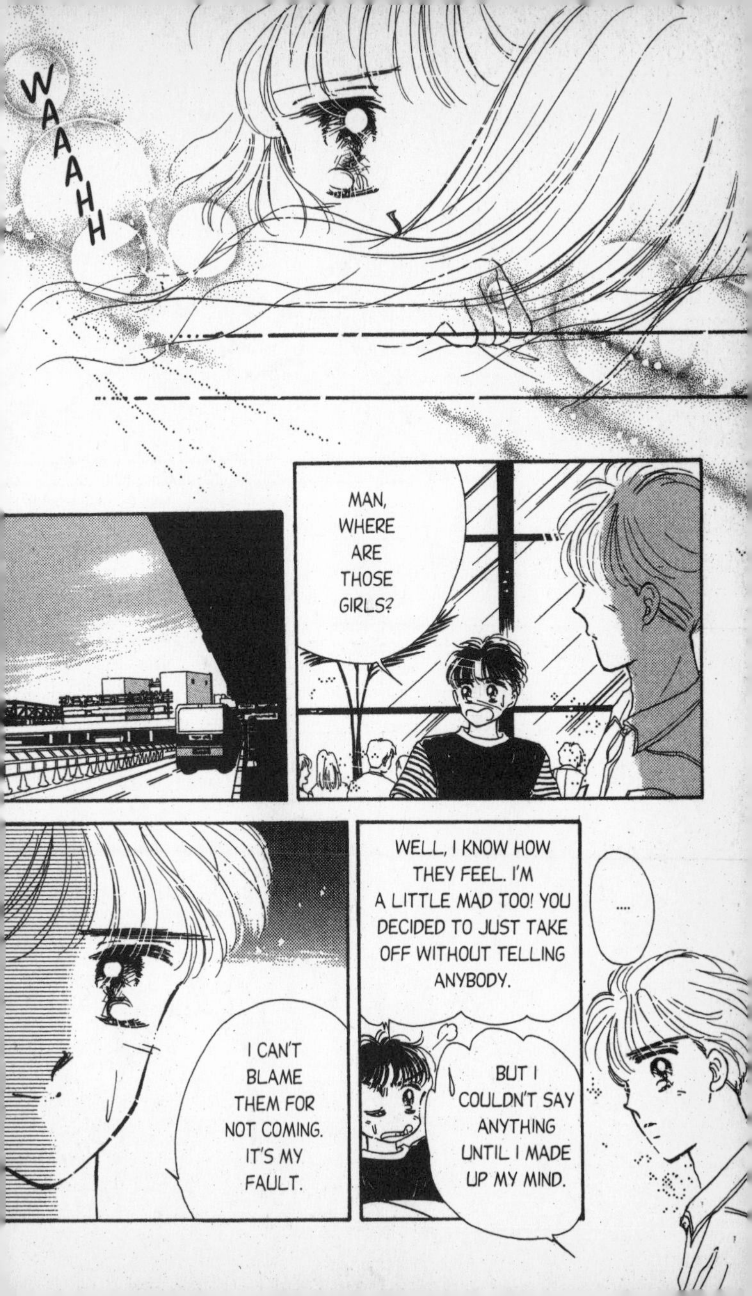
WAAAHH
MAN, WHERE ARE THOSE GIRLS?
I CAN'T BLAME THEM FOR NOT COMING. IT'S MY FAULT.
WELL, I KNOW HOW THEY FEEL. I'M A LITTLE MAD TOO! YOU DECIDED TO JUST TAKE OFF WITHOUT TELLING ANYBODY.
....
BUT I COULDN'T SAY ANYTHING UNTIL I MADE UP MY MIND.

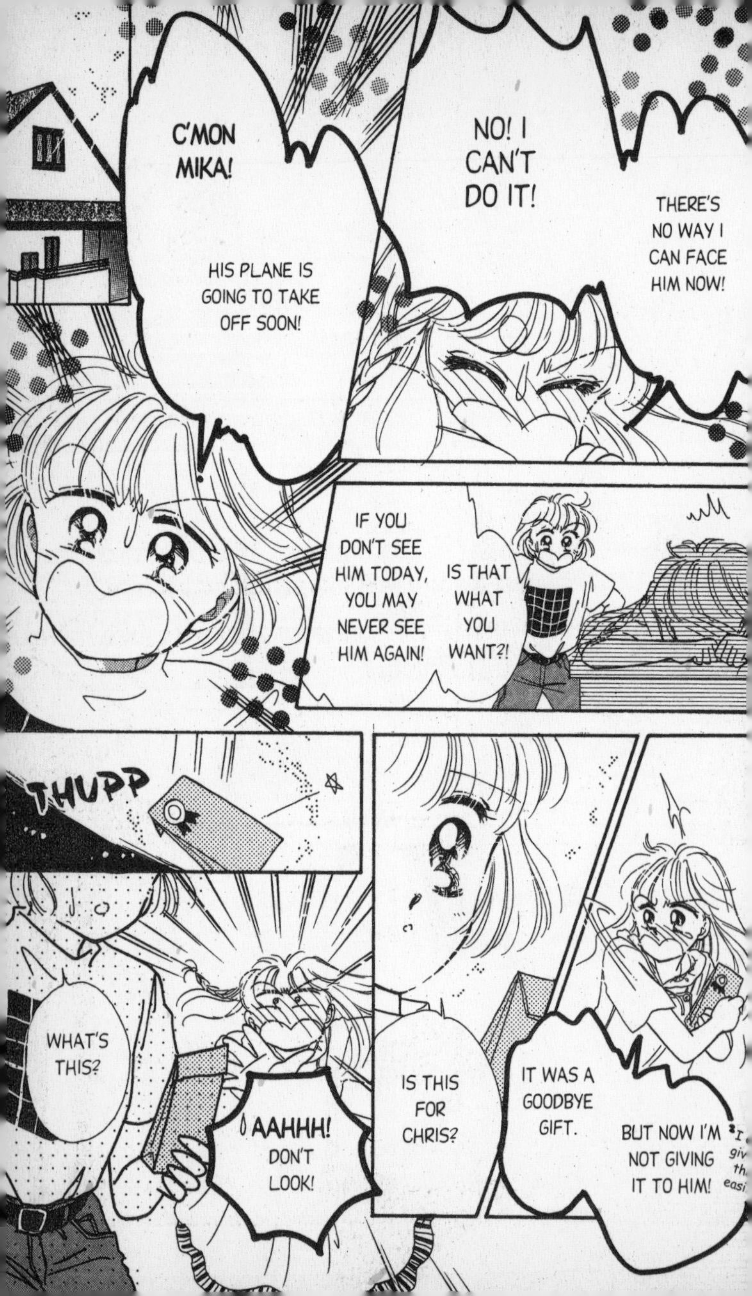
C'MON MIKA!
HIS PLANE IS GOING TO TAKE OFF SOON!
NO! I CAN'T DO IT!
THERE'S NO WAY I CAN FACE HIM NOW!
IF YOU DON'T SEE HIM TODAY, YOU MAY NEVER SEE HIM AGAIN!
IS THAT WHAT YOU WANT?!
THUPP
WHAT'S THIS?
AAHHH! DON'T LOOK!
IS THIS FOR CHRIS?
IT WAS A GOODBYE GIFT.
BUT NOW I'M NOT GIVING IT TO HIM!

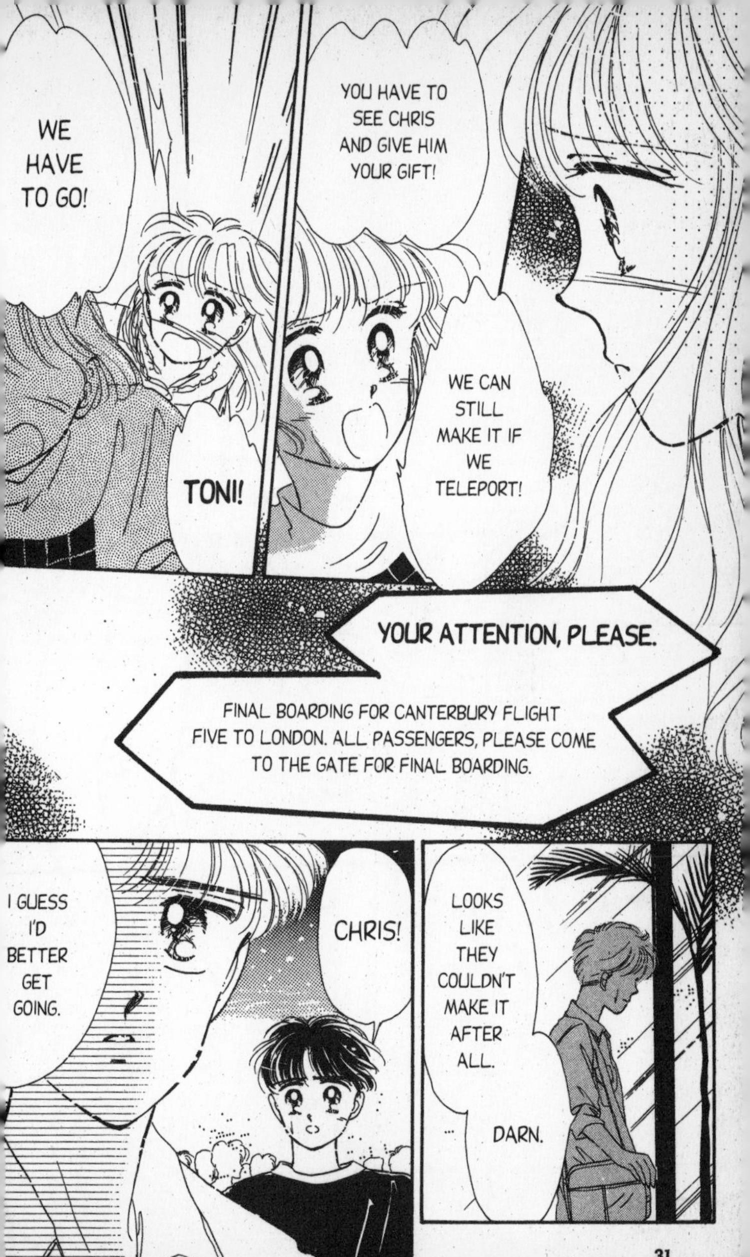
WE HAVE TO GO!
TONI!
YOU HAVE TO SEE CHRIS AND GIVE HIM YOUR GIFT!
WE CAN STILL MAKE IT IF WE TELEPORT!
YOUR ATTENTION, PLEASE.
FINAL BOARDING FOR CANTERBURY FLIGHT FIVE TO LONDON. ALL PASSENGERS, PLEASE COME TO THE GATE FOR FINAL BOARDING.
I GUESS I'D BETTER GET GOING.
CHRIS!
LOOKS LIKE THEY COULDN'T MAKE IT AFTER ALL.
...
DARN.

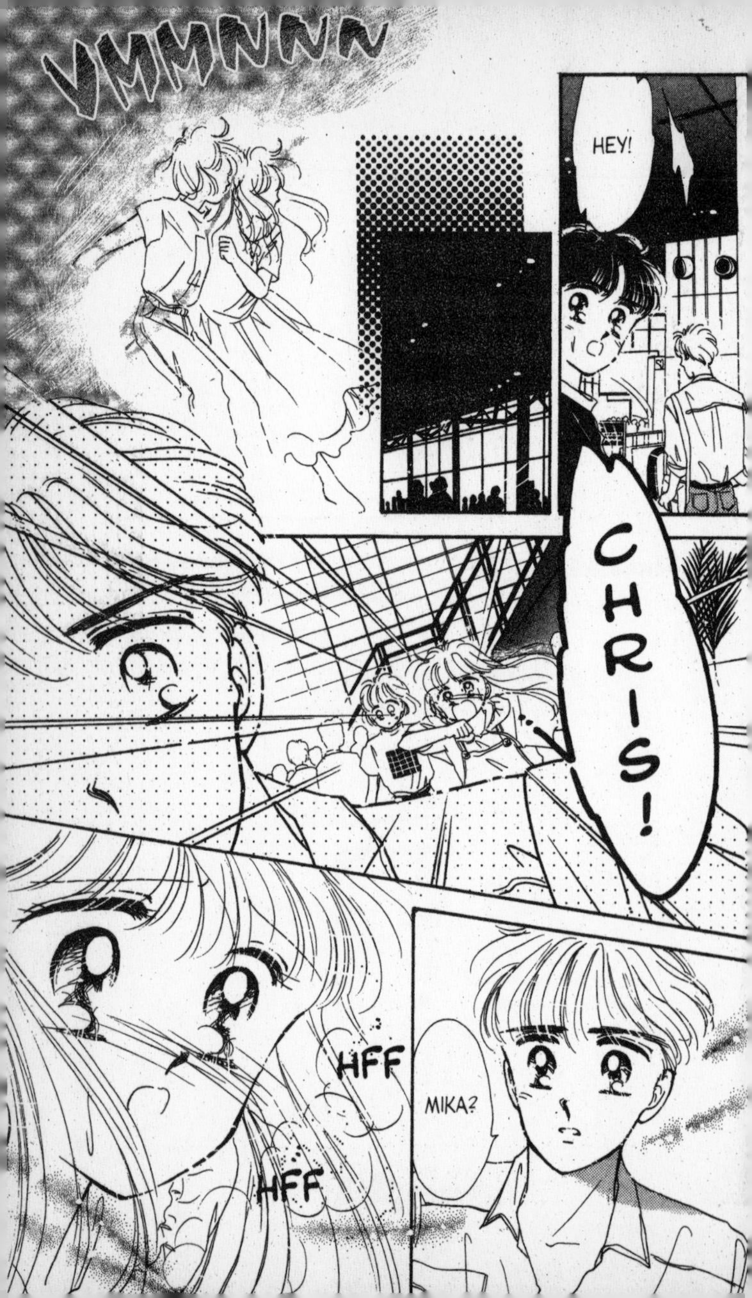
VMMNNN
HEY!
CHRIS!
HFF
HFF
MIKA?

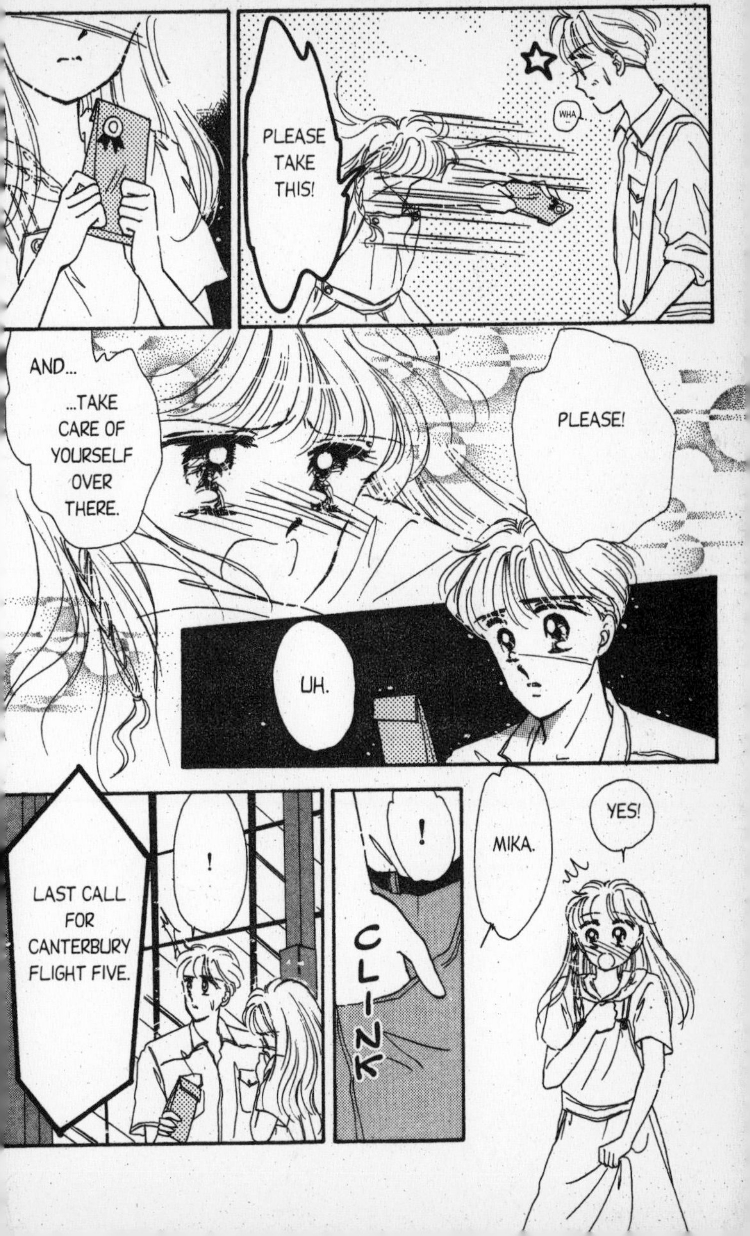
PLEASE TAKE THIS!
WHA...
AND...
...TAKE CARE OF YOURSELF OVER THERE.
PLEASE!
UH.
LAST CALL FOR CANTERBURY FLIGHT FIVE.
!
!
CLINK
MIKA.
YES!

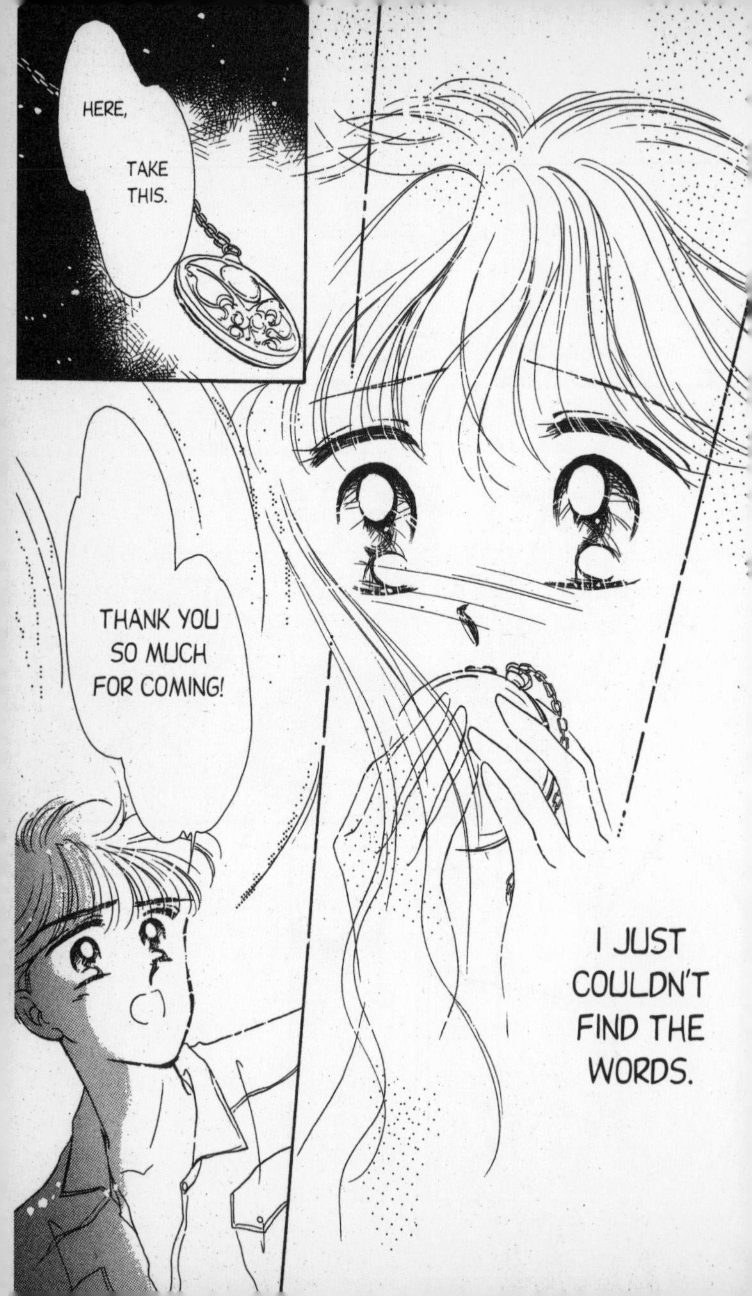
HERE,
TAKE THIS.
THANK YOU SO MUCH FOR COMING!
I JUST COULDN'T FIND THE WORDS.

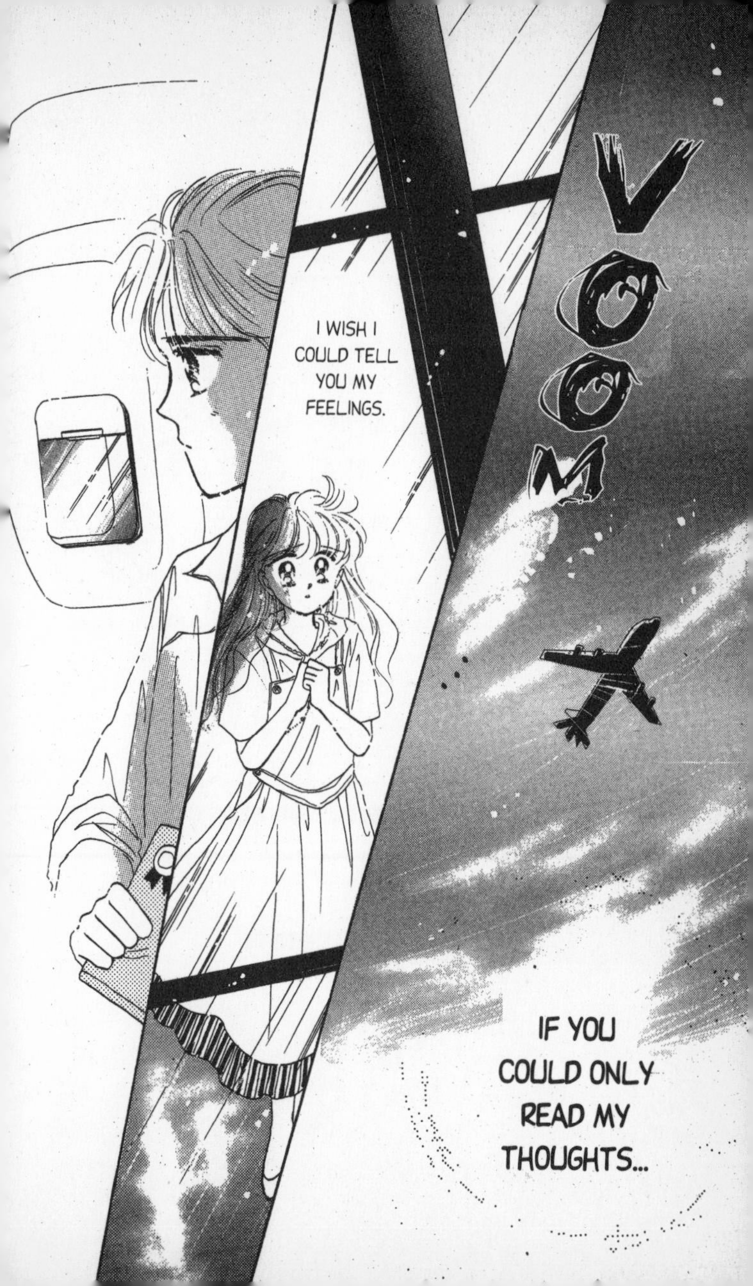
I WISH I COULD TELL YOU MY FEELINGS.
VOOM
IF YOU COULD ONLY READ MY THOUGHTS...

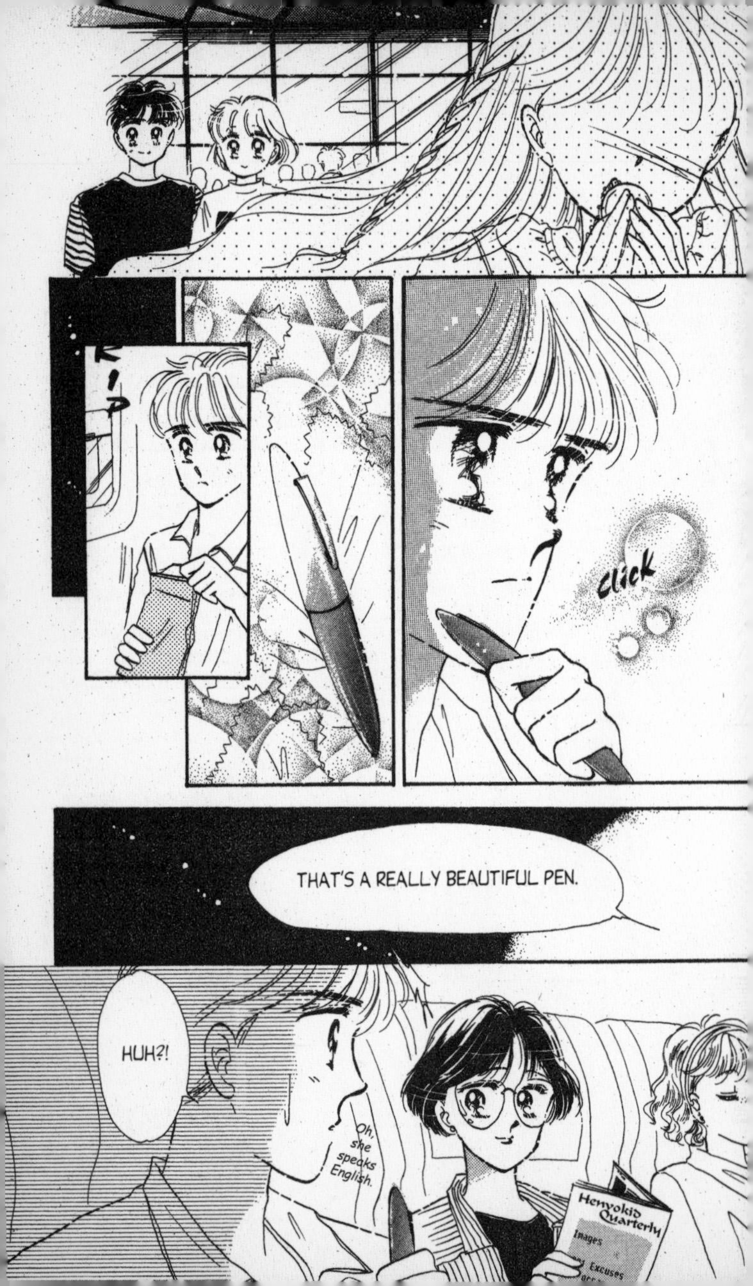
RIP
CLICK
THAT'S A REALLY BEAUTIFUL PEN.
HUH?!
Oh, she speaks English.
Henyokid Quarterly
Images
Excuses

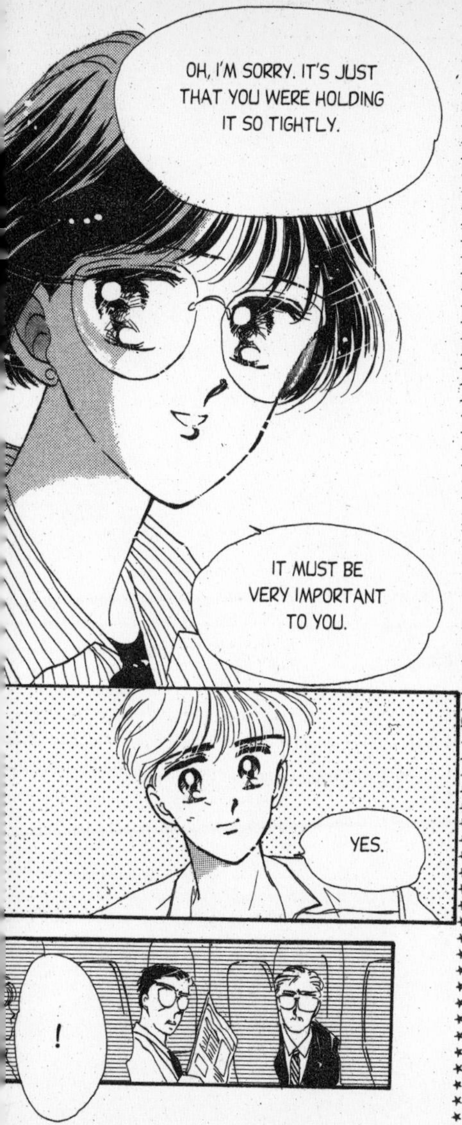
OH, I'M SORRY. IT'S JUST THAT YOU WERE HOLDING IT SO TIGHTLY.
IT MUST BE VERY IMPORTANT TO YOU.
YES.
!

BONUS

When I started "Miracle Girls," it was only meant to be a short run. (It was supposed to end with Part 1.) When I first pitched the story to my editor, he was a bit reluctant. But since he decided that the plot could be wrapped up rather quickly, he gave me the green light. So I began drawing my "girls' comic that had a demented teacher chasing after twin psychics subplot." Well, I considered it to be pretty normal and since it'd be over quickly, why not? But as it turns out–what's so short about it now? As you can see, I plan to keep adding episodes on through Part 3.

Well, I do enjoy what I do, you know...

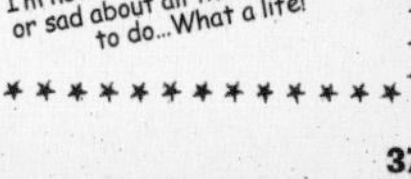

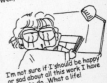

I'm not sure if I should be happy or sad about all this work I have to do... What a life!

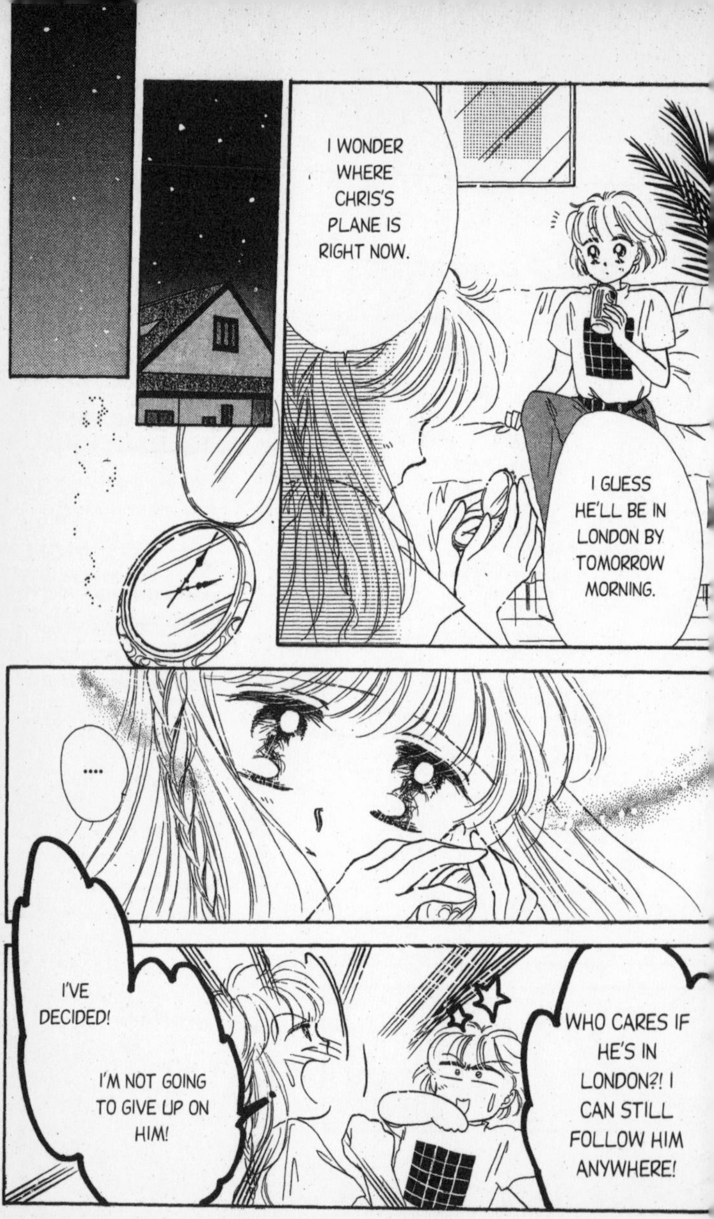
I WONDER WHERE CHRIS'S PLANE IS RIGHT NOW.
I GUESS HE'LL BE IN LONDON BY TOMORROW MORNING.
....
I'VE DECIDED!
I'M NOT GOING TO GIVE UP ON HIM!
WHO CARES IF HE'S IN LONDON?! I CAN STILL FOLLOW HIM ANYWHERE!

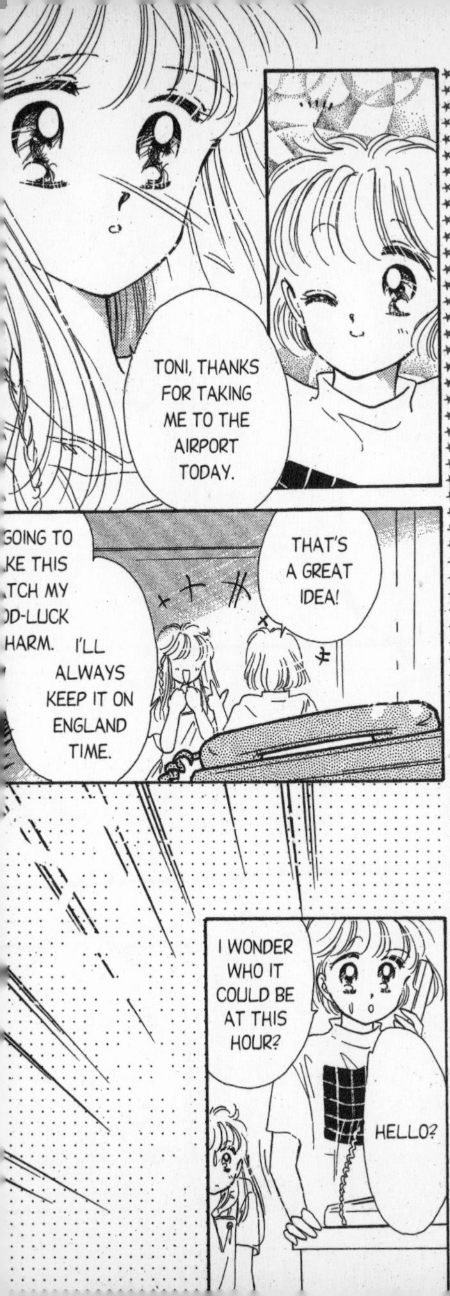
TONI, THANKS FOR TAKING ME TO THE AIRPORT TODAY.
GOING TO KE THIS TCH MY D-LUCK HARM. I'LL ALWAYS KEEP IT ON ENGLAND TIME.
THAT'S A GREAT IDEA!
I WONDER WHO IT COULD BE AT THIS HOUR?
HELLO?

BONUS

I was so exhausted after writing Part 2 that I decided to plan a vacation. However, I ended up completing Part 2 earlier than expected, so my editors ordered me to go straight into Part 3 without a break!

I began to panic. I hadn't thought about what kind of story to develop for Part 3 – plus, I didn't have the time. But then my editor suggested a plotline. A gift from heaven! So I decided to throw away all my attitude and ego and eagerly awaited my editor's suggestions. What did it turn out to be? "Miracle Girls, in Saudi Arabia!" Forget it. Never mind. I needed to figure out my problems on my own. But I was running out of time! One night, I awoke to a strange fragrance in my room. One of my perfume bottles had spilled all over my cabinet. And that's how I got the inspiration for the perfume "NAHEMA" in Part 3.

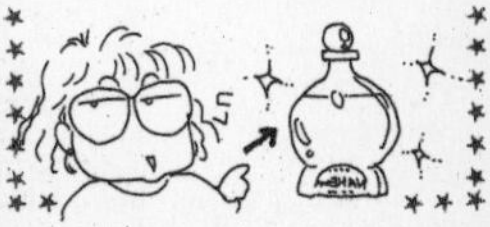

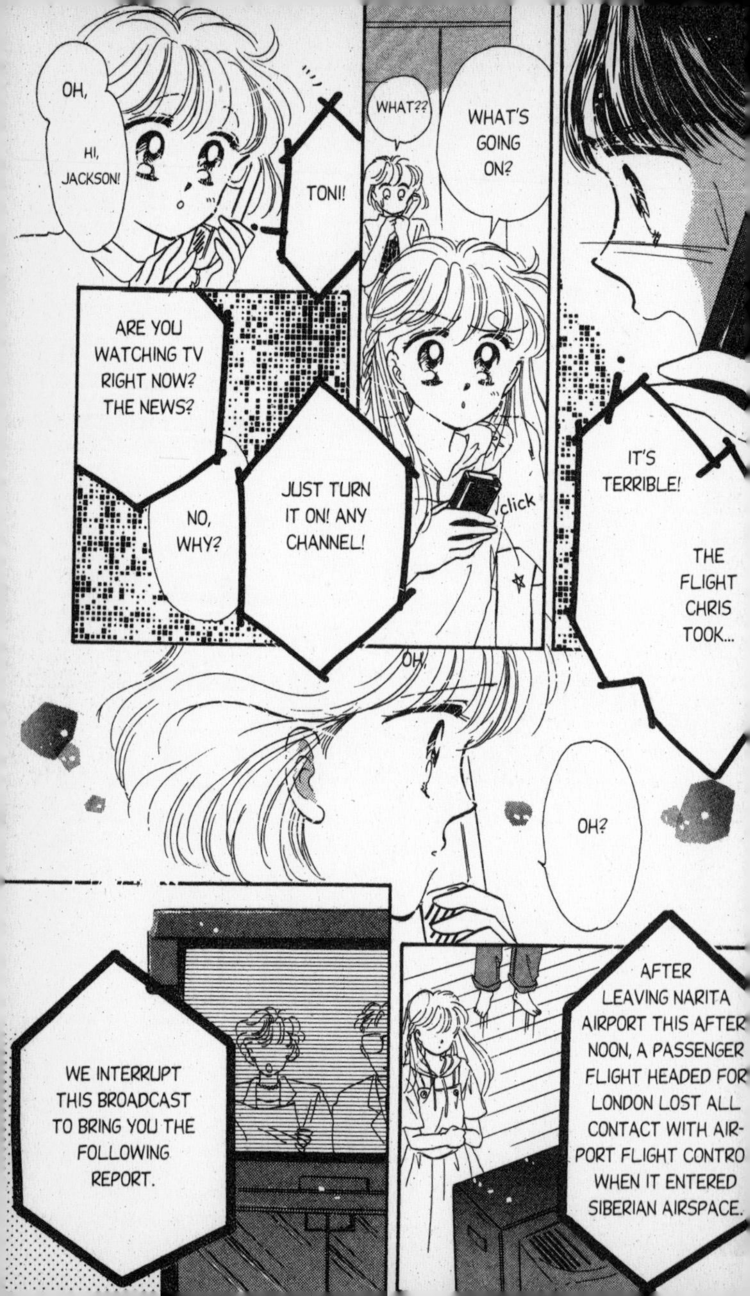
OH,
HI, JACKSON!
TONI!
ARE YOU WATCHING TV RIGHT NOW? THE NEWS?
NO, WHY?
JUST TURN IT ON! ANY CHANNEL!
WHAT??
WHAT'S GOING ON?
click
IT'S TERRIBLE!
THE FLIGHT CHRIS TOOK...
OH,
OH?
WE INTERRUPT THIS BROADCAST TO BRING YOU THE FOLLOWING REPORT.
AFTER LEAVING NARITA AIRPORT THIS AFTER NOON, A PASSENGER FLIGHT HEADED FOR LONDON LOST ALL CONTACT WITH AIR-PORT FLIGHT CONTRO WHEN IT ENTERED SIBERIAN AIRSPACE.

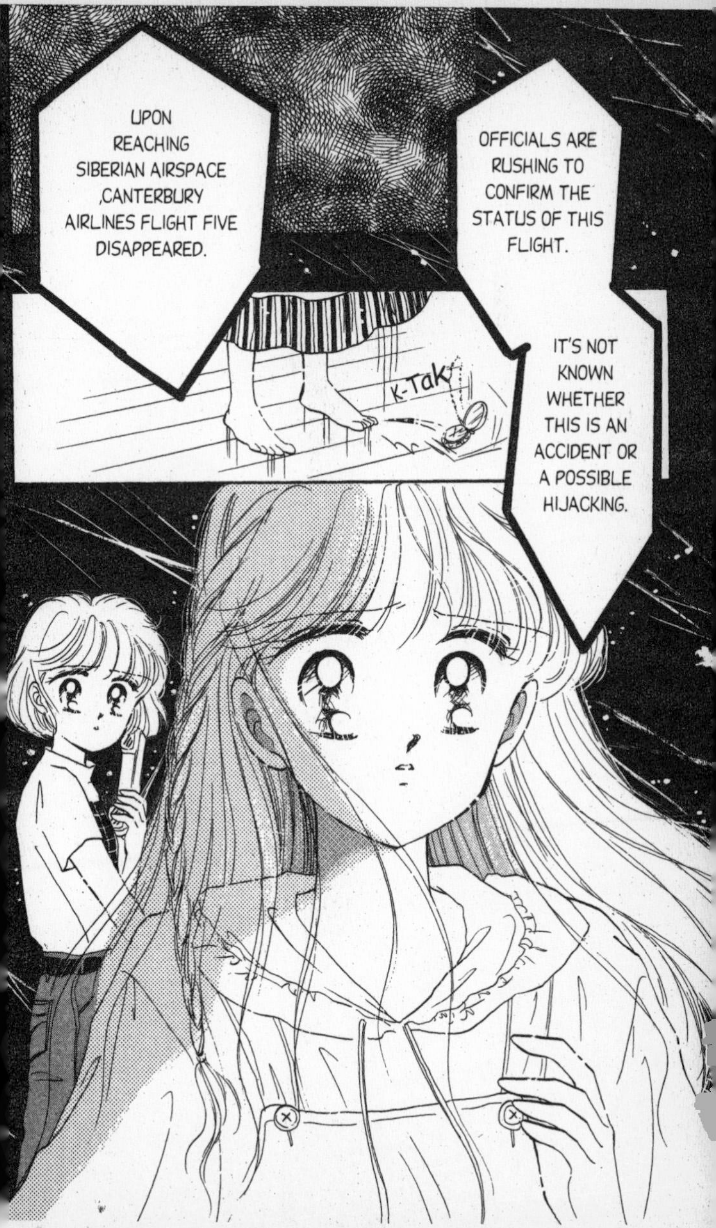
UPON REACHING SIBERIAN AIRSPACE ,CANTERBURY AIRLINES FLIGHT FIVE DISAPPEARED.
OFFICIALS ARE RUSHING TO CONFIRM THE STATUS OF THIS FLIGHT.
K-TAK
IT'S NOT KNOWN WHETHER THIS IS AN ACCIDENT OR A POSSIBLE HIJACKING.

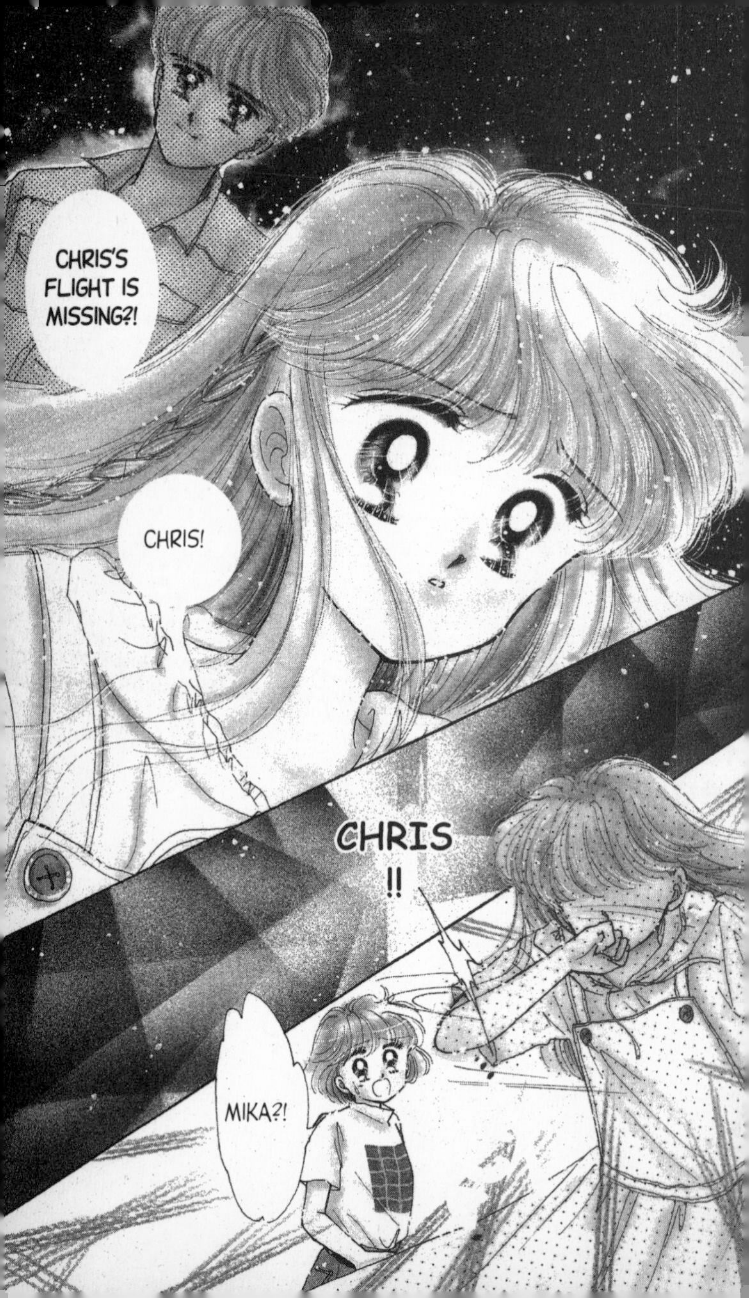
CHRIS'S FLIGHT IS MISSING?!
CHRIS!
CHRIS !!
MIKA?!

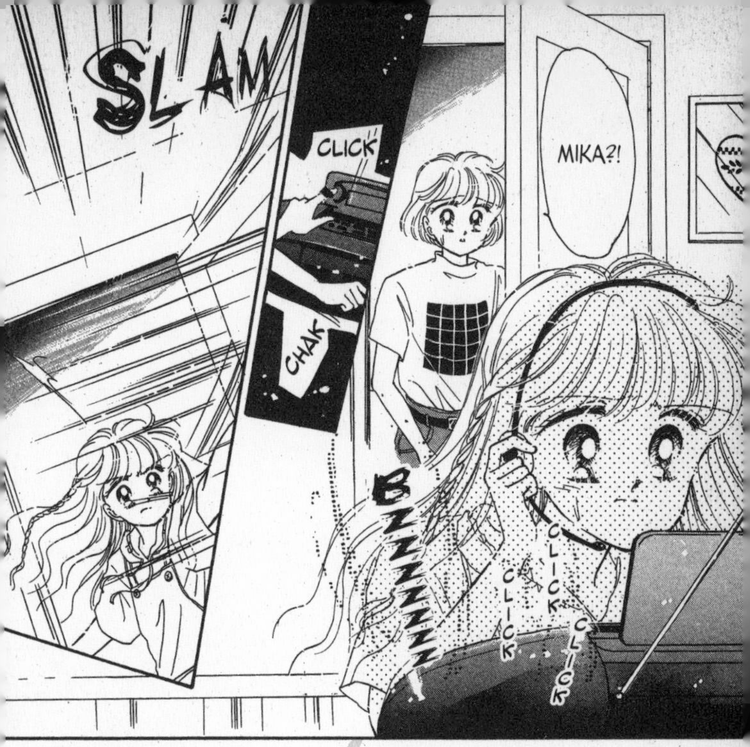
SLAM
CLICK
CHAK
MIKA?!
BZZZZZZZ
CLICK
CLICK
CLICK

BONUS

Nahema perfume was created to evoke the imaginary world of twin queens in a fairy tale world. Although I don't wear perfume, I actually like to collect fragrances as a hobby. This hobby began around the time I began drawing "Miracle Girls," so I was intrigued by the concept of "twins!"

I dreamed up my own concept of Nahema as I inhaled the fragrance. (To tell you the truth, it kinda stinks!) Although I only vaguely hint at it in the story, I wanted to evoke a strange and romantic world for the country of Diamas. And there, the adventures of Toni, Mika, Chris, Jackson, and Mr. Kageura began.

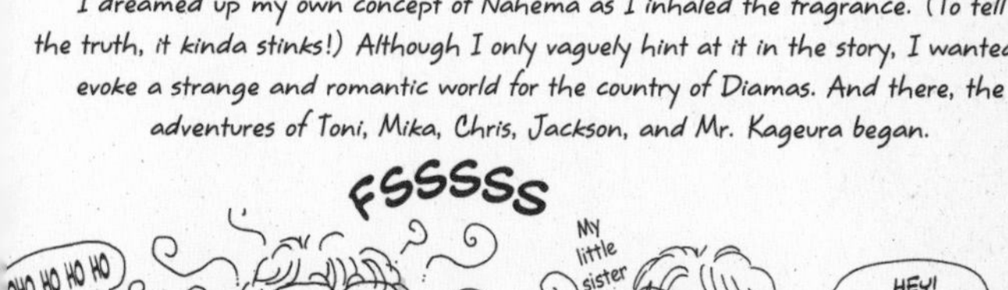
FSSSSS
OHO HO HO HO
My little sister
HEY! THIS STINKS

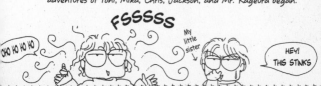

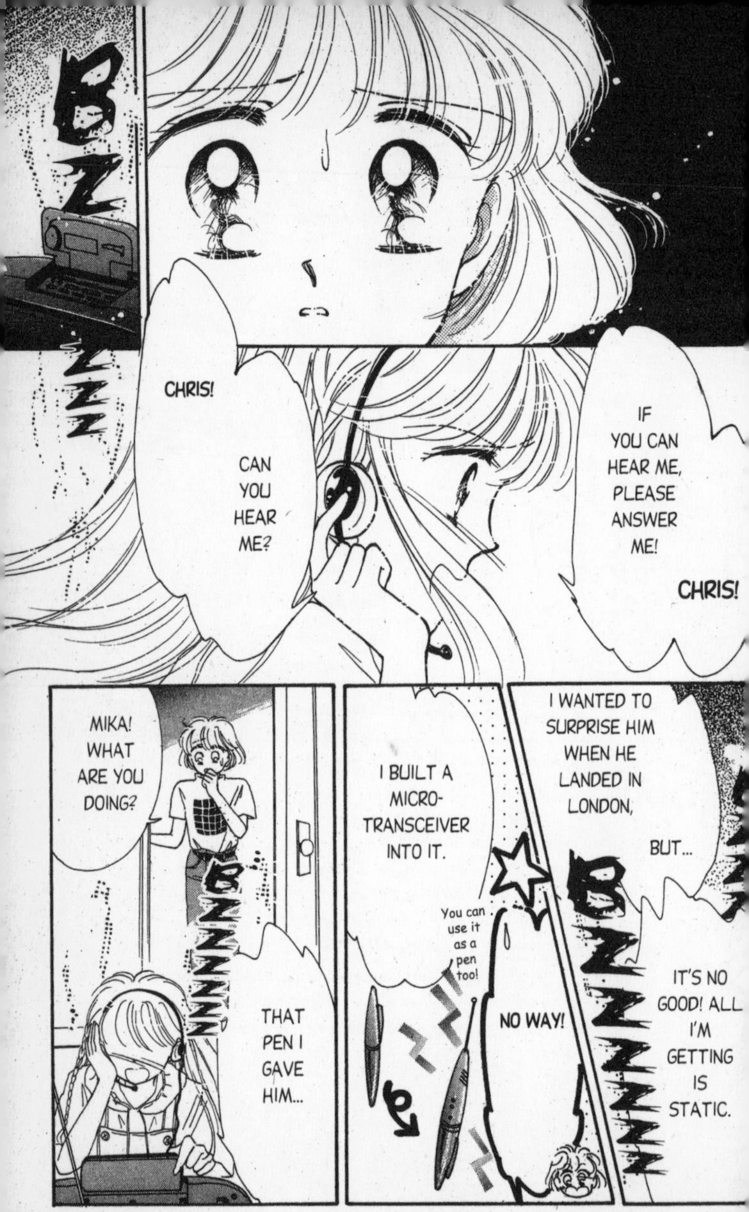
BZZ
ZZZ
CHRIS!
CAN YOU HEAR ME?
IF YOU CAN HEAR ME, PLEASE ANSWER ME!
CHRIS!
MIKA! WHAT ARE YOU DOING?
BZZZZZZZZ
THAT PEN I GAVE HIM...
I BUILT A MICRO-TRANSCEIVER INTO IT.
You can use it as a pen too!
NO WAY!
I WANTED TO SURPRISE HIM WHEN HE LANDED IN LONDON,
BUT...
BZZZZZZZ
IT'S NO GOOD! ALL I'M GETTING IS STATIC.

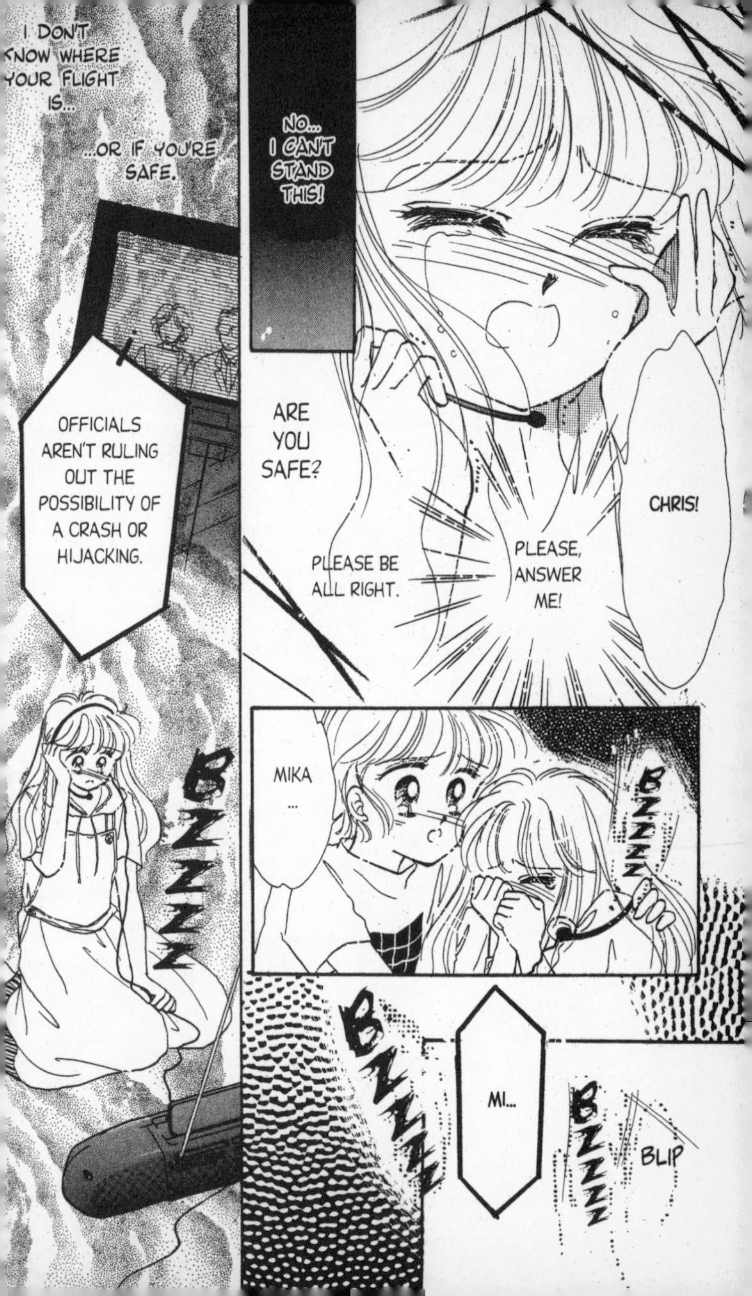
I DON'T KNOW WHERE YOUR FLIGHT IS...
...OR IF YOU'RE SAFE.
OFFICIALS AREN'T RULING OUT THE POSSIBILITY OF A CRASH OR HIJACKING.
BZZZZZ
NO... I CAN'T STAND THIS!
ARE YOU SAFE?
CHRIS!
PLEASE BE ALL RIGHT.
PLEASE, ANSWER ME!
MIKA ...
BZZZZ
BZZZZ
MI...
BZZZZ
BLIP

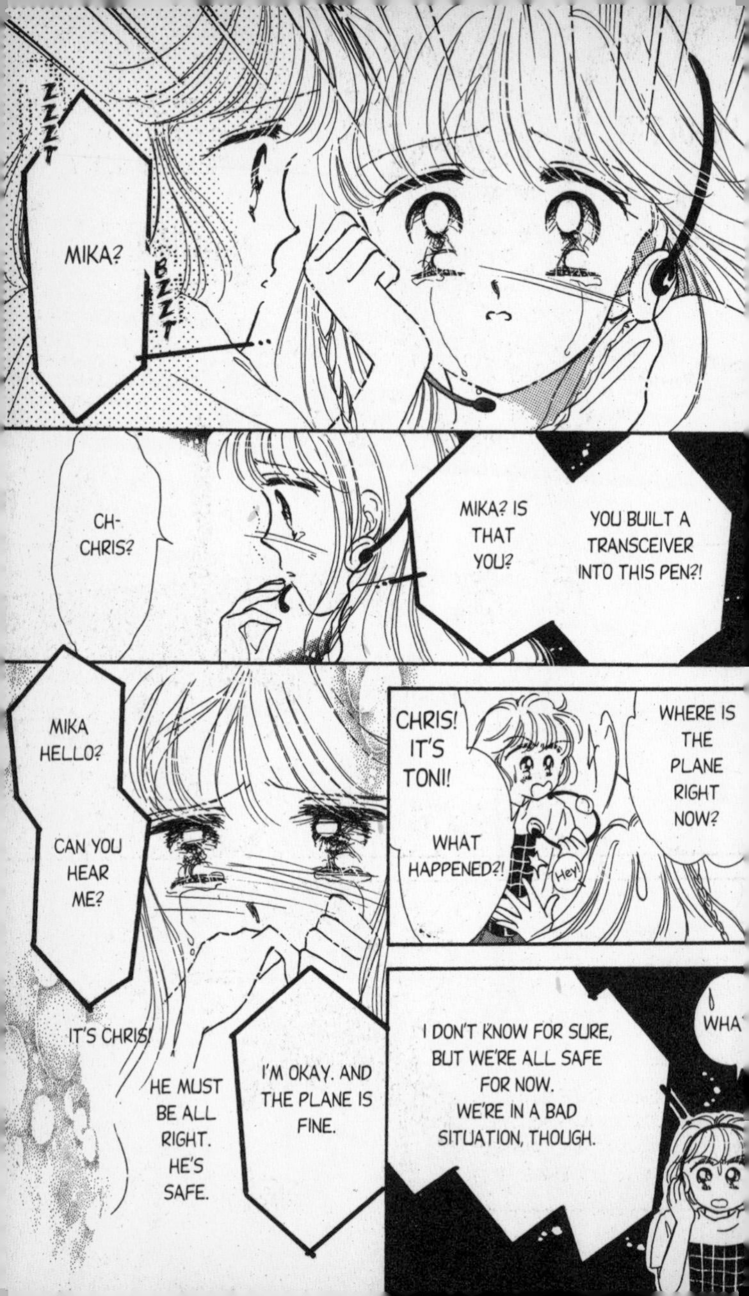
ZZZT
MIKA?
BZZZT
CH-CHRIS?
MIKA? IS THAT YOU?
YOU BUILT A TRANSCEIVER INTO THIS PEN?!
MIKA HELLO?
CAN YOU HEAR ME?
IT'S CHRIS!
HE MUST BE ALL RIGHT. HE'S SAFE.
CHRIS! IT'S TONI!
WHAT HAPPENED?!
Hey!
WHERE IS THE PLANE RIGHT NOW?
I'M OKAY. AND THE PLANE IS FINE.
I DON'T KNOW FOR SURE, BUT WE'RE ALL SAFE FOR NOW. WE'RE IN A BAD SITUATION, THOUGH.
WHA

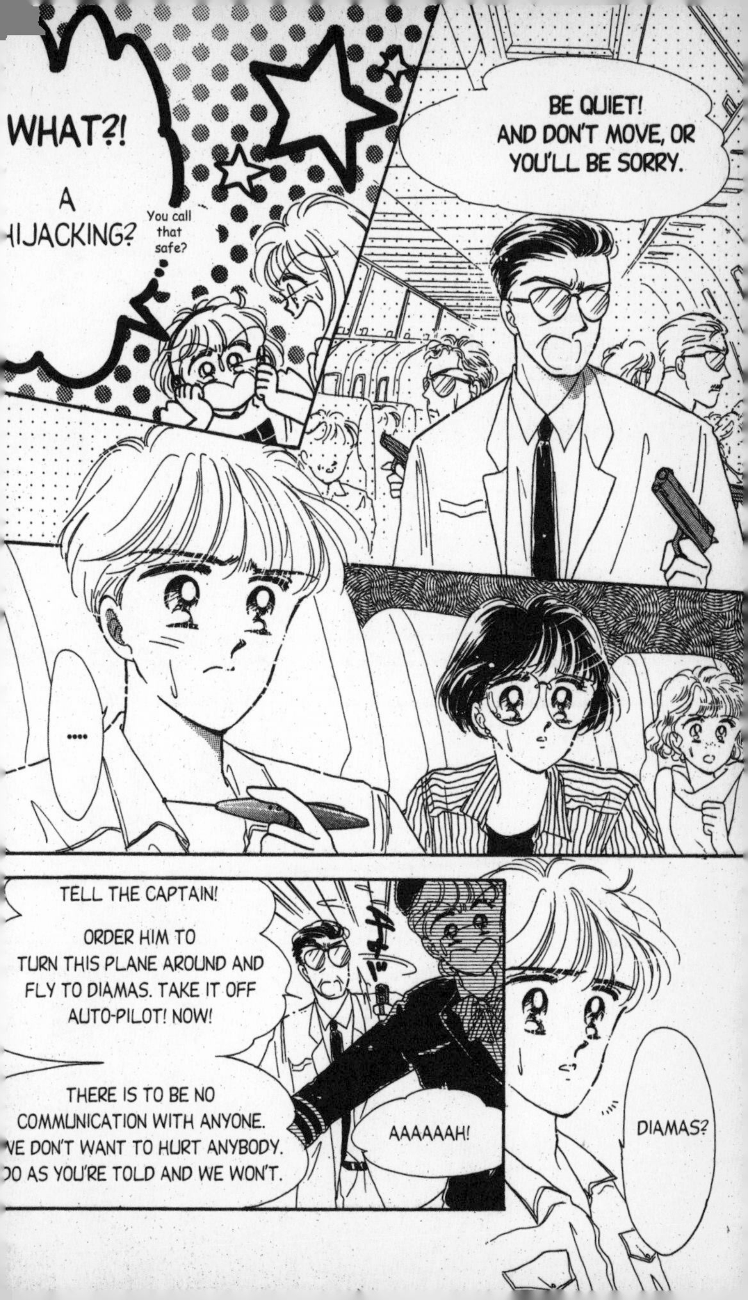
WHAT?!
A
HIJACKING?
You call that safe?
BE QUIET! AND DON'T MOVE, OR YOU'LL BE SORRY.
....
TELL THE CAPTAIN!
ORDER HIM TO TURN THIS PLANE AROUND AND FLY TO DIAMAS. TAKE IT OFF AUTO-PILOT! NOW!
THERE IS TO BE NO COMMUNICATION WITH ANYONE. WE DON'T WANT TO HURT ANYBODY. DO AS YOU'RE TOLD AND WE WON'T.
AAAAAAH!
DIAMAS?

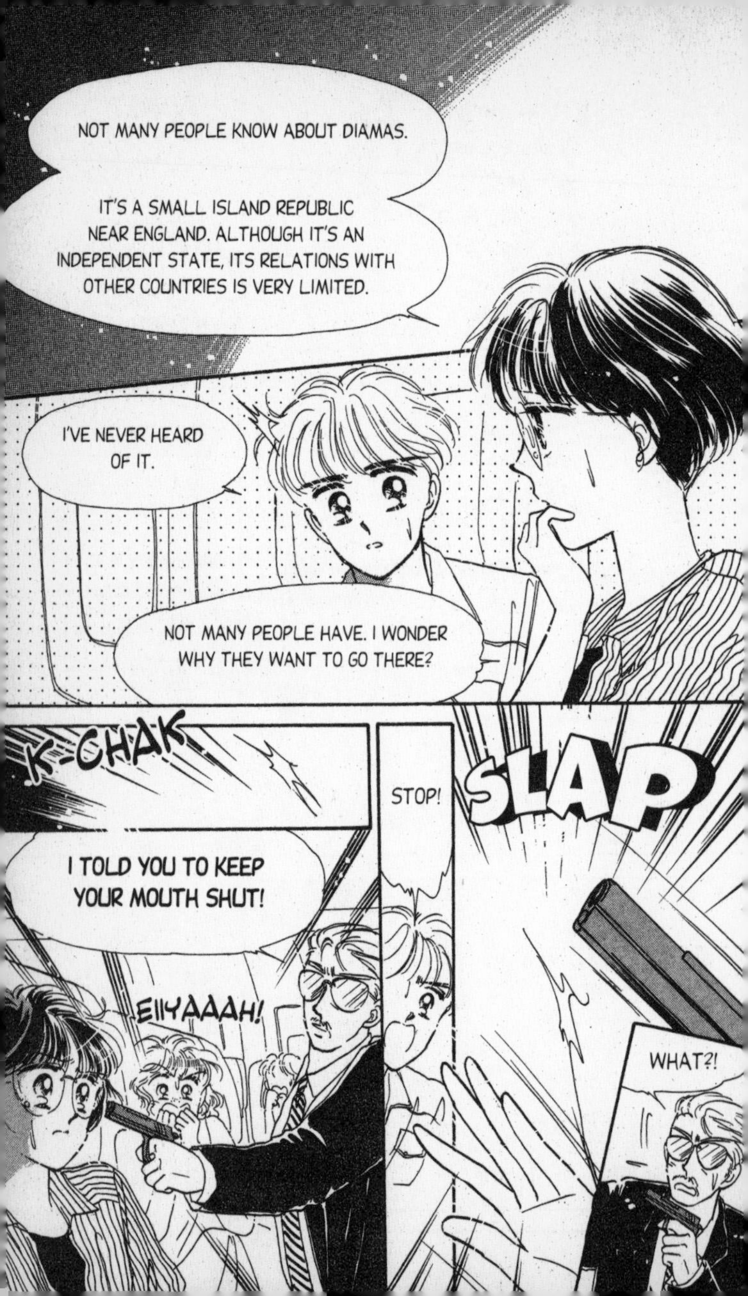

NOT MANY PEOPLE KNOW ABOUT DIAMAS.
IT'S A SMALL ISLAND REPUBLIC NEAR ENGLAND. ALTHOUGH IT'S AN INDEPENDENT STATE, ITS RELATIONS WITH OTHER COUNTRIES IS VERY LIMITED.
I'VE NEVER HEARD OF IT.
NOT MANY PEOPLE HAVE. I WONDER WHY THEY WANT TO GO THERE?
K-CHAK
I TOLD YOU TO KEEP YOUR MOUTH SHUT!
EIIYAAAH!
STOP!
SLAP
WHAT?!

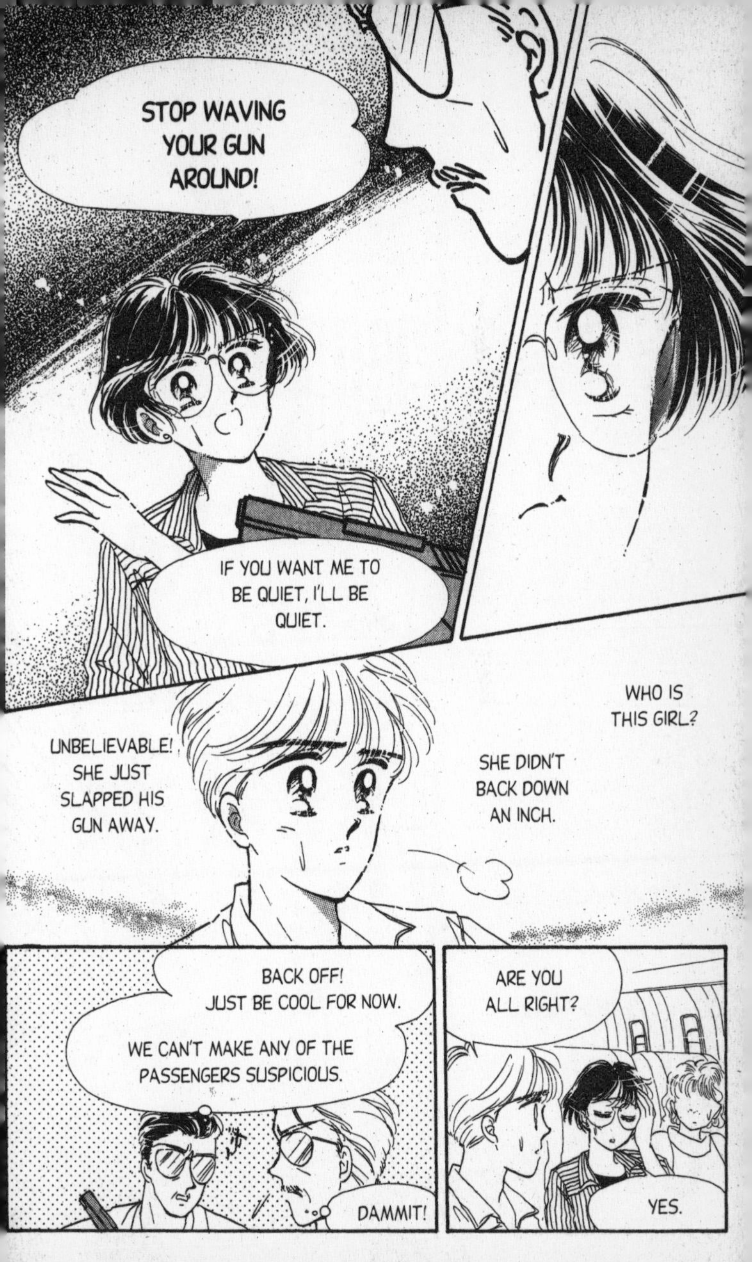
STOP WAVING YOUR GUN AROUND!
IF YOU WANT ME TO BE QUIET, I'LL BE QUIET.
UNBELIEVABLE! SHE JUST SLAPPED HIS GUN AWAY.
SHE DIDN'T BACK DOWN AN INCH.
WHO IS THIS GIRL?
BACK OFF! JUST BE COOL FOR NOW.
WE CAN'T MAKE ANY OF THE PASSENGERS SUSPICIOUS.
DAMMIT!
ARE YOU ALL RIGHT?
YES.

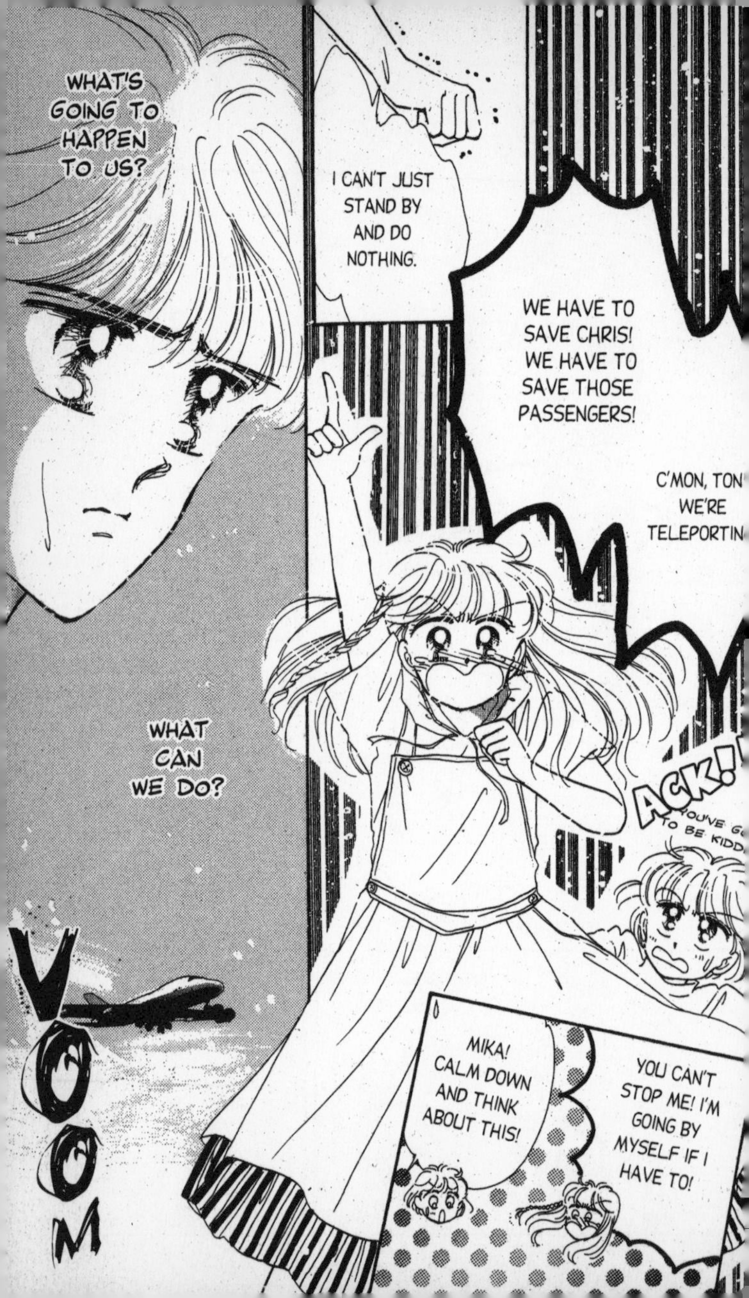
WHAT'S GOING TO HAPPEN TO US?
WHAT CAN WE DO?
VOOM
I CAN'T JUST STAND BY AND DO NOTHING.
WE HAVE TO SAVE CHRIS! WE HAVE TO SAVE THOSE PASSENGERS!
C'MON, TON WE'RE TELEPORTIN
ACK!
YOU'VE G TO BE KIDD
MIKA! CALM DOWN AND THINK ABOUT THIS!
YOU CAN'T STOP ME! I'M GOING BY MYSELF IF I HAVE TO!

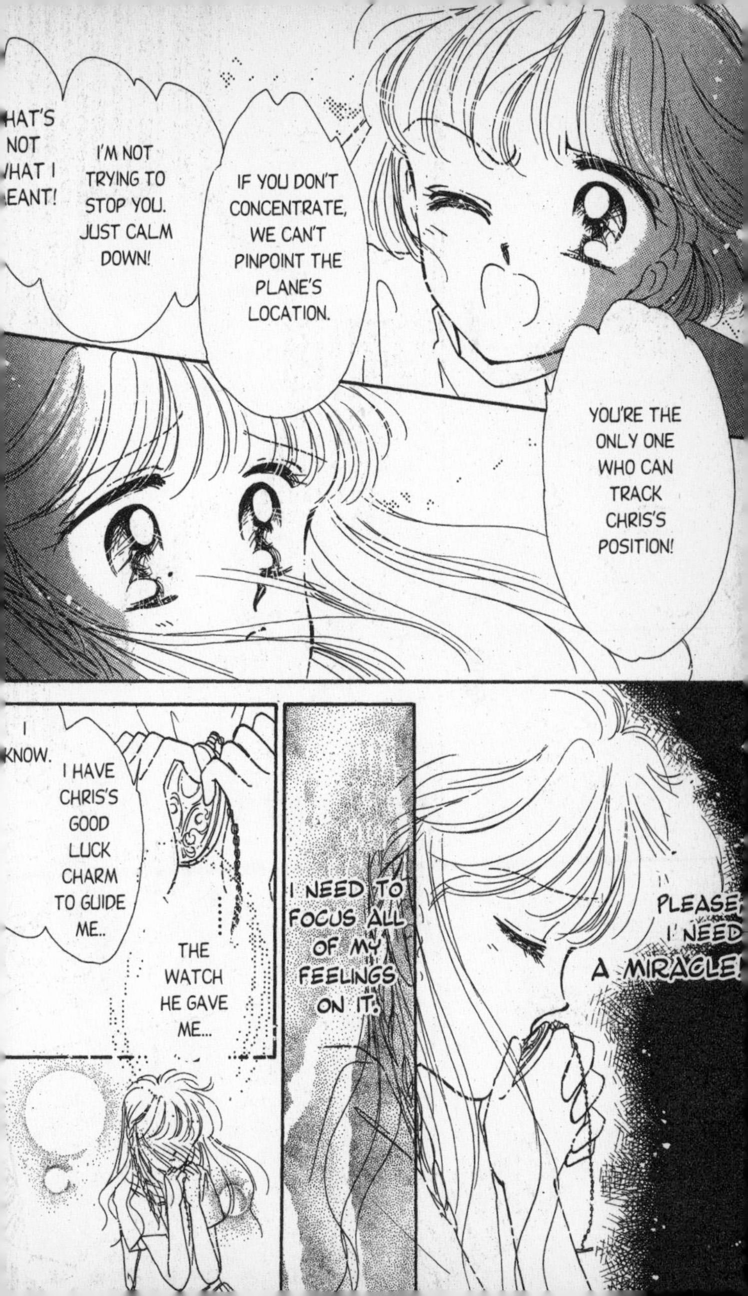
HAT'S NOT HAT I EANT!
I'M NOT TRYING TO STOP YOU. JUST CALM DOWN!
IF YOU DON'T CONCENTRATE, WE CAN'T PINPOINT THE PLANE'S LOCATION.
YOU'RE THE ONLY ONE WHO CAN TRACK CHRIS'S POSITION!
I KNOW.
I HAVE CHRIS'S GOOD LUCK CHARM TO GUIDE ME..
THE WATCH HE GAVE ME...
I NEED TO FOCUS ALL OF MY FEELINGS ON IT.
PLEASE, I NEED A MIRACLE!

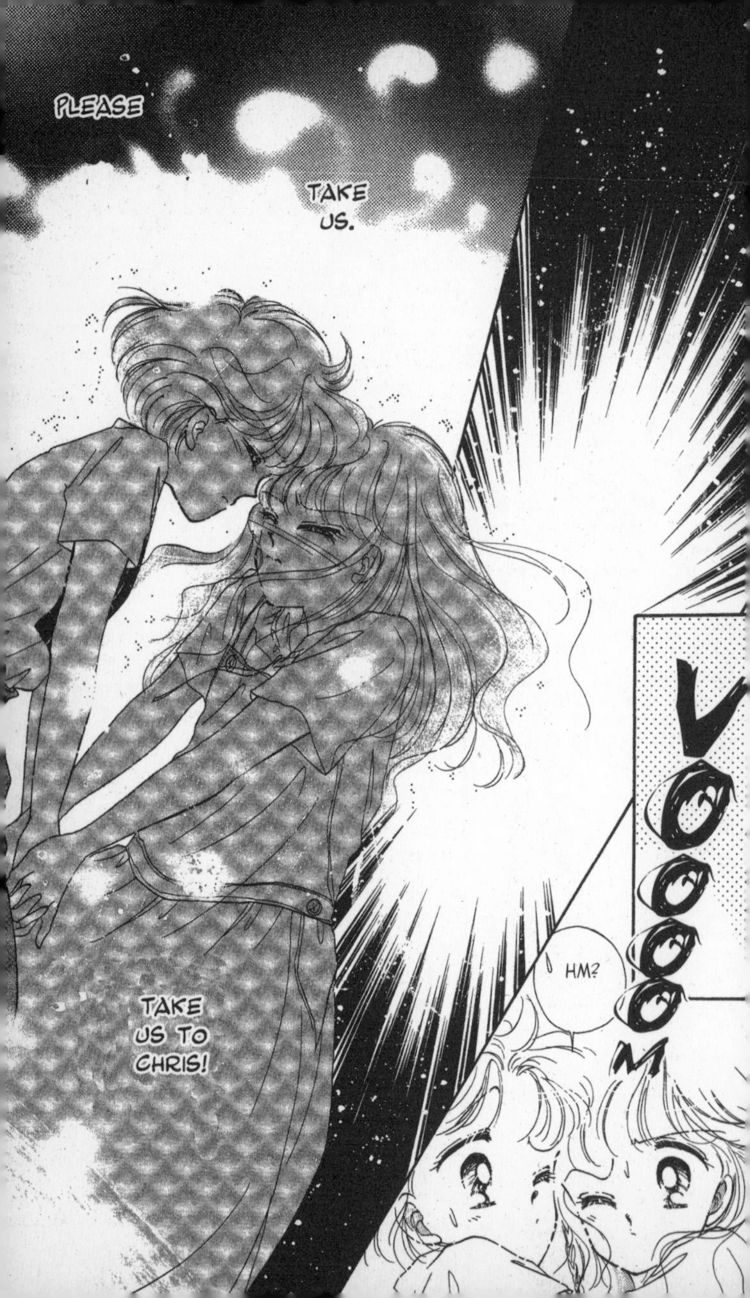
PLEASE
TAKE US.
TAKE US TO CHRIS!
VOOOOOM
HM?

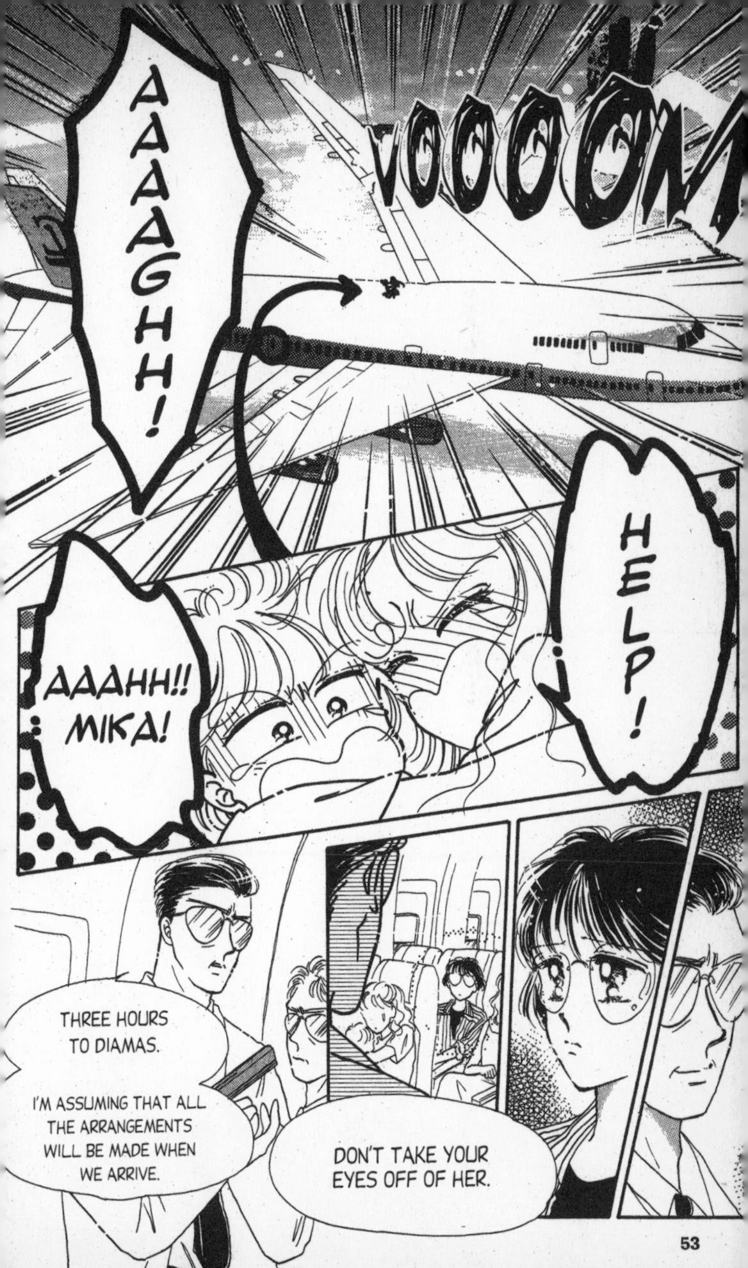
AAAAGHH!
VOOOOOM
AAAHH!! MIKA!
HELP!
THREE HOURS TO DIAMAS.
I'M ASSUMING THAT ALL THE ARRANGEMENTS WILL BE MADE WHEN WE ARRIVE.
DON'T TAKE YOUR EYES OFF OF HER.

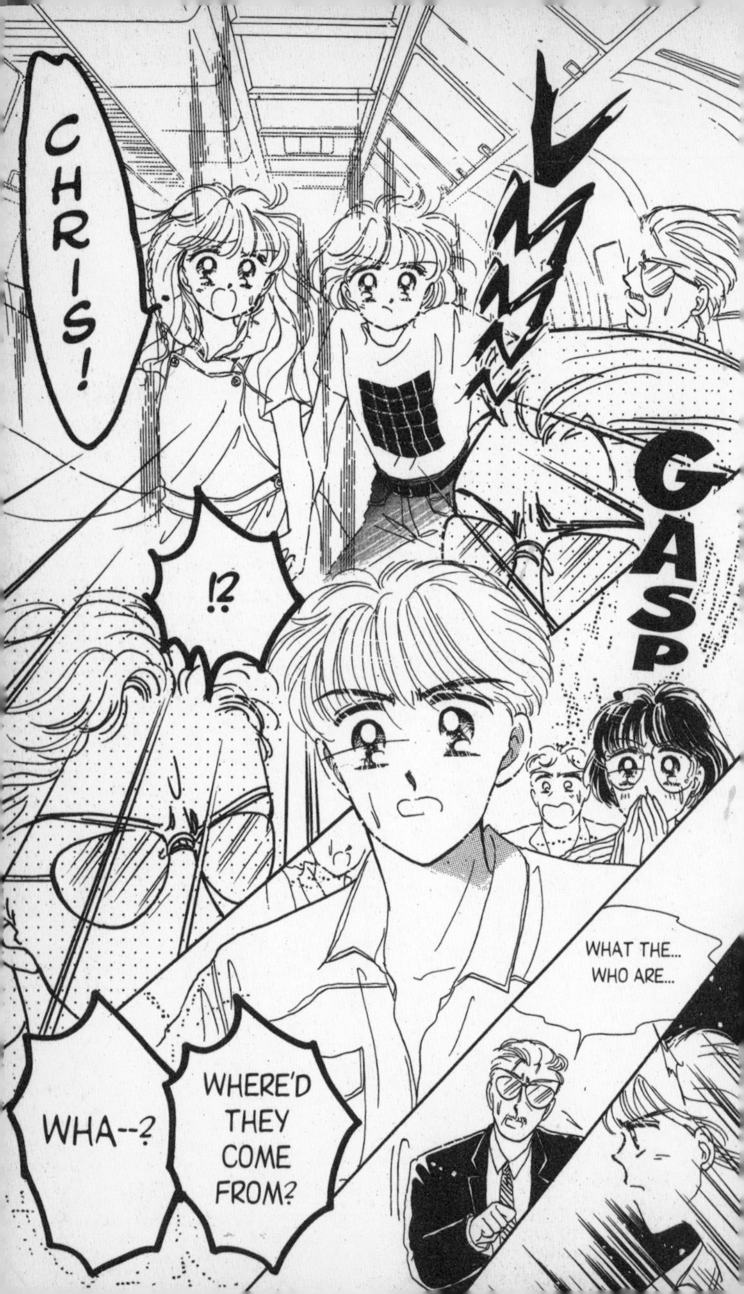
CHRIS!
GASP
!?
WHAT THE... WHO ARE...
WHA--?
WHERE'D THEY COME FROM?

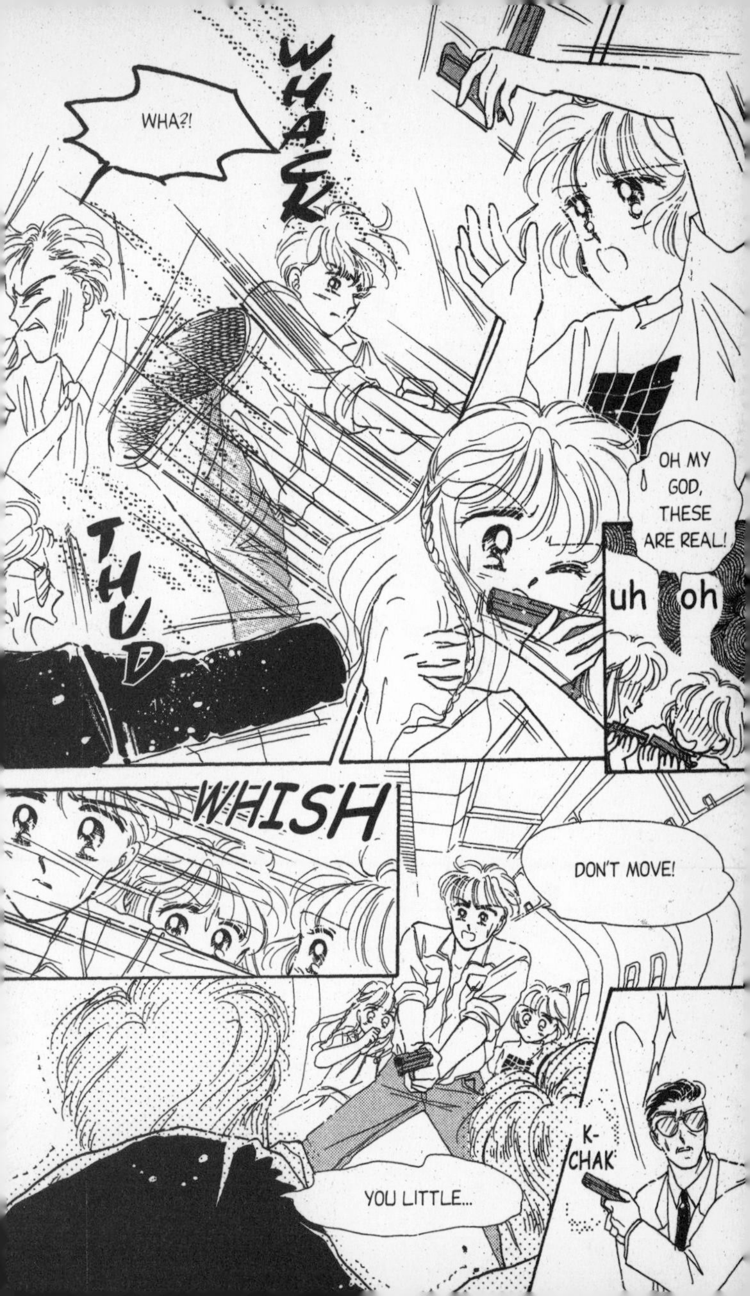
WHA?!
WHACK
THUD
OH MY GOD, THESE ARE REAL!
uh oh
WHISH
DON'T MOVE!
YOU LITTLE...
K-CHAK

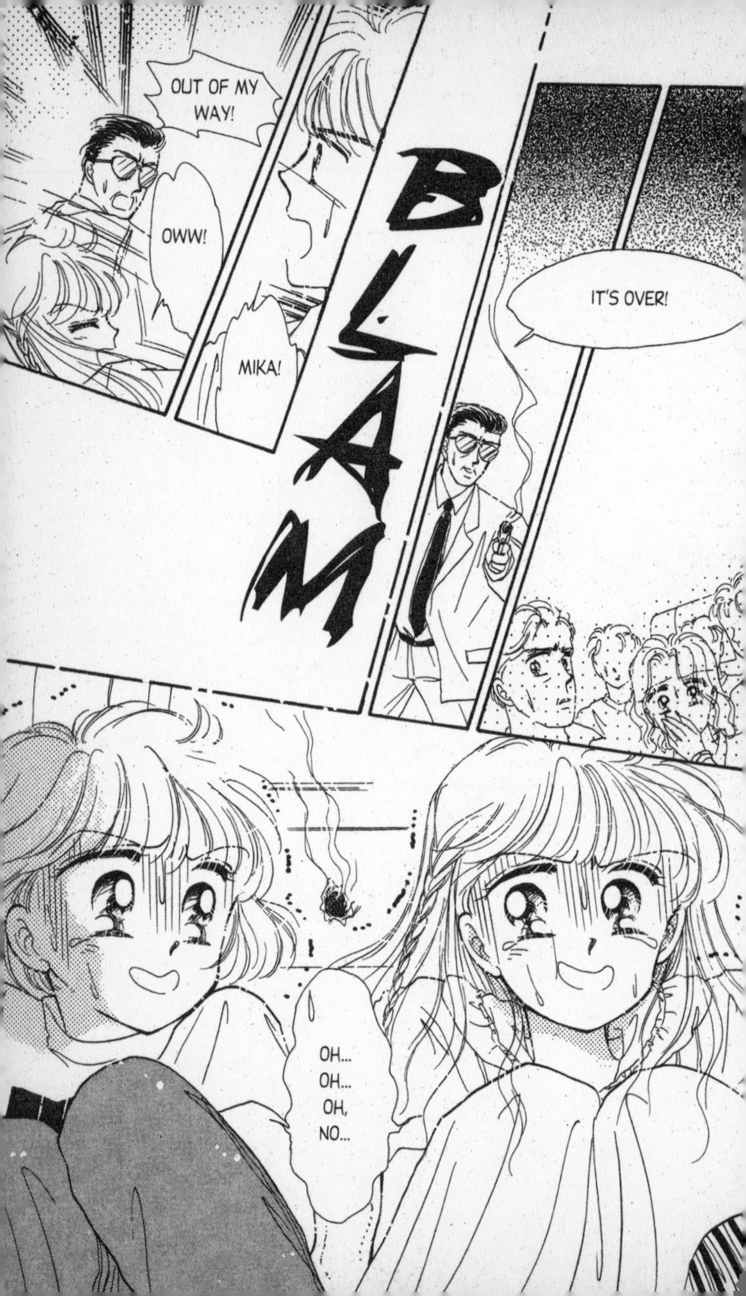
OUT OF MY WAY!
OWW!
MIKA!
BLAM!
IT'S OVER!
OH... OH... OH, NO...

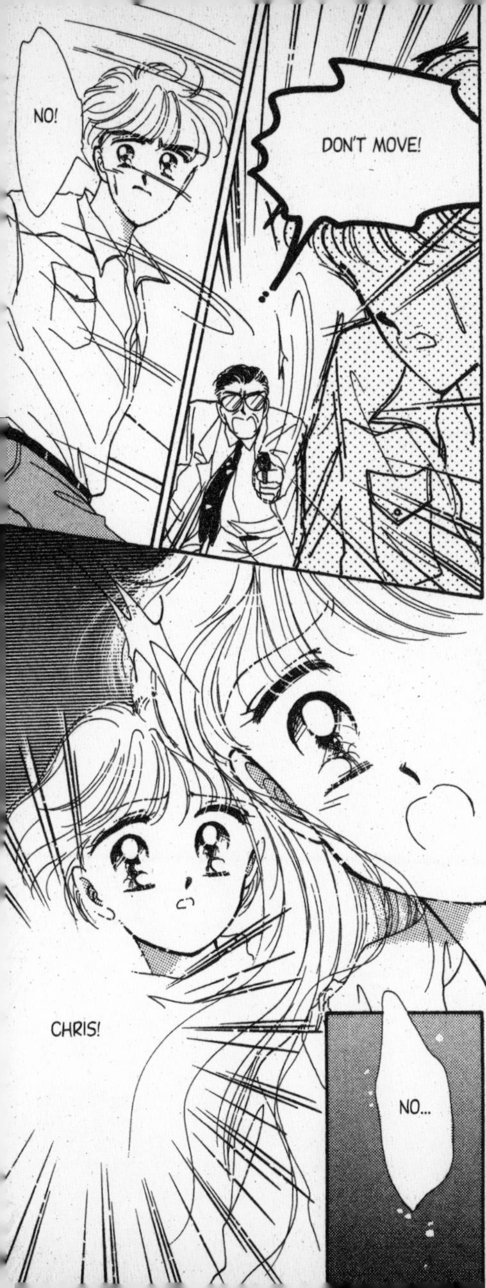
NO!
DON'T MOVE!
CHRIS!
NO...

BONUS

So, I have my idea for Part 3. But that still leaves the issue of what to do with Chris. He has been becoming such a minor character since Part 2. Well, the thing to do in situations like this one is to get rid of him somehow. Okay, I'm not going to kill him off, but I need to get rid of him gently. Like, say, having him go overseas to study. Since I've always wanted to go to England, I thought, Why don't I send him there? I could have had him go to America, but everyone seems to go there just to have fun. I'd hate it if my boyfriend came back with some blonde girlfriend. Okay, I'm taking this way too seriously! I didn't mean to offend all the serious exchange students out there. Anyway, I know this is hard on Mika, but it is a little more dramatic this way—having a long-distance love affair. Oh, I'm so evil...

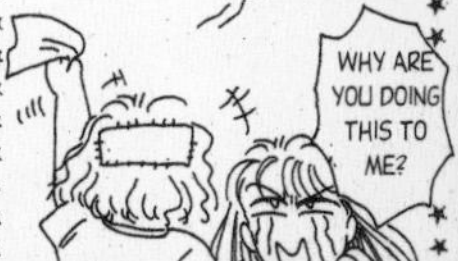
WHY ARE YOU DOING THIS TO ME?

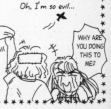

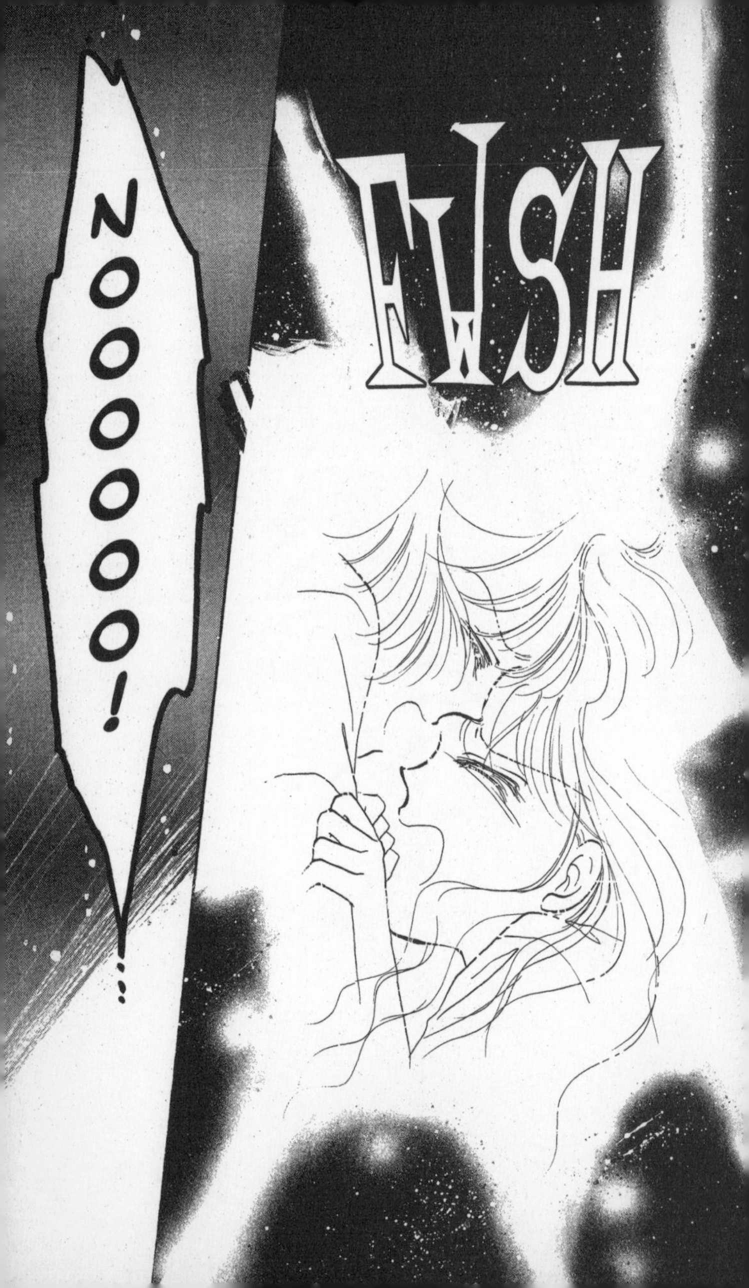
NOOOOOO!
FWSH

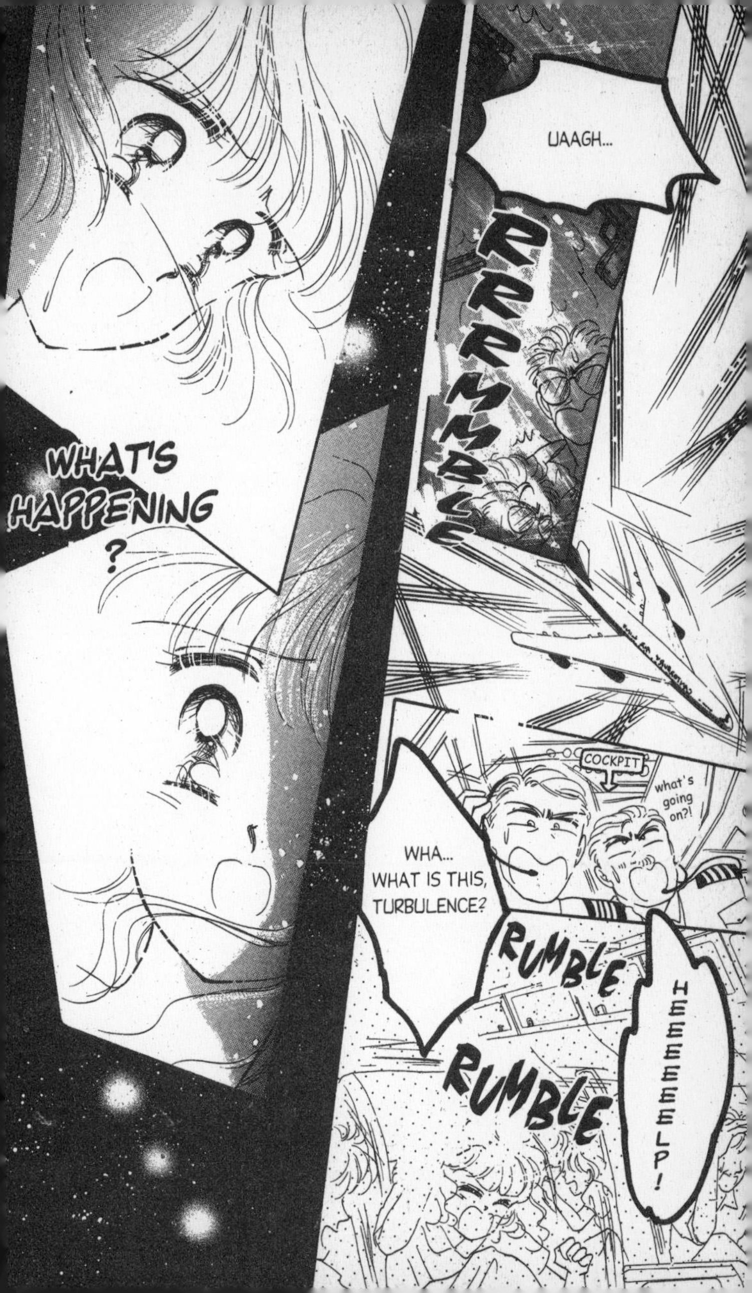
WHAT'S HAPPENING ?
UAAGH...
RRRMMBLE
COCKPIT
WHA... WHAT IS THIS, TURBULENCE?
what's going on?!
RUMBLE
RUMBLE
HEEEEELP!

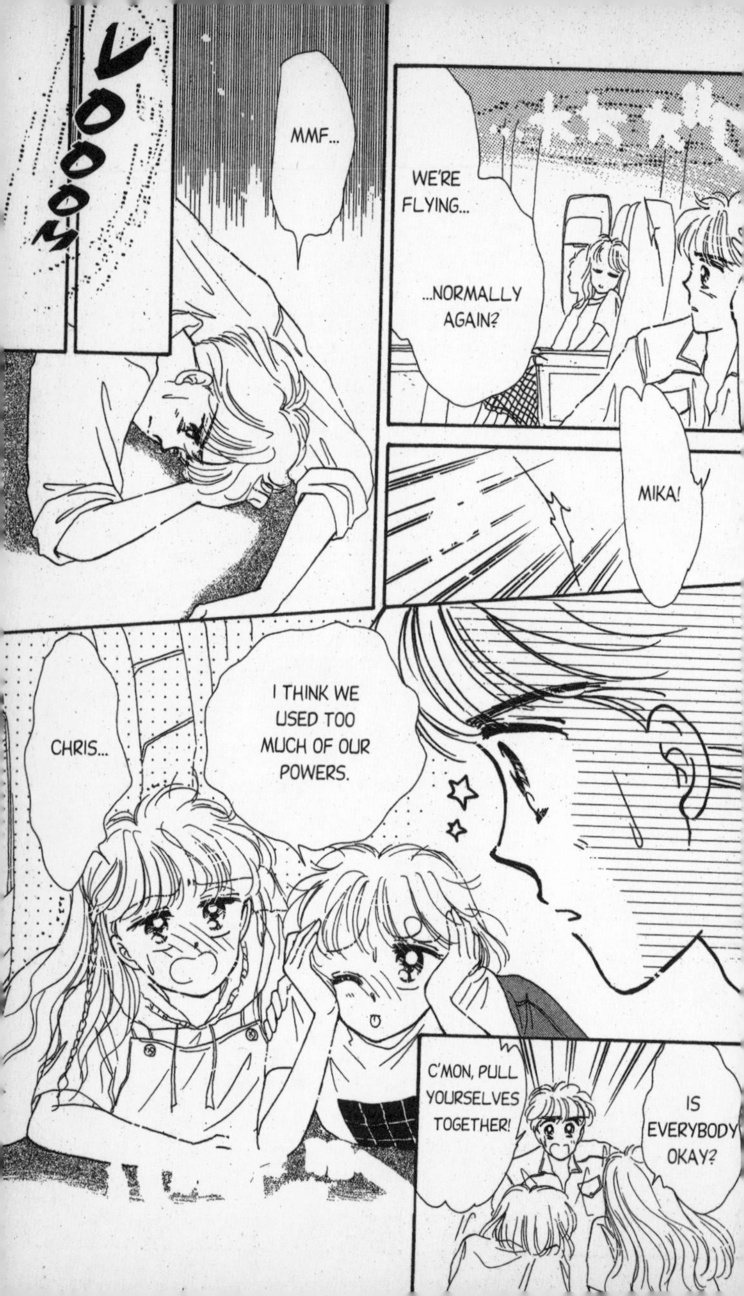
VOOOOM
MMF...
WE'RE FLYING...
...NORMALLY AGAIN?
MIKA!
CHRIS...
I THINK WE USED TOO MUCH OF OUR POWERS.
C'MON, PULL YOURSELVES TOGETHER!
IS EVERYBODY OKAY?

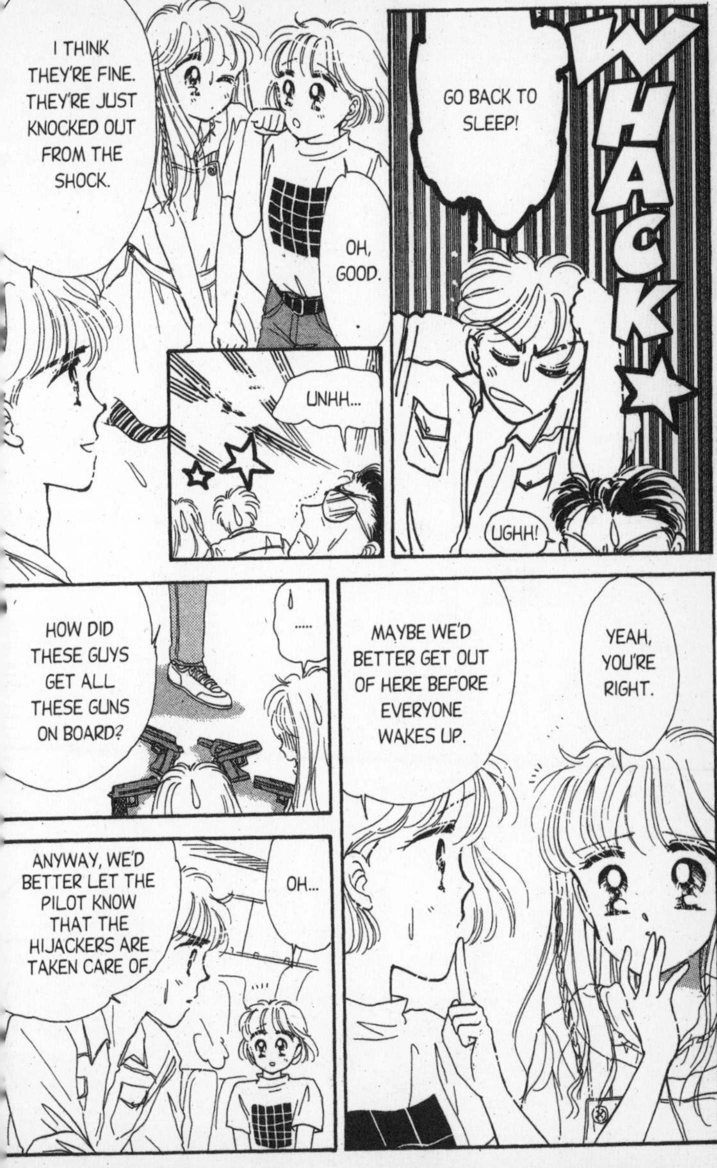
I THINK THEY'RE FINE. THEY'RE JUST KNOCKED OUT FROM THE SHOCK.
OH, GOOD.
UNHH...
GO BACK TO SLEEP!
WHACK
UGHH!
HOW DID THESE GUYS GET ALL THESE GUNS ON BOARD?
.....
ANYWAY, WE'D BETTER LET THE PILOT KNOW THAT THE HIJACKERS ARE TAKEN CARE OF.
OH...
MAYBE WE'D BETTER GET OUT OF HERE BEFORE EVERYONE WAKES UP.
YEAH, YOU'RE RIGHT.

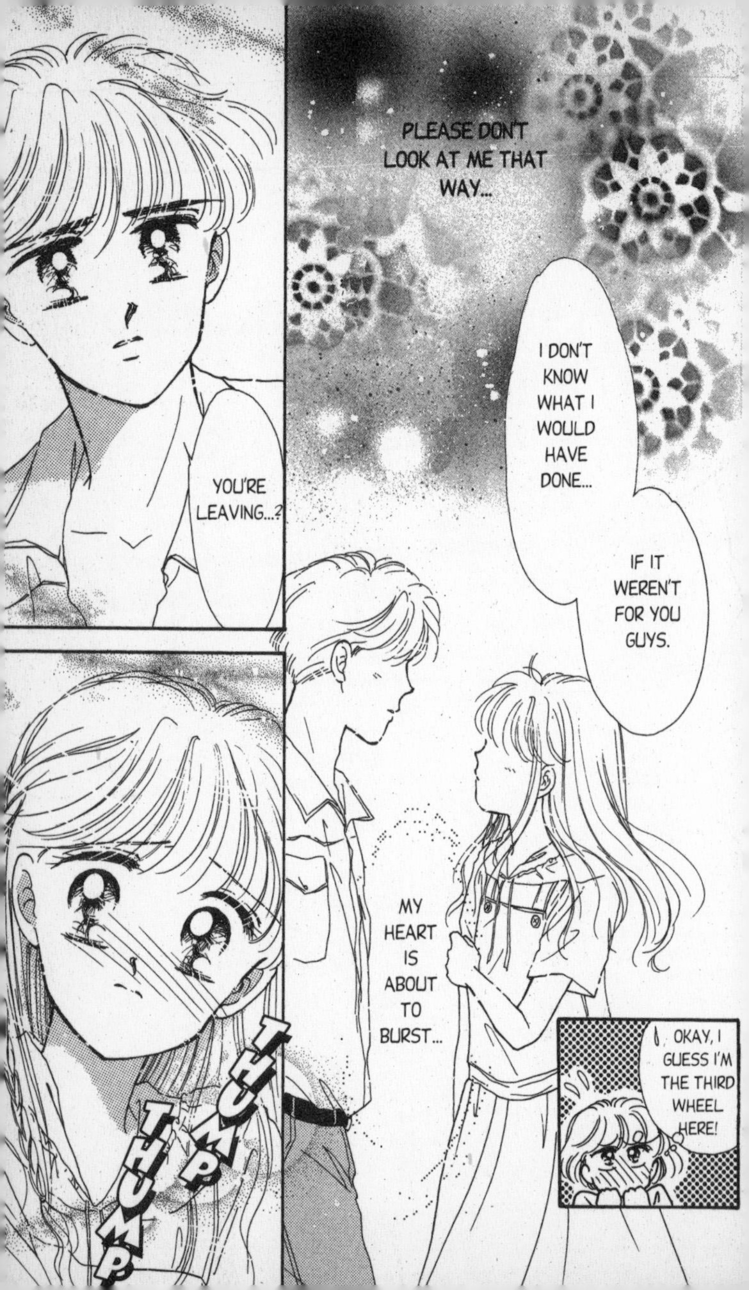
YOU'RE LEAVING...?
THUMP THUMP
PLEASE DON'T LOOK AT ME THAT WAY...
I DON'T KNOW WHAT I WOULD HAVE DONE...
IF IT WEREN'T FOR YOU GUYS.
MY HEART IS ABOUT TO BURST...
OKAY, I GUESS I'M THE THIRD WHEEL HERE!

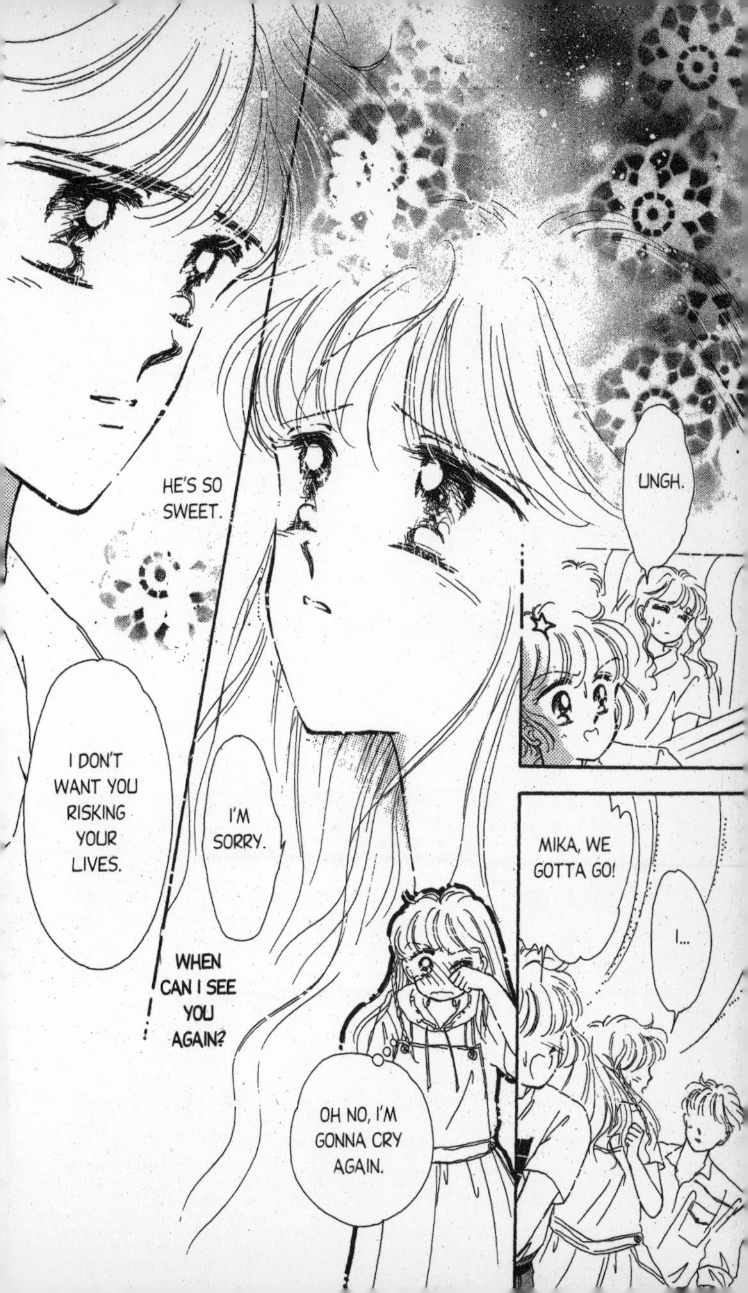
HE'S SO SWEET.
I DON'T WANT YOU RISKING YOUR LIVES.
I'M SORRY.
WHEN CAN I SEE YOU AGAIN?
OH NO, I'M GONNA CRY AGAIN.
UNGH.
MIKA, WE GOTTA GO!
I...

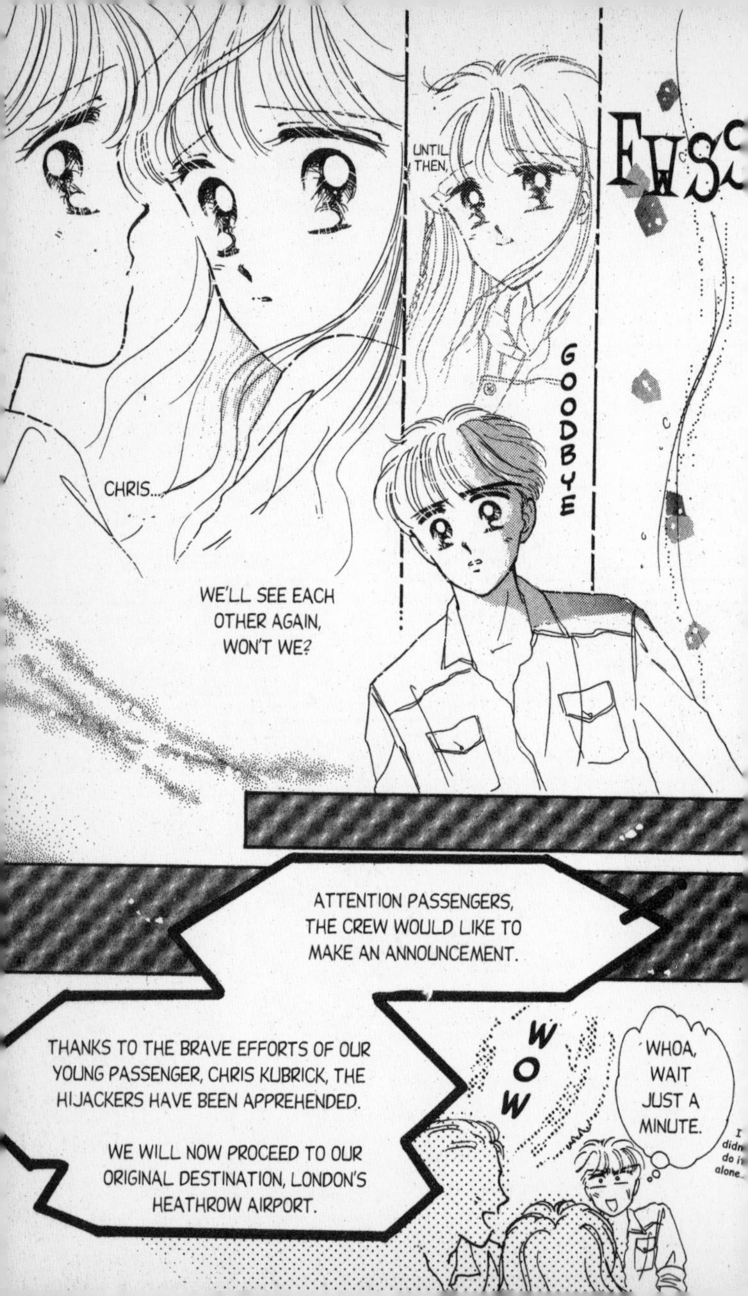
CHRIS...
WE'LL SEE EACH OTHER AGAIN, WON'T WE?
UNTIL THEN,
GOODBYE
ATTENTION PASSENGERS, THE CREW WOULD LIKE TO MAKE AN ANNOUNCEMENT.
THANKS TO THE BRAVE EFFORTS OF OUR YOUNG PASSENGER, CHRIS KUBRICK, THE HIJACKERS HAVE BEEN APPREHENDED.
WE WILL NOW PROCEED TO OUR ORIGINAL DESTINATION, LONDON'S HEATHROW AIRPORT.
WOW
WHOA, WAIT JUST A MINUTE.

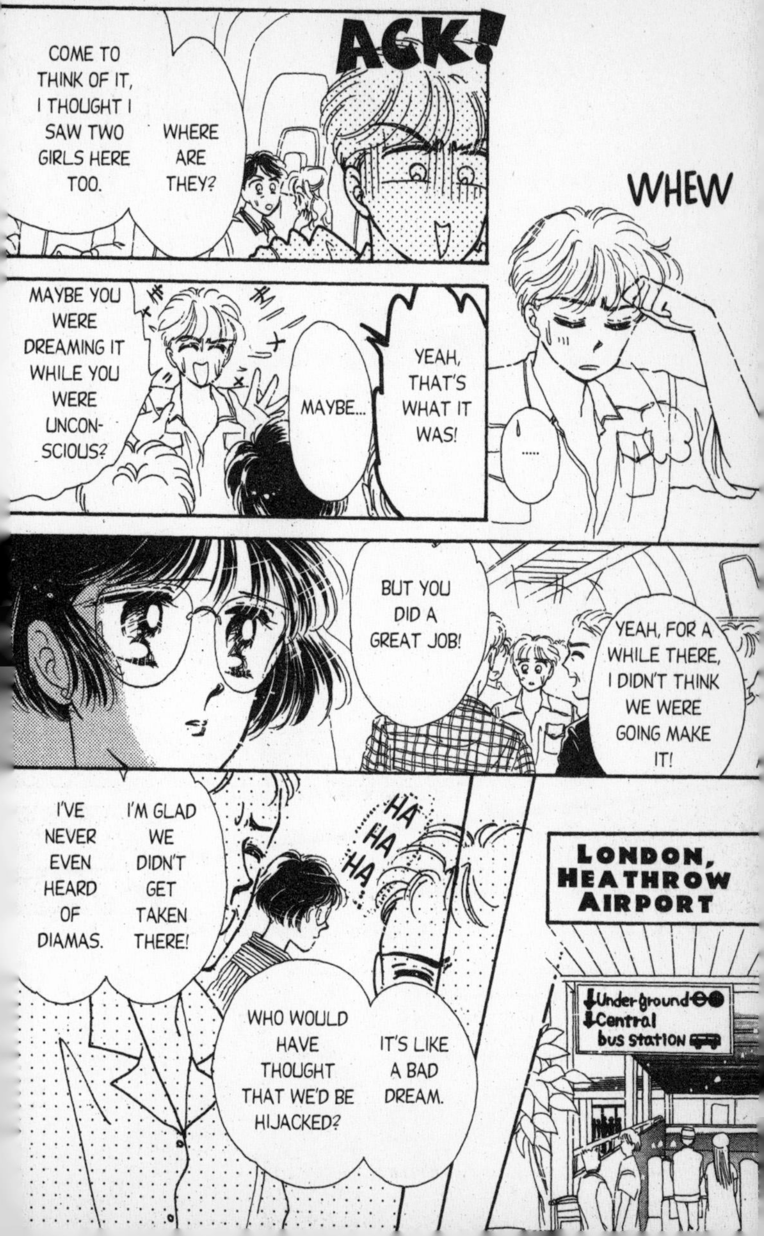
COME TO THINK OF IT, I THOUGHT I SAW TWO GIRLS HERE TOO.
WHERE ARE THEY?
ACK!
WHEW
MAYBE YOU WERE DREAMING IT WHILE YOU WERE UNCON-SCIOUS?
MAYBE...
YEAH, THAT'S WHAT IT WAS!
!
.....
BUT YOU DID A GREAT JOB!
YEAH, FOR A WHILE THERE, I DIDN'T THINK WE WERE GOING MAKE IT!
I'VE NEVER EVEN HEARD OF DIAMAS.
I'M GLAD WE DIDN'T GET TAKEN THERE!
HA HA HA
WHO WOULD HAVE THOUGHT THAT WE'D BE HIJACKED?
IT'S LIKE A BAD DREAM.
LONDON, HEATHROW AIRPORT
Underground
Central bus station

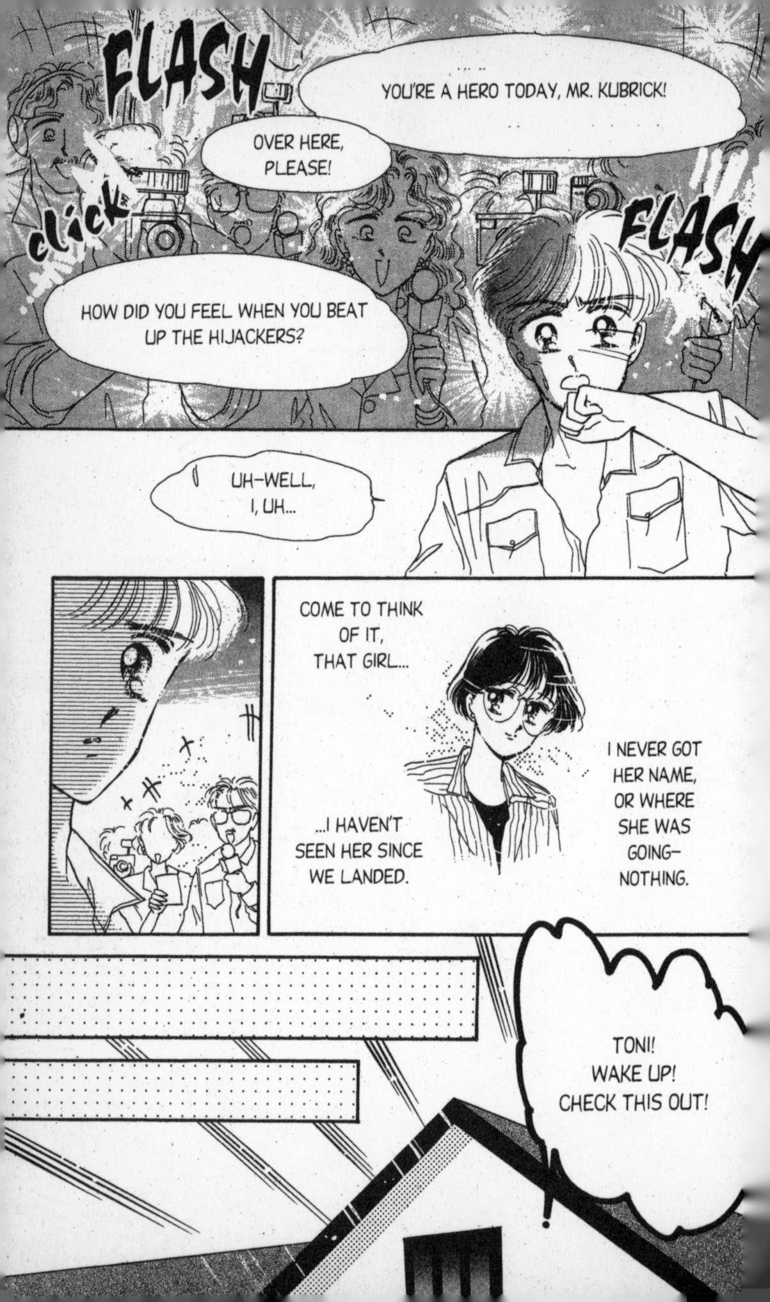
FLASH
YOU'RE A HERO TODAY, MR. KUBRICK!
OVER HERE, PLEASE!
click
FLASH
HOW DID YOU FEEL WHEN YOU BEAT UP THE HIJACKERS?
UH-WELL, I, UH...
COME TO THINK OF IT, THAT GIRL...
...I HAVEN'T SEEN HER SINCE WE LANDED.
I NEVER GOT HER NAME, OR WHERE SHE WAS GOING-NOTHING.
TONI! WAKE UP! CHECK THIS OUT!

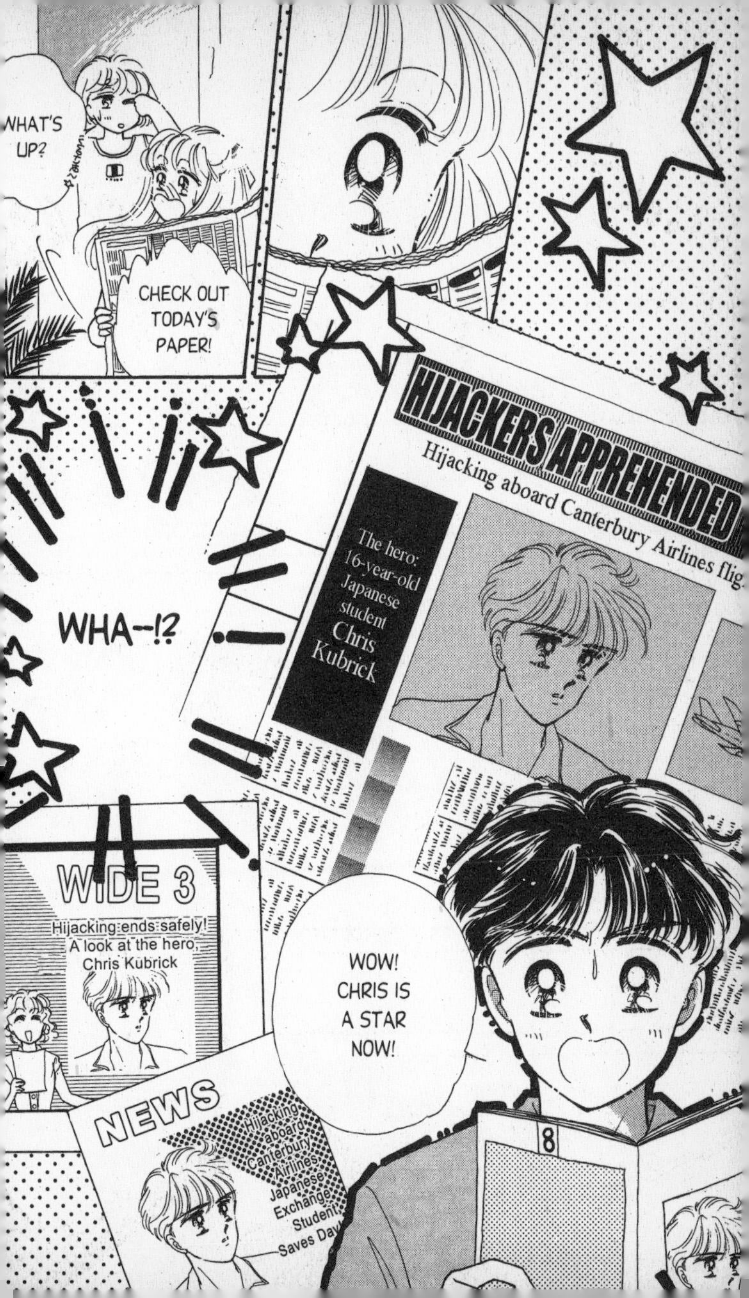
WHAT'S UP?
CHECK OUT TODAY'S PAPER!
WHA--!?
HIJACKERS APPREHENDED
Hijacking aboard Canterbury Airlines flig
The hero: 16-year-old Japanese student Chris Kubrick
WIDE 3
Hijacking ends safely! A look at the hero, Chris Kubrick
NEWS
Hijacking aboard Canterbury Airlines Japanese Exchange Student Saves Day
WOW! CHRIS IS A STAR NOW!
8

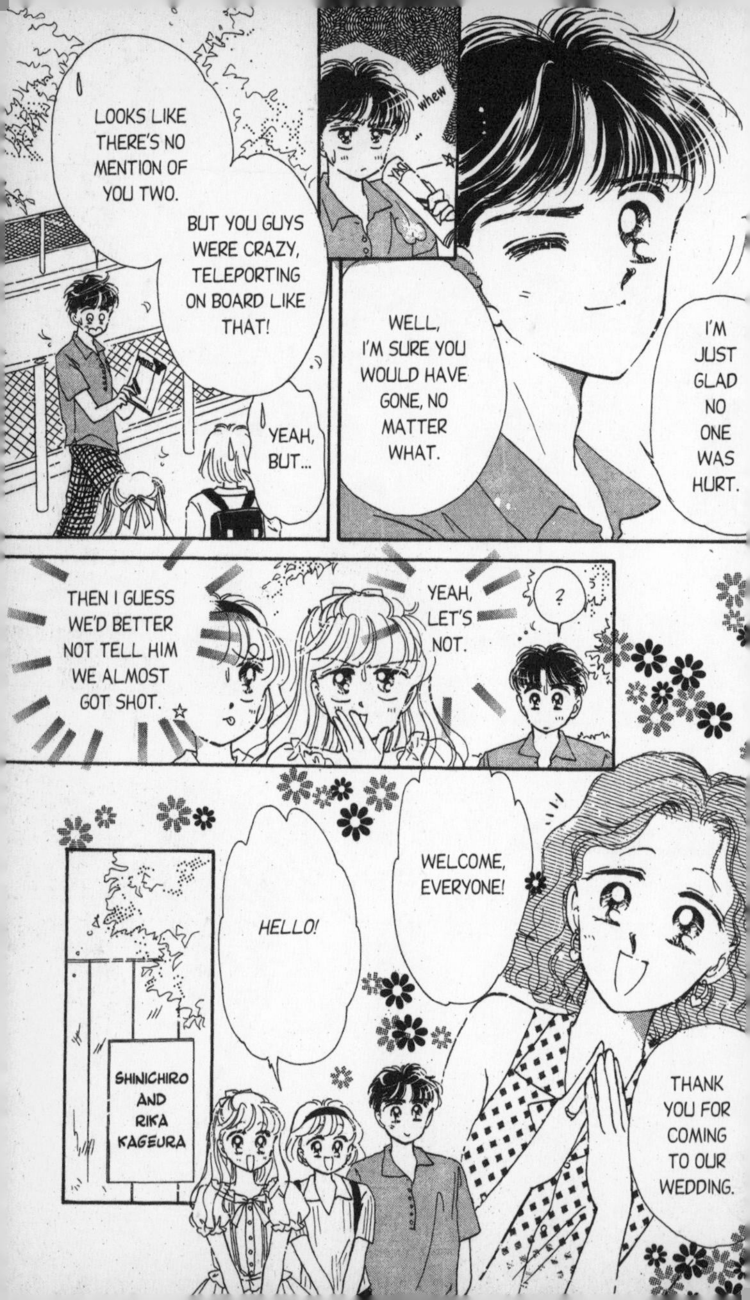
LOOKS LIKE THERE'S NO MENTION OF YOU TWO.
BUT YOU GUYS WERE CRAZY, TELEPORTING ON BOARD LIKE THAT!
YEAH, BUT...
whew
WELL, I'M SURE YOU WOULD HAVE GONE, NO MATTER WHAT.
I'M JUST GLAD NO ONE WAS HURT.
THEN I GUESS WE'D BETTER NOT TELL HIM WE ALMOST GOT SHOT.
YEAH, LET'S NOT.
?
SHINICHIRO AND RIKA KAGEURA
HELLO!
WELCOME, EVERYONE!
THANK YOU FOR COMING TO OUR WEDDING.

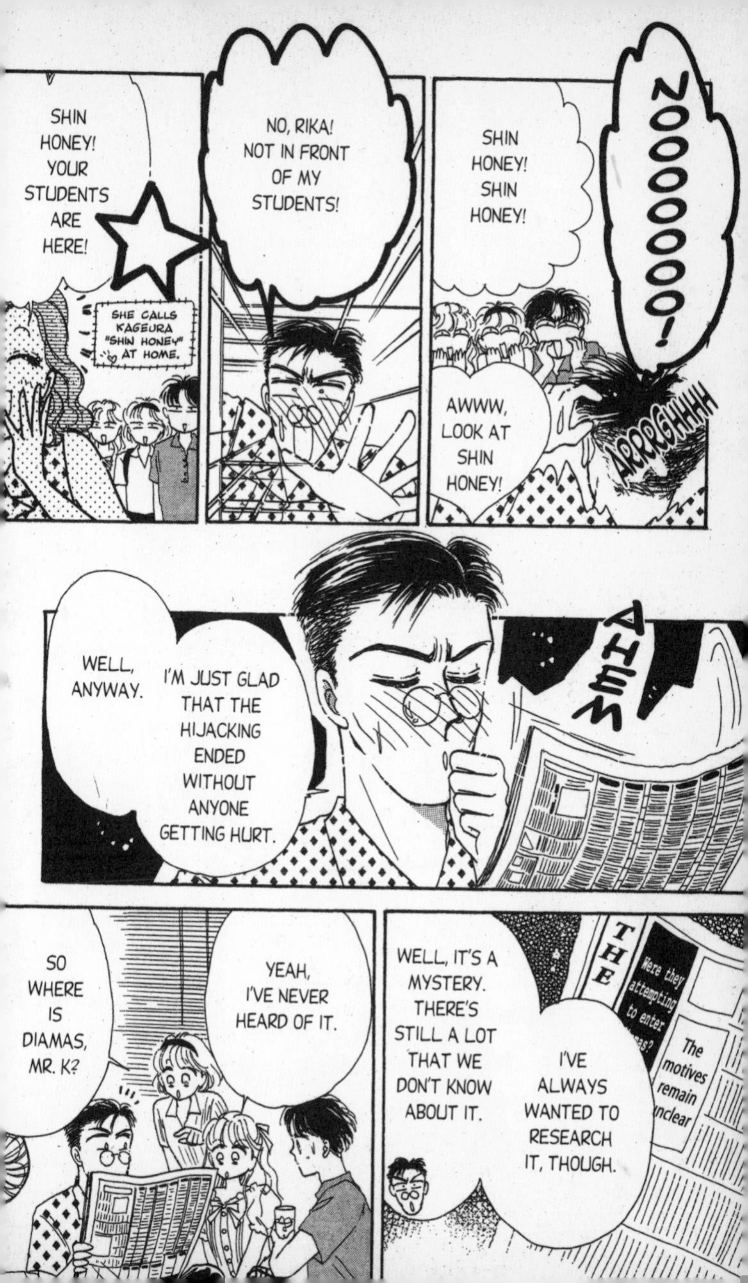
SHIN HONEY! YOUR STUDENTS ARE HERE!
SHE CALLS KAGEURA "SHIN HONEY" AT HOME.
NO, RIKA! NOT IN FRONT OF MY STUDENTS!
SHIN HONEY! SHIN HONEY!
AWWW, LOOK AT SHIN HONEY!
NOOOOOOOO!
ARRRGHHHH
WELL, ANYWAY.
I'M JUST GLAD THAT THE HIJACKING ENDED WITHOUT ANYONE GETTING HURT.
AHEM
SO WHERE IS DIAMAS, MR. K?
YEAH, I'VE NEVER HEARD OF IT.
WELL, IT'S A MYSTERY. THERE'S STILL A LOT THAT WE DON'T KNOW ABOUT IT.
I'VE ALWAYS WANTED TO RESEARCH IT, THOUGH.
THE
The motives remain unclear

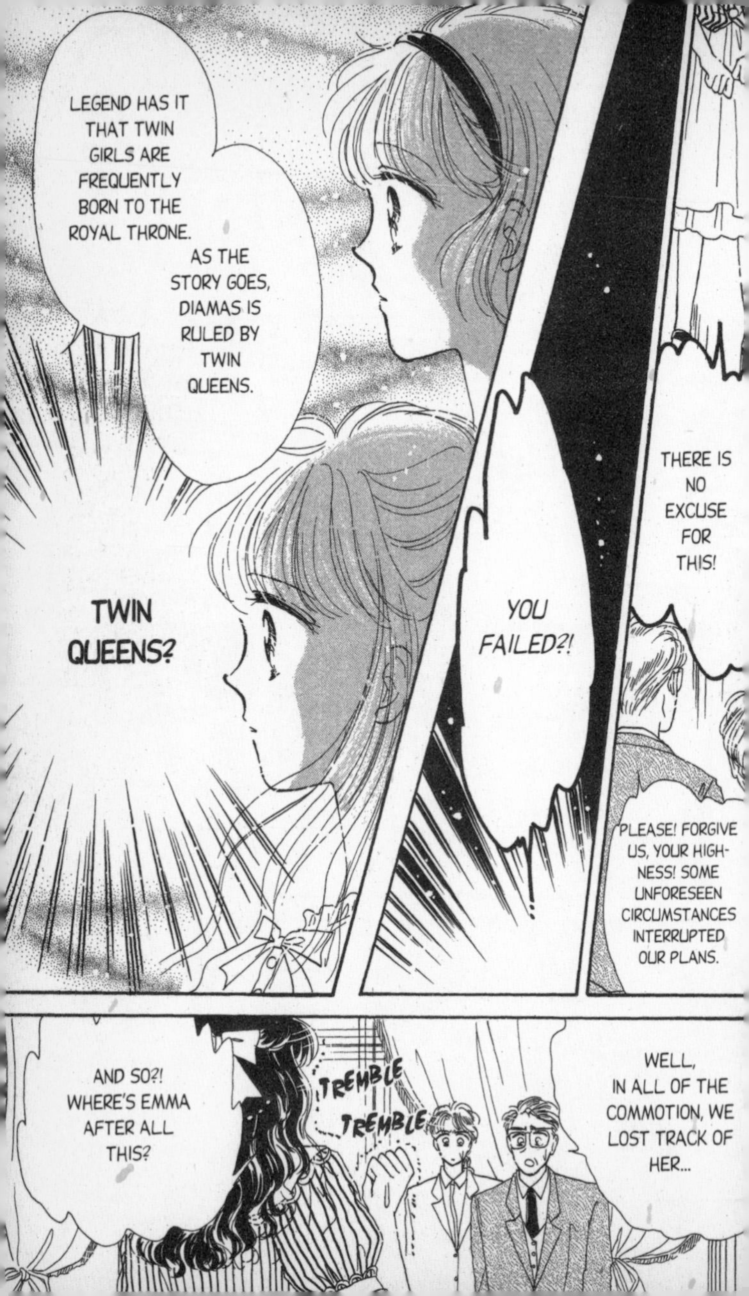
LEGEND HAS IT THAT TWIN GIRLS ARE FREQUENTLY BORN TO THE ROYAL THRONE.
AS THE STORY GOES, DIAMAS IS RULED BY TWIN QUEENS.
TWIN QUEENS?
YOU FAILED?!
THERE IS NO EXCUSE FOR THIS!
PLEASE! FORGIVE US, YOUR HIGH-NESS! SOME UNFORESEEN CIRCUMSTANCES INTERRUPTED OUR PLANS.
AND SO?! WHERE'S EMMA AFTER ALL THIS?
TREMBLE
TREMBLE
WELL, IN ALL OF THE COMMOTION, WE LOST TRACK OF HER...

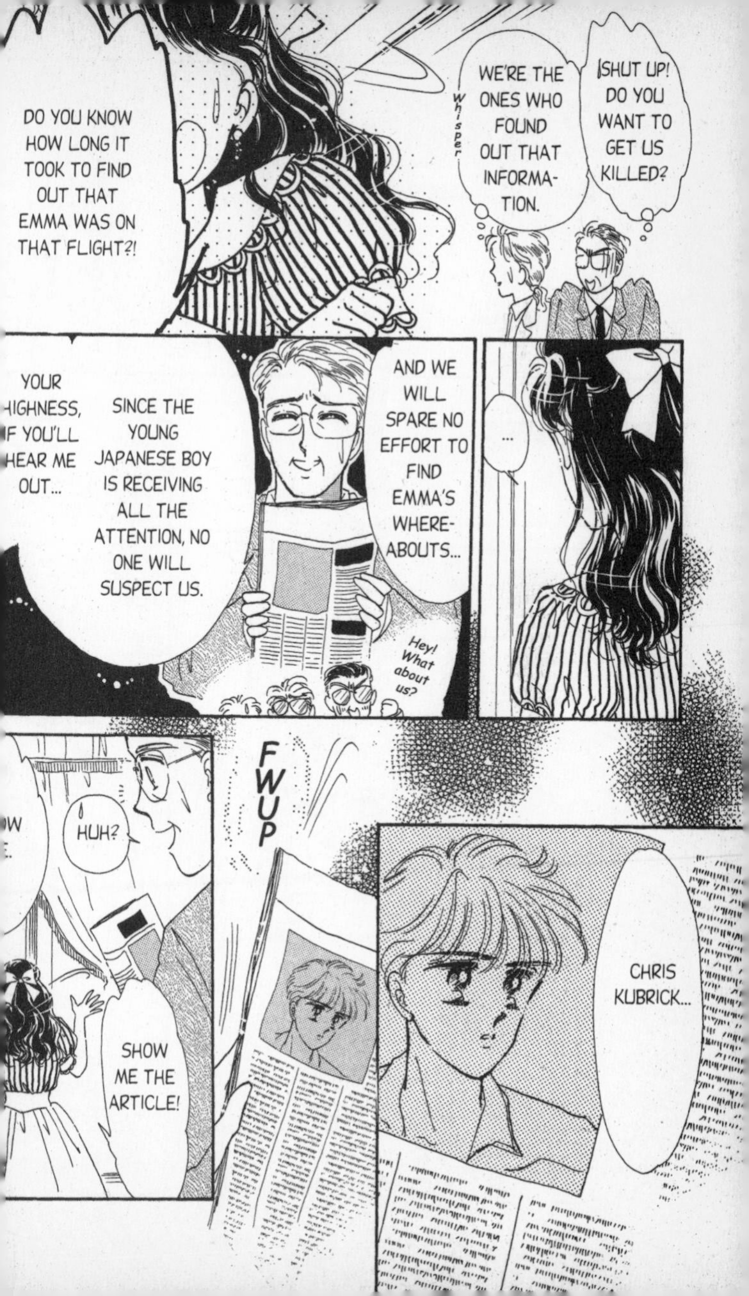
DO YOU KNOW HOW LONG IT TOOK TO FIND OUT THAT EMMA WAS ON THAT FLIGHT?!
Whisper
WE'RE THE ONES WHO FOUND OUT THAT INFORMATION.
SHUT UP! DO YOU WANT TO GET US KILLED?
YOUR HIGHNESS, IF YOU'LL HEAR ME OUT...
SINCE THE YOUNG JAPANESE BOY IS RECEIVING ALL THE ATTENTION, NO ONE WILL SUSPECT US.
AND WE WILL SPARE NO EFFORT TO FIND EMMA'S WHEREABOUTS...
Hey! What about us?
...
HUH?
SHOW ME THE ARTICLE!
FWUP
CHRIS KUBRICK...

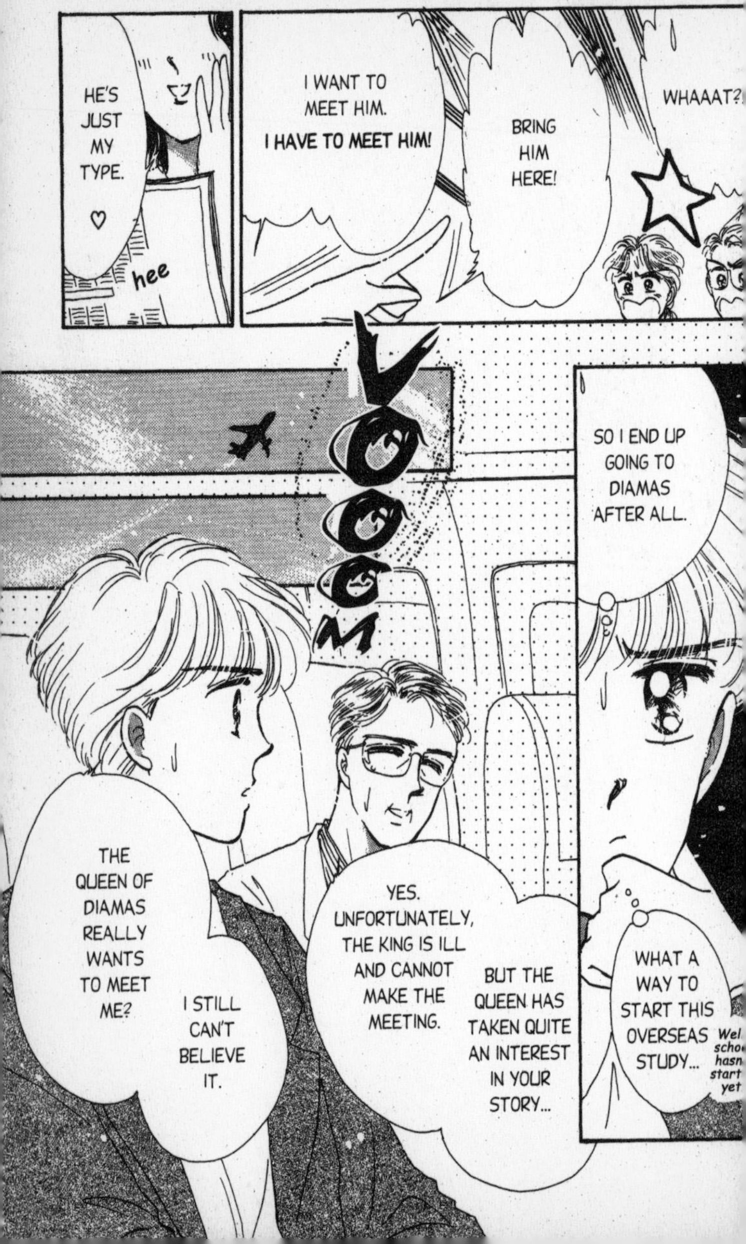
HE'S JUST MY TYPE. ♡
hee
I WANT TO MEET HIM. I HAVE TO MEET HIM!
BRING HIM HERE!
WHAAAT?!
VOOOM
THE QUEEN OF DIAMAS REALLY WANTS TO MEET ME?
I STILL CAN'T BELIEVE IT.
YES. UNFORTUNATELY, THE KING IS ILL AND CANNOT MAKE THE MEETING.
BUT THE QUEEN HAS TAKEN QUITE AN INTEREST IN YOUR STORY...
SO I END UP GOING TO DIAMAS AFTER ALL.
WHAT A WAY TO START THIS OVERSEAS STUDY...

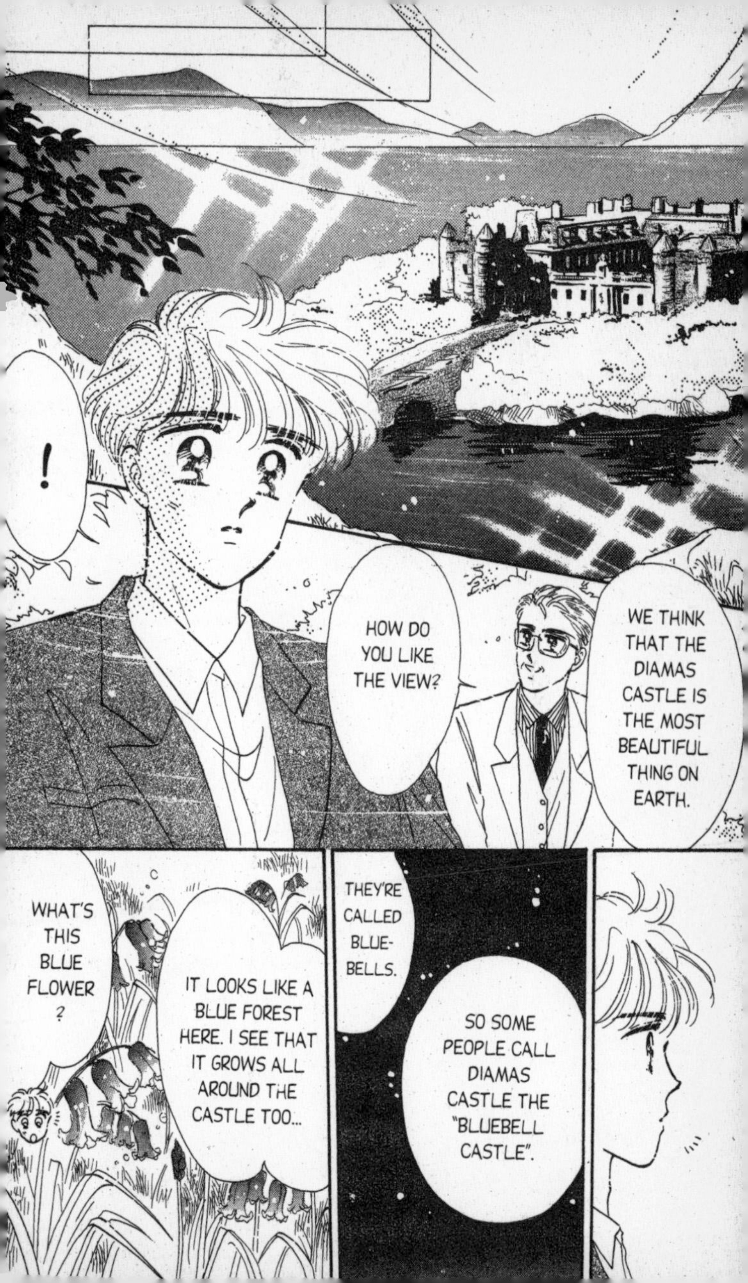
!
HOW DO YOU LIKE THE VIEW?
WE THINK THAT THE DIAMAS CASTLE IS THE MOST BEAUTIFUL THING ON EARTH.
WHAT'S THIS BLUE FLOWER ?
IT LOOKS LIKE A BLUE FOREST HERE. I SEE THAT IT GROWS ALL AROUND THE CASTLE TOO...
THEY'RE CALLED BLUE-BELLS.
SO SOME PEOPLE CALL DIAMAS CASTLE THE "BLUEBELL CASTLE".

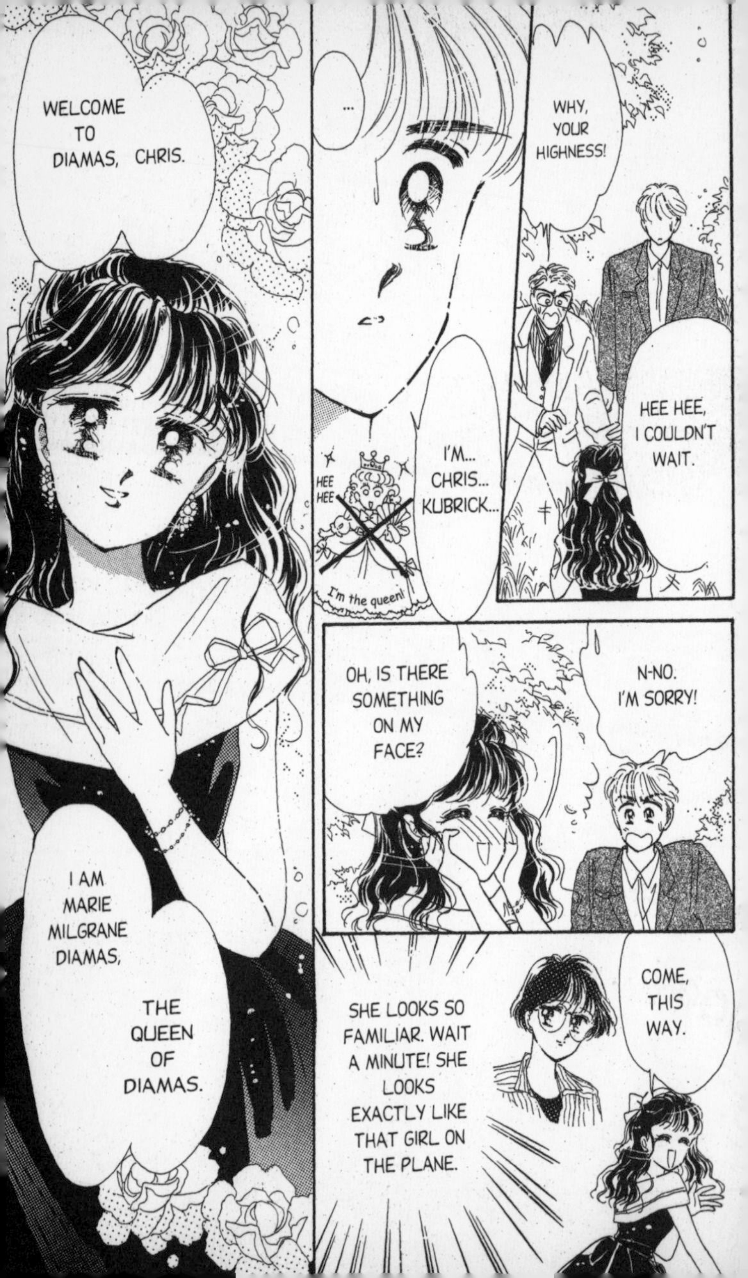
WELCOME TO DIAMAS, CHRIS.
I AM MARIE MILGRANE DIAMAS,
THE QUEEN OF DIAMAS.
...
I'M... CHRIS... KUBRICK...
HEE HEE
I'm the queen!
WHY, YOUR HIGHNESS!
HEE HEE, I COULDN'T WAIT.
OH, IS THERE SOMETHING ON MY FACE?
N-NO. I'M SORRY!
SHE LOOKS SO FAMILIAR. WAIT A MINUTE! SHE LOOKS EXACTLY LIKE THAT GIRL ON THE PLANE.
COME, THIS WAY.

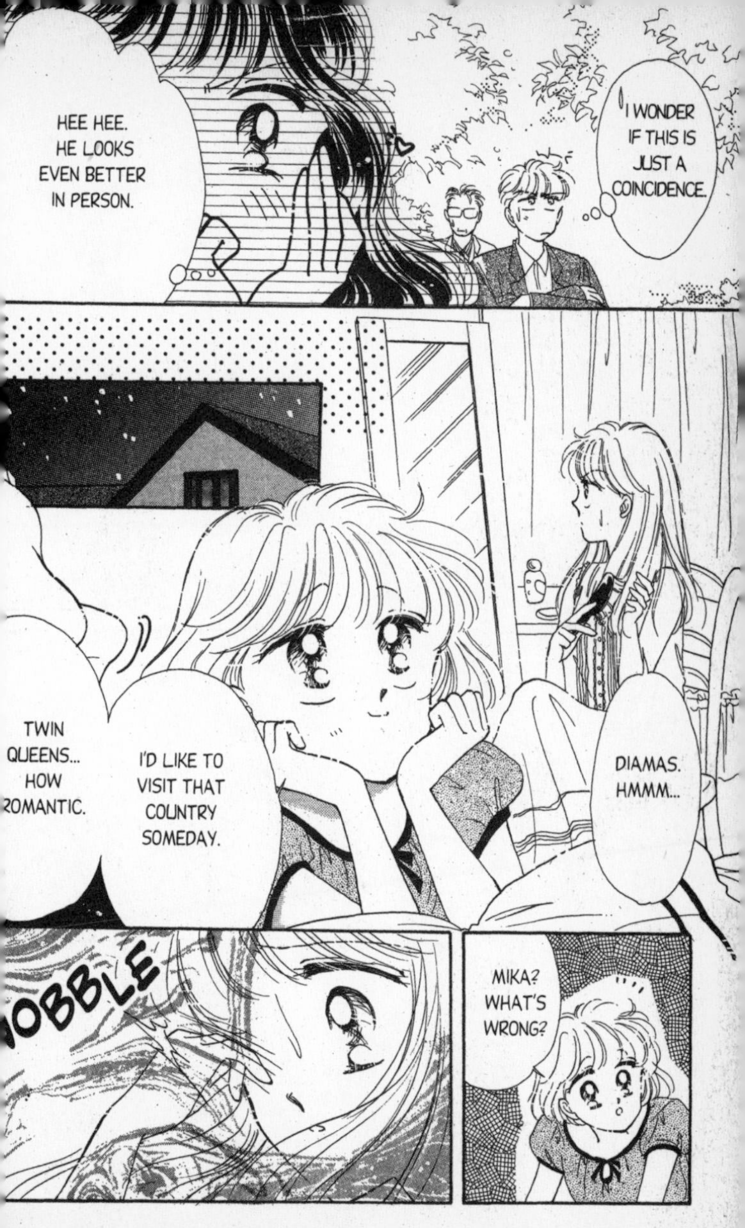
HEE HEE. HE LOOKS EVEN BETTER IN PERSON.
I WONDER IF THIS IS JUST A COINCIDENCE.
TWIN QUEENS... HOW ROMANTIC.
I'D LIKE TO VISIT THAT COUNTRY SOMEDAY.
DIAMAS. HMMM...
OBBLE
MIKA? WHAT'S WRONG?

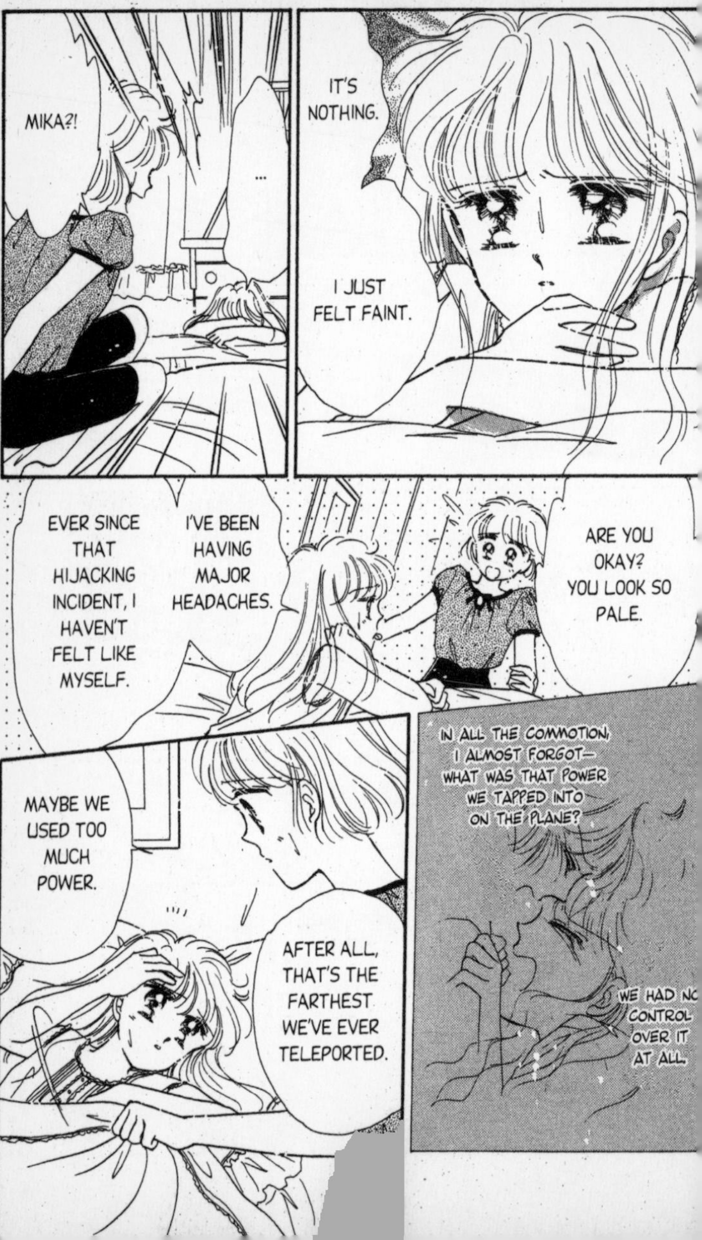
MIKA?!
...
IT'S NOTHING.
I JUST FELT FAINT.
EVER SINCE THAT HIJACKING INCIDENT, I HAVEN'T FELT LIKE MYSELF.
I'VE BEEN HAVING MAJOR HEADACHES.
ARE YOU OKAY? YOU LOOK SO PALE.
MAYBE WE USED TOO MUCH POWER.
...
AFTER ALL, THAT'S THE FARTHEST WE'VE EVER TELEPORTED.
IN ALL THE COMMOTION, I ALMOST FORGOT— WHAT WAS THAT POWER WE TAPPED INTO ON THE PLANE?
WE HAD NO CONTROL OVER IT AT ALL.

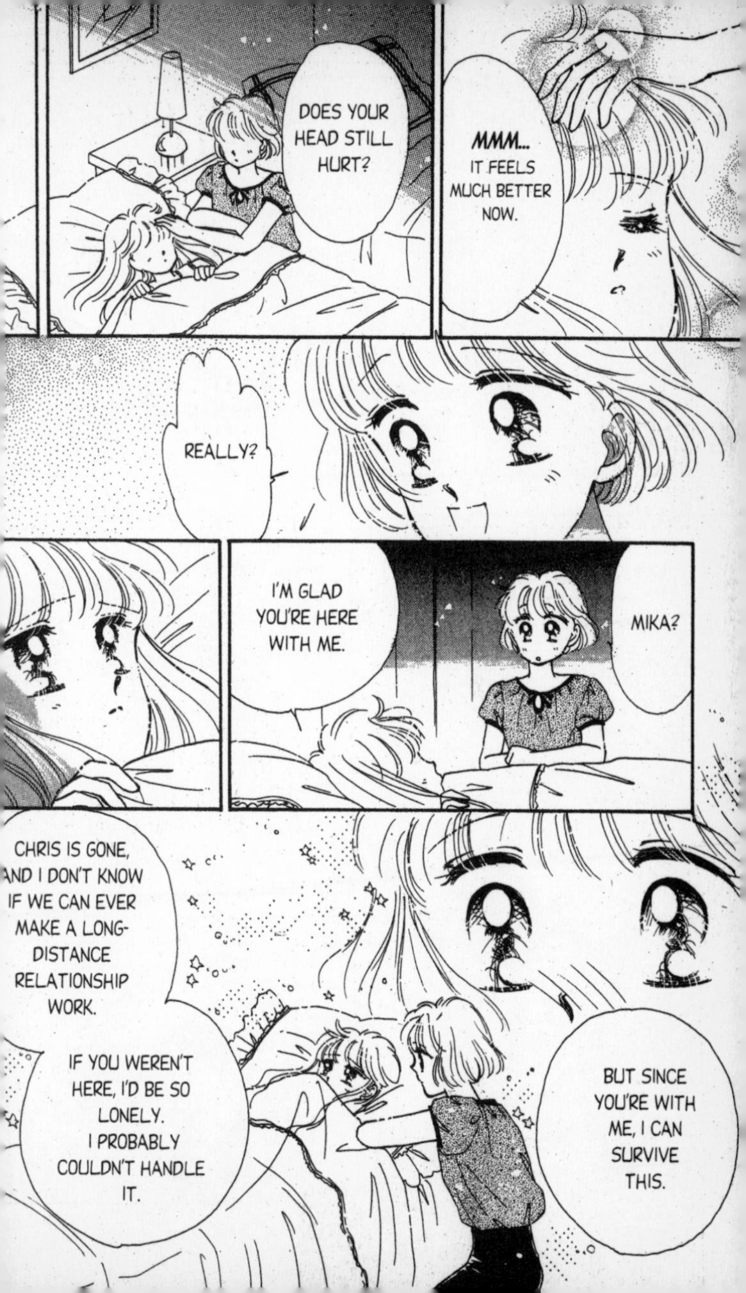
DOES YOUR HEAD STILL HURT?
MMM... IT FEELS MUCH BETTER NOW.
REALLY?
I'M GLAD YOU'RE HERE WITH ME.
MIKA?
CHRIS IS GONE, AND I DON'T KNOW IF WE CAN EVER MAKE A LONG-DISTANCE RELATIONSHIP WORK.
IF YOU WEREN'T HERE, I'D BE SO LONELY. I PROBABLY COULDN'T HANDLE IT.
BUT SINCE YOU'RE WITH ME, I CAN SURVIVE THIS.

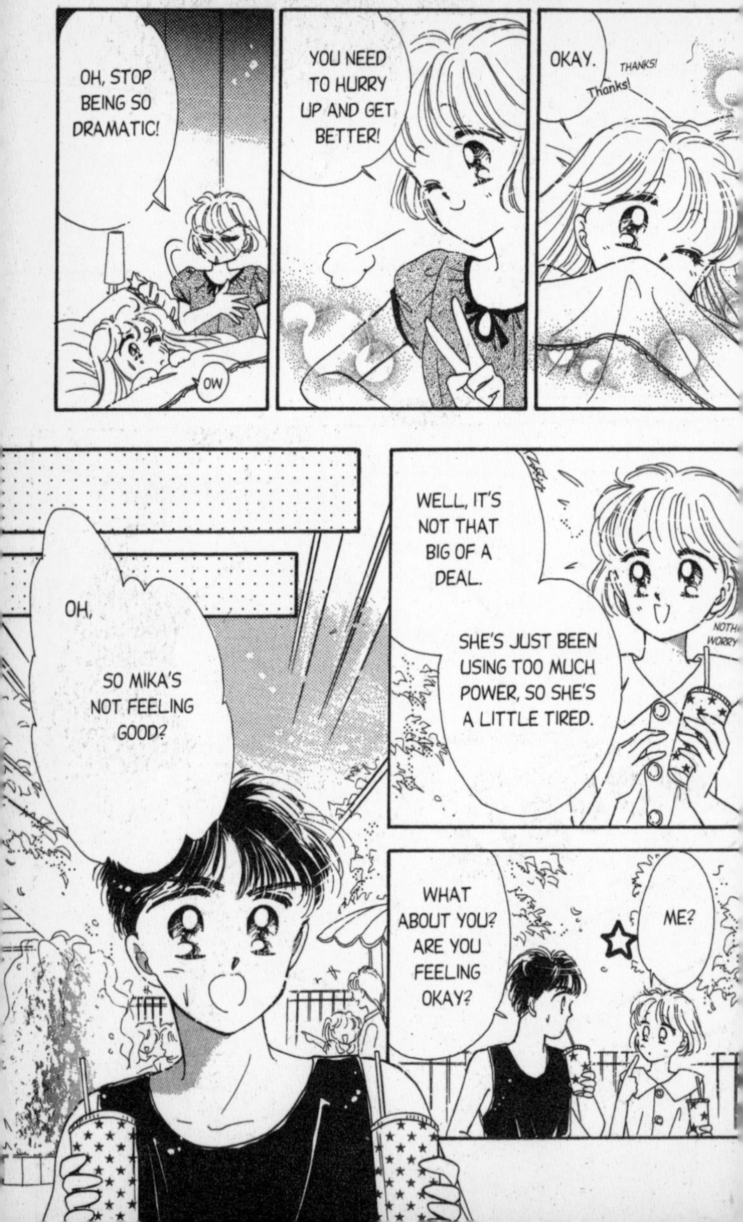
OH, STOP BEING SO DRAMATIC!
OW
YOU NEED TO HURRY UP AND GET BETTER!
OKAY.
THANKS!
Thanks!
OH,
SO MIKA'S NOT FEELING GOOD?
WELL, IT'S NOT THAT BIG OF A DEAL.
SHE'S JUST BEEN USING TOO MUCH POWER, SO SHE'S A LITTLE TIRED.
WHAT ABOUT YOU? ARE YOU FEELING OKAY?
ME?

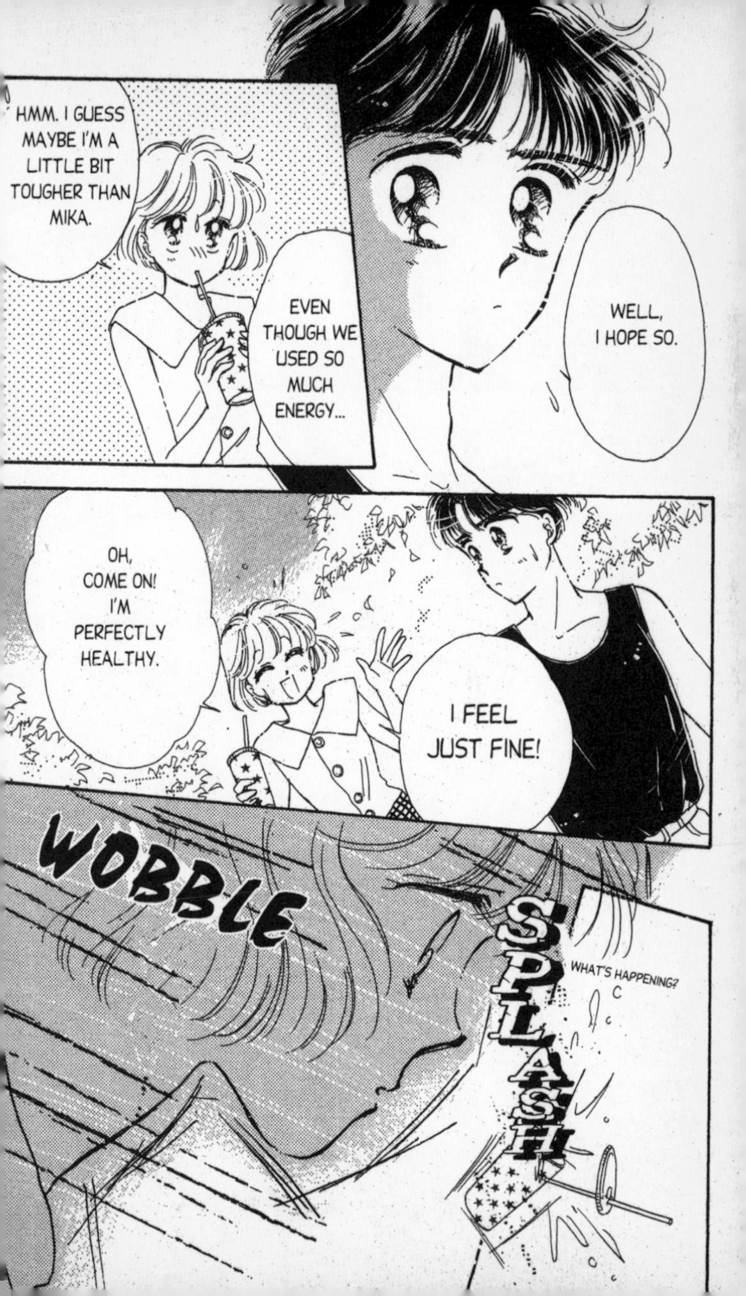
HMM. I GUESS MAYBE I'M A LITTLE BIT TOUGHER THAN MIKA.
EVEN THOUGH WE USED SO MUCH ENERGY...
WELL, I HOPE SO.
OH, COME ON! I'M PERFECTLY HEALTHY.
I FEEL JUST FINE!
WOBBLE
SPLASH
WHAT'S HAPPENING?

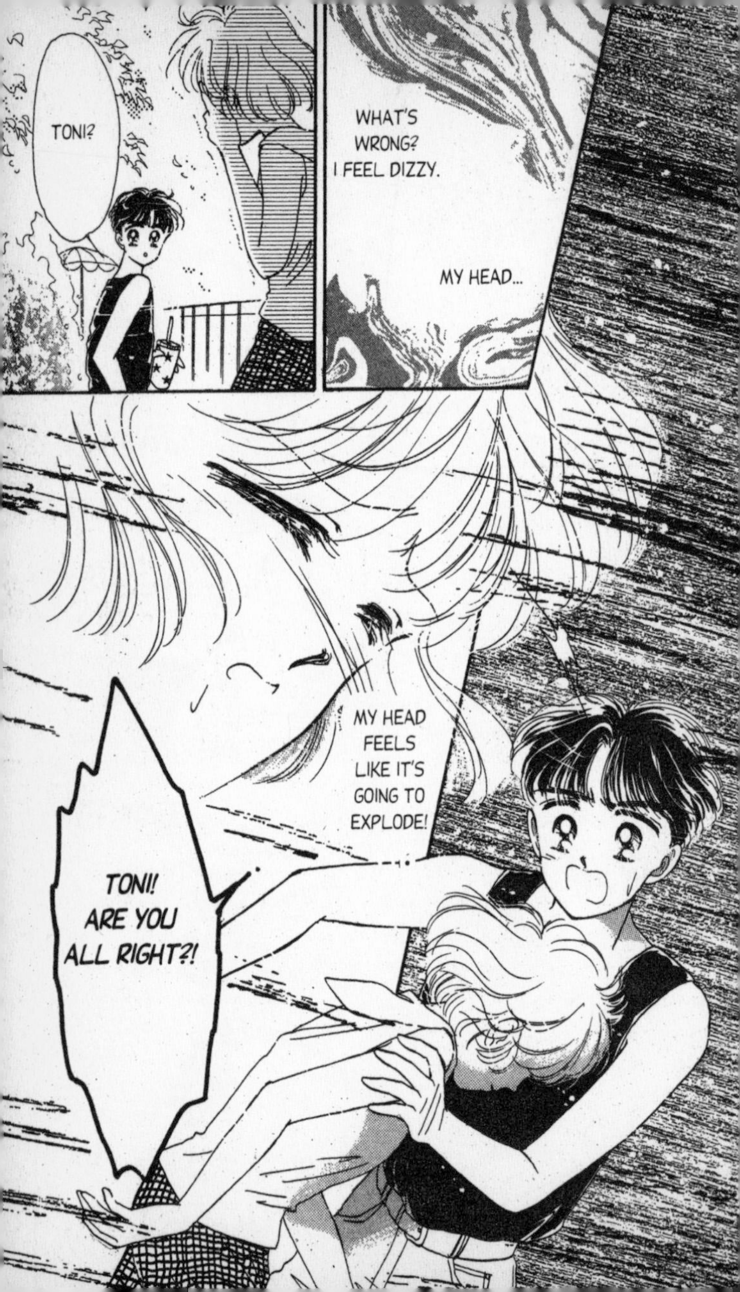
TONI?
WHAT'S WRONG? I FEEL DIZZY.
MY HEAD...
MY HEAD FEELS LIKE IT'S GOING TO EXPLODE!
TONI! ARE YOU ALL RIGHT?!

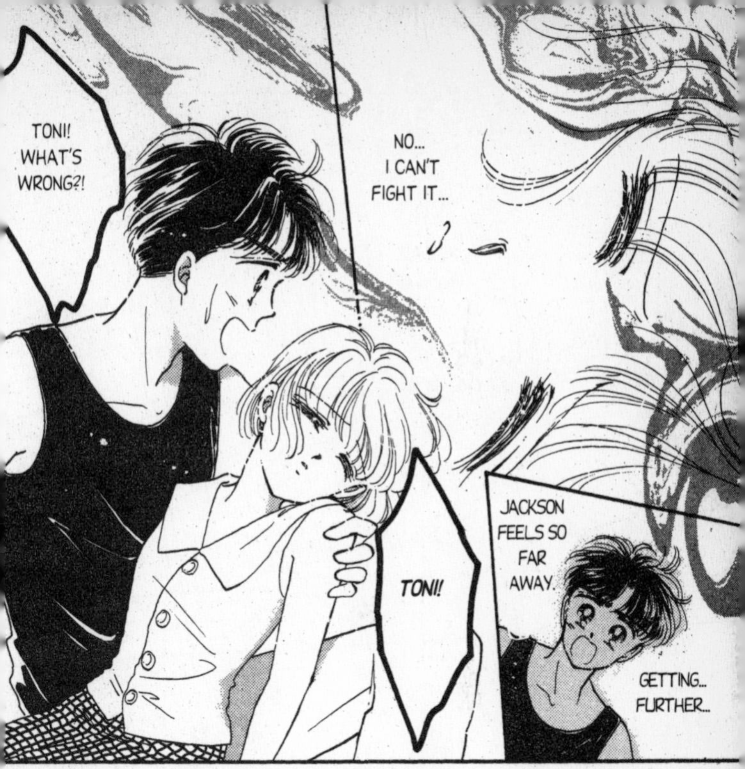
TONI! WHAT'S WRONG?!
NO... I CAN'T FIGHT IT...
TONI!
JACKSON FEELS SO FAR AWAY.
GETTING... FURTHER...

BONUS

The first big surprises in Part 3 are Chris's sudden overseas journey and, of course, Mr. Kageura's wedding. It appears I took my readers by surprise. Everyone's been sending me letters! It was only a month ago (Book 4) that Mr. Kageura was still shooting laser beams out of his eyes. And now he's getting married?!

I just wanted to get a fresh start for Part 3, so I didn't think it was that weird. There's a chapel near my studio, so I've been wanting to draw some wedding scenes. Maybe that's the only reason why... heh heh.

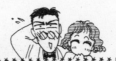

Mr. Kageura IS human... He can get married just like anyone else.

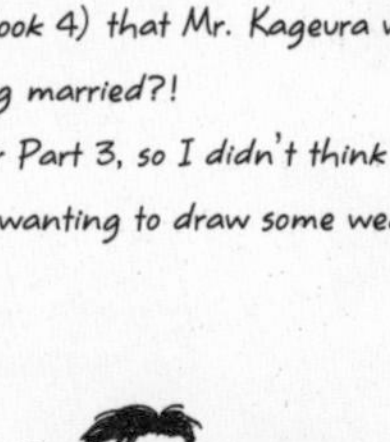

But still, his new wife Rika's a brave one. Good luck!

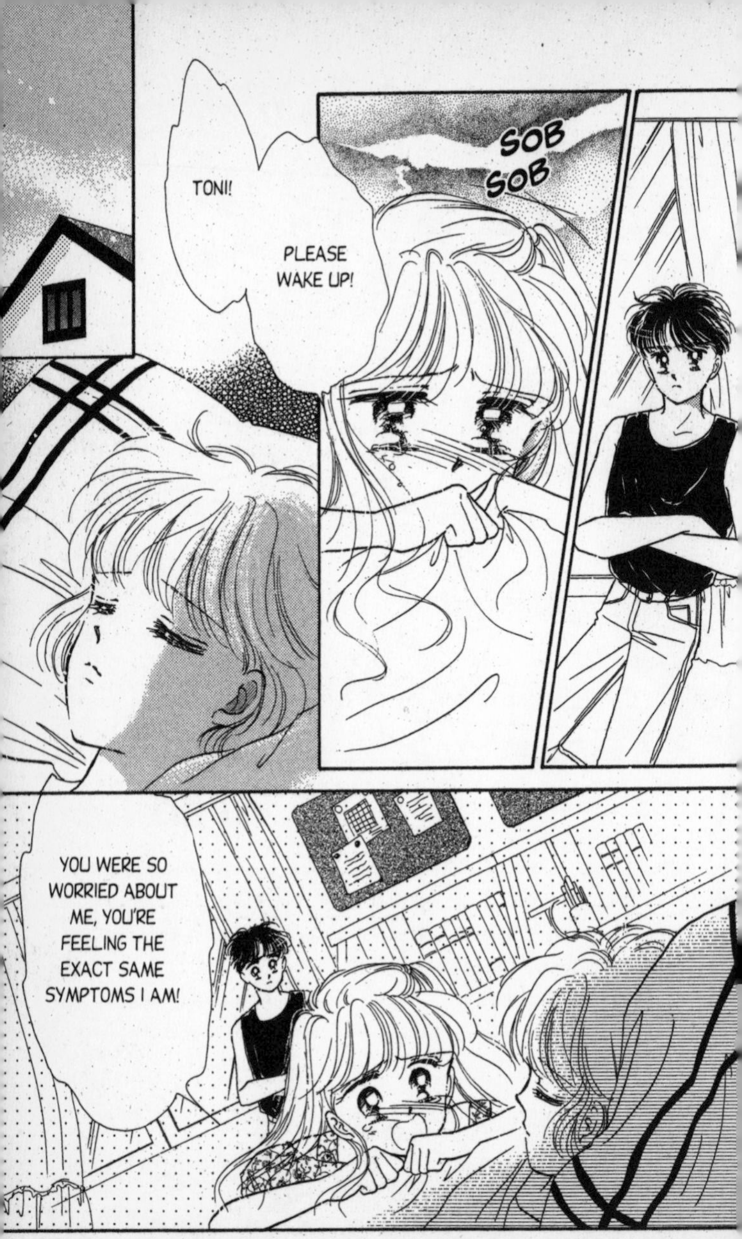
TONI!
PLEASE WAKE UP!
SOB SOB
YOU WERE SO WORRIED ABOUT ME, YOU'RE FEELING THE EXACT SAME SYMPTOMS I AM!

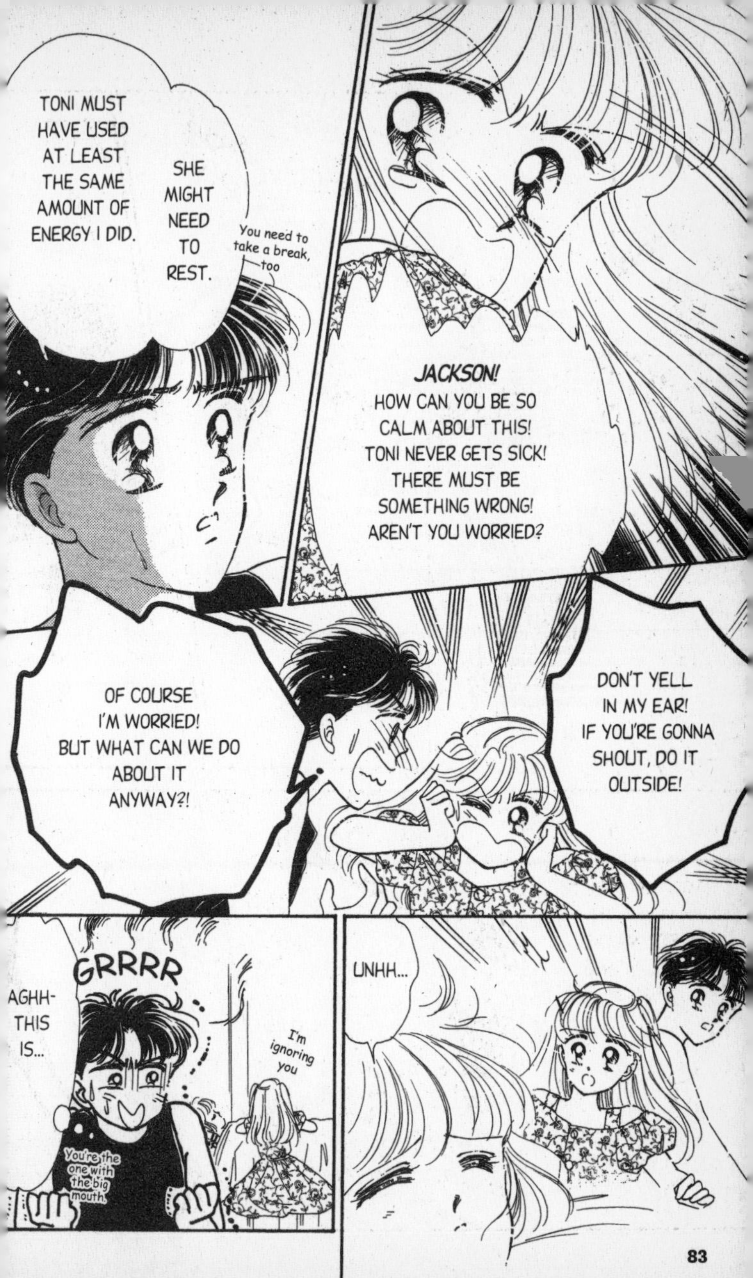
TONI MUST HAVE USED AT LEAST THE SAME AMOUNT OF ENERGY I DID.
SHE MIGHT NEED TO REST.
You need to take a break, too
JACKSON! HOW CAN YOU BE SO CALM ABOUT THIS! TONI NEVER GETS SICK! THERE MUST BE SOMETHING WRONG! AREN'T YOU WORRIED?
OF COURSE I'M WORRIED! BUT WHAT CAN WE DO ABOUT IT ANYWAY?!
DON'T YELL IN MY EAR! IF YOU'RE GONNA SHOUT, DO IT OUTSIDE!
GRRRR
AGHH- THIS IS...
You're the one with the big mouth.
I'm ignoring you
UNHH...

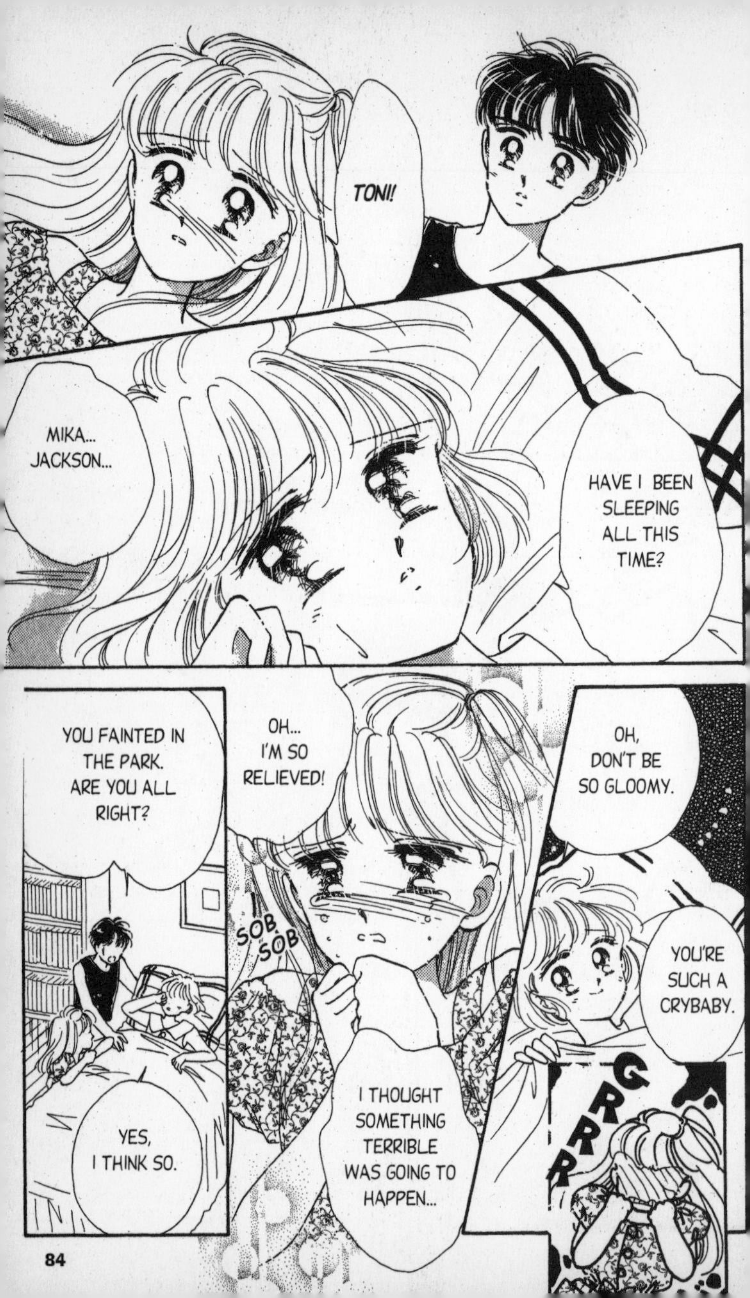
TONI!
MIKA... JACKSON...
HAVE I BEEN SLEEPING ALL THIS TIME?
YOU FAINTED IN THE PARK. ARE YOU ALL RIGHT?
YES, I THINK SO.
OH... I'M SO RELIEVED!
SOB SOB
I THOUGHT SOMETHING TERRIBLE WAS GOING TO HAPPEN...
OH, DON'T BE SO GLOOMY.
YOU'RE SUCH A CRYBABY.
GRRR

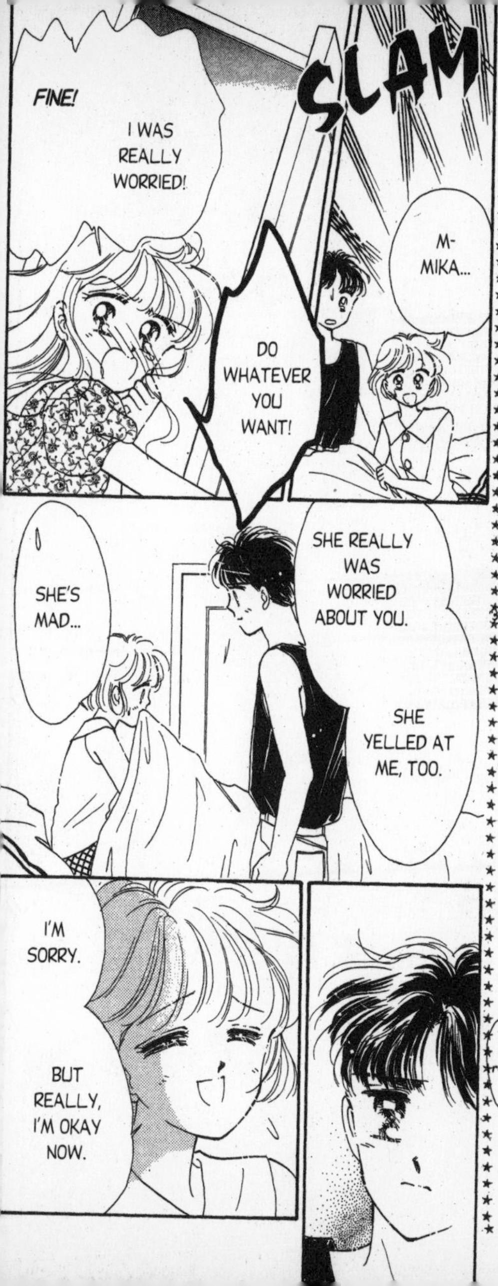
FINE!
I WAS REALLY WORRIED!
SLAM
M-MIKA...
DO WHATEVER YOU WANT!
SHE'S MAD...
SHE REALLY WAS WORRIED ABOUT YOU.
SHE YELLED AT ME, TOO.
I'M SORRY.
BUT REALLY, I'M OKAY NOW.

BONUS

Mr. Kageura actually has a real-life model. He was someone in the editorial department who has since been transferred to a different division. Although I didn't really work with him, I just thought he might make for an interesting character. And no, I don't have a grudge against him! But I thought, I've got to use this guy, so I did. Well, I thought this was going be a short run, but hey... Sorry! (I know it's too late, but...) Mr. Kageura is just one of those characters you can play around with for fun. But since I didn't have much time in Part 1, he turned out much more normal than I originally intended. In my original draft, I was going to have his pet turtle Rika (who he keeps inside his mouth!) transform into a human, and then he was going to marry her!

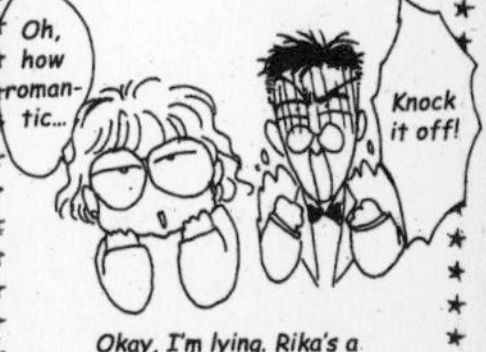
Oh, how roman-tic...
Knock it off!

Okay, I'm lying. Rika's a normal human being.

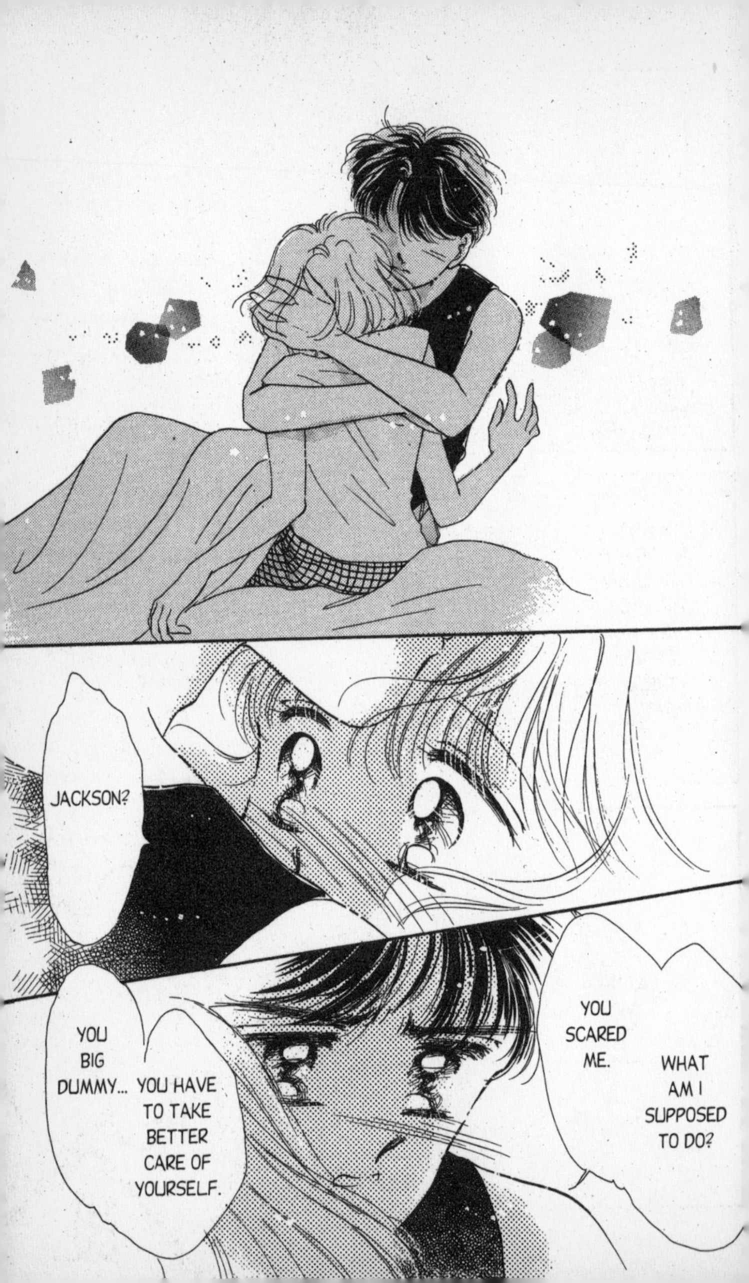
JACKSON?
YOU BIG DUMMY...
YOU HAVE TO TAKE BETTER CARE OF YOURSELF.
YOU SCARED ME.
WHAT AM I SUPPOSED TO DO?

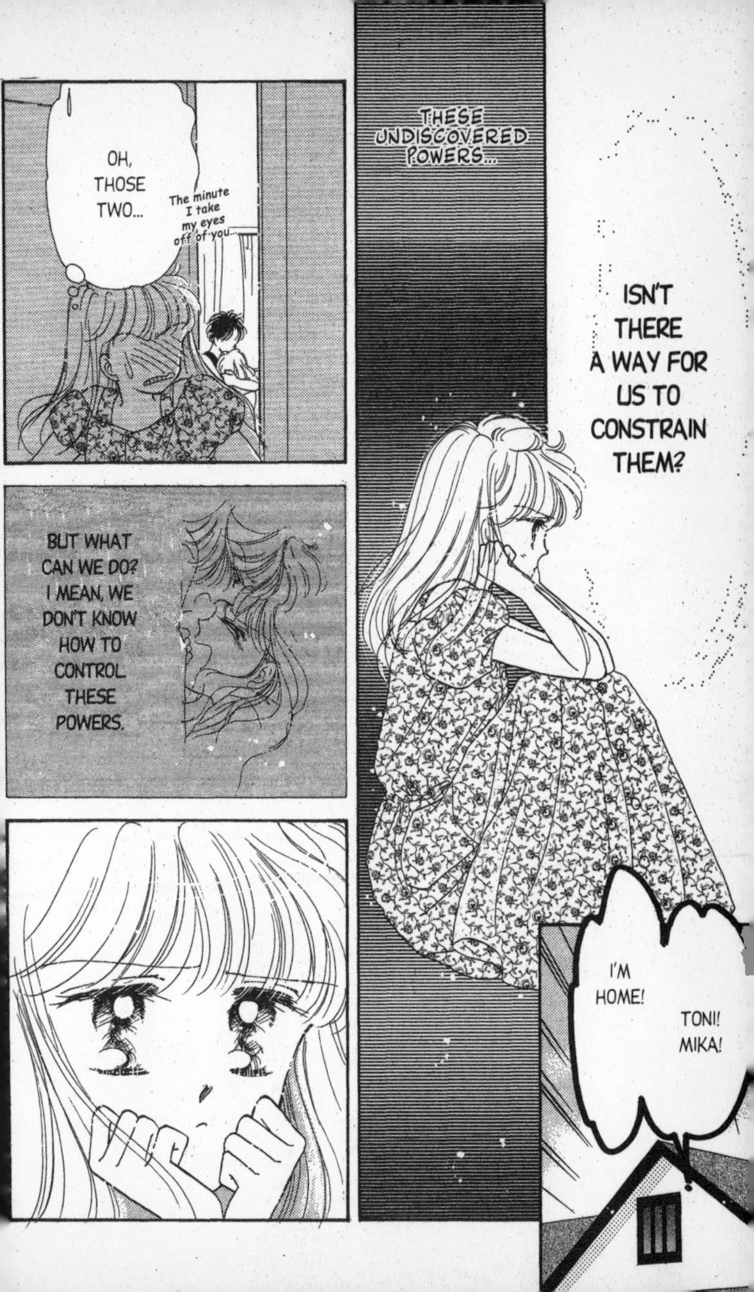
OH, THOSE TWO...
The minute I take my eyes off of you...
BUT WHAT CAN WE DO? I MEAN, WE DON'T KNOW HOW TO CONTROL THESE POWERS.
THESE UNDISCOVERED POWERS...
ISN'T THERE A WAY FOR US TO CONSTRAIN THEM?
I'M HOME!
TONI! MIKA!

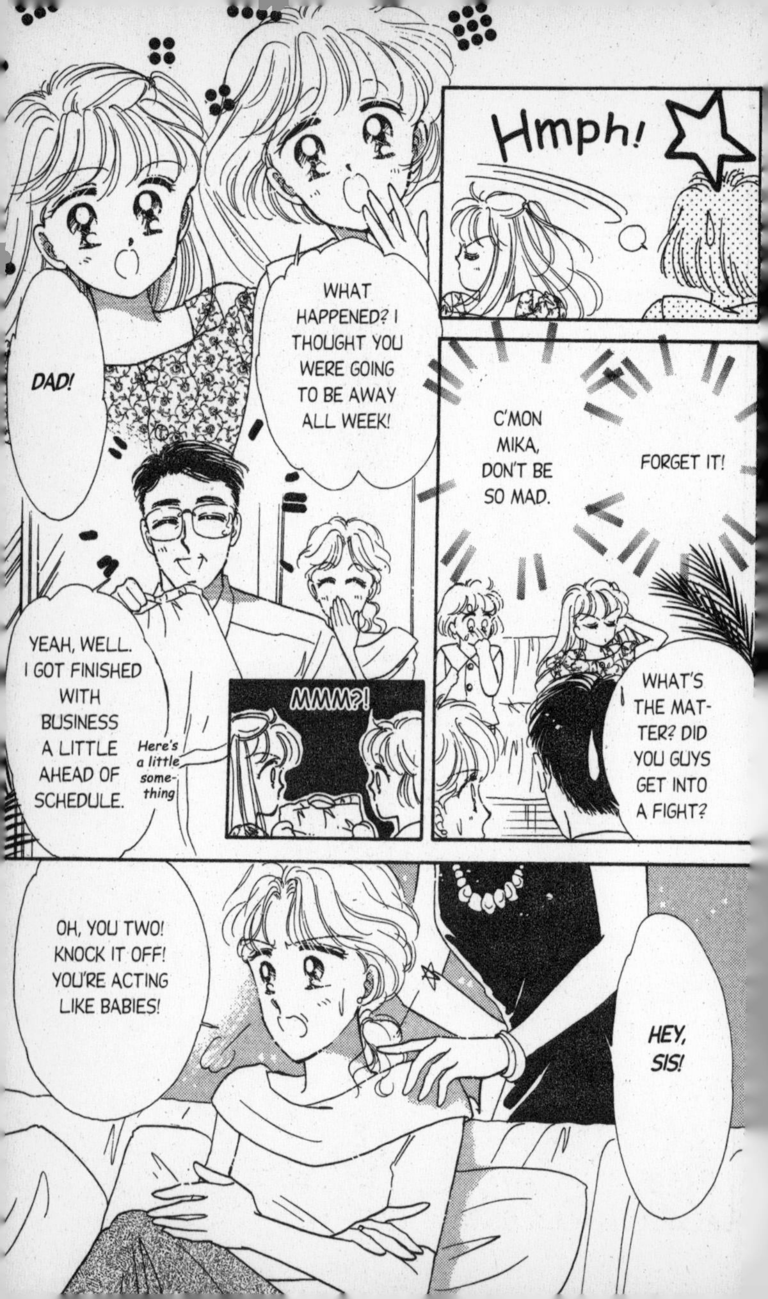
DAD!
WHAT HAPPENED? I THOUGHT YOU WERE GOING TO BE AWAY ALL WEEK!
YEAH, WELL. I GOT FINISHED WITH BUSINESS A LITTLE AHEAD OF SCHEDULE.
Here's a little some-thing
MMM?!
Hmph!
C'MON MIKA, DON'T BE SO MAD.
FORGET IT!
WHAT'S THE MAT-TER? DID YOU GUYS GET INTO A FIGHT?
OH, YOU TWO! KNOCK IT OFF! YOU'RE ACTING LIKE BABIES!
HEY, SIS!

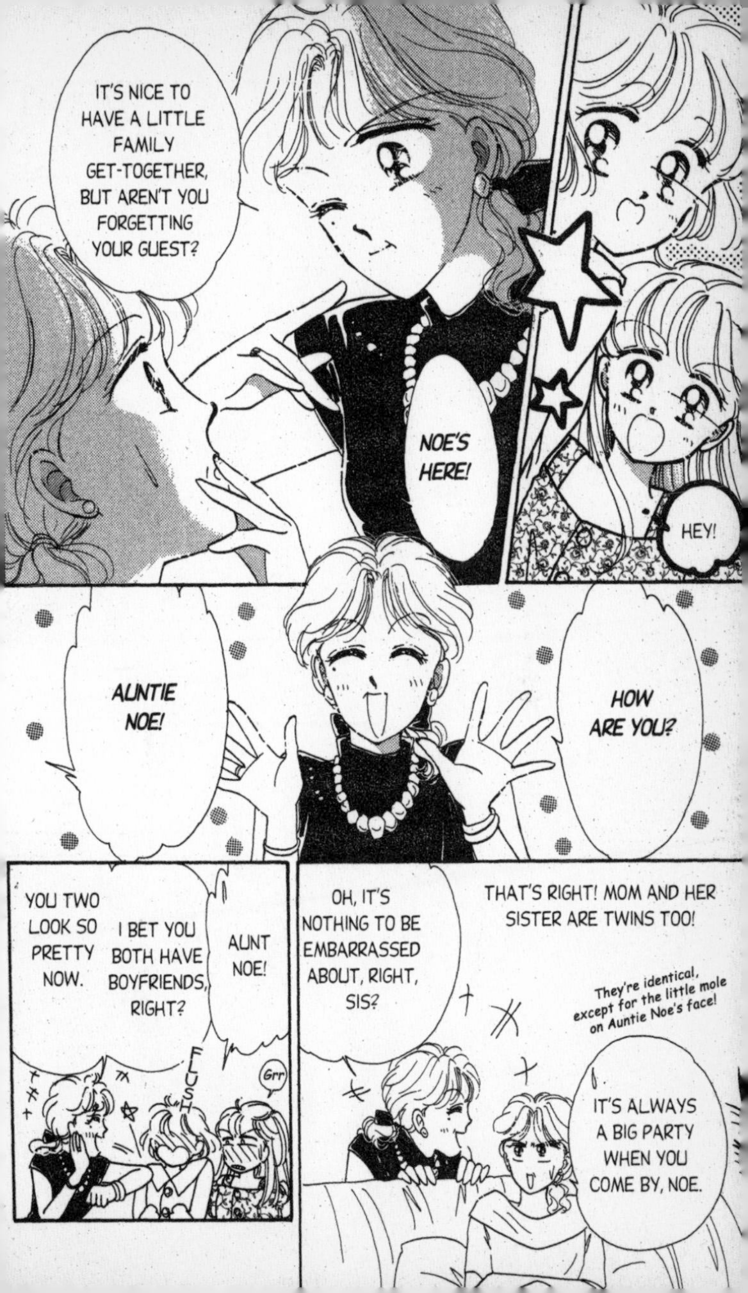
IT'S NICE TO HAVE A LITTLE FAMILY GET-TOGETHER, BUT AREN'T YOU FORGETTING YOUR GUEST?
NOE'S HERE!
HEY!
AUNTIE NOE!
HOW ARE YOU?
YOU TWO LOOK SO PRETTY NOW.
I BET YOU BOTH HAVE BOYFRIENDS, RIGHT?
AUNT NOE!
FLUSH
Grr
OH, IT'S NOTHING TO BE EMBARRASSED ABOUT, RIGHT, SIS?
THAT'S RIGHT! MOM AND HER SISTER ARE TWINS TOO!
They're identical, except for the little mole on Auntie Noe's face!
IT'S ALWAYS A BIG PARTY WHEN YOU COME BY, NOE.

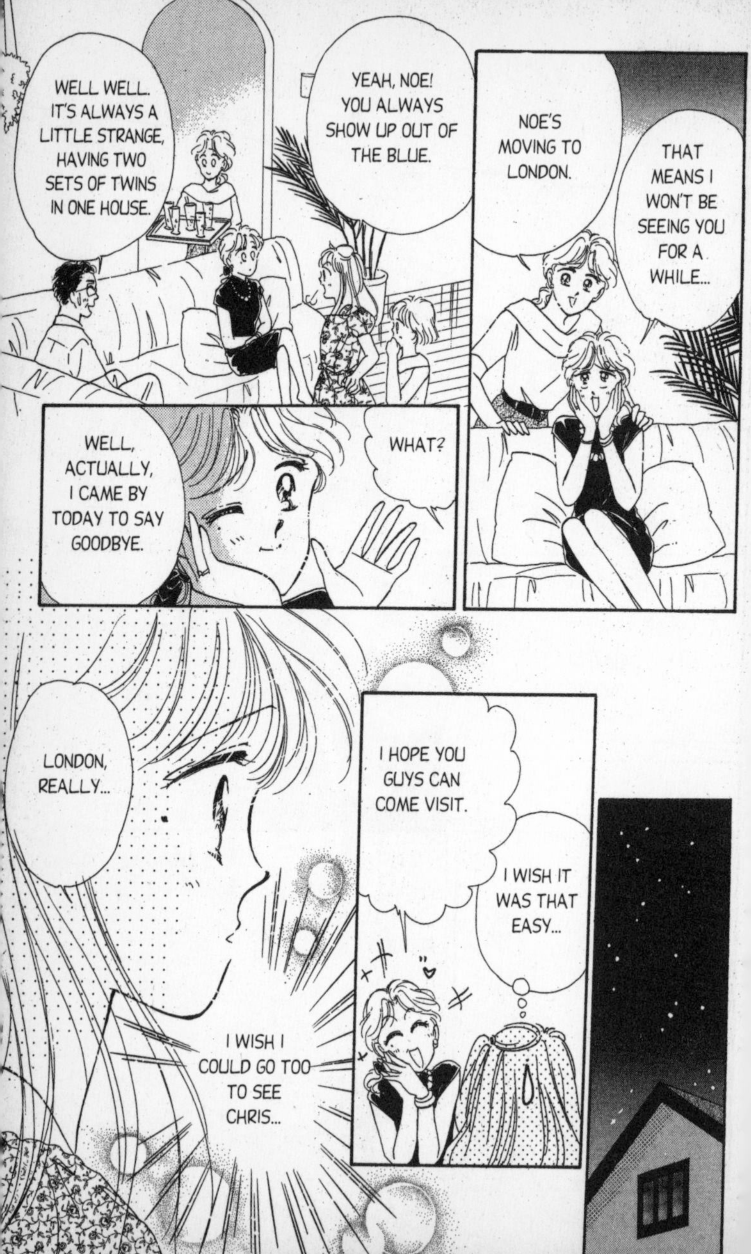
WELL WELL. IT'S ALWAYS A LITTLE STRANGE, HAVING TWO SETS OF TWINS IN ONE HOUSE.
YEAH, NOE! YOU ALWAYS SHOW UP OUT OF THE BLUE.
WELL, ACTUALLY, I CAME BY TODAY TO SAY GOODBYE.
WHAT?
NOE'S MOVING TO LONDON.
THAT MEANS I WON'T BE SEEING YOU FOR A WHILE...
LONDON, REALLY...
I WISH I COULD GO TOO TO SEE CHRIS...
I HOPE YOU GUYS CAN COME VISIT.
I WISH IT WAS THAT EASY...

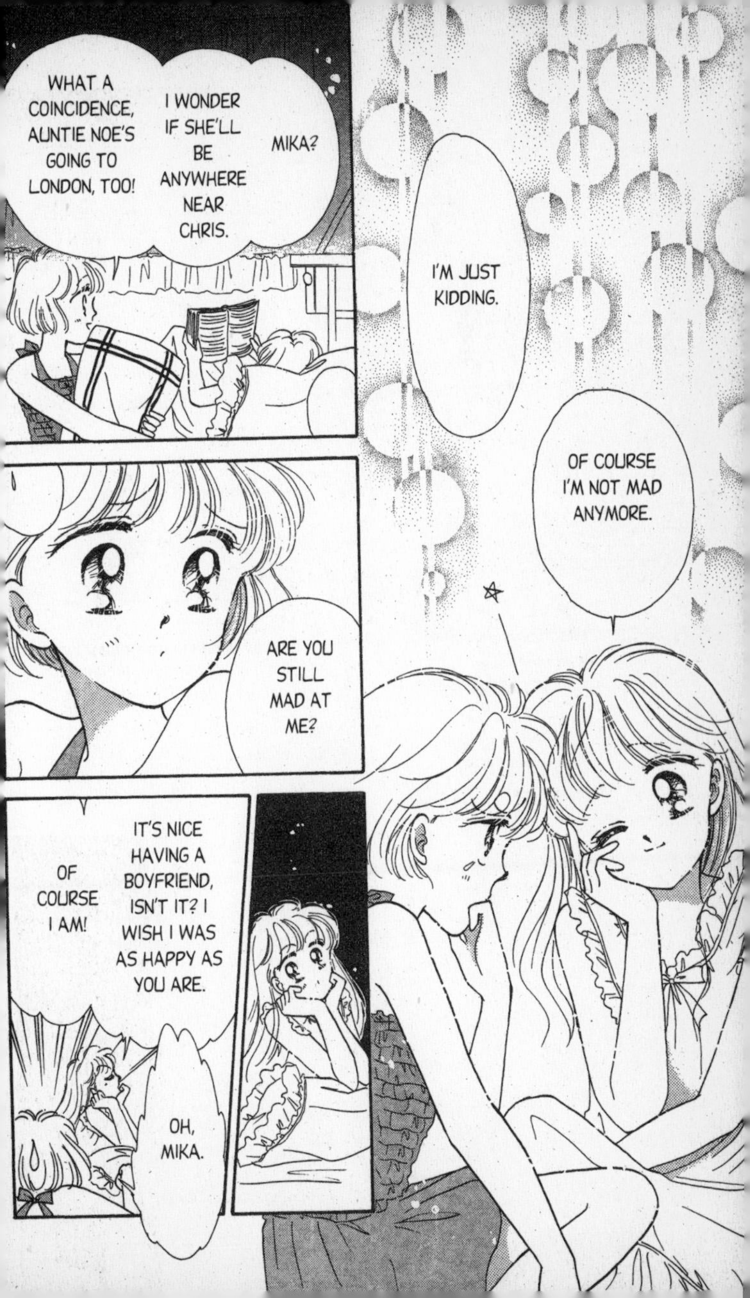
WHAT A COINCIDENCE, AUNTIE NOE'S GOING TO LONDON, TOO!
I WONDER IF SHE'LL BE ANYWHERE NEAR CHRIS.
MIKA?
ARE YOU STILL MAD AT ME?
OF COURSE I AM!
IT'S NICE HAVING A BOYFRIEND, ISN'T IT? I WISH I WAS AS HAPPY AS YOU ARE.
OH, MIKA.
I'M JUST KIDDING.
OF COURSE I'M NOT MAD ANYMORE.

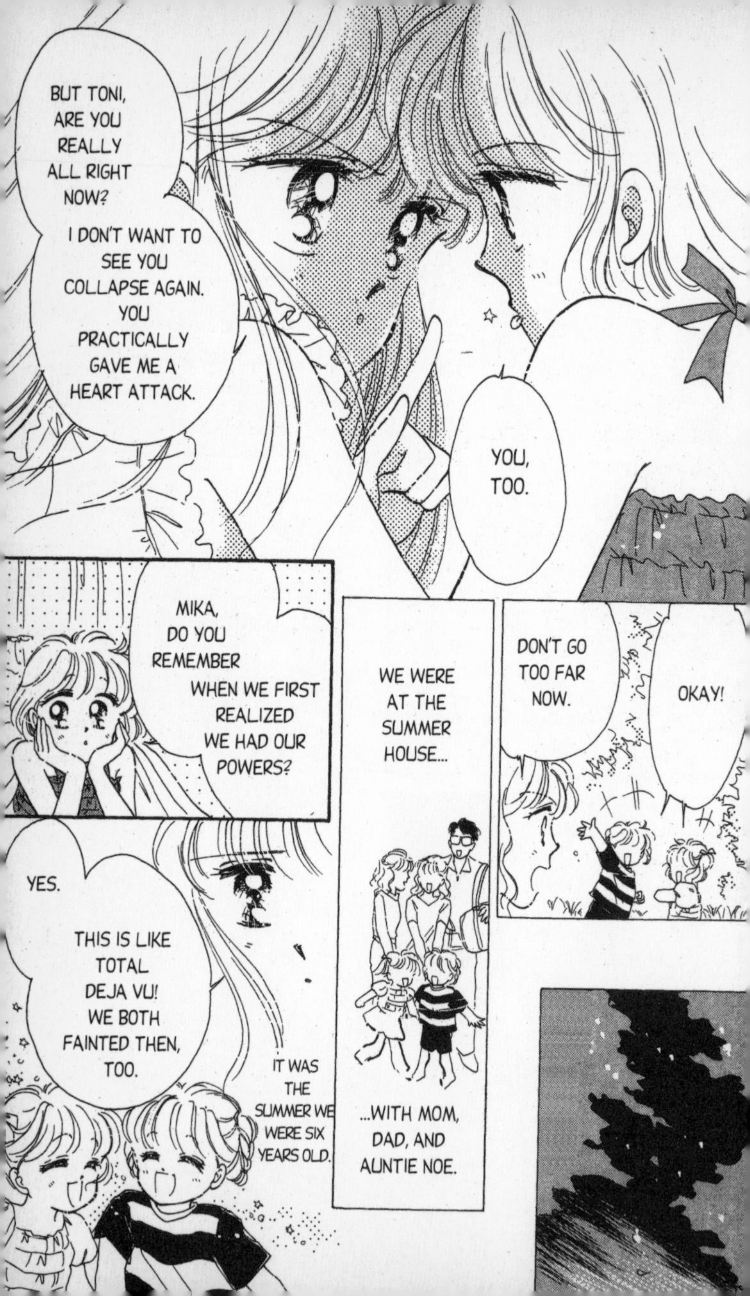
BUT TONI, ARE YOU REALLY ALL RIGHT NOW?
I DON'T WANT TO SEE YOU COLLAPSE AGAIN. YOU PRACTICALLY GAVE ME A HEART ATTACK.
YOU, TOO.
MIKA, DO YOU REMEMBER
WHEN WE FIRST REALIZED WE HAD OUR POWERS?
WE WERE AT THE SUMMER HOUSE...
...WITH MOM, DAD, AND AUNTIE NOE.
DON'T GO TOO FAR NOW.
OKAY!
YES.
THIS IS LIKE TOTAL DEJA VU! WE BOTH FAINTED THEN, TOO.
IT WAS THE SUMMER WE WERE SIX YEARS OLD.

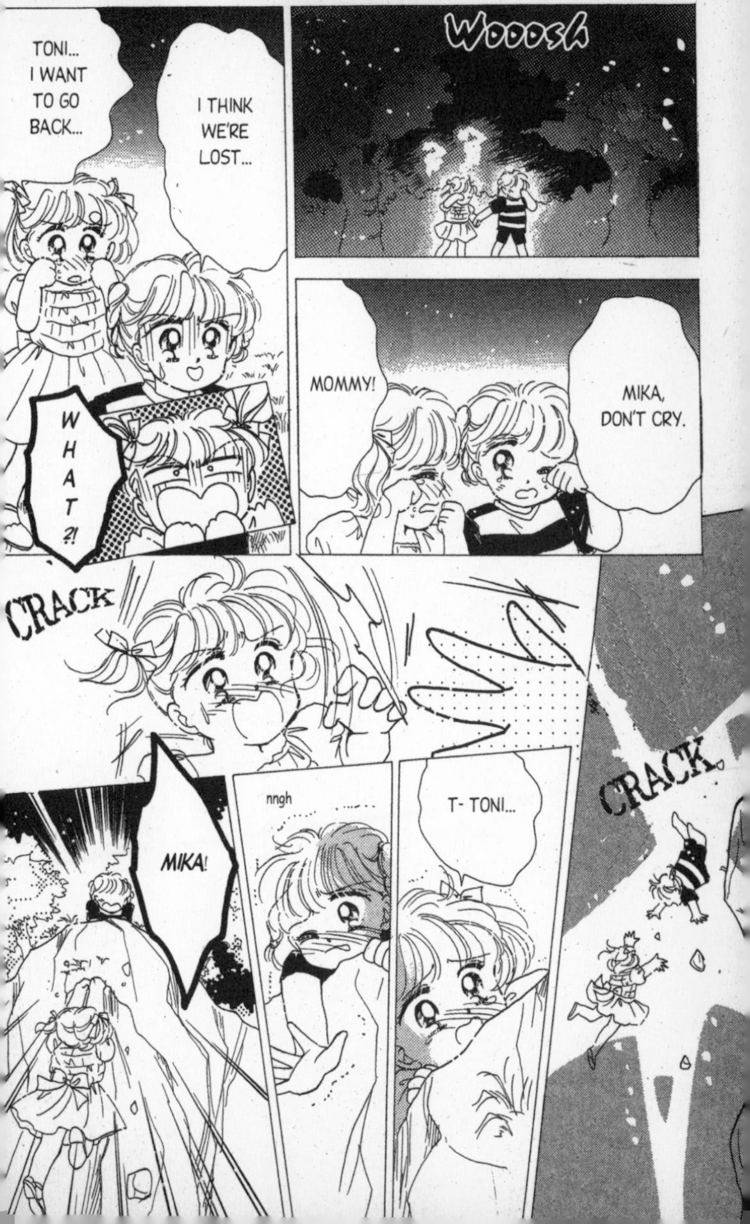
TONI... I WANT TO GO BACK...
I THINK WE'RE LOST...
WHAT?!
Wooosh
MOMMY!
MIKA, DON'T CRY.
CRACK
MIKA!
nngh
T- TONI...
CRACK

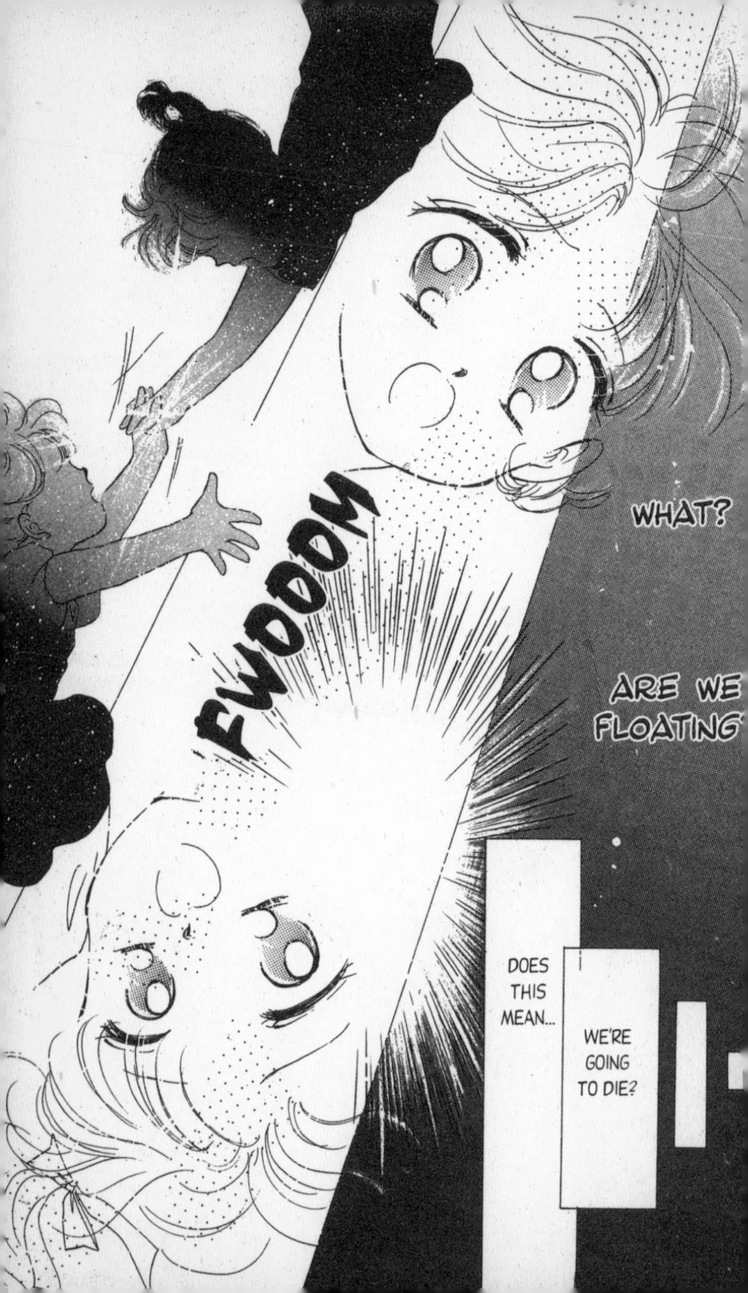
FWOOOM
WHAT?
ARE WE FLOATING?
DOES THIS MEAN...
WE'RE GOING TO DIE?

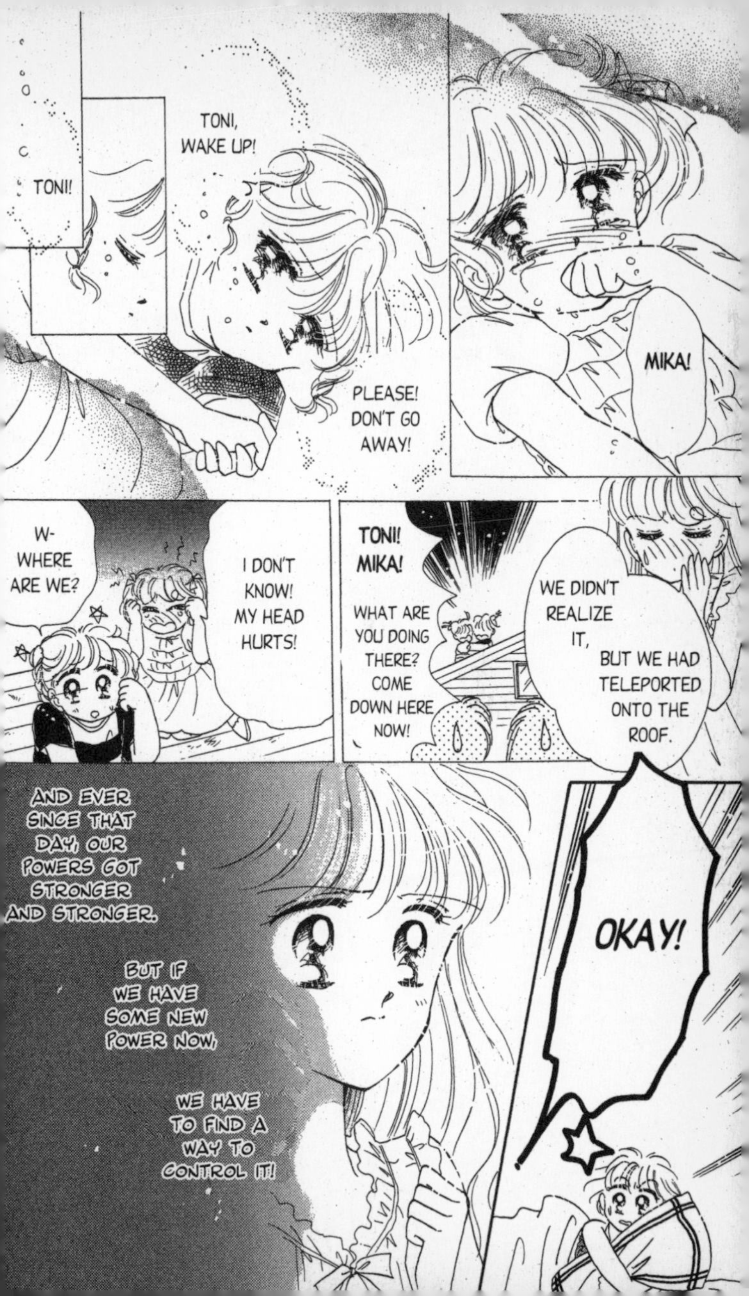
TONI!
TONI, WAKE UP!
PLEASE! DON'T GO AWAY!
MIKA!
W- WHERE ARE WE?
I DON'T KNOW! MY HEAD HURTS!
TONI! MIKA!
WHAT ARE YOU DOING THERE? COME DOWN HERE NOW!
WE DIDN'T REALIZE IT,
BUT WE HAD TELEPORTED ONTO THE ROOF.
AND EVER SINCE THAT DAY, OUR POWERS GOT STRONGER AND STRONGER.
BUT IF WE HAVE SOME NEW POWER NOW,
WE HAVE TO FIND A WAY TO CONTROL IT!
OKAY!

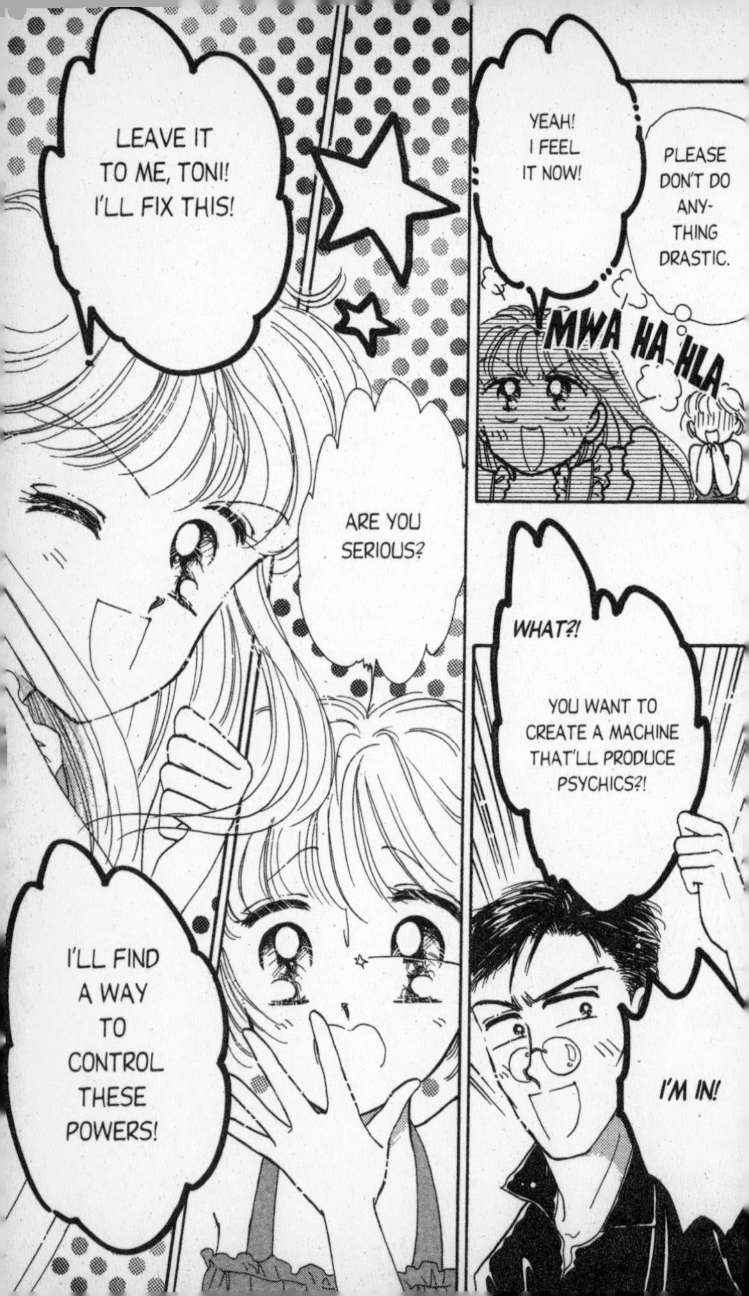
LEAVE IT TO ME, TONI! I'LL FIX THIS!
ARE YOU SERIOUS?
I'LL FIND A WAY TO CONTROL THESE POWERS!
YEAH! I FEEL IT NOW!
PLEASE DON'T DO ANY-THING DRASTIC.
MWA HA HLA
WHAT?!
YOU WANT TO CREATE A MACHINE THAT'LL PRODUCE PSYCHICS?!
I'M IN!

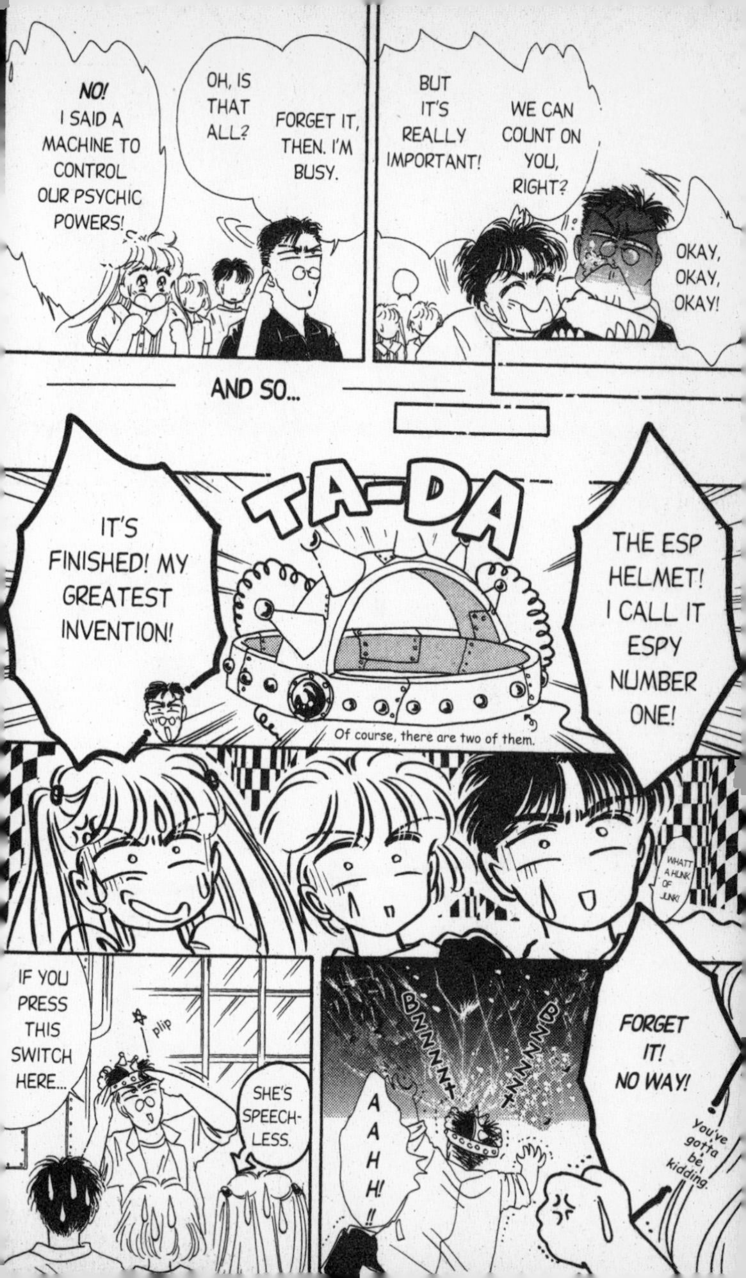
NO! I SAID A MACHINE TO CONTROL OUR PSYCHIC POWERS!
OH, IS THAT ALL?
FORGET IT, THEN. I'M BUSY.
BUT IT'S REALLY IMPORTANT!
WE CAN COUNT ON YOU, RIGHT?
OKAY, OKAY, OKAY!
AND SO...
IT'S FINISHED! MY GREATEST INVENTION!
TA-DA
THE ESP HELMET! I CALL IT ESPY NUMBER ONE!
Of course, there are two of them.
WHAT A HUNK OF JUNK!
IF YOU PRESS THIS SWITCH HERE...
plip
SHE'S SPEECHLESS.
AAAH!!
BZZZZZT
NNNNNB
FORGET IT! NO WAY!
You've gotta be kidding.

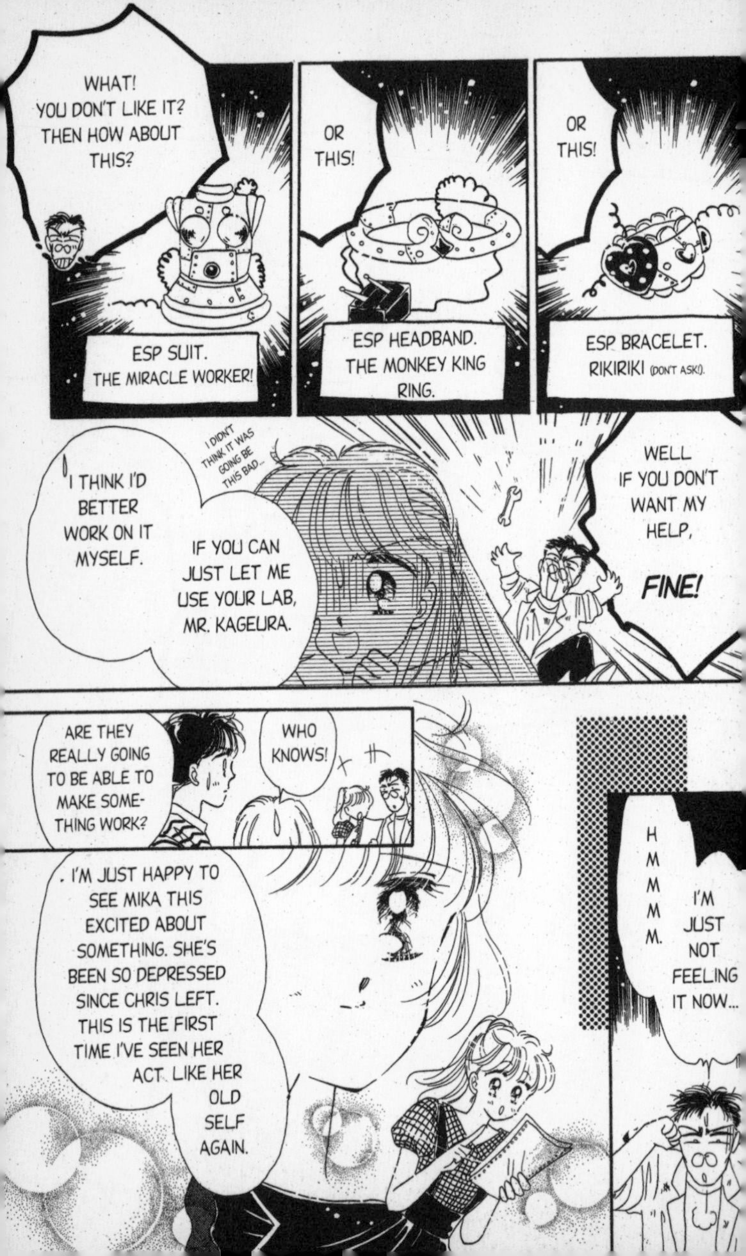
WHAT! YOU DON'T LIKE IT? THEN HOW ABOUT THIS?
ESP SUIT. THE MIRACLE WORKER!
OR THIS!
ESP HEADBAND. THE MONKEY KING RING.
OR THIS!
ESP BRACELET. RIKIRIKI (DON'T ASK!).
I THINK I'D BETTER WORK ON IT MYSELF.
I DIDN'T THINK IT WAS GOING BE THIS BAD...
IF YOU CAN JUST LET ME USE YOUR LAB, MR. KAGEURA.
WELL IF YOU DON'T WANT MY HELP,
FINE!
ARE THEY REALLY GOING TO BE ABLE TO MAKE SOME-THING WORK?
WHO KNOWS!
. I'M JUST HAPPY TO SEE MIKA THIS EXCITED ABOUT SOMETHING. SHE'S BEEN SO DEPRESSED SINCE CHRIS LEFT. THIS IS THE FIRST TIME I'VE SEEN HER ACT LIKE HER OLD SELF AGAIN.
HMMMM.
I'M JUST NOT FEELING IT NOW...

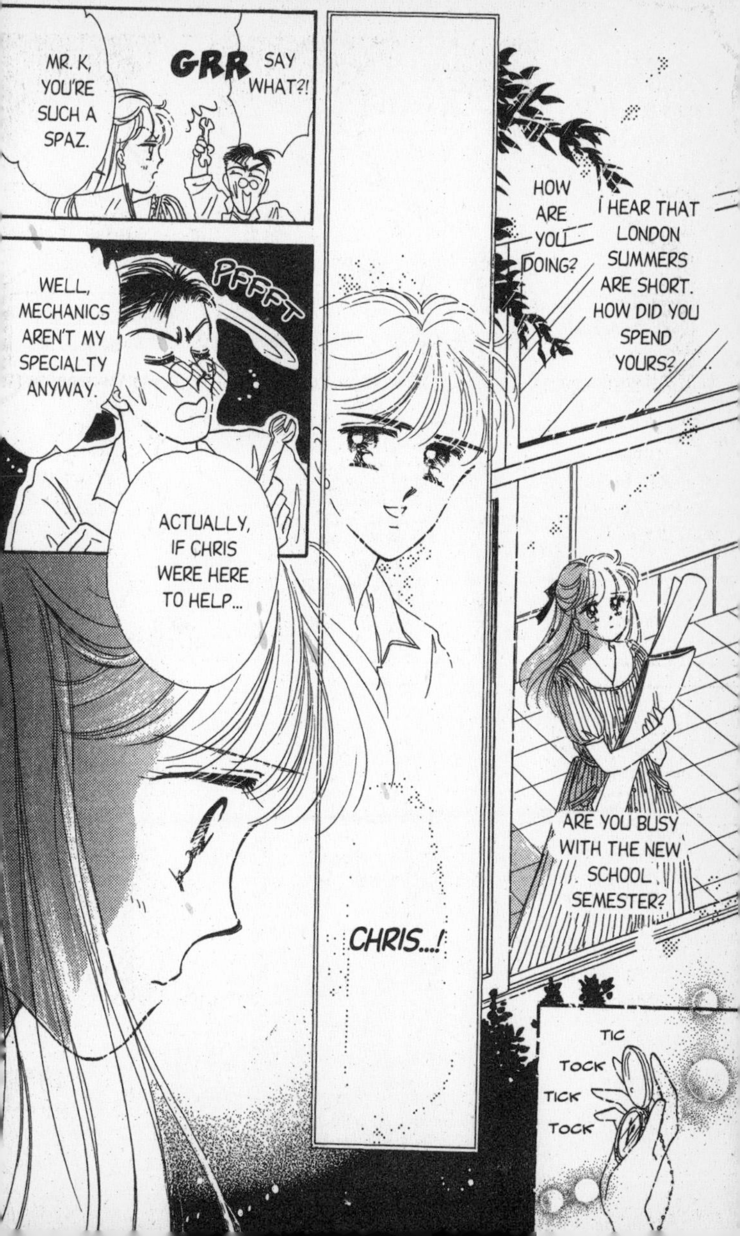
MR. K, YOU'RE SUCH A SPAZ.
GRR
SAY WHAT?!
WELL, MECHANICS AREN'T MY SPECIALTY ANYWAY.
PFFFT
ACTUALLY, IF CHRIS WERE HERE TO HELP...
CHRIS...!
HOW ARE YOU DOING?
I HEAR THAT LONDON SUMMERS ARE SHORT. HOW DID YOU SPEND YOURS?
ARE YOU BUSY WITH THE NEW SCHOOL SEMESTER?
TIC
TOCK
TICK
TOCK

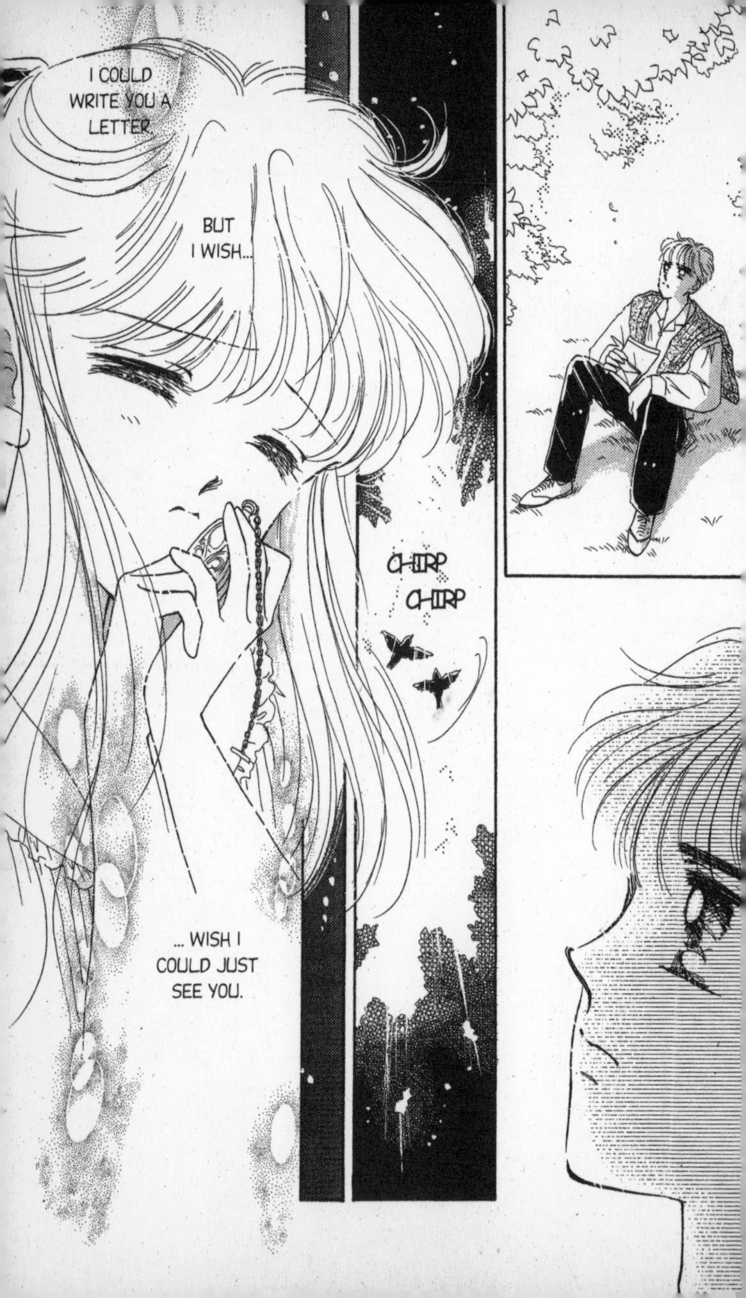
I COULD WRITE YOU A LETTER
BUT I WISH...
... WISH I COULD JUST SEE YOU.
CHIRP
CHIRP

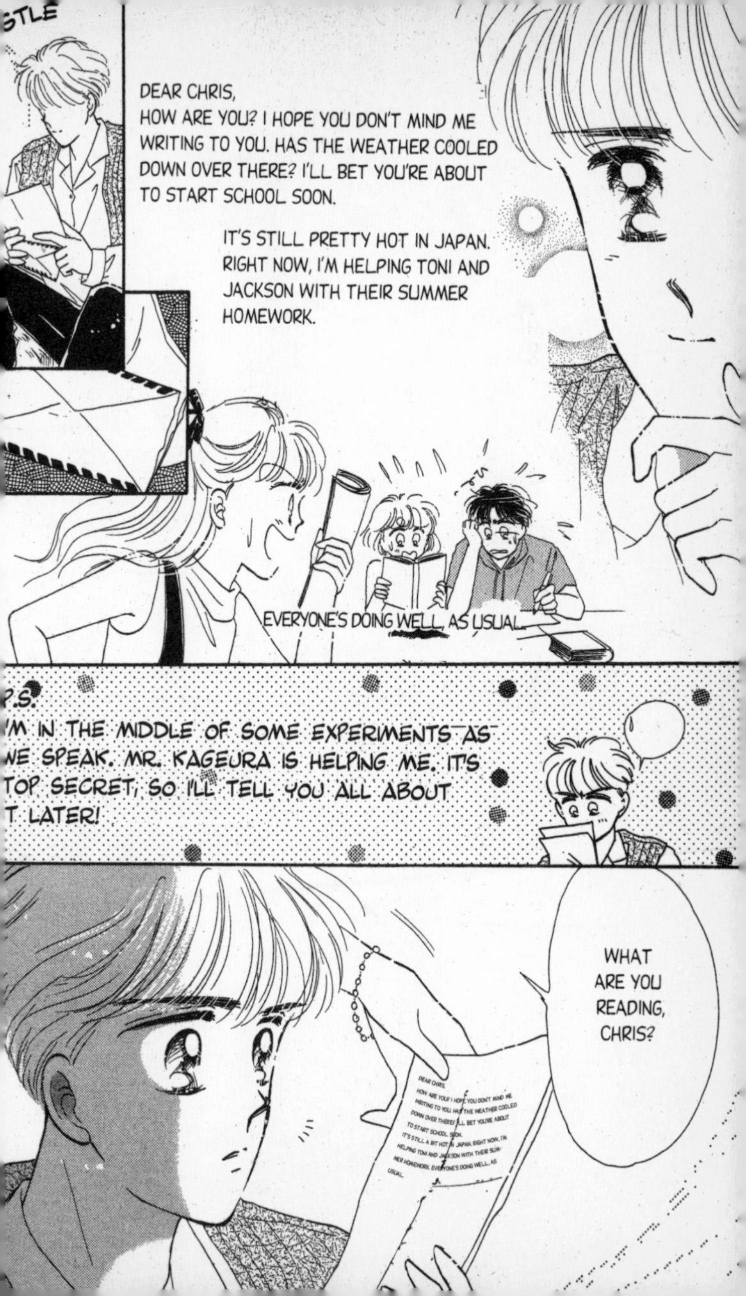
STLE
DEAR CHRIS,
HOW ARE YOU? I HOPE YOU DON'T MIND ME WRITING TO YOU. HAS THE WEATHER COOLED DOWN OVER THERE? I'LL BET YOU'RE ABOUT TO START SCHOOL SOON.
IT'S STILL PRETTY HOT IN JAPAN. RIGHT NOW, I'M HELPING TONI AND JACKSON WITH THEIR SUMMER HOMEWORK.
EVERYONE'S DOING WELL, AS USUAL.
P.S.
'M IN THE MIDDLE OF SOME EXPERIMENTS AS WE SPEAK. MR. KAGEURA IS HELPING ME. IT'S TOP SECRET, SO I'LL TELL YOU ALL ABOUT T LATER!
WHAT ARE YOU READING, CHRIS?

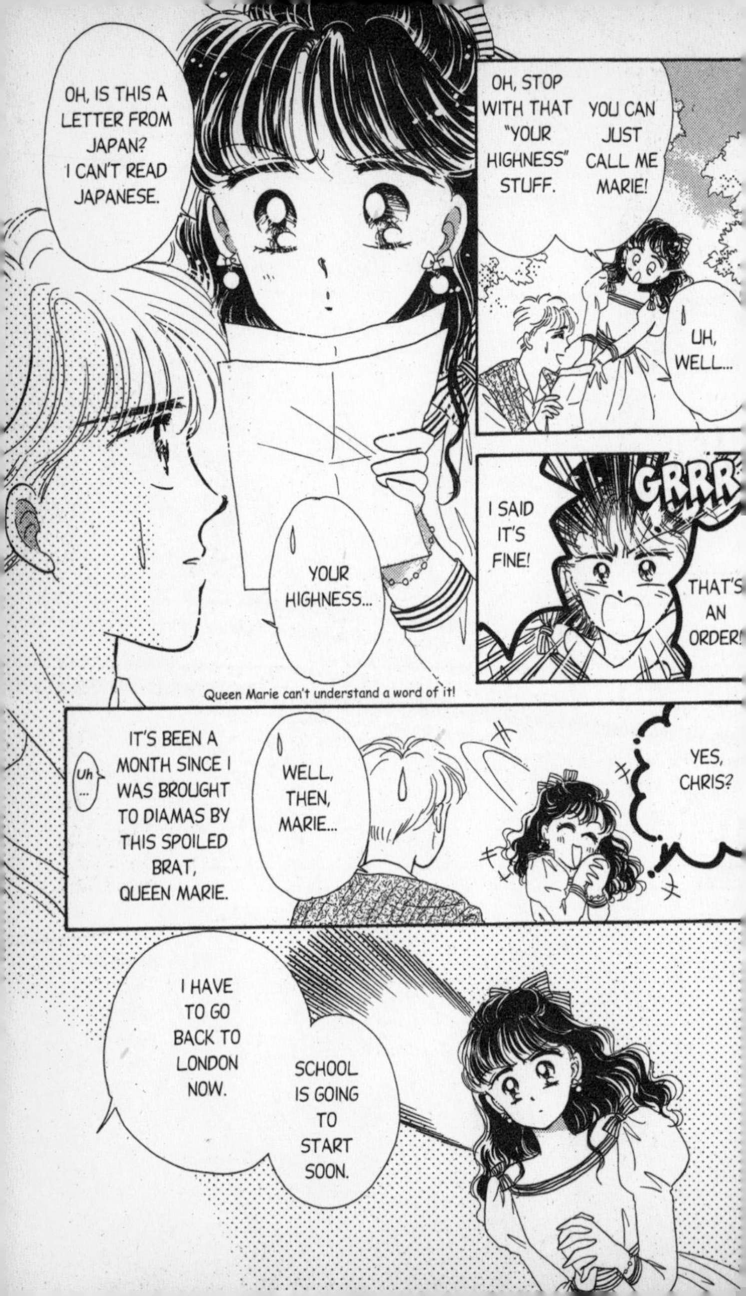
OH, IS THIS A LETTER FROM JAPAN? I CAN'T READ JAPANESE.
YOUR HIGHNESS...
Queen Marie can't understand a word of it!
OH, STOP WITH THAT "YOUR HIGHNESS" STUFF.
YOU CAN JUST CALL ME MARIE!
UH, WELL...
GRRR
I SAID IT'S FINE!
THAT'S AN ORDER!
Uh...
IT'S BEEN A MONTH SINCE I WAS BROUGHT TO DIAMAS BY THIS SPOILED BRAT, QUEEN MARIE.
WELL, THEN, MARIE...
YES, CHRIS?
I HAVE TO GO BACK TO LONDON NOW.
SCHOOL IS GOING TO START SOON.

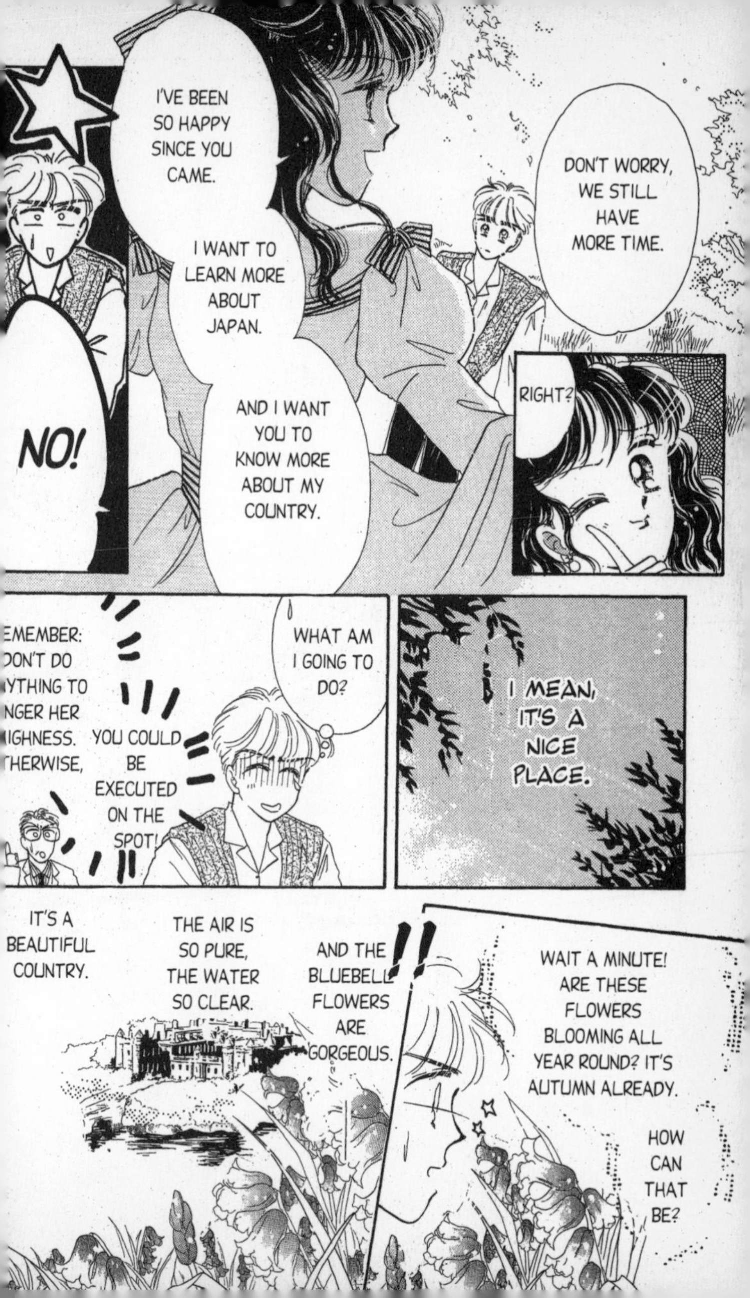

I'VE BEEN SO HAPPY SINCE YOU CAME.
I WANT TO LEARN MORE ABOUT JAPAN.
AND I WANT YOU TO KNOW MORE ABOUT MY COUNTRY.
NO!
DON'T WORRY, WE STILL HAVE MORE TIME.
RIGHT?
EMEMBER: DON'T DO YTHING TO NGER HER IGHNESS. THERWISE,
YOU COULD BE EXECUTED ON THE SPOT!
WHAT AM I GOING TO DO?
I MEAN, IT'S A NICE PLACE.
IT'S A BEAUTIFUL COUNTRY.
THE AIR IS SO PURE, THE WATER SO CLEAR.
AND THE BLUEBELL FLOWERS ARE GORGEOUS.
WAIT A MINUTE! ARE THESE FLOWERS BLOOMING ALL YEAR ROUND? IT'S AUTUMN ALREADY.
HOW CAN THAT BE?

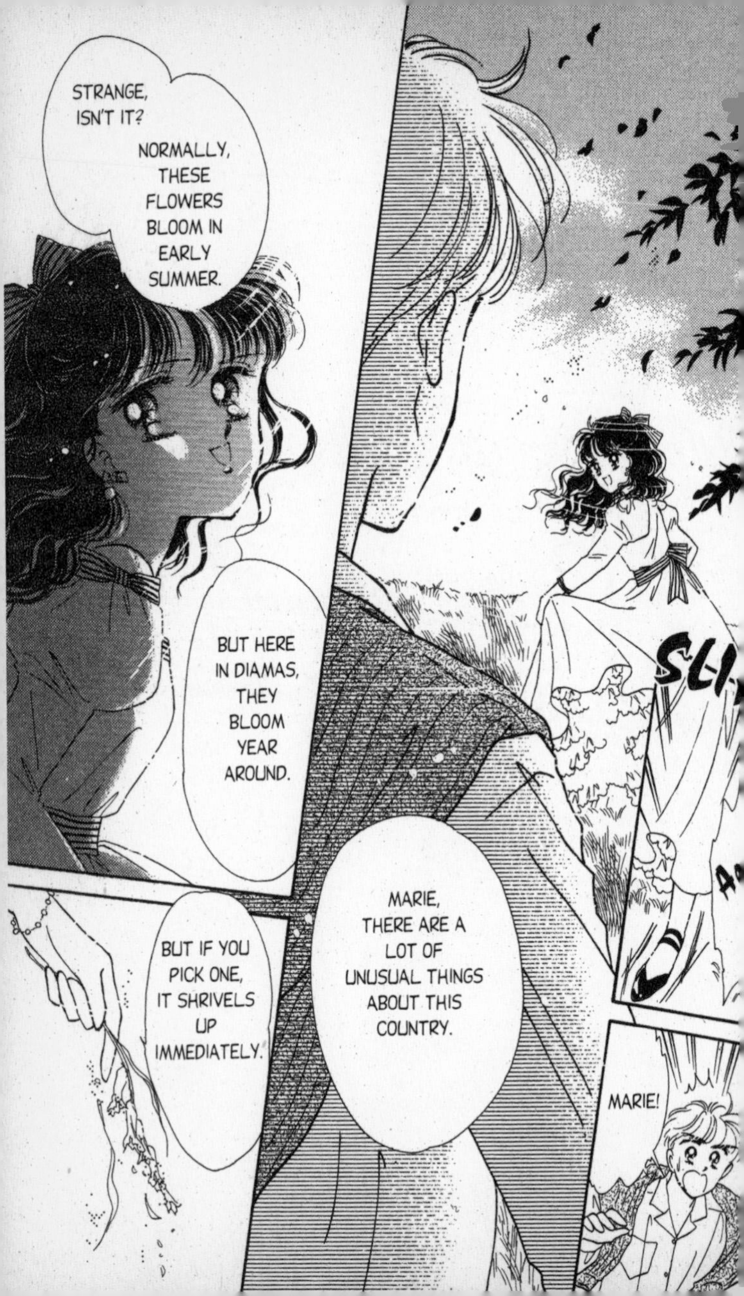
STRANGE, ISN'T IT? NORMALLY, THESE FLOWERS BLOOM IN EARLY SUMMER.
BUT HERE IN DIAMAS, THEY BLOOM YEAR AROUND.
BUT IF YOU PICK ONE, IT SHRIVELS UP IMMEDIATELY.
MARIE, THERE ARE A LOT OF UNUSUAL THINGS ABOUT THIS COUNTRY.
SLI-
MARIE!

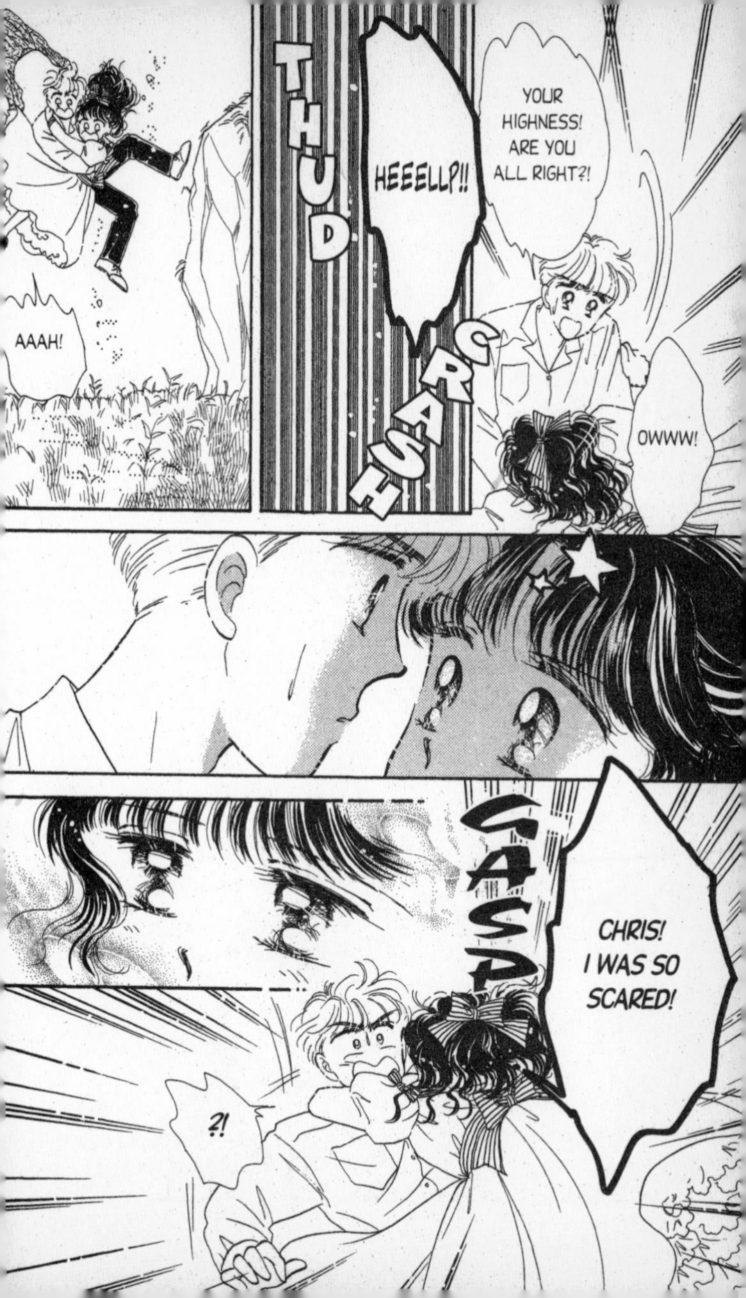
AAAH!
THUD
HEEELLP!!
CRASH
YOUR HIGHNESS! ARE YOU ALL RIGHT?!
OWWW!
GASP
CHRIS! I WAS SO SCARED!
?!

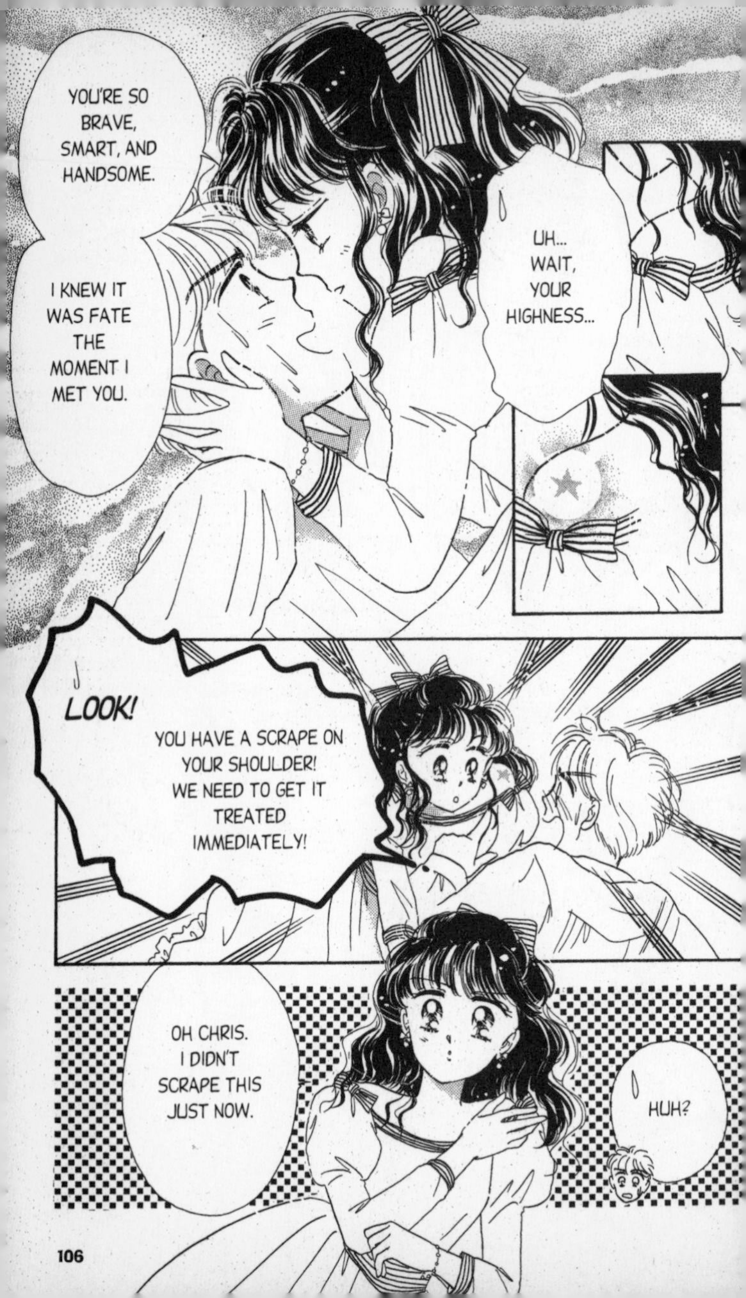
YOU'RE SO BRAVE, SMART, AND HANDSOME.
I KNEW IT WAS FATE THE MOMENT I MET YOU.
UH... WAIT, YOUR HIGHNESS...
LOOK!
YOU HAVE A SCRAPE ON YOUR SHOULDER! WE NEED TO GET IT TREATED IMMEDIATELY!
OH CHRIS. I DIDN'T SCRAPE THIS JUST NOW.
HUH?

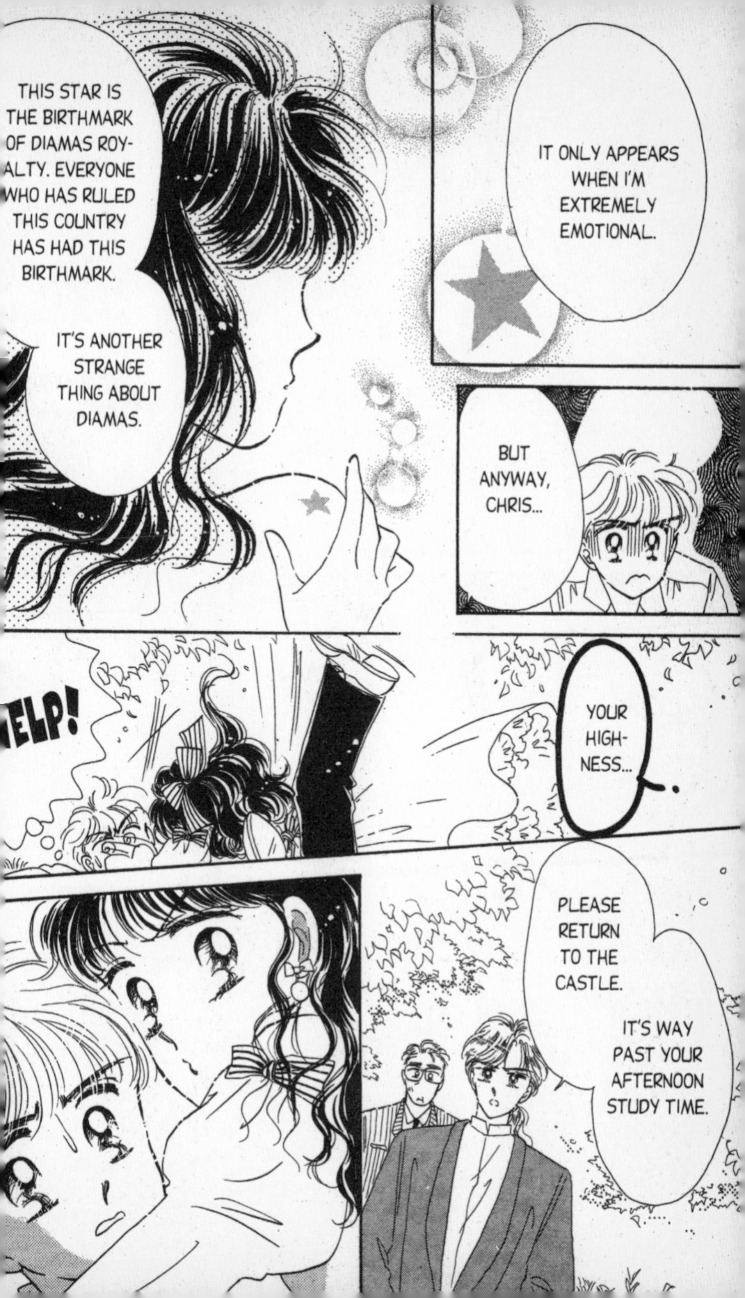
THIS STAR IS THE BIRTHMARK OF DIAMAS ROY-ALTY. EVERYONE WHO HAS RULED THIS COUNTRY HAS HAD THIS BIRTHMARK.
IT'S ANOTHER STRANGE THING ABOUT DIAMAS.
IT ONLY APPEARS WHEN I'M EXTREMELY EMOTIONAL.
BUT ANYWAY, CHRIS...
ELP!
YOUR HIGH-NESS...
PLEASE RETURN TO THE CASTLE.
IT'S WAY PAST YOUR AFTERNOON STUDY TIME.

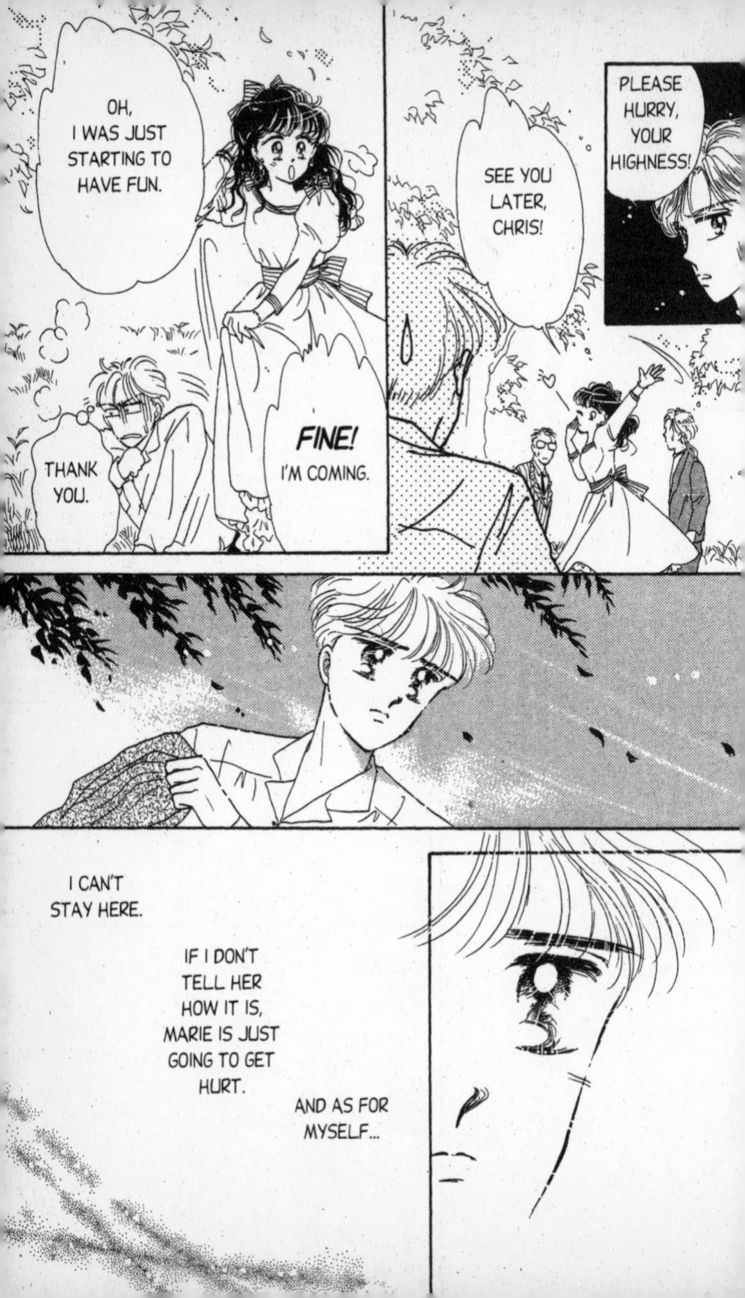
OH, I WAS JUST STARTING TO HAVE FUN.
THANK YOU.
FINE! I'M COMING.
SEE YOU LATER, CHRIS!
PLEASE HURRY, YOUR HIGHNESS!
I CAN'T STAY HERE.
IF I DON'T TELL HER HOW IT IS, MARIE IS JUST GOING TO GET HURT.
AND AS FOR MYSELF...

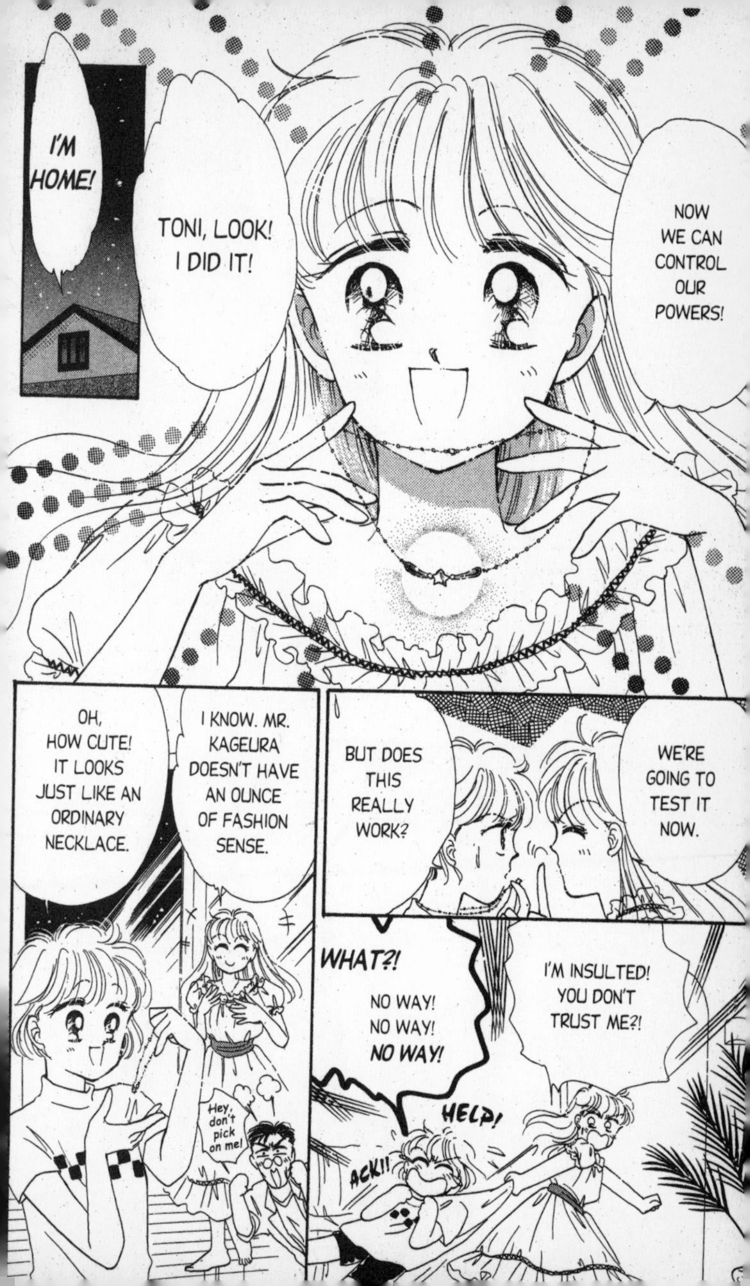
I'M HOME!
TONI, LOOK! I DID IT!
NOW WE CAN CONTROL OUR POWERS!
OH, HOW CUTE! IT LOOKS JUST LIKE AN ORDINARY NECKLACE.
I KNOW. MR. KAGEURA DOESN'T HAVE AN OUNCE OF FASHION SENSE.
Hey, don't pick on me!
BUT DOES THIS REALLY WORK?
WE'RE GOING TO TEST IT NOW.
WHAT?!
NO WAY! NO WAY! NO WAY!
I'M INSULTED! YOU DON'T TRUST ME?!
HELP!
ACK!!

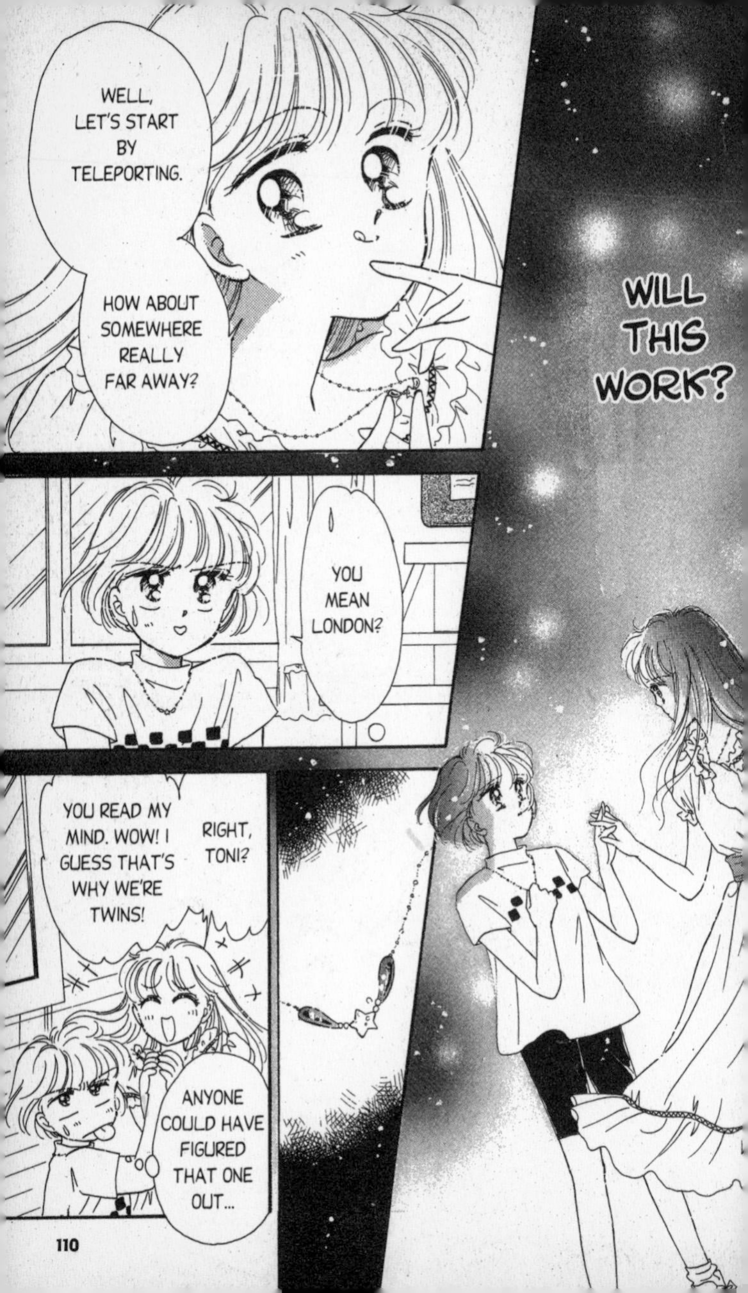
WELL, LET'S START BY TELEPORTING.
HOW ABOUT SOMEWHERE REALLY FAR AWAY?
YOU MEAN LONDON?
YOU READ MY MIND. WOW! I GUESS THAT'S WHY WE'RE TWINS!
RIGHT, TONI?
ANYONE COULD HAVE FIGURED THAT ONE OUT...
WILL THIS WORK?

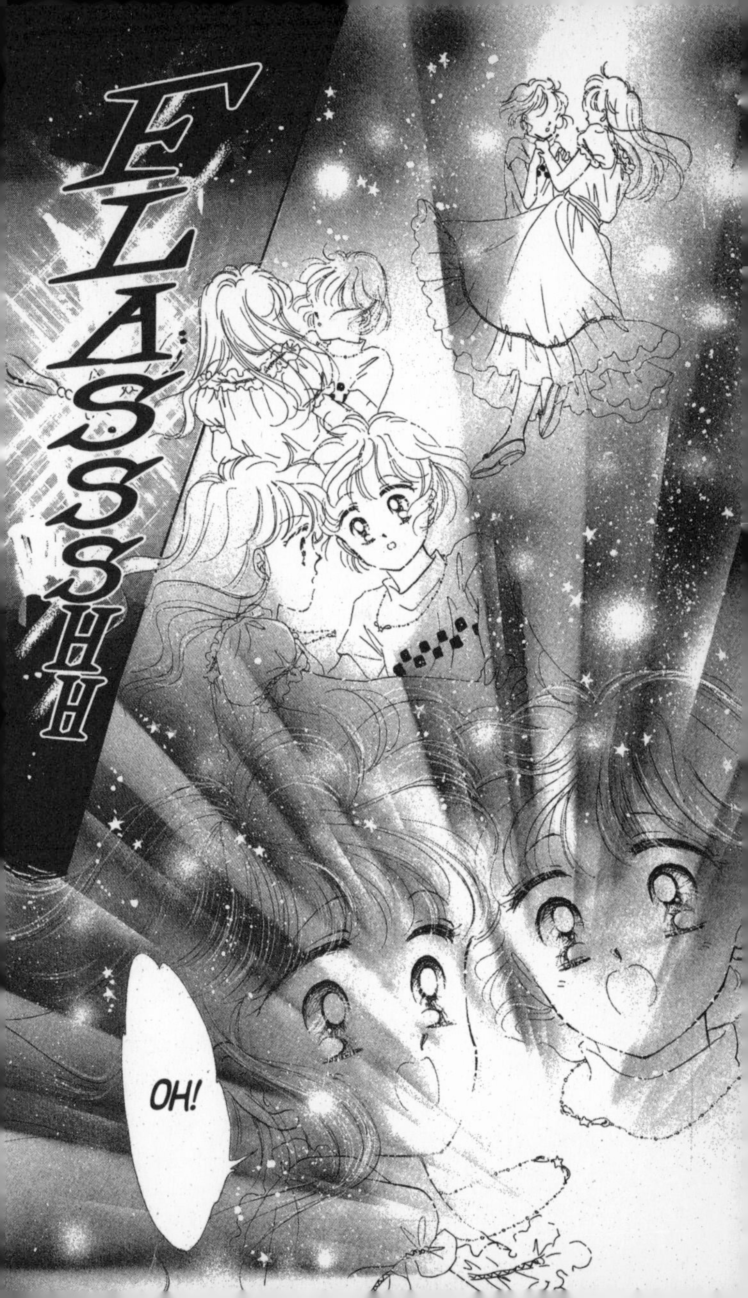
FLASSSHH
OH!

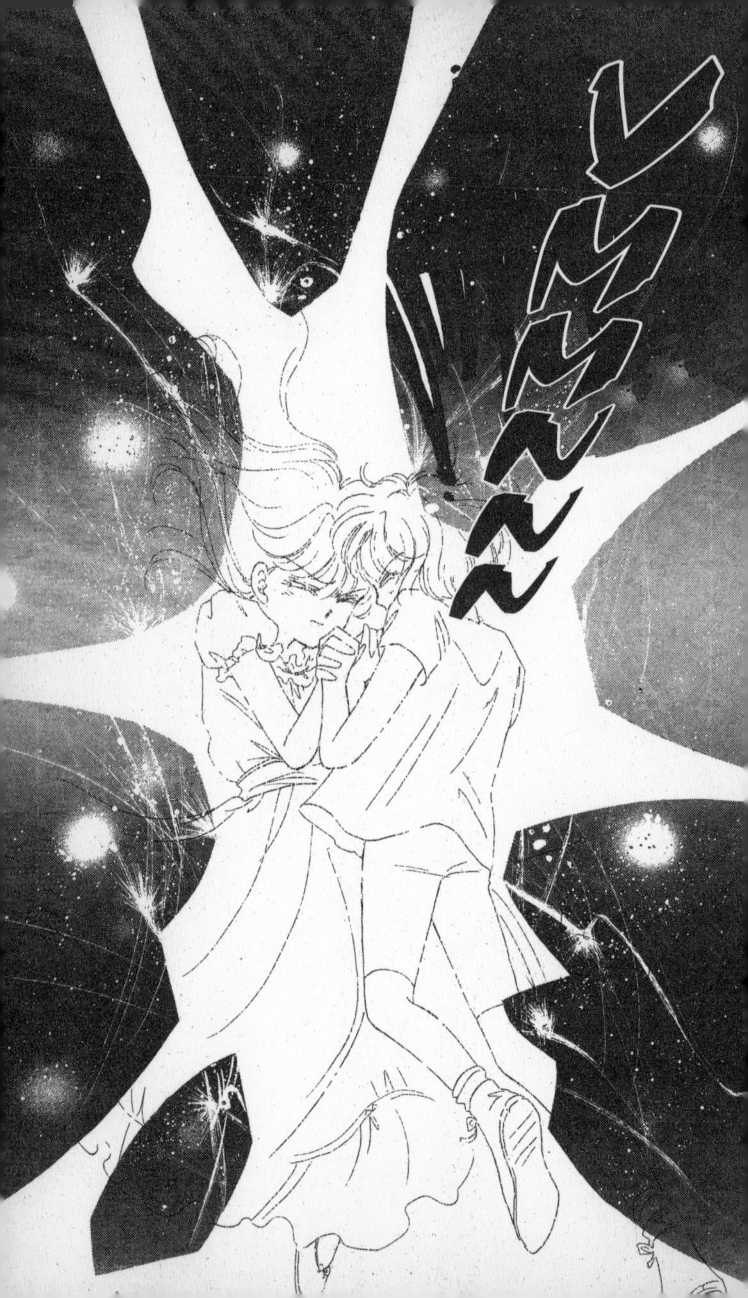

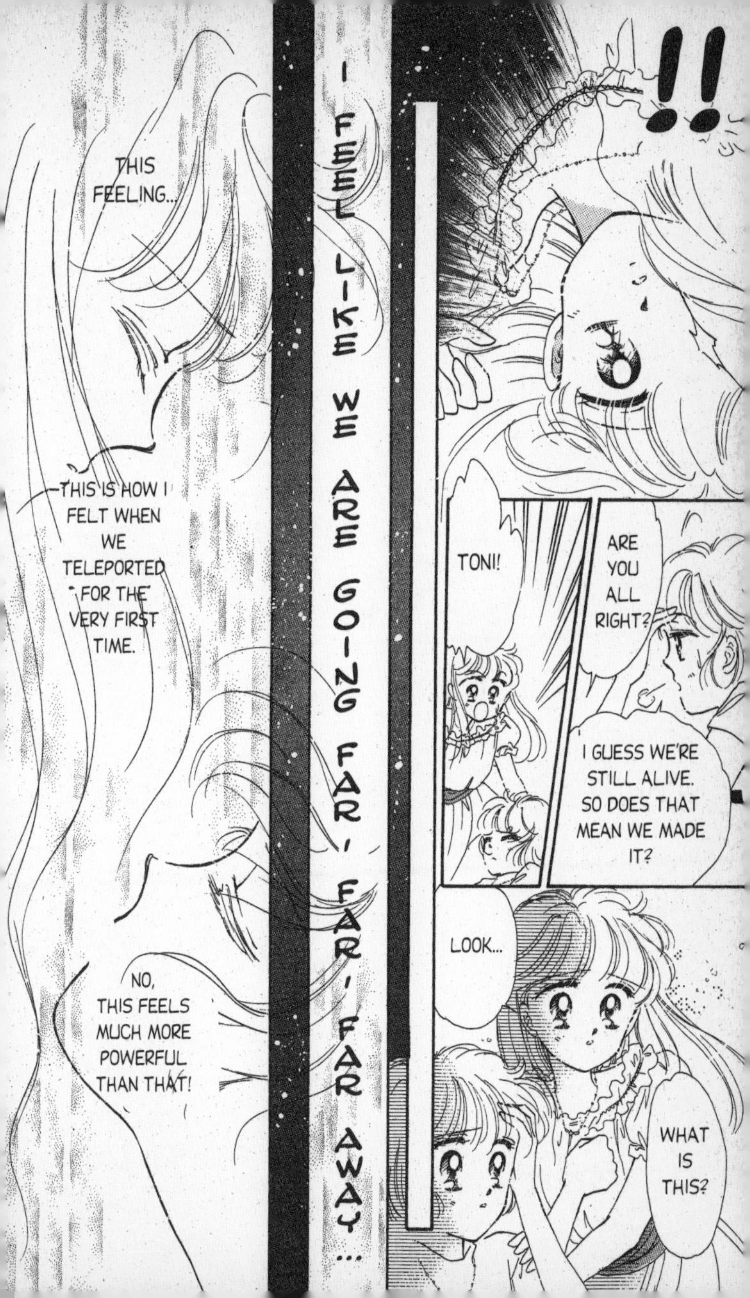
THIS FEELING...
—THIS IS HOW I FELT WHEN WE TELEPORTED FOR THE VERY FIRST TIME.
NO, THIS FEELS MUCH MORE POWERFUL THAN THAT!
I FEEL LIKE WE ARE GOING FAR, FAR, FAR AWAY...
!!
TONI!
ARE YOU ALL RIGHT?
I GUESS WE'RE STILL ALIVE. SO DOES THAT MEAN WE MADE IT?
LOOK...
WHAT IS THIS?

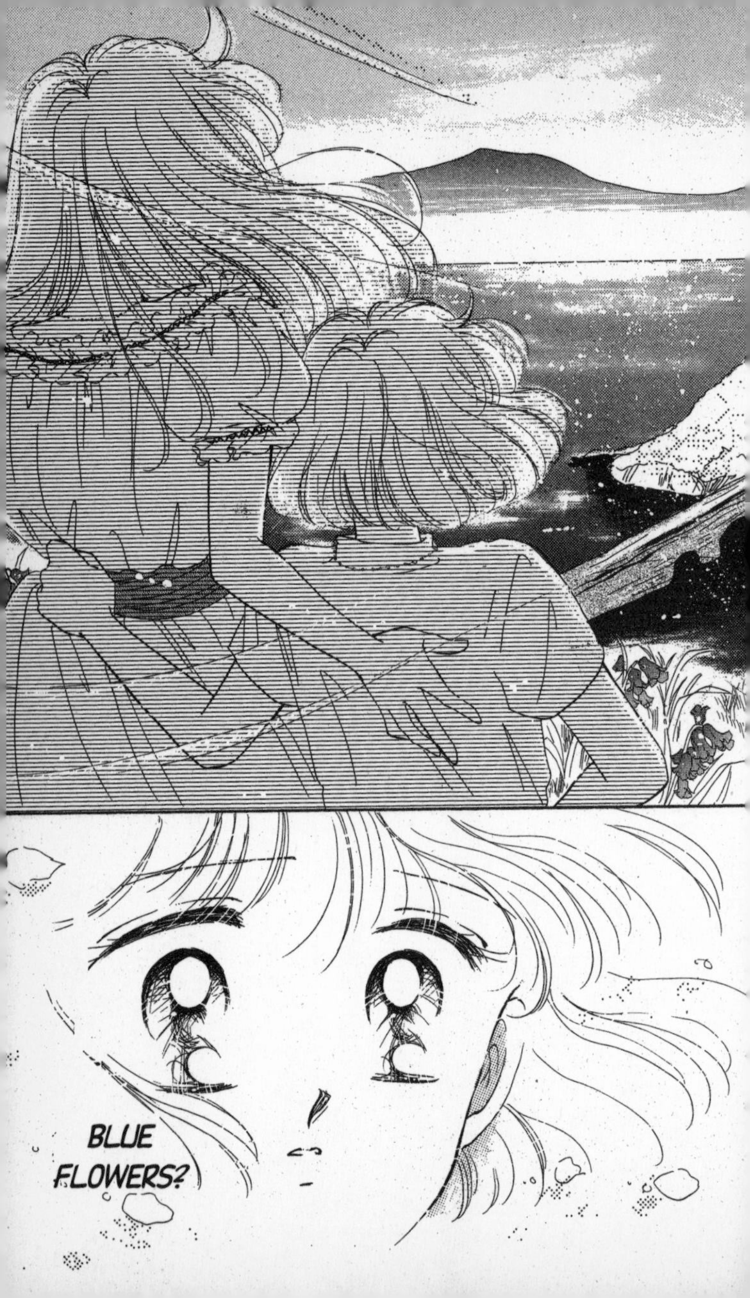
BLUE
FLOWERS?

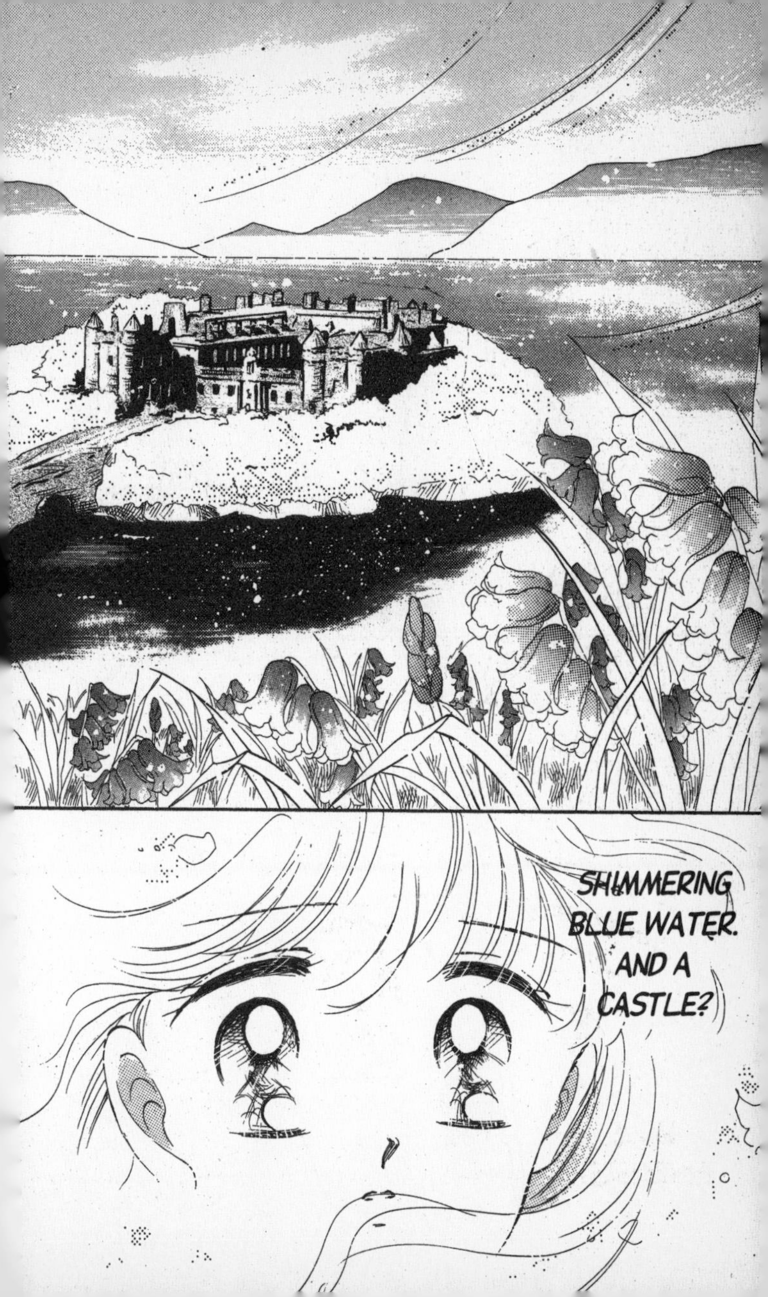
SHIMMERING BLUE WATER. AND A CASTLE?

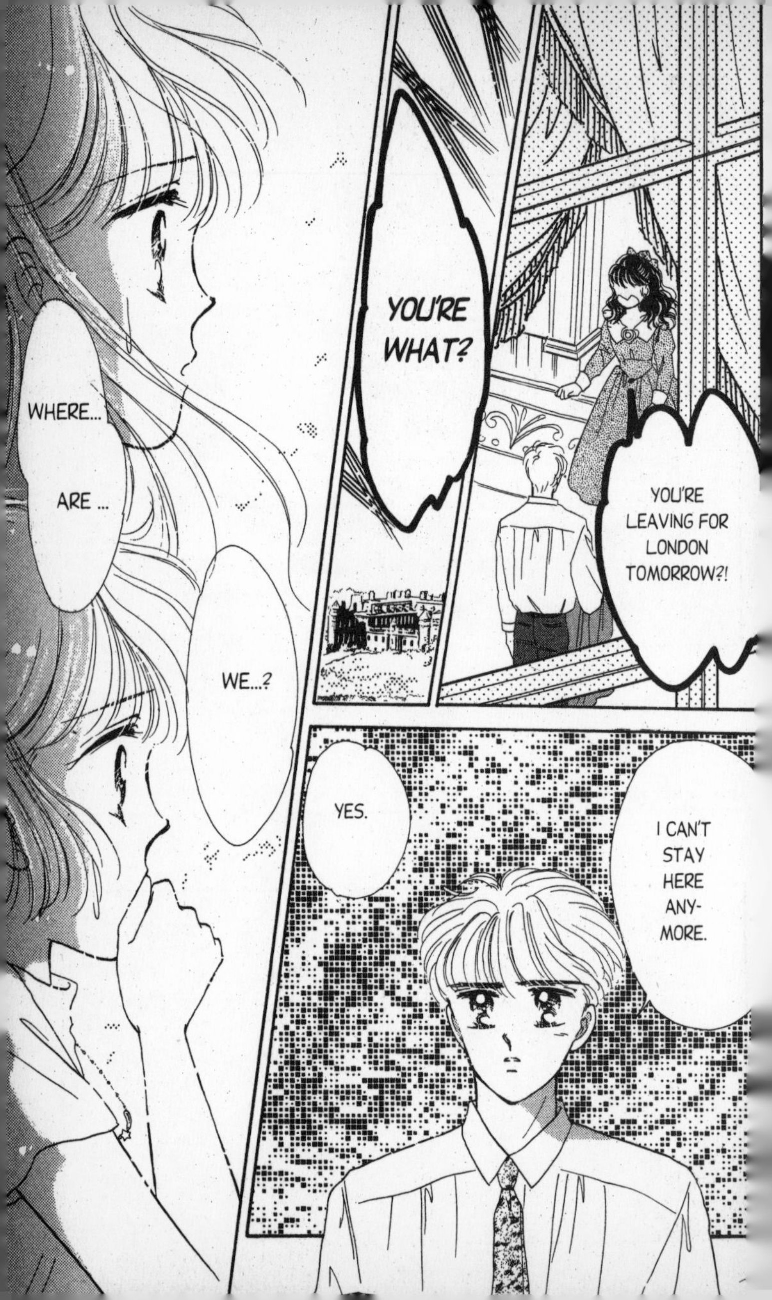
WHERE...
ARE ...
WE...?
YOU'RE WHAT?
YOU'RE LEAVING FOR LONDON TOMORROW?!
YES.
I CAN'T STAY HERE ANY-MORE.

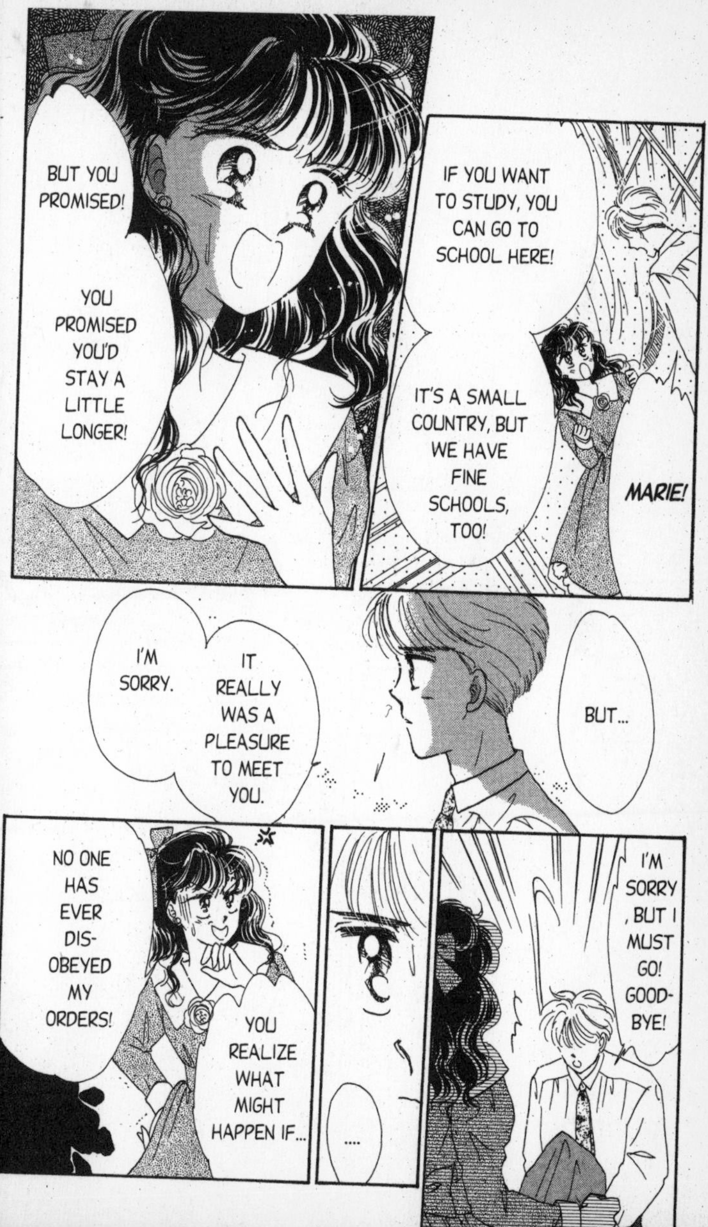
BUT YOU PROMISED!
YOU PROMISED YOU'D STAY A LITTLE LONGER!
IF YOU WANT TO STUDY, YOU CAN GO TO SCHOOL HERE!
IT'S A SMALL COUNTRY, BUT WE HAVE FINE SCHOOLS, TOO!
MARIE!
I'M SORRY.
IT REALLY WAS A PLEASURE TO MEET YOU.
BUT...
NO ONE HAS EVER DIS-OBEYED MY ORDERS!
YOU REALIZE WHAT MIGHT HAPPEN IF...
....
I'M SORRY, BUT I MUST GO! GOOD-BYE!

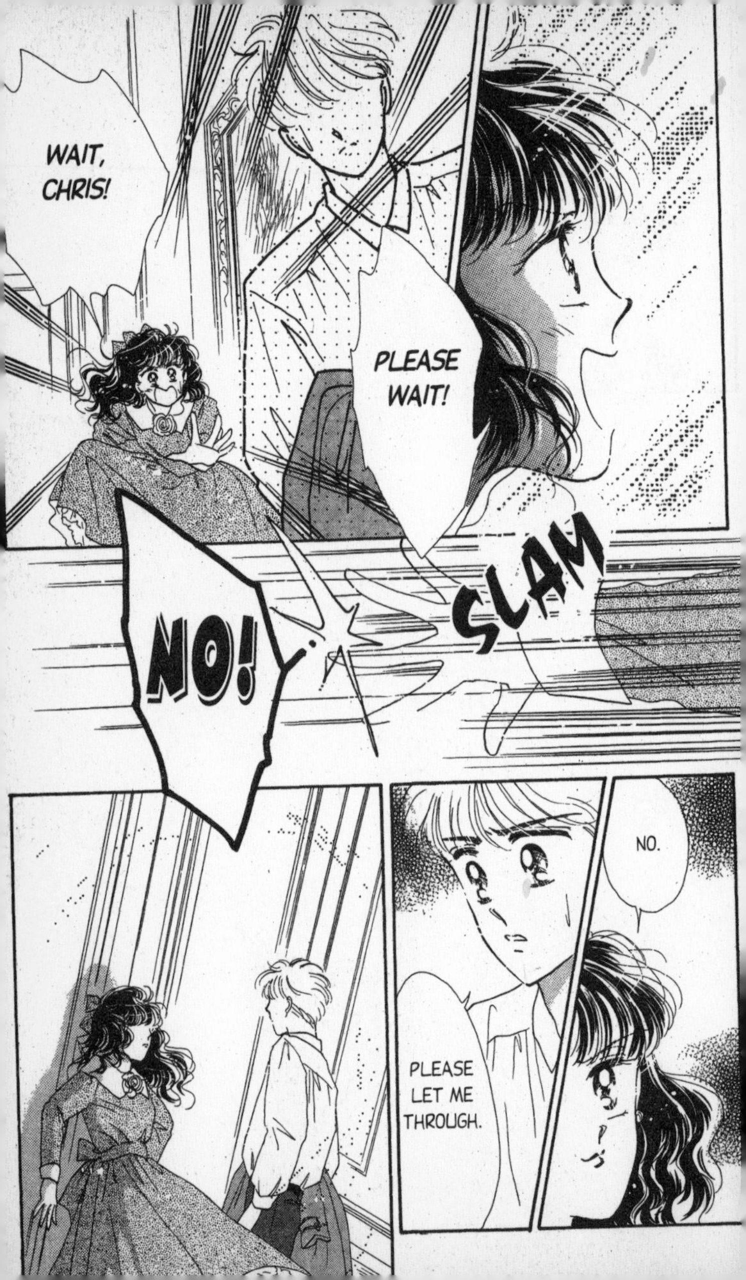
WAIT, CHRIS!
PLEASE WAIT!
NO!
SLAM
NO.
PLEASE LET ME THROUGH.

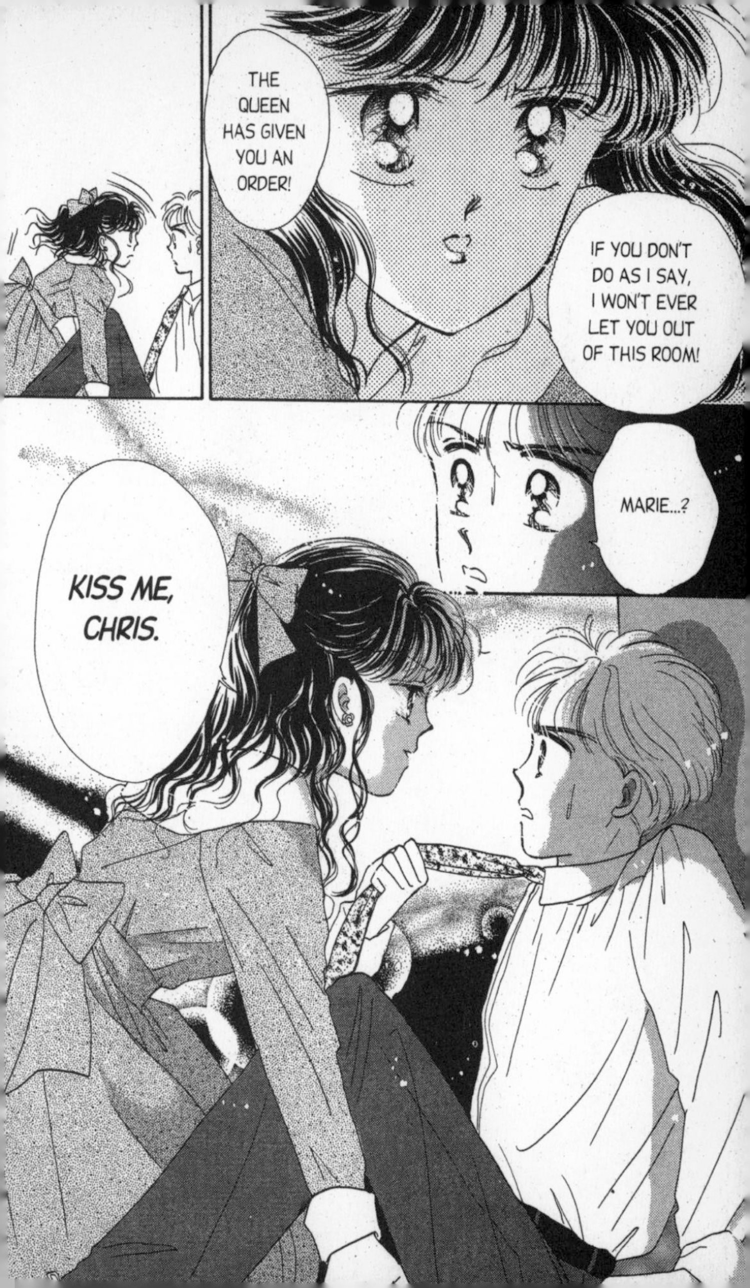
THE QUEEN HAS GIVEN YOU AN ORDER!
IF YOU DON'T DO AS I SAY, I WON'T EVER LET YOU OUT OF THIS ROOM!
KISS ME, CHRIS.
MARIE...?

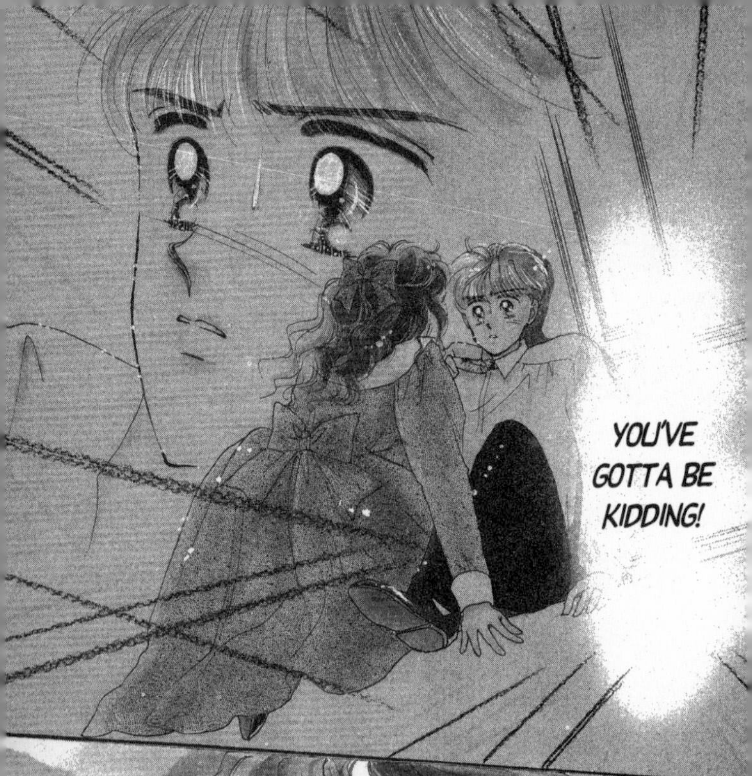
YOU'VE GOTTA BE KIDDING!

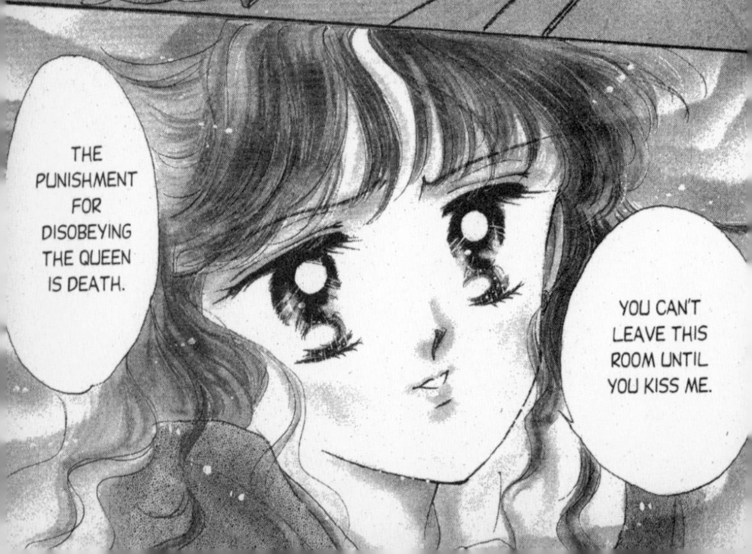
THE PUNISHMENT FOR DISOBEYING THE QUEEN IS DEATH.
YOU CAN'T LEAVE THIS ROOM UNTIL YOU KISS ME.

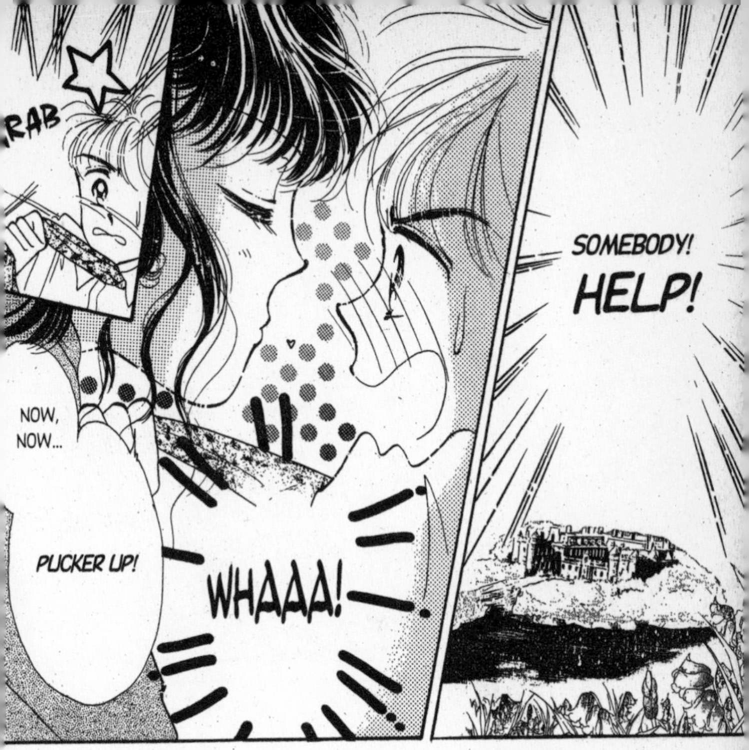
RAB
NOW, NOW...
PUCKER UP!
WHAAA!
SOMEBODY! HELP!

BONUS

In Parts 1 and 2, I ended up concentrating on Toni and Jackson's relationship, but in Part 3, Mika and Chris take center stage. Everyone could pretty much figure that sparks were going to fly between Toni and Jackson as early as Part 1. But I got a lot of mail asking me to fix Mika and Chris up! Well, the wait is over! But then again, I also got quite a bit of mail saying I could go ahead and get rid of Chris, too. Well, anyway, I think this love story will be a little bit different than Toni and Jackson's.

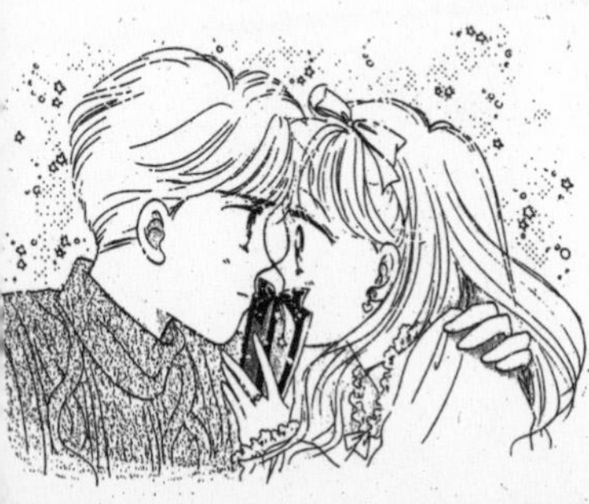

YOU'VE GOT TO BE STRONG AND ENDURE, MIKA

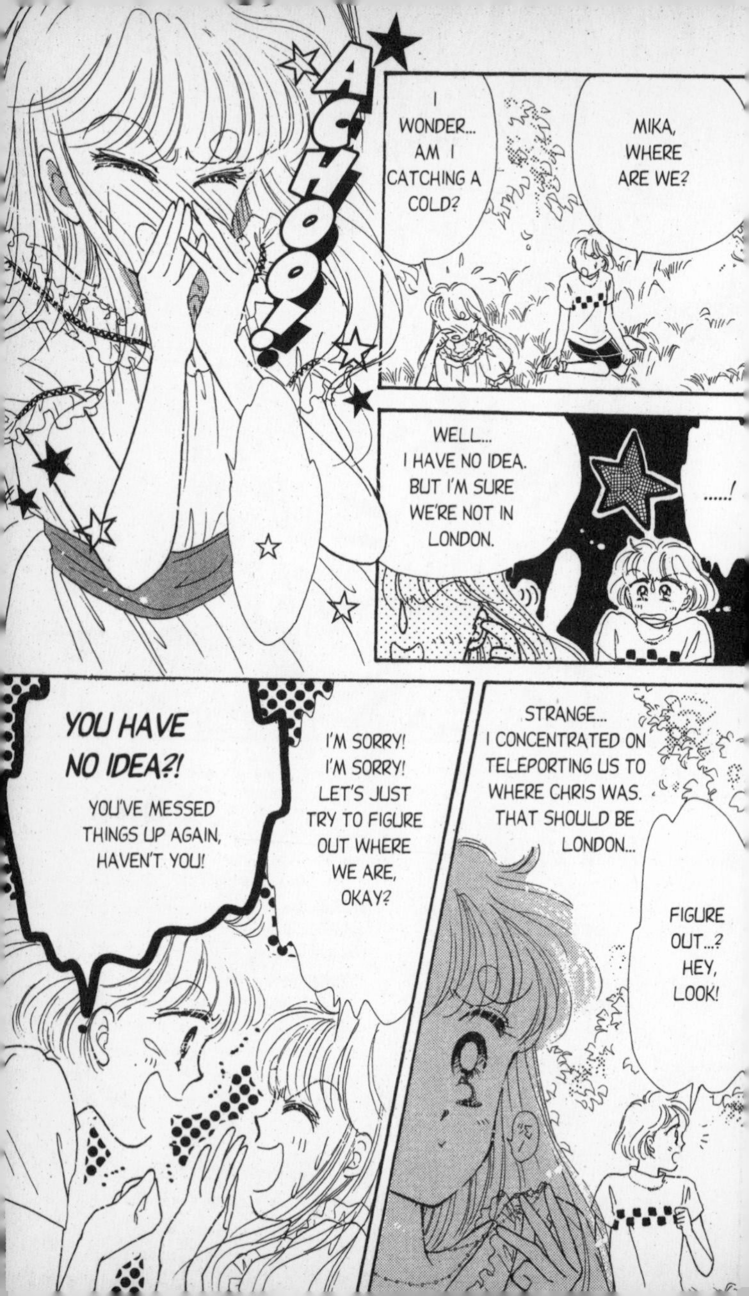
ACHOO!
I WONDER... AM I CATCHING A COLD?
MIKA, WHERE ARE WE?
WELL... I HAVE NO IDEA. BUT I'M SURE WE'RE NOT IN LONDON.
......!
YOU HAVE NO IDEA?!
YOU'VE MESSED THINGS UP AGAIN, HAVEN'T YOU!
I'M SORRY! I'M SORRY! LET'S JUST TRY TO FIGURE OUT WHERE WE ARE, OKAY?
STRANGE... I CONCENTRATED ON TELEPORTING US TO WHERE CHRIS WAS. THAT SHOULD BE LONDON...
FIGURE OUT...? HEY, LOOK!

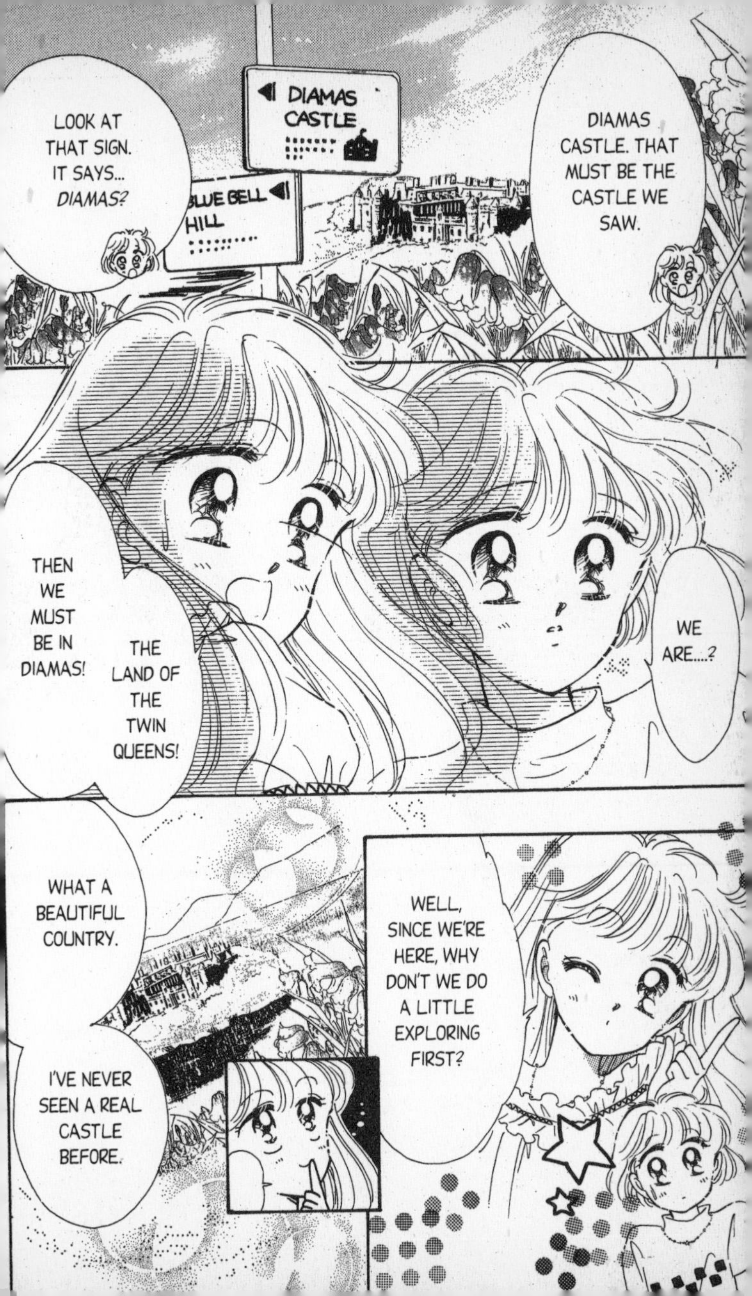
LOOK AT THAT SIGN. IT SAYS... *DIAMAS?*
DIAMAS CASTLE
BLUE BELL HILL
DIAMAS CASTLE. THAT MUST BE THE CASTLE WE SAW.
THEN WE MUST BE IN DIAMAS!
THE LAND OF THE TWIN QUEENS!
WE ARE...?
WHAT A BEAUTIFUL COUNTRY.
I'VE NEVER SEEN A REAL CASTLE BEFORE.
WELL, SINCE WE'RE HERE, WHY DON'T WE DO A LITTLE EXPLORING FIRST?

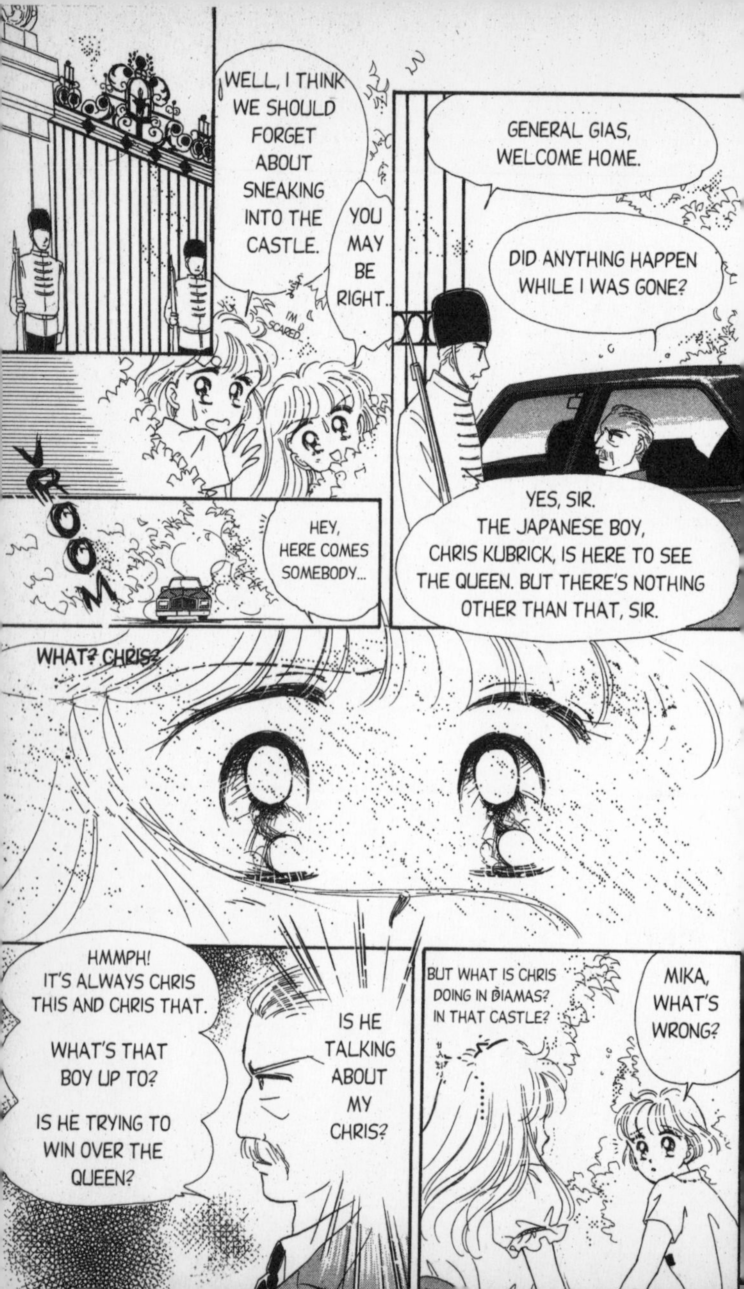

WELL, I THINK WE SHOULD FORGET ABOUT SNEAKING INTO THE CASTLE.
YOU MAY BE RIGHT...
I'M SCARED
VROOM
HEY, HERE COMES SOMEBODY...
GENERAL GIAS, WELCOME HOME.
DID ANYTHING HAPPEN WHILE I WAS GONE?
YES, SIR. THE JAPANESE BOY, CHRIS KUBRICK, IS HERE TO SEE THE QUEEN. BUT THERE'S NOTHING OTHER THAN THAT, SIR.
WHAT? CHRIS?
HMMPH! IT'S ALWAYS CHRIS THIS AND CHRIS THAT. WHAT'S THAT BOY UP TO? IS HE TRYING TO WIN OVER THE QUEEN?
IS HE TALKING ABOUT MY CHRIS?
BUT WHAT IS CHRIS DOING IN DIAMAS? IN THAT CASTLE?
MIKA, WHAT'S WRONG?

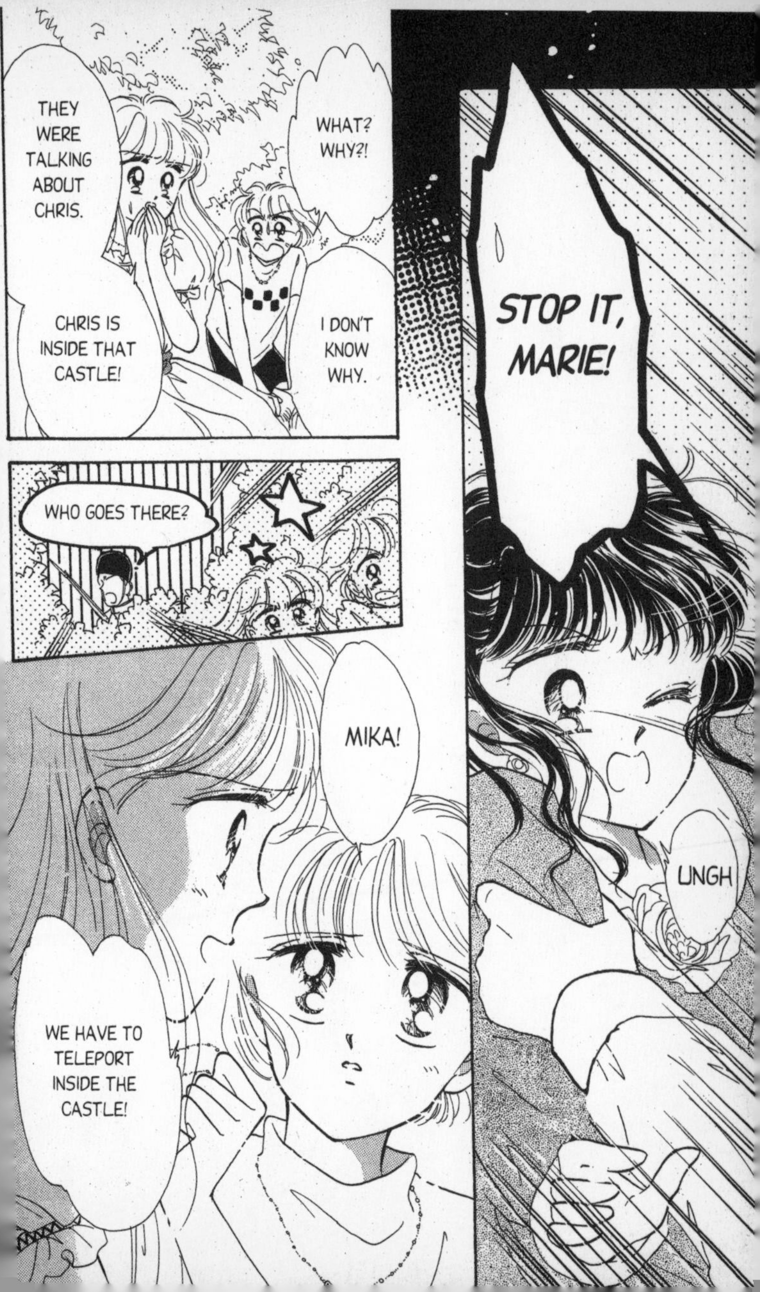
THEY WERE TALKING ABOUT CHRIS.
WHAT? WHY?!
CHRIS IS INSIDE THAT CASTLE!
I DON'T KNOW WHY.
WHO GOES THERE?
MIKA!
WE HAVE TO TELEPORT INSIDE THE CASTLE!
STOP IT, MARIE!
UNGH

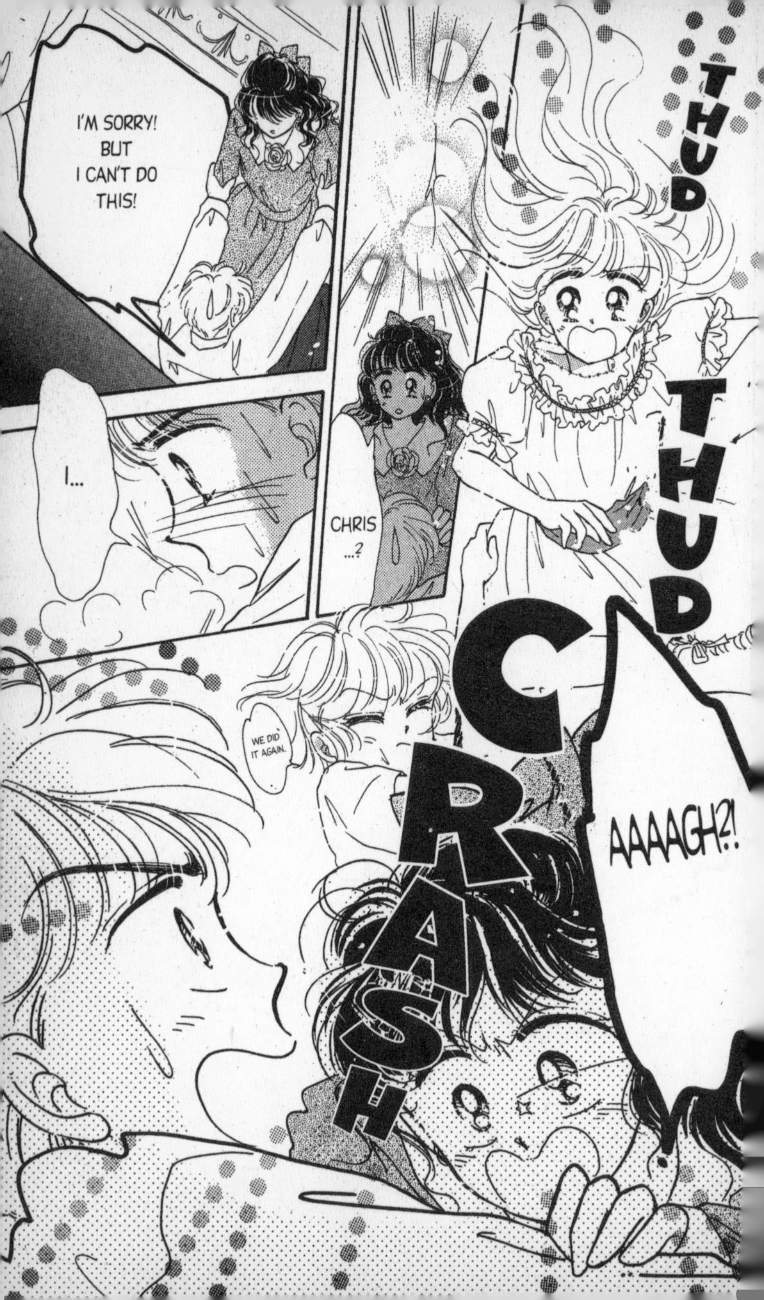
I'M SORRY! BUT I CAN'T DO THIS!
THUD
I...
CHRIS ...?
THUD THUD
WE DID IT AGAIN.
CRASH
AAAAGH?!

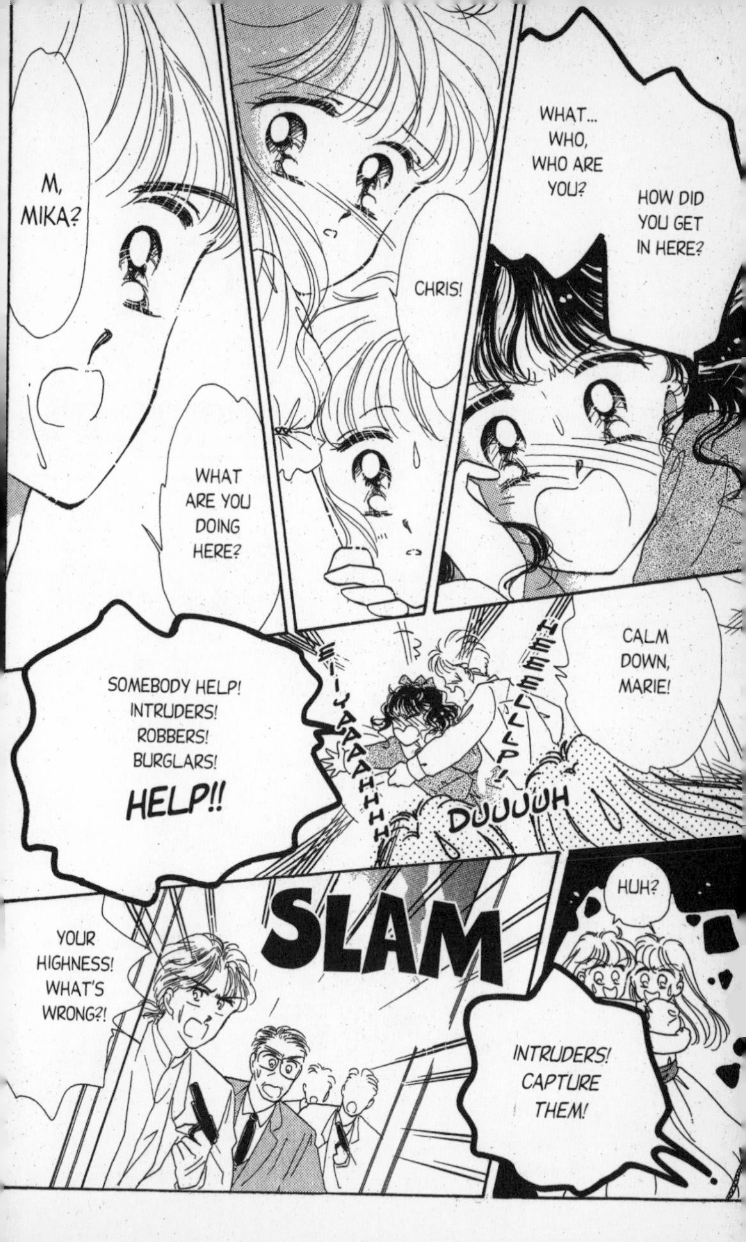
M, MIKA?
WHAT ARE YOU DOING HERE?
CHRIS!
WHAT... WHO, WHO ARE YOU?
HOW DID YOU GET IN HERE?
SOMEBODY HELP! INTRUDERS! ROBBERS! BURGLARS! HELP!!
EI-YAAAAHHHH
HEEELLLP!
CALM DOWN, MARIE!
DUUUUH
YOUR HIGHNESS! WHAT'S WRONG?!
SLAM
HUH?
INTRUDERS! CAPTURE THEM!

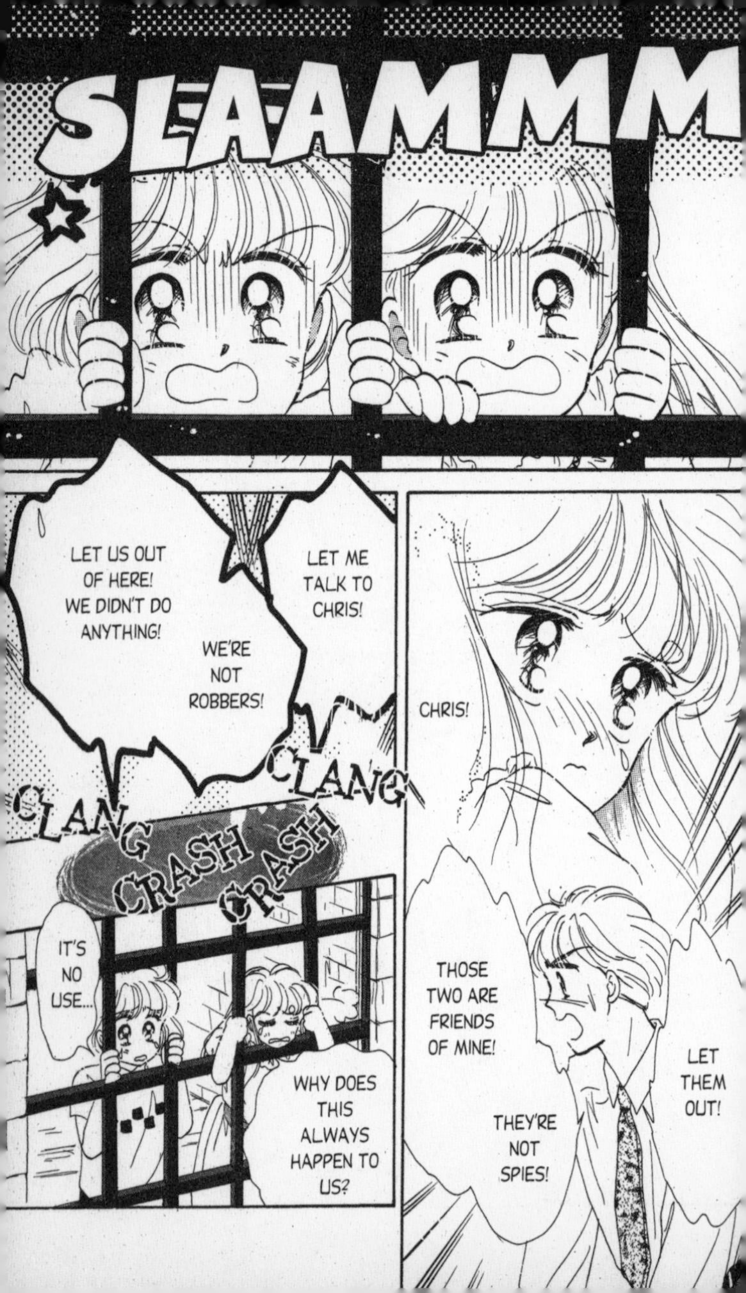
SLAAMMM
LET US OUT OF HERE! WE DIDN'T DO ANYTHING!
WE'RE NOT ROBBERS!
LET ME TALK TO CHRIS!
CLANG
CLANG
CRASH
CRASH
IT'S NO USE...
WHY DOES THIS ALWAYS HAPPEN TO US?
CHRIS!
THOSE TWO ARE FRIENDS OF MINE!
THEY'RE NOT SPIES!
LET THEM OUT!

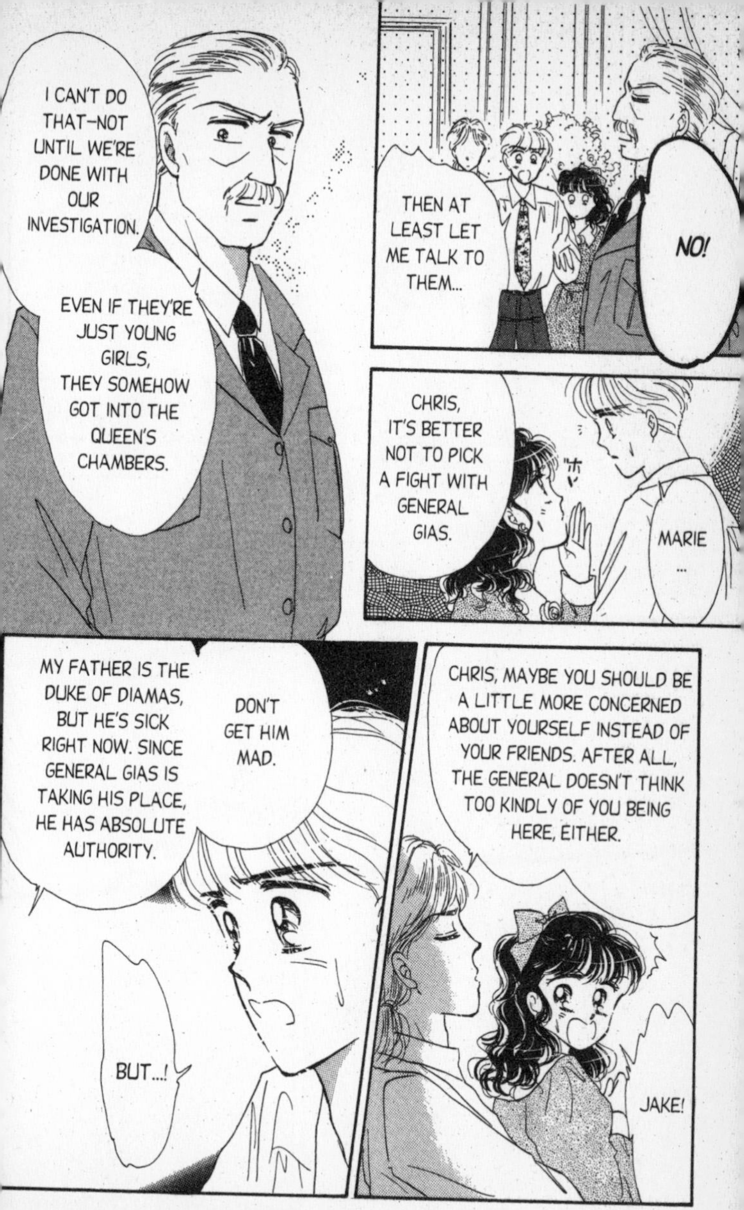
I CAN'T DO THAT–NOT UNTIL WE'RE DONE WITH OUR INVESTIGATION.
EVEN IF THEY'RE JUST YOUNG GIRLS, THEY SOMEHOW GOT INTO THE QUEEN'S CHAMBERS.
THEN AT LEAST LET ME TALK TO THEM...
NO!
CHRIS, IT'S BETTER NOT TO PICK A FIGHT WITH GENERAL GIAS.
MARIE...
MY FATHER IS THE DUKE OF DIAMAS, BUT HE'S SICK RIGHT NOW. SINCE GENERAL GIAS IS TAKING HIS PLACE, HE HAS ABSOLUTE AUTHORITY.
DON'T GET HIM MAD.
BUT...!
CHRIS, MAYBE YOU SHOULD BE A LITTLE MORE CONCERNED ABOUT YOURSELF INSTEAD OF YOUR FRIENDS. AFTER ALL, THE GENERAL DOESN'T THINK TOO KINDLY OF YOU BEING HERE, EITHER.
JAKE!

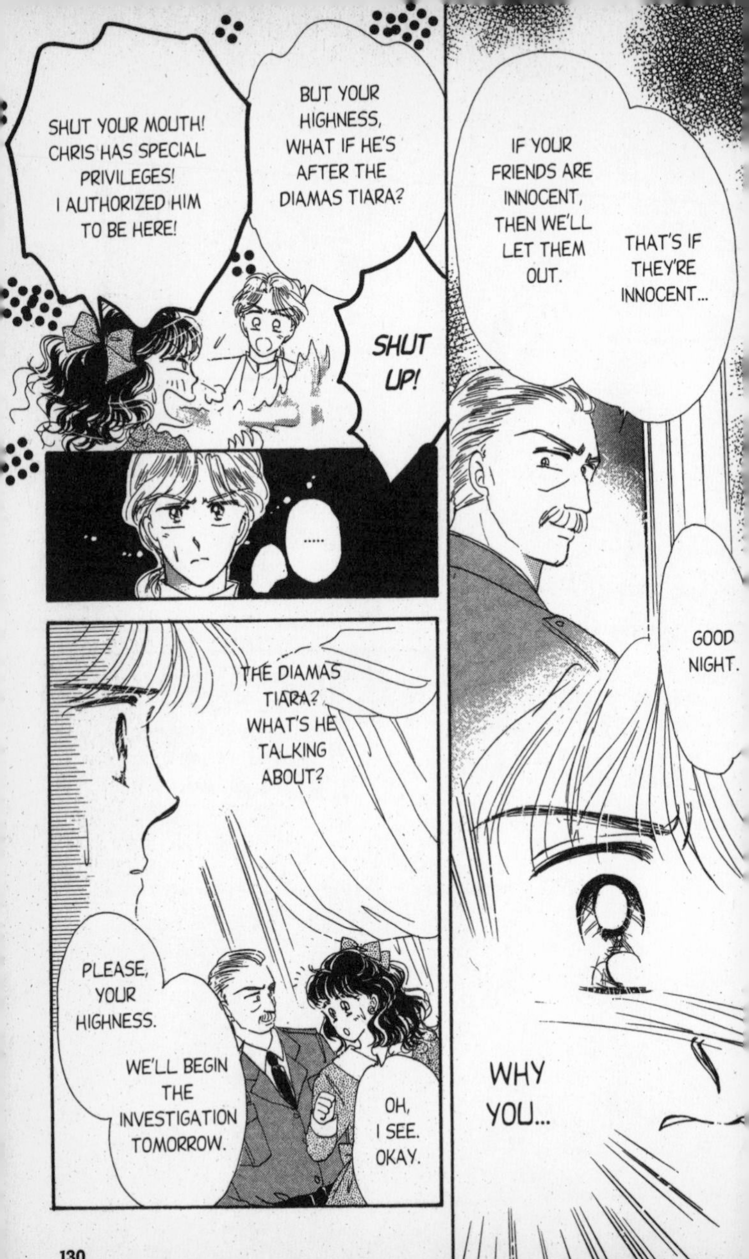

SHUT YOUR MOUTH! CHRIS HAS SPECIAL PRIVILEGES! I AUTHORIZED HIM TO BE HERE!
BUT YOUR HIGHNESS, WHAT IF HE'S AFTER THE DIAMAS TIARA?
SHUT UP!
.....
THE DIAMAS TIARA? WHAT'S HE TALKING ABOUT?
PLEASE, YOUR HIGHNESS.
WE'LL BEGIN THE INVESTIGATION TOMORROW.
OH, I SEE. OKAY.
IF YOUR FRIENDS ARE INNOCENT, THEN WE'LL LET THEM OUT.
THAT'S IF THEY'RE INNOCENT...
GOOD NIGHT.
WHY YOU...

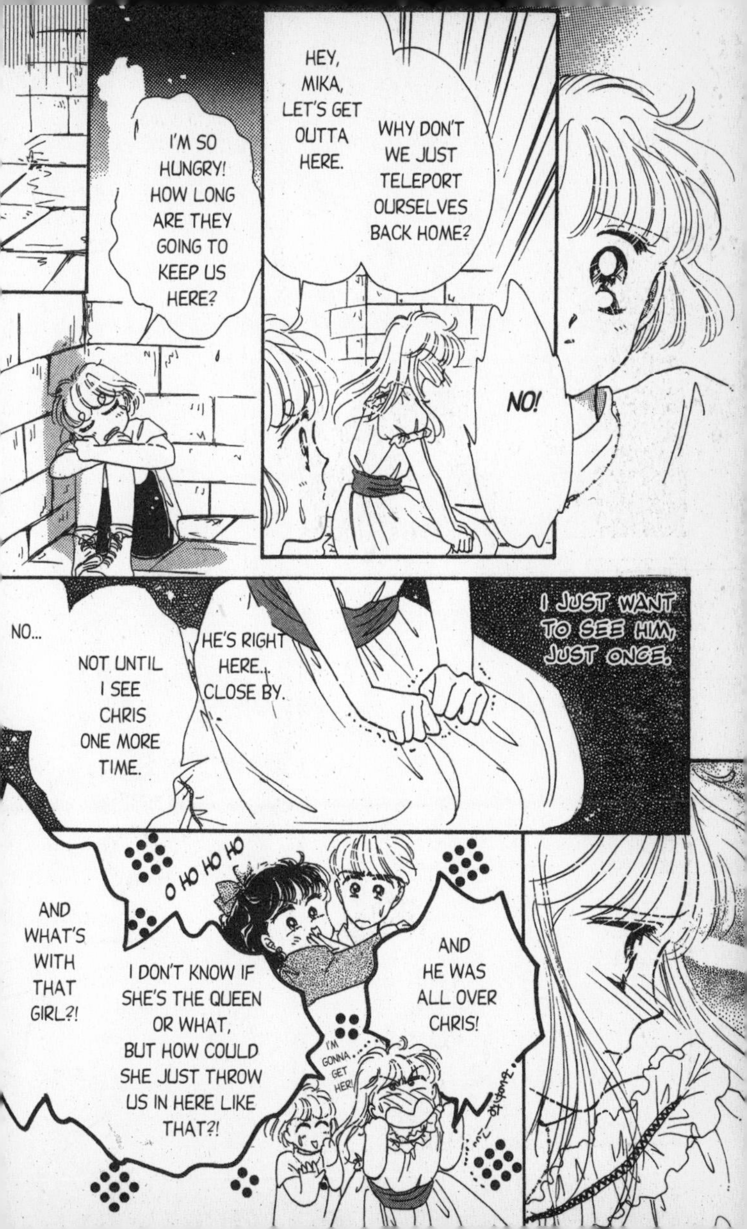
I'M SO HUNGRY! HOW LONG ARE THEY GOING TO KEEP US HERE?
HEY, MIKA, LET'S GET OUTTA HERE.
WHY DON'T WE JUST TELEPORT OURSELVES BACK HOME?
NO!
NO...
NOT UNTIL I SEE CHRIS ONE MORE TIME.
HE'S RIGHT HERE.. CLOSE BY.
I JUST WANT TO SEE HIM, JUST ONCE.
O HO HO HO
AND WHAT'S WITH THAT GIRL?!
I DON'T KNOW IF SHE'S THE QUEEN OR WHAT, BUT HOW COULD SHE JUST THROW US IN HERE LIKE THAT?!
AND HE WAS ALL OVER CHRIS!
I'M GONNA GET HER!

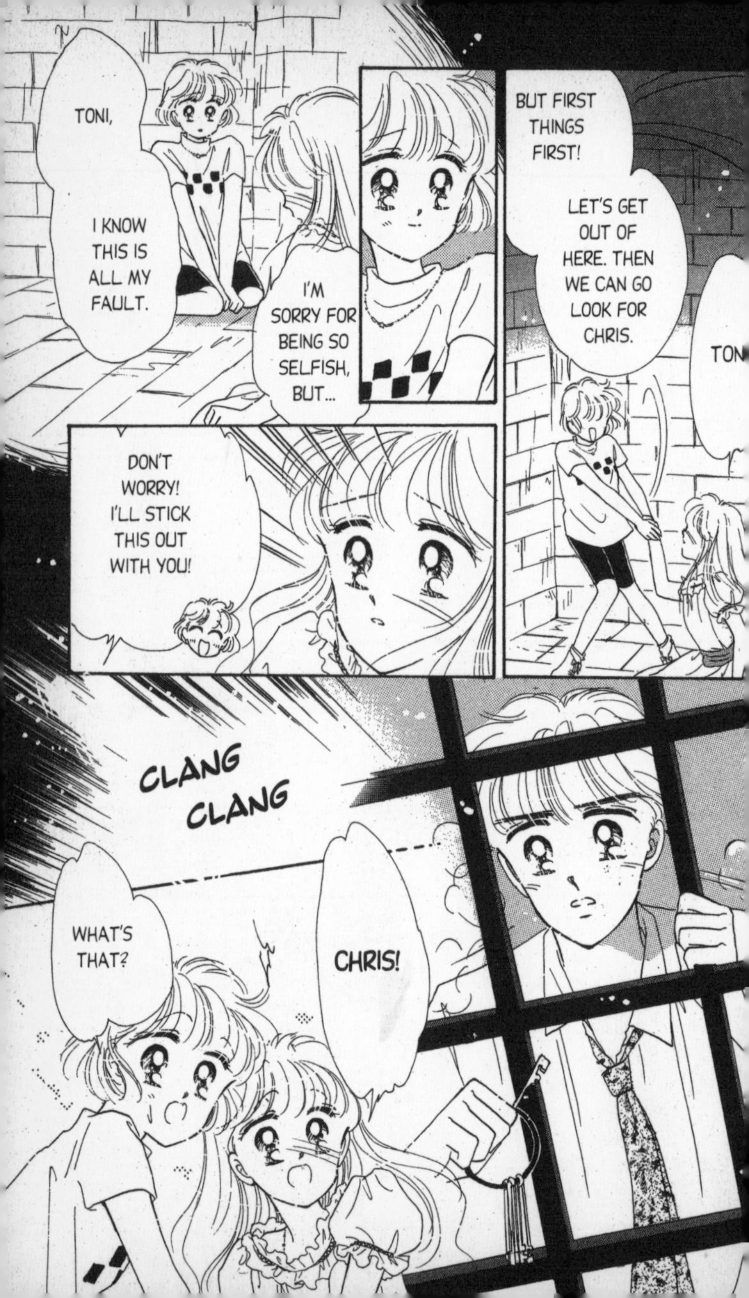
TONI,
I KNOW THIS IS ALL MY FAULT.
I'M SORRY FOR BEING SO SELFISH, BUT...
BUT FIRST THINGS FIRST!
LET'S GET OUT OF HERE. THEN WE CAN GO LOOK FOR CHRIS.
TON
DON'T WORRY! I'LL STICK THIS OUT WITH YOU!
CLANG
CLANG
WHAT'S THAT?
CHRIS!

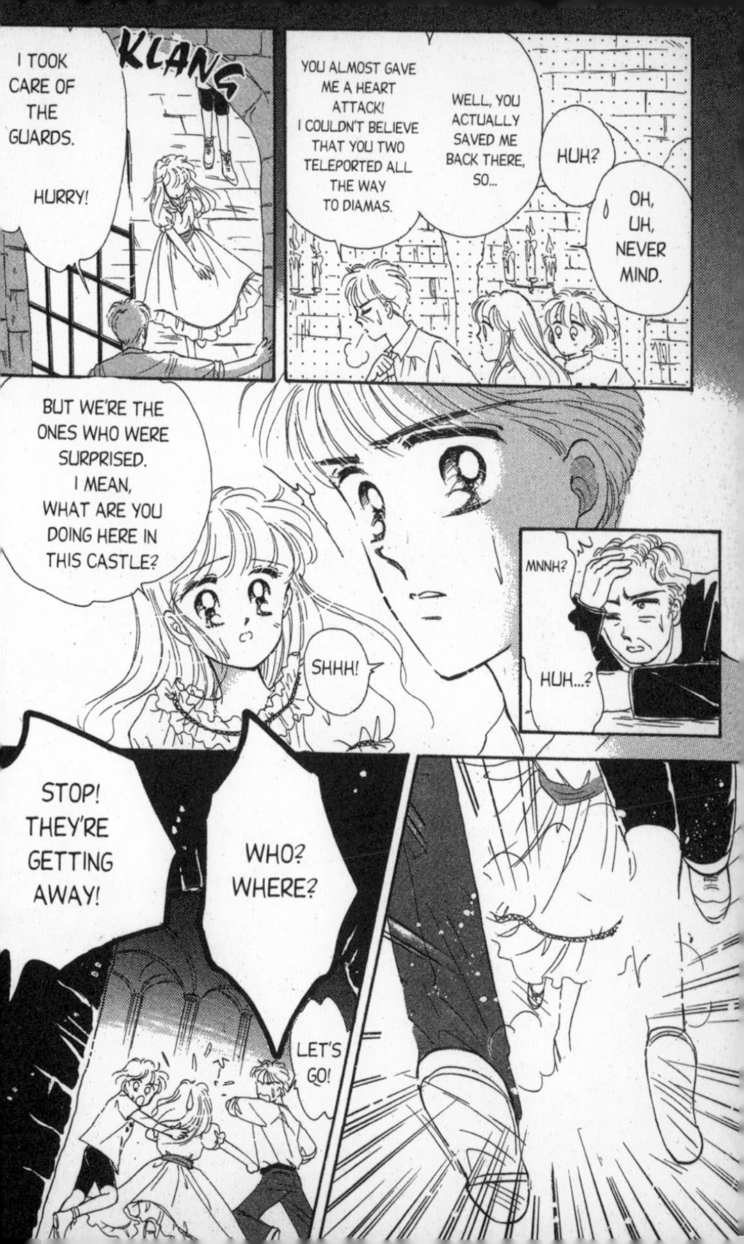
I TOOK CARE OF THE GUARDS.
HURRY!
KLANS
YOU ALMOST GAVE ME A HEART ATTACK! I COULDN'T BELIEVE THAT YOU TWO TELEPORTED ALL THE WAY TO DIAMAS.
WELL, YOU ACTUALLY SAVED ME BACK THERE, SO...
HUH?
OH, UH, NEVER MIND.
BUT WE'RE THE ONES WHO WERE SURPRISED. I MEAN, WHAT ARE YOU DOING HERE IN THIS CASTLE?
SHHH!
MNNH?
HUH...?
STOP! THEY'RE GETTING AWAY!
WHO? WHERE?
LET'S GO!

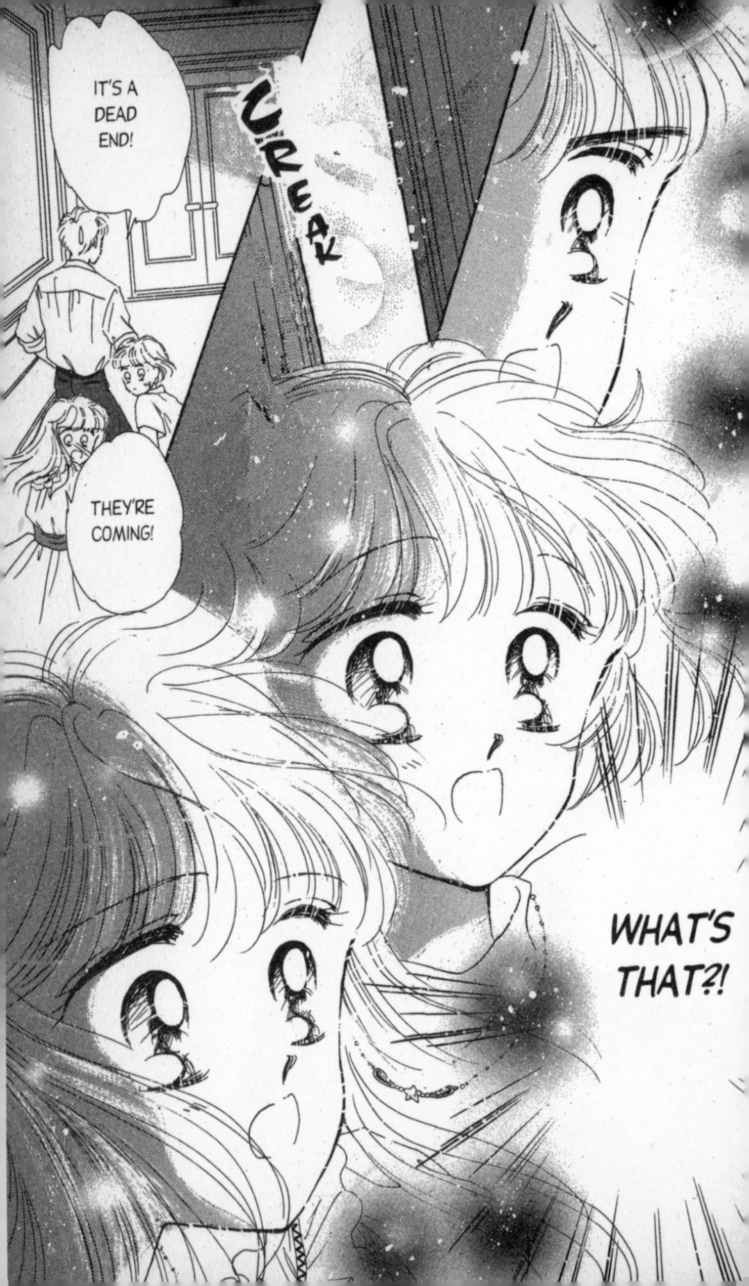
IT'S A DEAD END!
CREAK
THEY'RE COMING!
WHAT'S THAT?!

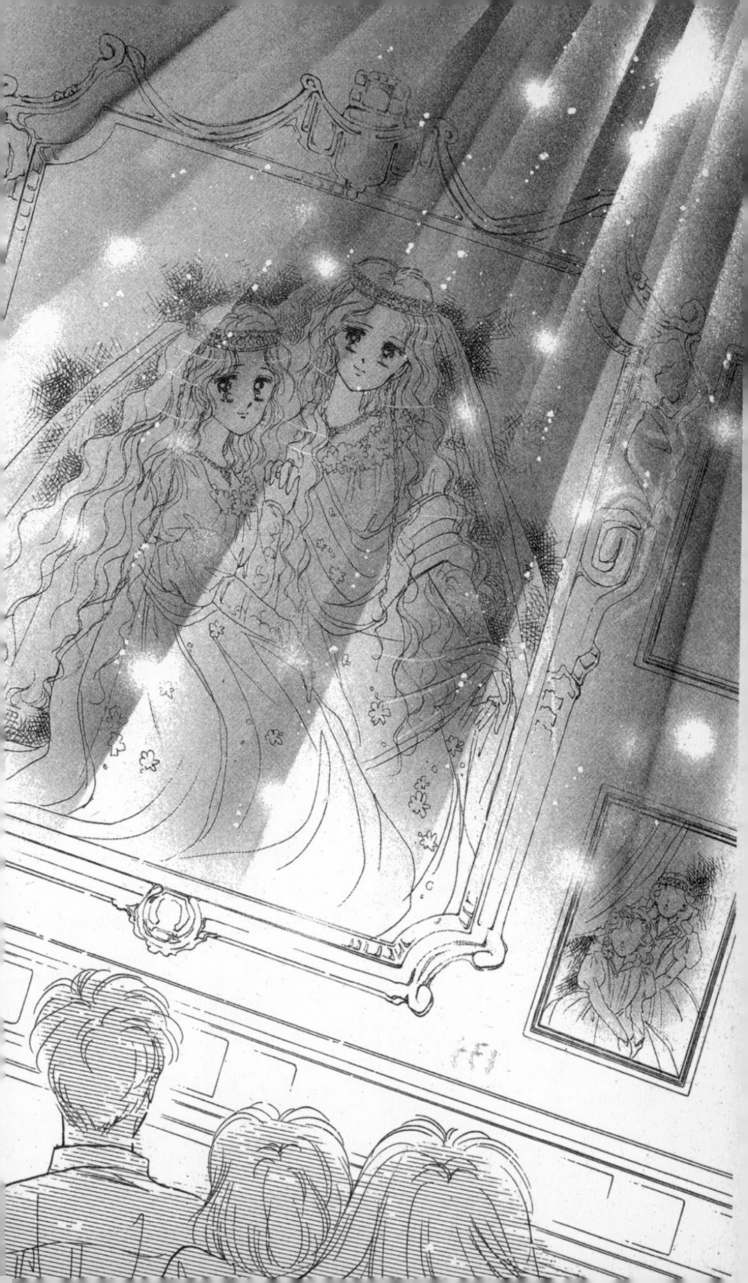

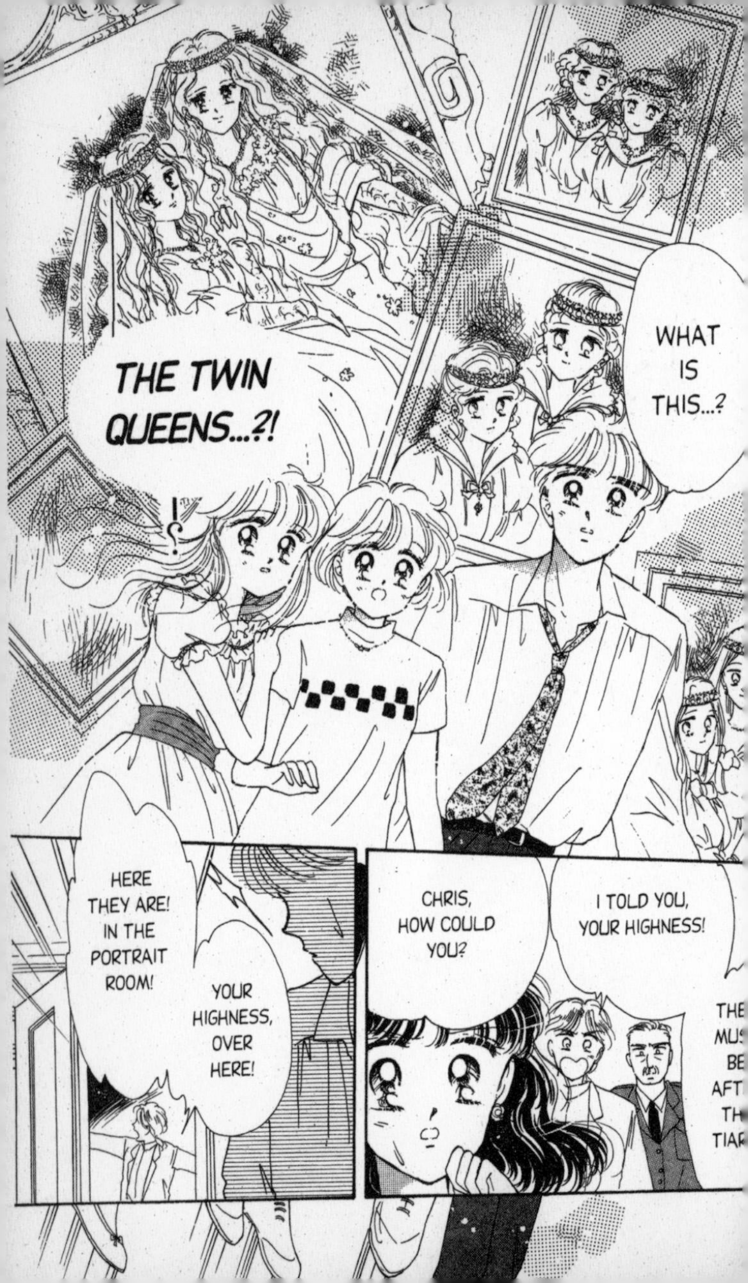
THE TWIN QUEENS...?!
!?
WHAT IS THIS...?
HERE THEY ARE! IN THE PORTRAIT ROOM!
YOUR HIGHNESS, OVER HERE!
CHRIS, HOW COULD YOU?
I TOLD YOU, YOUR HIGHNESS!

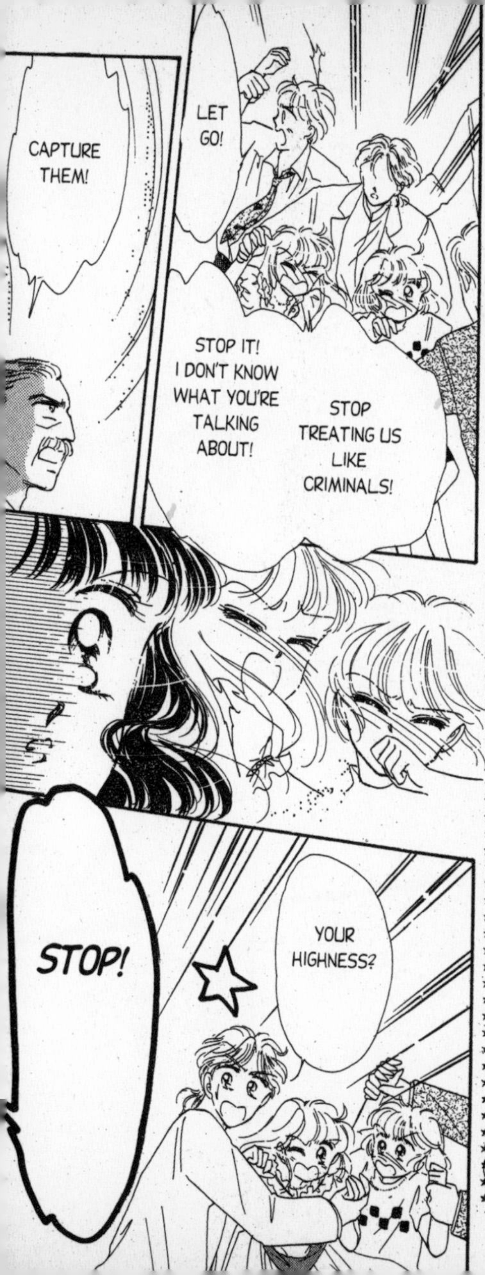
CAPTURE THEM!
LET GO!
STOP IT! I DON'T KNOW WHAT YOU'RE TALKING ABOUT!
STOP TREATING US LIKE CRIMINALS!
STOP!
YOUR HIGHNESS?

BONUS

Even though Toni and Jackson are a couple now, I've been getting letters saying, "I hate Toni!" I try to treat Toni and Mika equally, so it hurts me when I get letters like that. But I sat down to try to see why people might feel that way.

Here's what I came up with:

1. Toni is an airhead, but that's my fault. It's not that she's dumb. It's just that Mika is so smart. Toni is someone who tries really hard! Besides, they made it into the same high school, right?

2. Sure, she gets silly when she's with Jackson. But wouldn't you, too?

3. She's too cute.

Well...Anyway, the reason Mika is so spoiled is because Toni is there to support her. So please don't beat up on Toni!

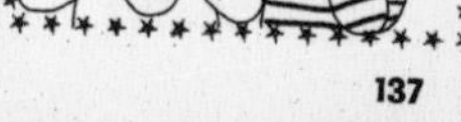
Yeah, leave her alone!

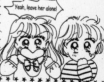

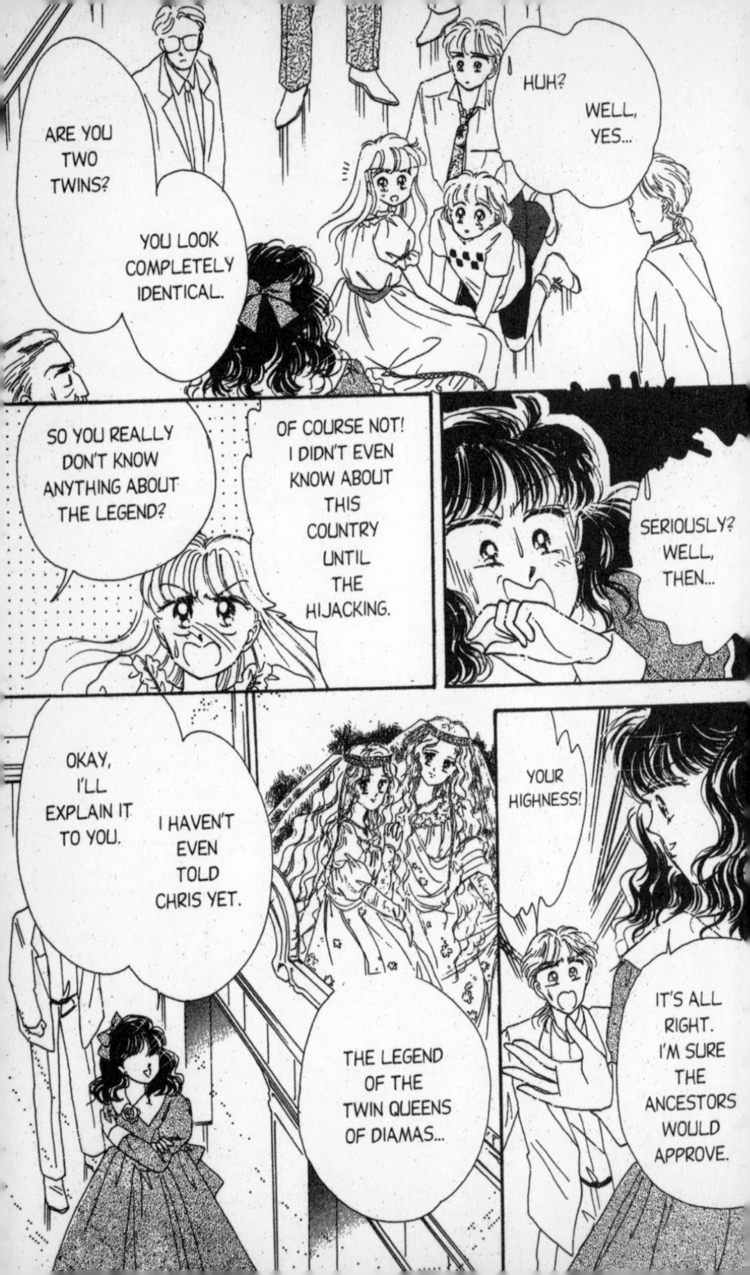
ARE YOU TWO TWINS?
YOU LOOK COMPLETELY IDENTICAL.
HUH?
WELL, YES...
SO YOU REALLY DON'T KNOW ANYTHING ABOUT THE LEGEND?
OF COURSE NOT! I DIDN'T EVEN KNOW ABOUT THIS COUNTRY UNTIL THE HIJACKING.
SERIOUSLY? WELL, THEN...
OKAY, I'LL EXPLAIN IT TO YOU.
I HAVEN'T EVEN TOLD CHRIS YET.
THE LEGEND OF THE TWIN QUEENS OF DIAMAS...
YOUR HIGHNESS!
IT'S ALL RIGHT. I'M SURE THE ANCESTORS WOULD APPROVE.

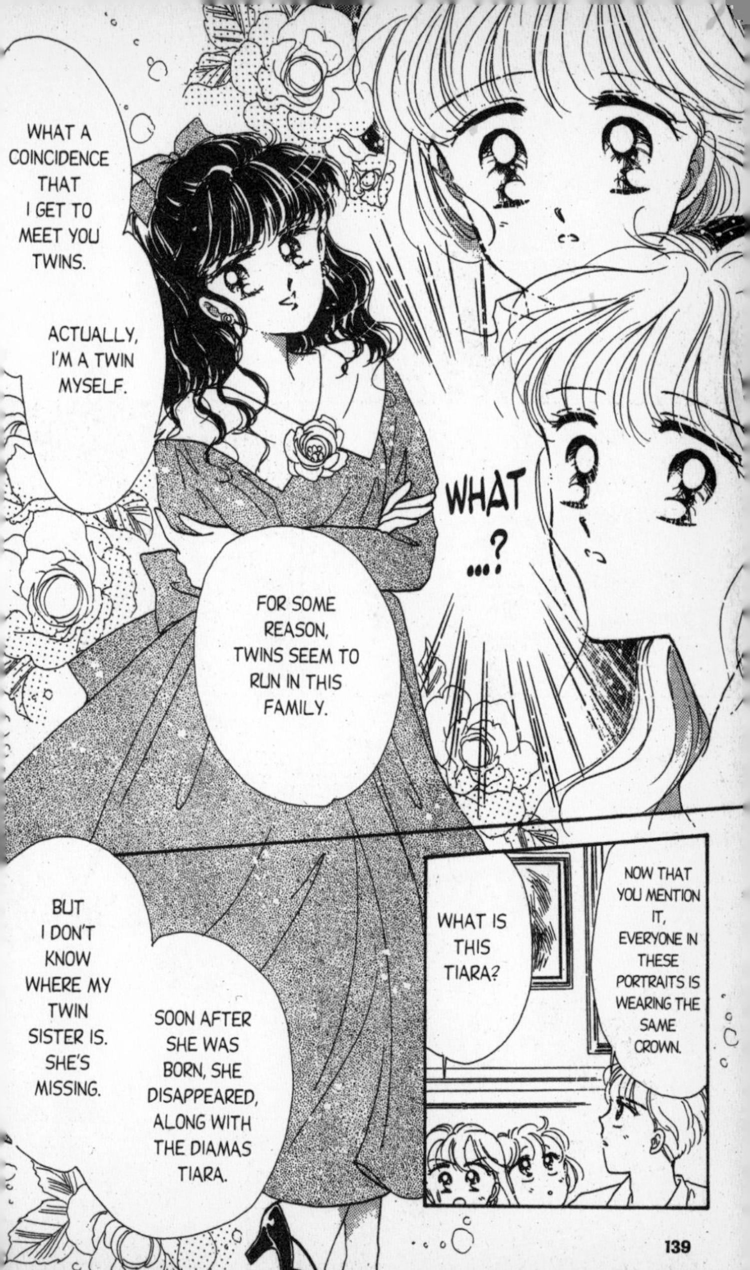
WHAT A COINCIDENCE THAT I GET TO MEET YOU TWINS.
ACTUALLY, I'M A TWIN MYSELF.
FOR SOME REASON, TWINS SEEM TO RUN IN THIS FAMILY.
WHAT ...?
BUT I DON'T KNOW WHERE MY TWIN SISTER IS. SHE'S MISSING.
SOON AFTER SHE WAS BORN, SHE DISAPPEARED, ALONG WITH THE DIAMAS TIARA.
WHAT IS THIS TIARA?
NOW THAT YOU MENTION IT, EVERYONE IN THESE PORTRAITS IS WEARING THE SAME CROWN.

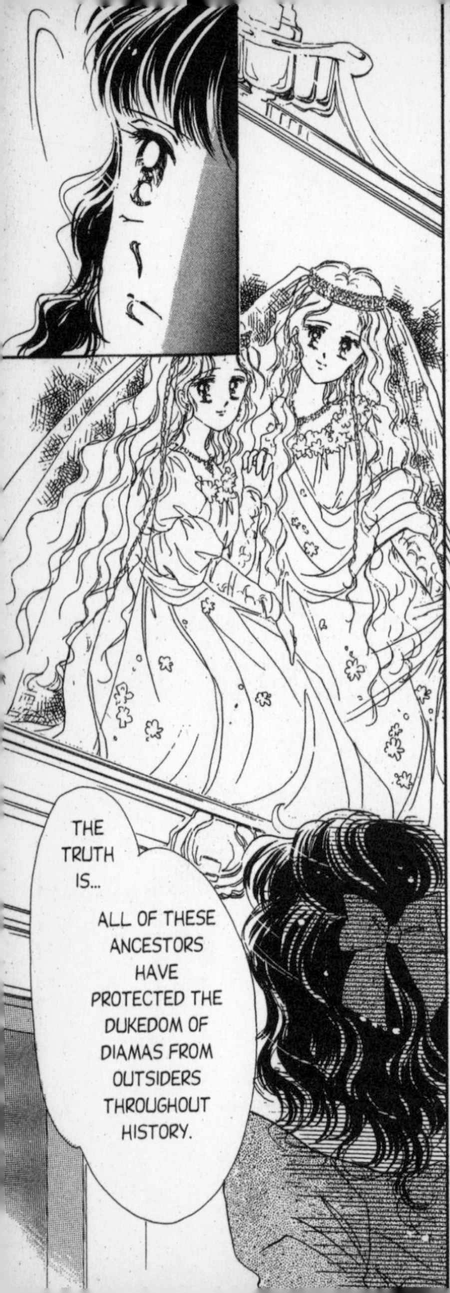
THE TRUTH IS...
ALL OF THESE ANCESTORS HAVE PROTECTED THE DUKEDOM OF DIAMAS FROM OUTSIDERS THROUGHOUT HISTORY.
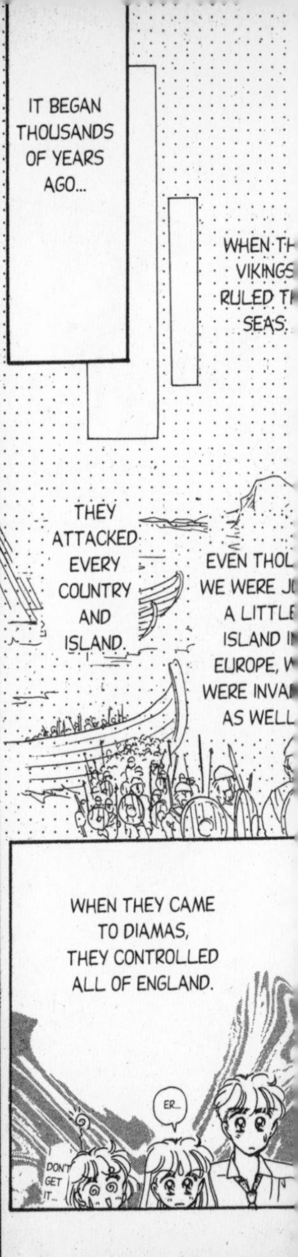
IT BEGAN THOUSANDS OF YEARS AGO...
WHEN TH VIKINGS RULED T SEAS.
THEY ATTACKED EVERY COUNTRY AND ISLAND.
EVEN THOU WE WERE JU A LITTLE ISLAND I EUROPE, W WERE INVA AS WELL
WHEN THEY CAME TO DIAMAS, THEY CONTROLLED ALL OF ENGLAND.
ER...
DON'T GET IT...

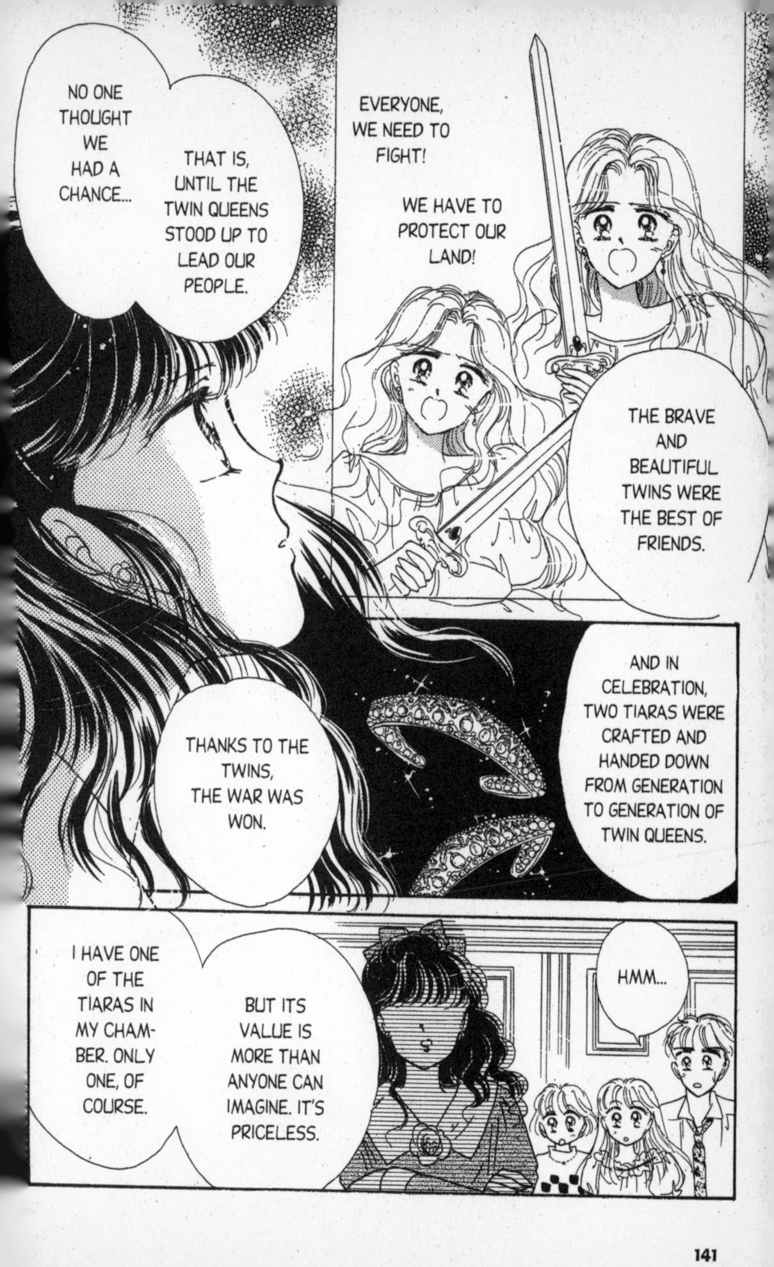
NO ONE THOUGHT WE HAD A CHANCE...
THAT IS, UNTIL THE TWIN QUEENS STOOD UP TO LEAD OUR PEOPLE.
EVERYONE, WE NEED TO FIGHT!
WE HAVE TO PROTECT OUR LAND!
THE BRAVE AND BEAUTIFUL TWINS WERE THE BEST OF FRIENDS.
THANKS TO THE TWINS, THE WAR WAS WON.
AND IN CELEBRATION, TWO TIARAS WERE CRAFTED AND HANDED DOWN FROM GENERATION TO GENERATION OF TWIN QUEENS.
I HAVE ONE OF THE TIARAS IN MY CHAM-BER. ONLY ONE, OF COURSE.
BUT ITS VALUE IS MORE THAN ANYONE CAN IMAGINE. IT'S PRICELESS.
HMM...

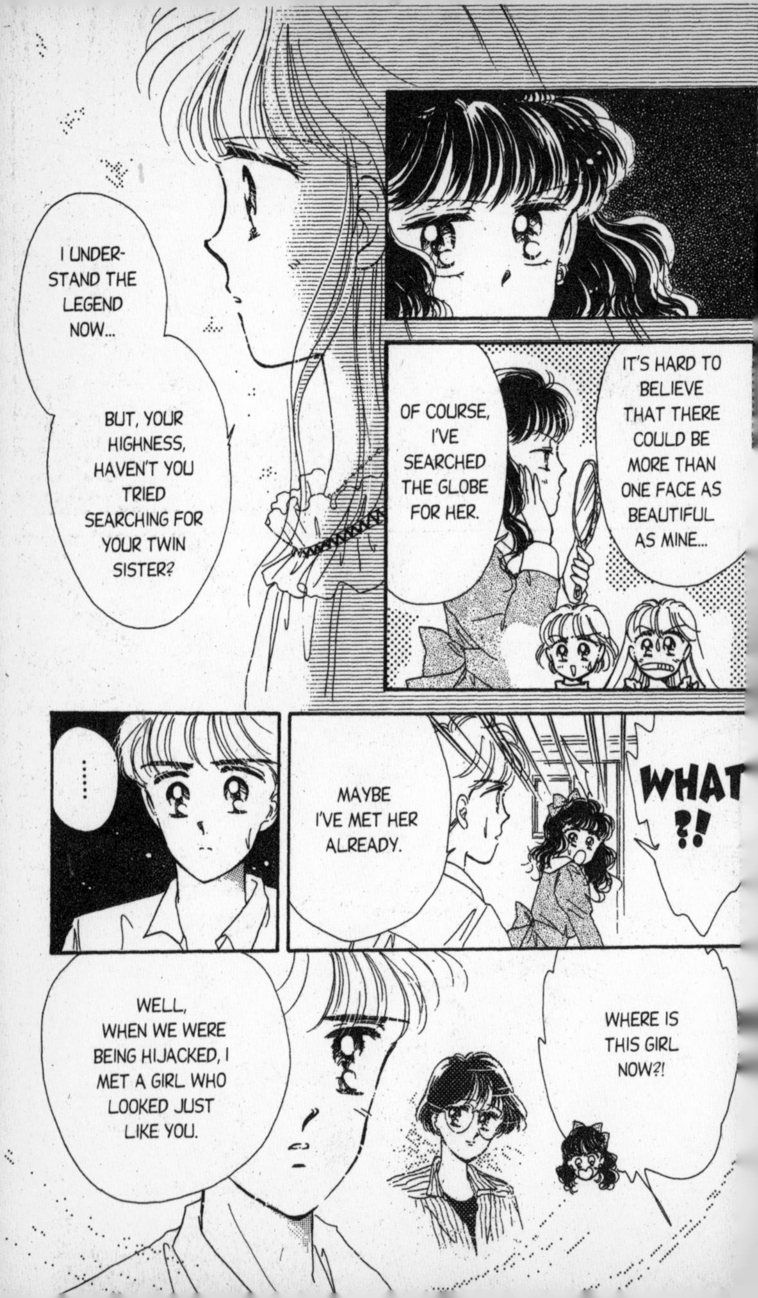
I UNDER-STAND THE LEGEND NOW...
BUT, YOUR HIGHNESS, HAVEN'T YOU TRIED SEARCHING FOR YOUR TWIN SISTER?
OF COURSE, I'VE SEARCHED THE GLOBE FOR HER.
IT'S HARD TO BELIEVE THAT THERE COULD BE MORE THAN ONE FACE AS BEAUTIFUL AS MINE...
......
MAYBE I'VE MET HER ALREADY.
WHAT ?!
WELL, WHEN WE WERE BEING HIJACKED, I MET A GIRL WHO LOOKED JUST LIKE YOU.
WHERE IS THIS GIRL NOW?!

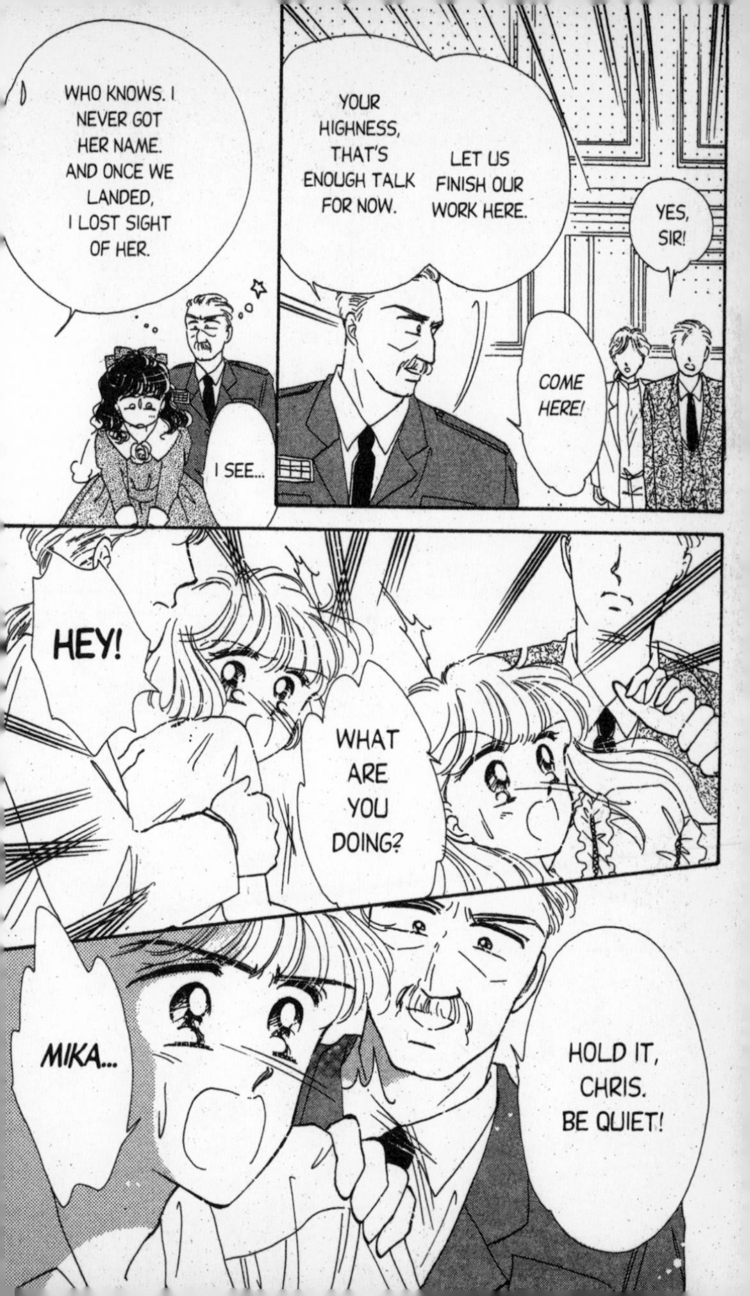
WHO KNOWS. I NEVER GOT HER NAME. AND ONCE WE LANDED, I LOST SIGHT OF HER.
I SEE...
YOUR HIGHNESS, THAT'S ENOUGH TALK FOR NOW.
LET US FINISH OUR WORK HERE.
COME HERE!
YES, SIR!
HEY!
WHAT ARE YOU DOING?
MIKA...
HOLD IT, CHRIS. BE QUIET!

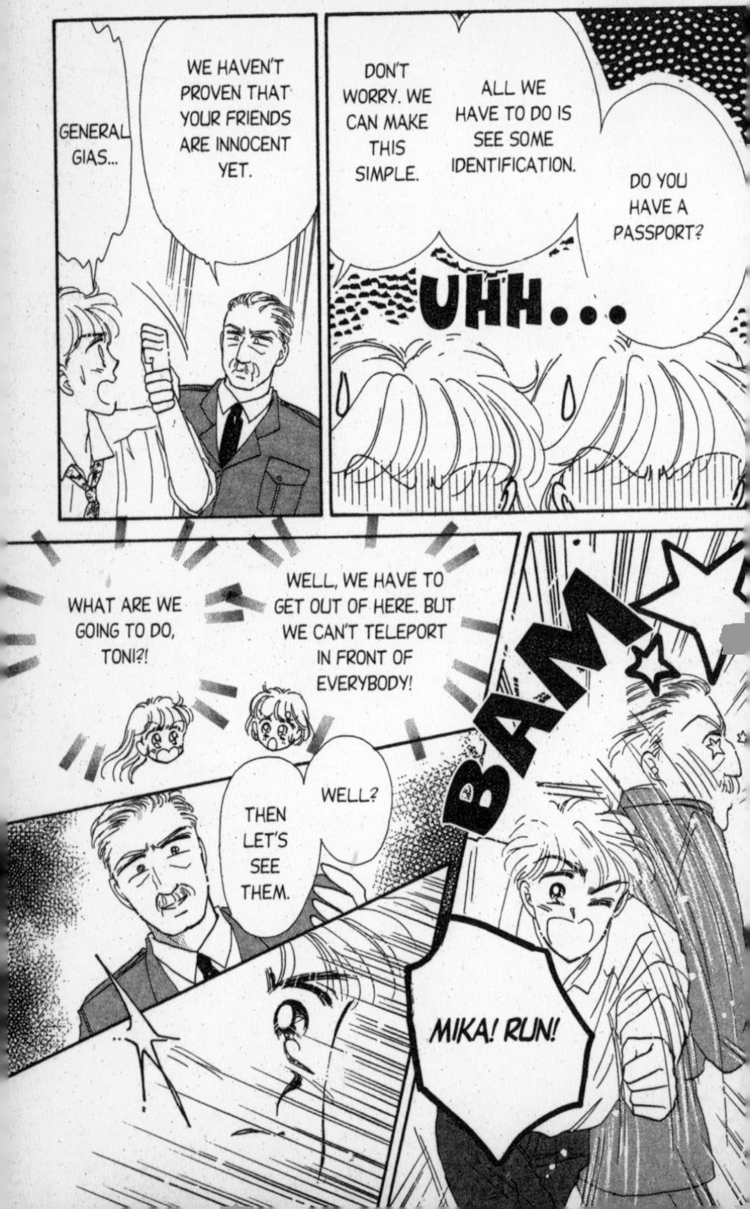
GENERAL GIAS...
WE HAVEN'T PROVEN THAT YOUR FRIENDS ARE INNOCENT YET.
DON'T WORRY. WE CAN MAKE THIS SIMPLE.
ALL WE HAVE TO DO IS SEE SOME IDENTIFICATION.
DO YOU HAVE A PASSPORT?
UHH...
WHAT ARE WE GOING TO DO, TONI?!
WELL, WE HAVE TO GET OUT OF HERE. BUT WE CAN'T TELEPORT IN FRONT OF EVERYBODY!
WELL?
THEN LET'S SEE THEM.
BAM
MIKA! RUN!

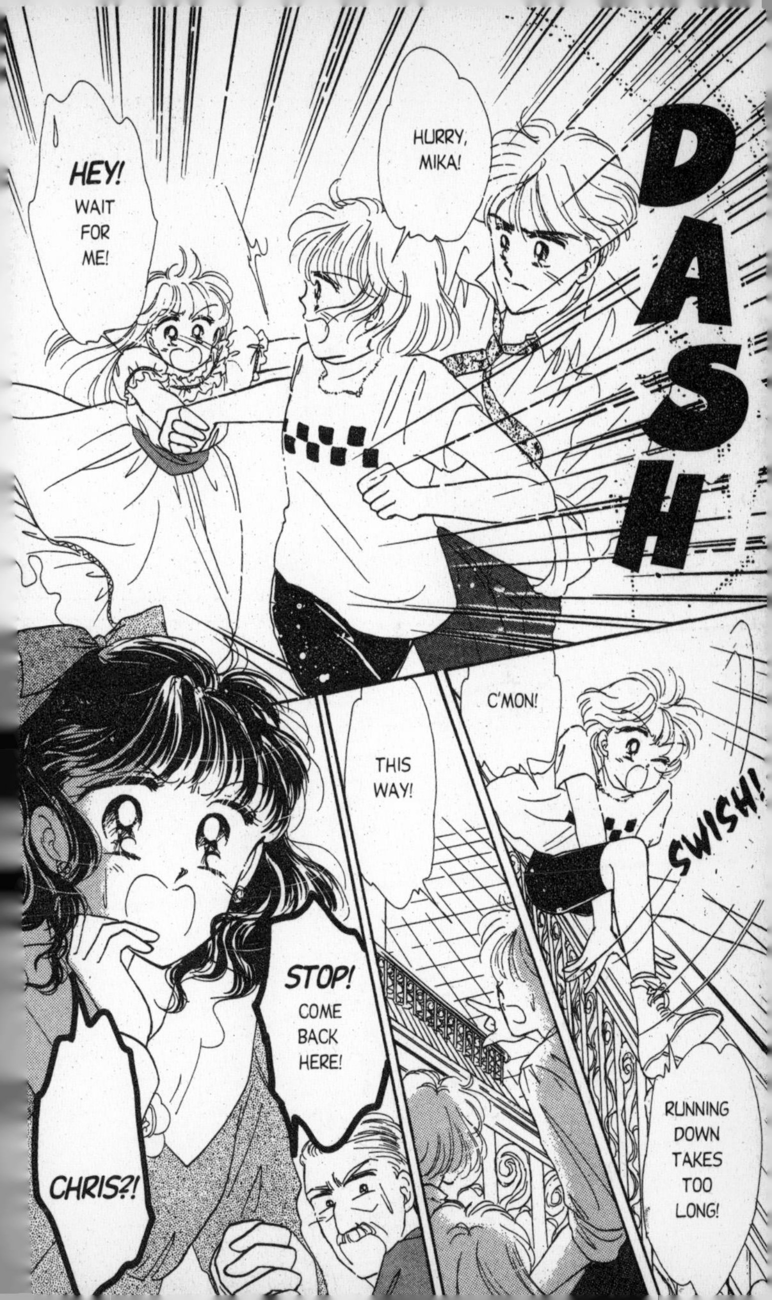
HEY! WAIT FOR ME!
HURRY, MIKA!
DASH
STOP! COME BACK HERE!
CHRIS?!
THIS WAY!
C'MON!
SWISH!
RUNNING DOWN TAKES TOO LONG!

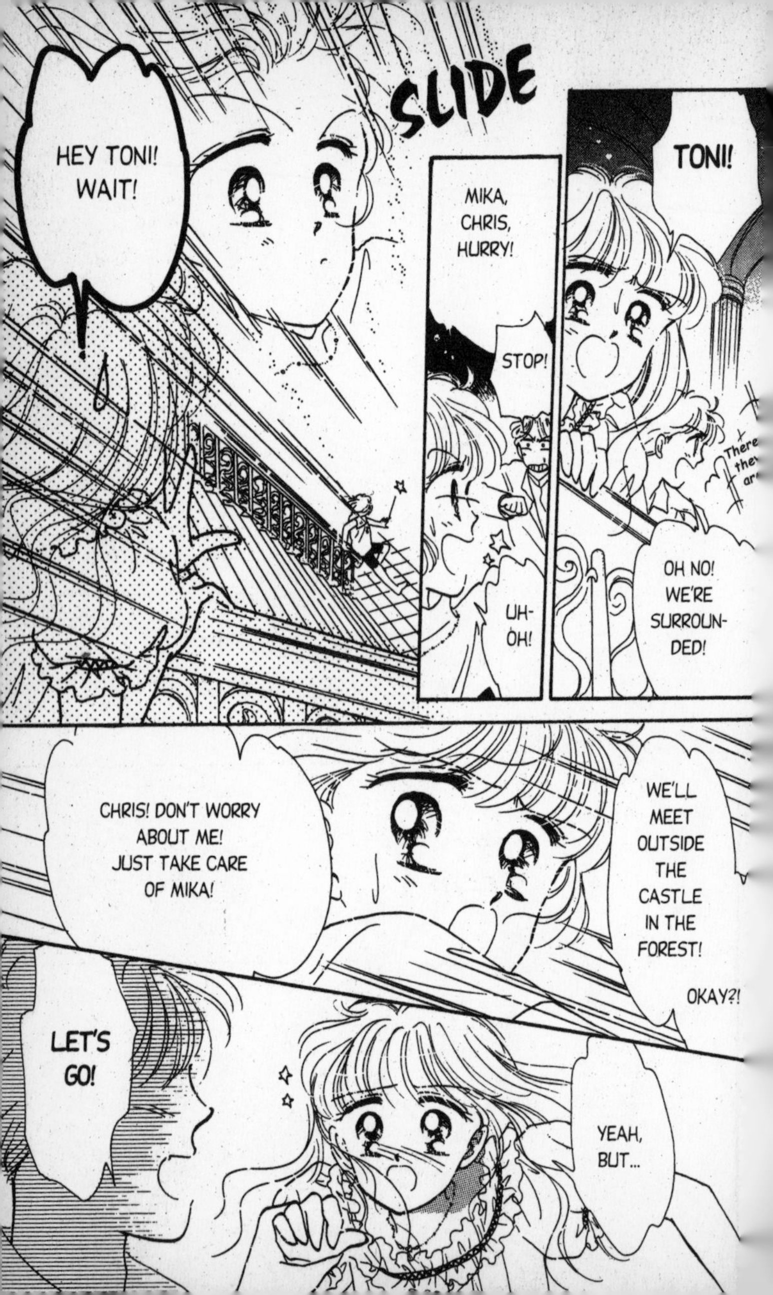
HEY TONI! WAIT!
SLIDE
MIKA, CHRIS, HURRY!
STOP!
UH-OH!
TONI!
OH NO! WE'RE SURROUN-DED!
CHRIS! DON'T WORRY ABOUT ME! JUST TAKE CARE OF MIKA!
WE'LL MEET OUTSIDE THE CASTLE IN THE FOREST!
OKAY?!
LET'S GO!
YEAH, BUT...

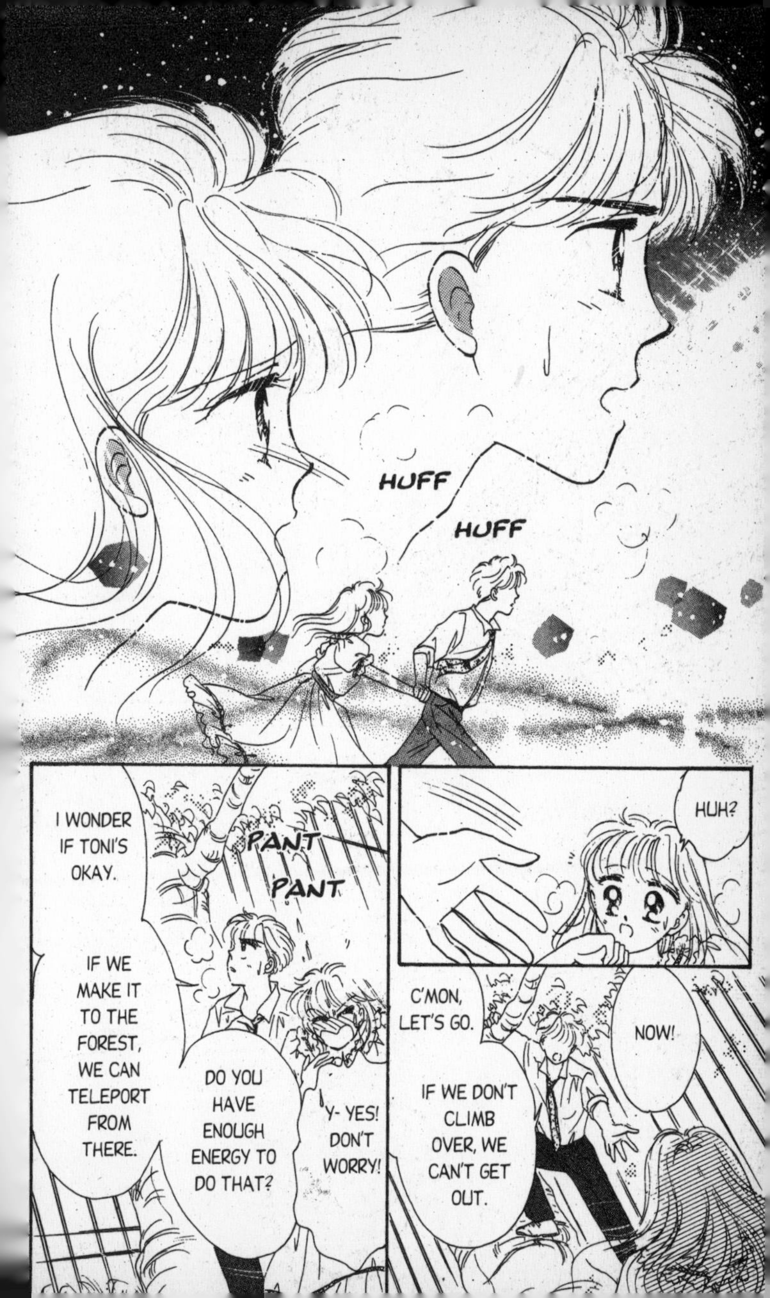
HUFF
HUFF
I WONDER IF TONI'S OKAY.
PANT
PANT
IF WE MAKE IT TO THE FOREST, WE CAN TELEPORT FROM THERE.
DO YOU HAVE ENOUGH ENERGY TO DO THAT?
Y- YES! DON'T WORRY!
HUH?
C'MON, LET'S GO.
NOW!
IF WE DON'T CLIMB OVER, WE CAN'T GET OUT.

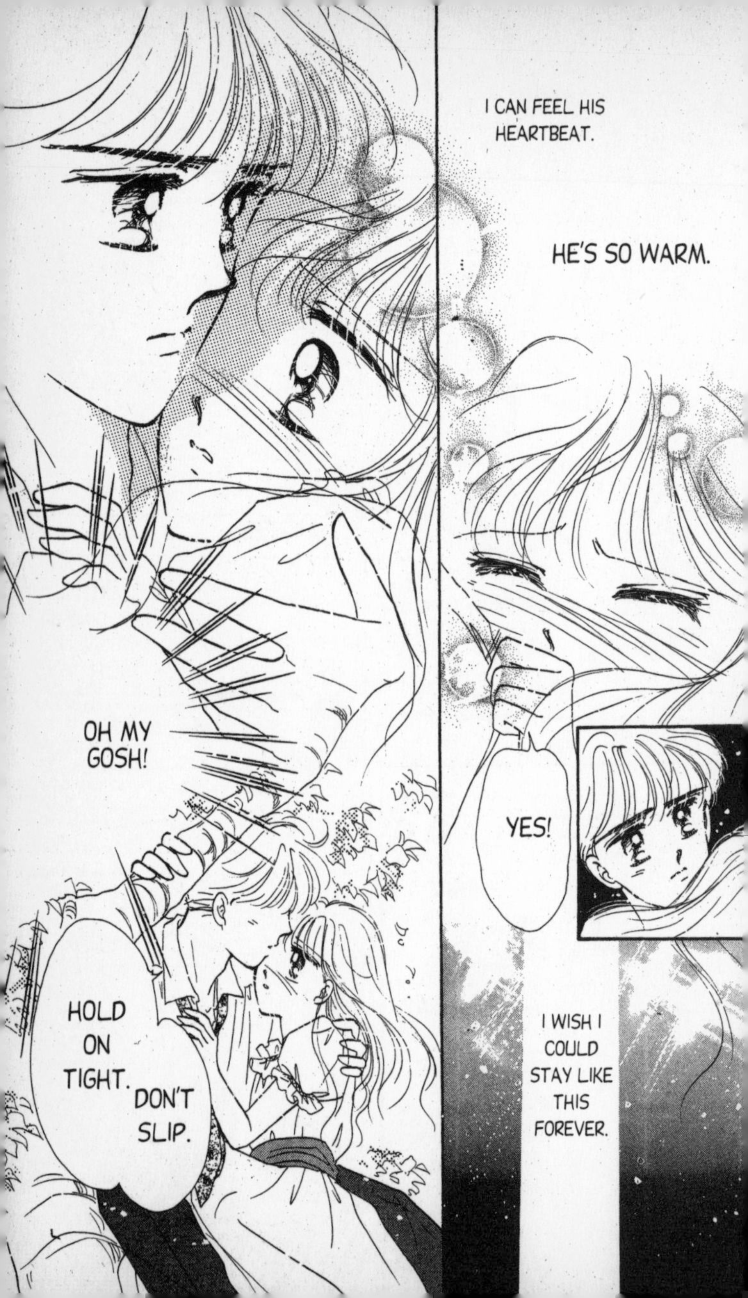
OH MY GOSH!
HOLD ON TIGHT.
DON'T SLIP.
I CAN FEEL HIS HEARTBEAT.
HE'S SO WARM.
YES!
I WISH I COULD STAY LIKE THIS FOREVER.

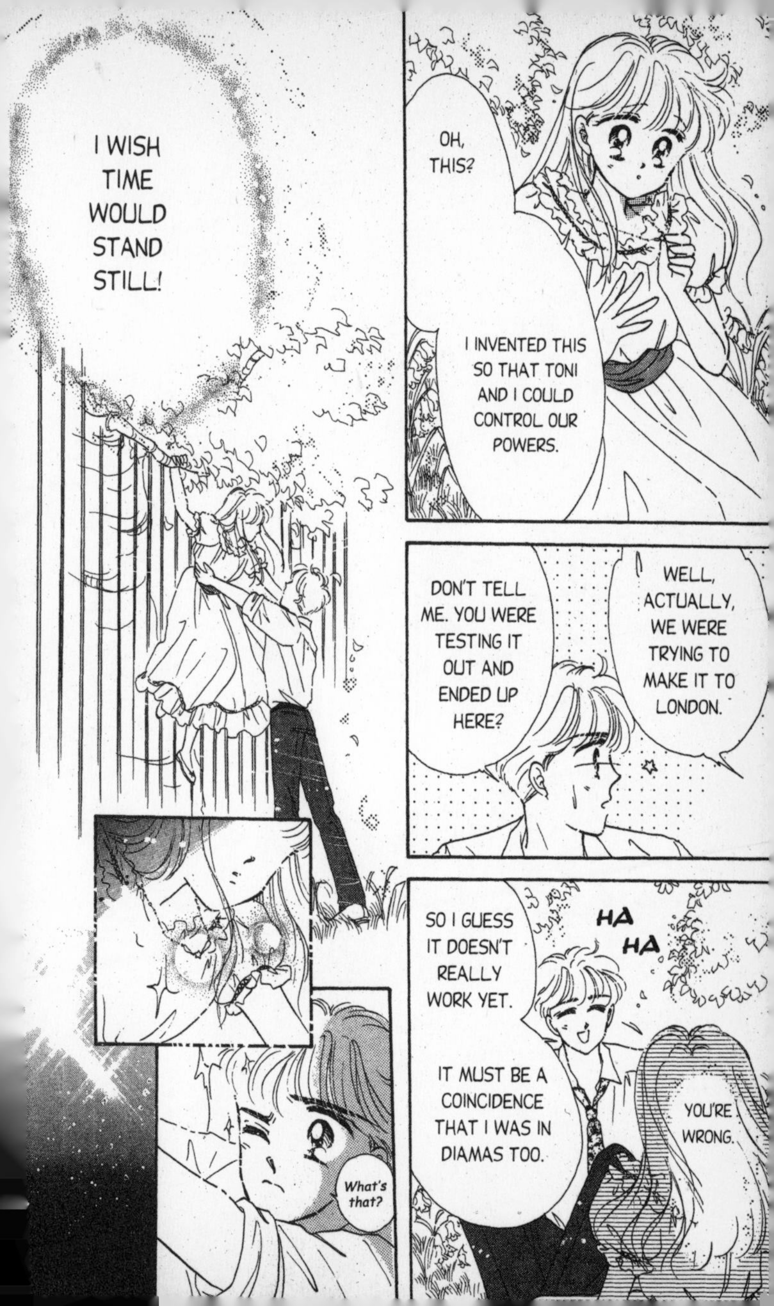
I WISH TIME WOULD STAND STILL!
What's that?
OH, THIS?
I INVENTED THIS SO THAT TONI AND I COULD CONTROL OUR POWERS.
DON'T TELL ME. YOU WERE TESTING IT OUT AND ENDED UP HERE?
WELL, ACTUALLY, WE WERE TRYING TO MAKE IT TO LONDON.
SO I GUESS IT DOESN'T REALLY WORK YET.
HA HA
IT MUST BE A COINCIDENCE THAT I WAS IN DIAMAS TOO.
YOU'RE WRONG.

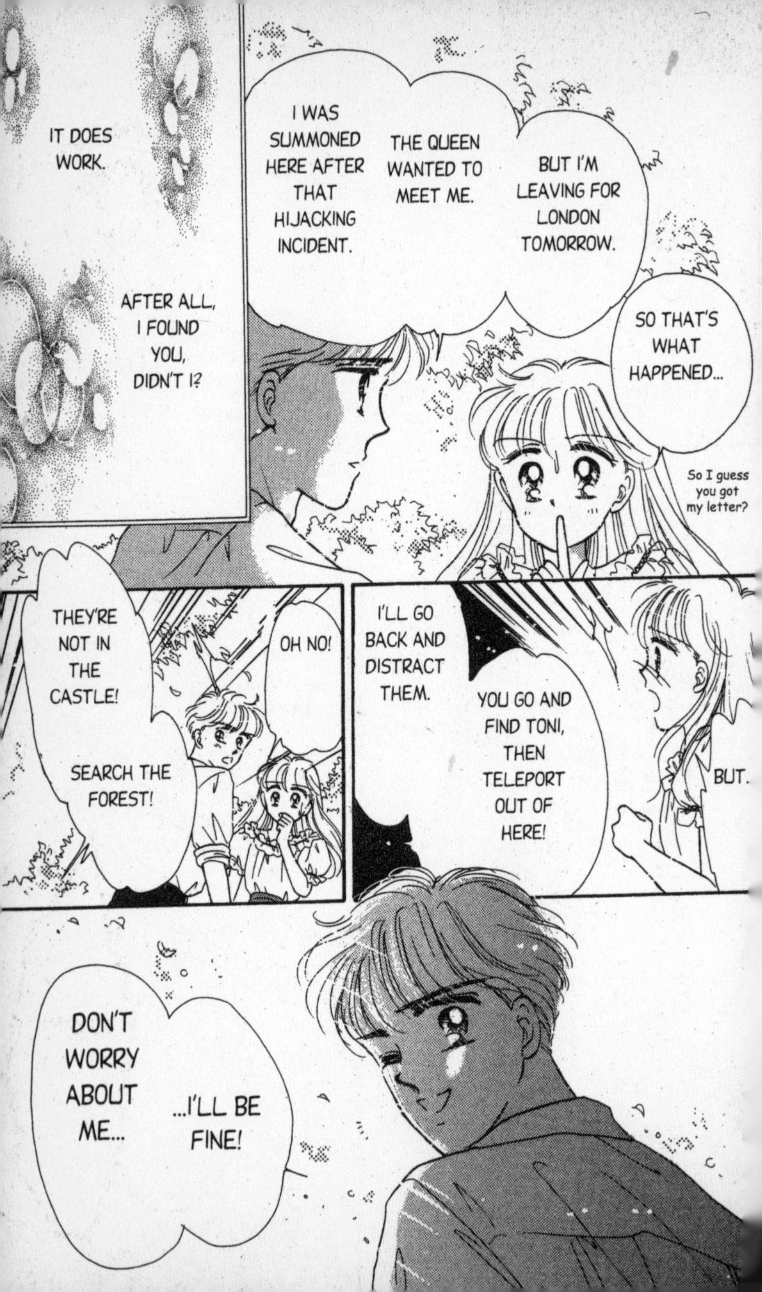
IT DOES WORK.
AFTER ALL, I FOUND YOU, DIDN'T I?
I WAS SUMMONED HERE AFTER THAT HIJACKING INCIDENT.
THE QUEEN WANTED TO MEET ME.
BUT I'M LEAVING FOR LONDON TOMORROW.
SO THAT'S WHAT HAPPENED...
So I guess you got my letter?
THEY'RE NOT IN THE CASTLE!
SEARCH THE FOREST!
OH NO!
I'LL GO BACK AND DISTRACT THEM.
YOU GO AND FIND TONI, THEN TELEPORT OUT OF HERE!
BUT.
DON'T WORRY ABOUT ME...
...I'LL BE FINE!

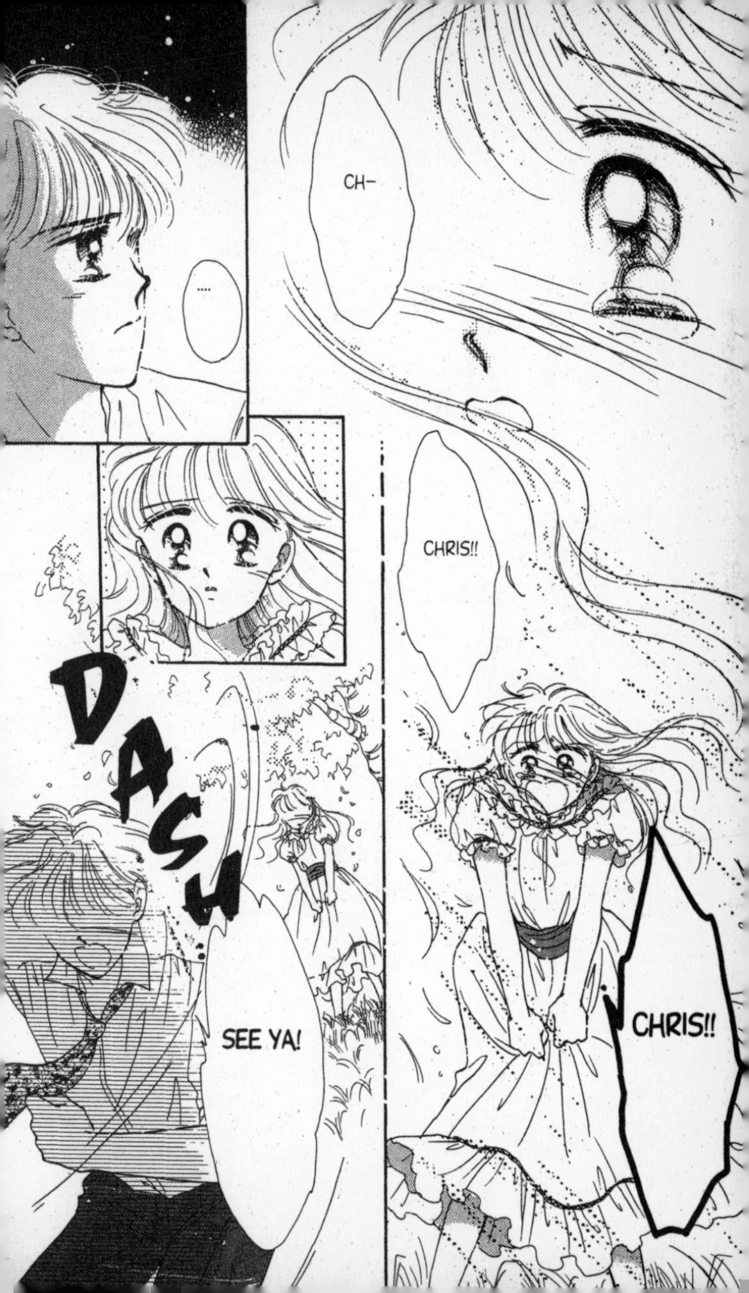
....
CH-
DASH
SEE YA!
CHRIS!!
CHRIS!!

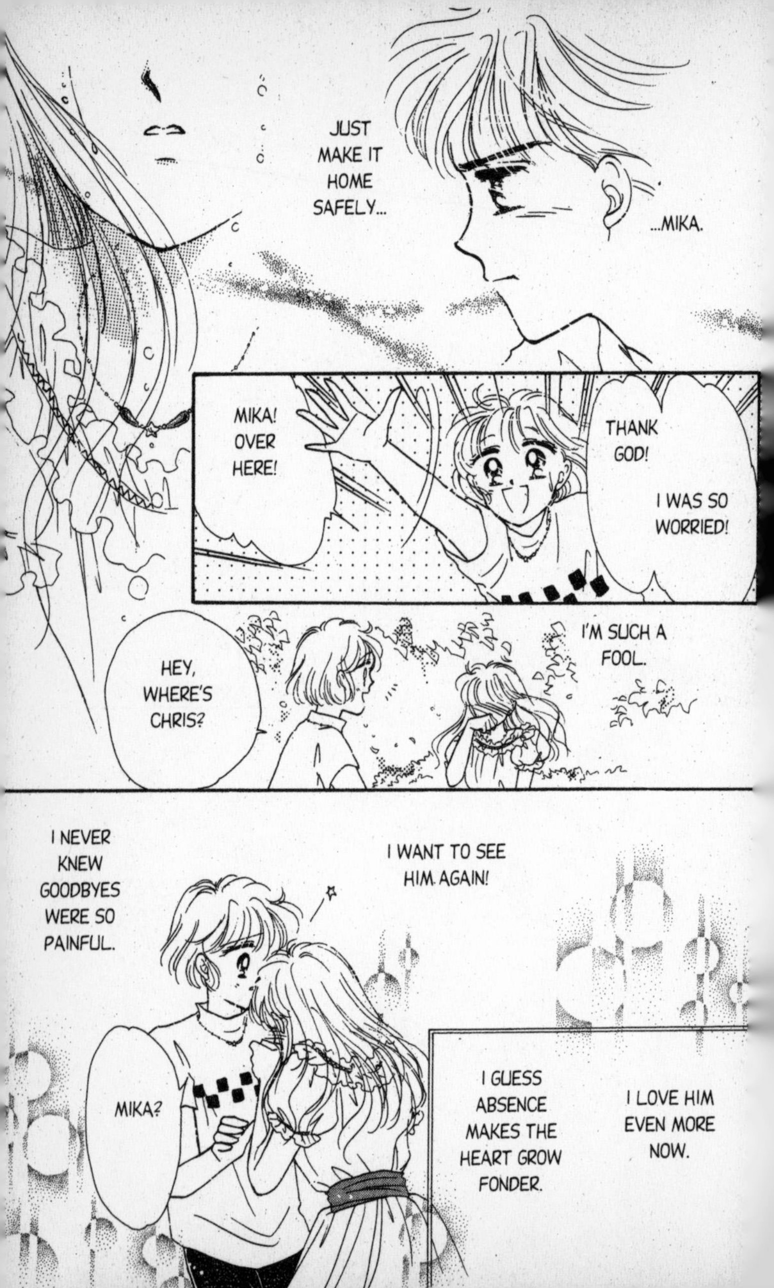
JUST MAKE IT HOME SAFELY...
...MIKA.
MIKA! OVER HERE!
THANK GOD!
I WAS SO WORRIED!
HEY, WHERE'S CHRIS?
I'M SUCH A FOOL.
I NEVER KNEW GOODBYES WERE SO PAINFUL.
I WANT TO SEE HIM AGAIN!
MIKA?
I GUESS ABSENCE MAKES THE HEART GROW FONDER.
I LOVE HIM EVEN MORE NOW.

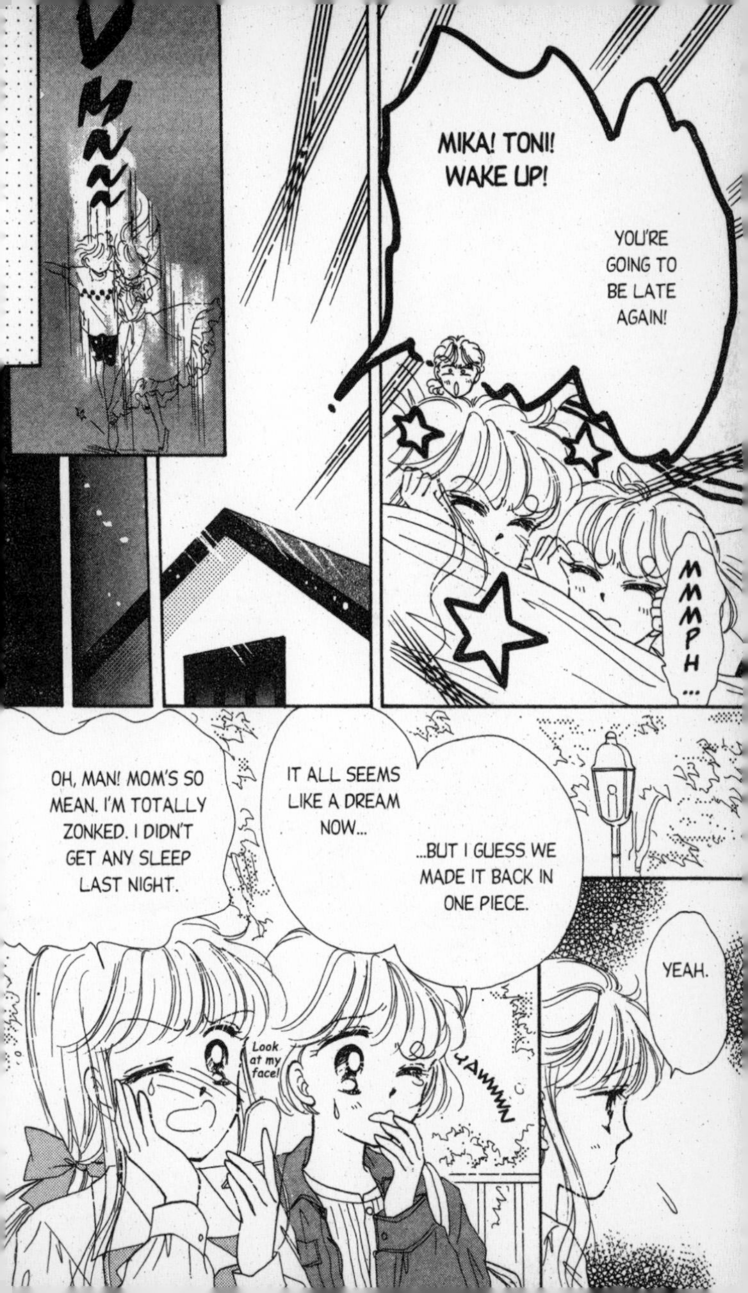
MIKA! TONI! WAKE UP!
YOU'RE GOING TO BE LATE AGAIN!
MMMPH...
OH, MAN! MOM'S SO MEAN. I'M TOTALLY ZONKED. I DIDN'T GET ANY SLEEP LAST NIGHT.
IT ALL SEEMS LIKE A DREAM NOW...
...BUT I GUESS WE MADE IT BACK IN ONE PIECE.
Look at my face!
YAWWWN
YEAH.

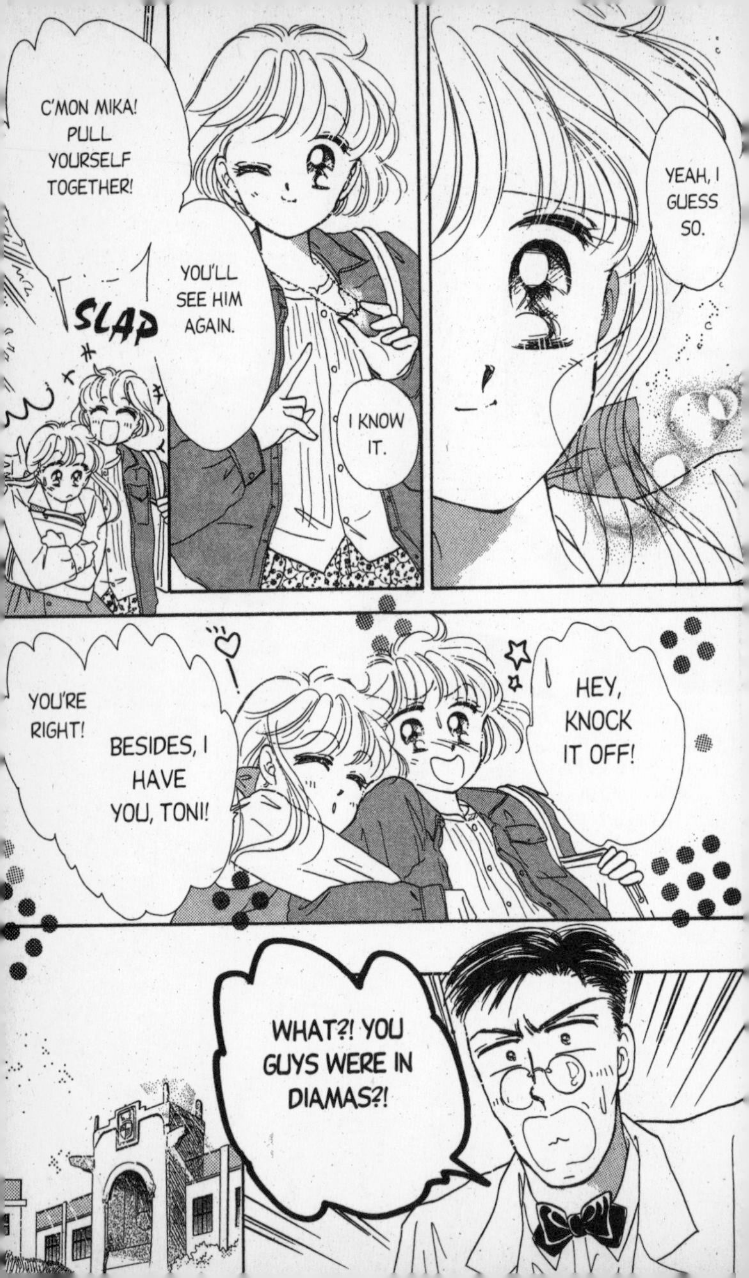
C'MON MIKA! PULL YOURSELF TOGETHER!
SLAP
YOU'LL SEE HIM AGAIN.
I KNOW IT.
YEAH, I GUESS SO.
YOU'RE RIGHT!
BESIDES, I HAVE YOU, TONI!
HEY, KNOCK IT OFF!
WHAT?! YOU GUYS WERE IN DIAMAS?!

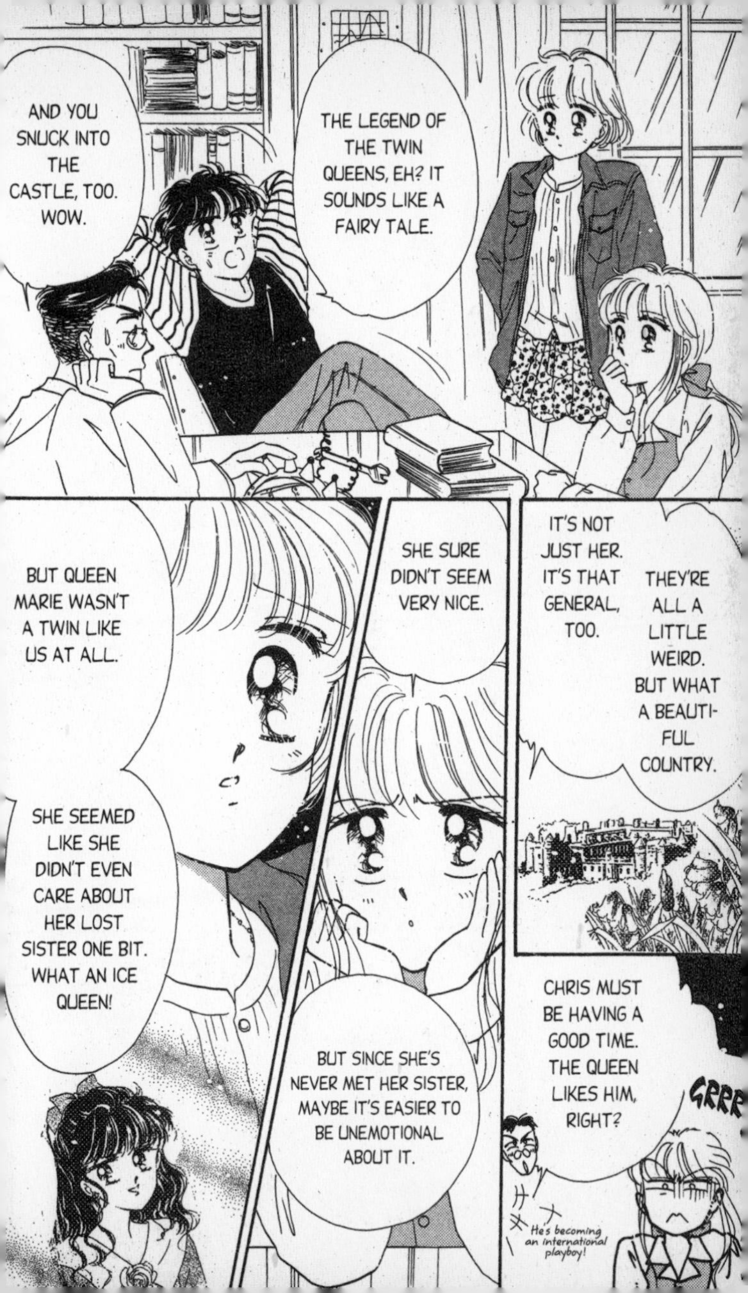
AND YOU SNUCK INTO THE CASTLE, TOO. WOW.
THE LEGEND OF THE TWIN QUEENS, EH? IT SOUNDS LIKE A FAIRY TALE.
BUT QUEEN MARIE WASN'T A TWIN LIKE US AT ALL.
SHE SEEMED LIKE SHE DIDN'T EVEN CARE ABOUT HER LOST SISTER ONE BIT. WHAT AN ICE QUEEN!
SHE SURE DIDN'T SEEM VERY NICE.
BUT SINCE SHE'S NEVER MET HER SISTER, MAYBE IT'S EASIER TO BE UNEMOTIONAL ABOUT IT.
IT'S NOT JUST HER. IT'S THAT GENERAL, TOO.
THEY'RE ALL A LITTLE WEIRD. BUT WHAT A BEAUTI-FUL COUNTRY.
CHRIS MUST BE HAVING A GOOD TIME. THE QUEEN LIKES HIM, RIGHT?
GRRR
He's becoming an international playboy!

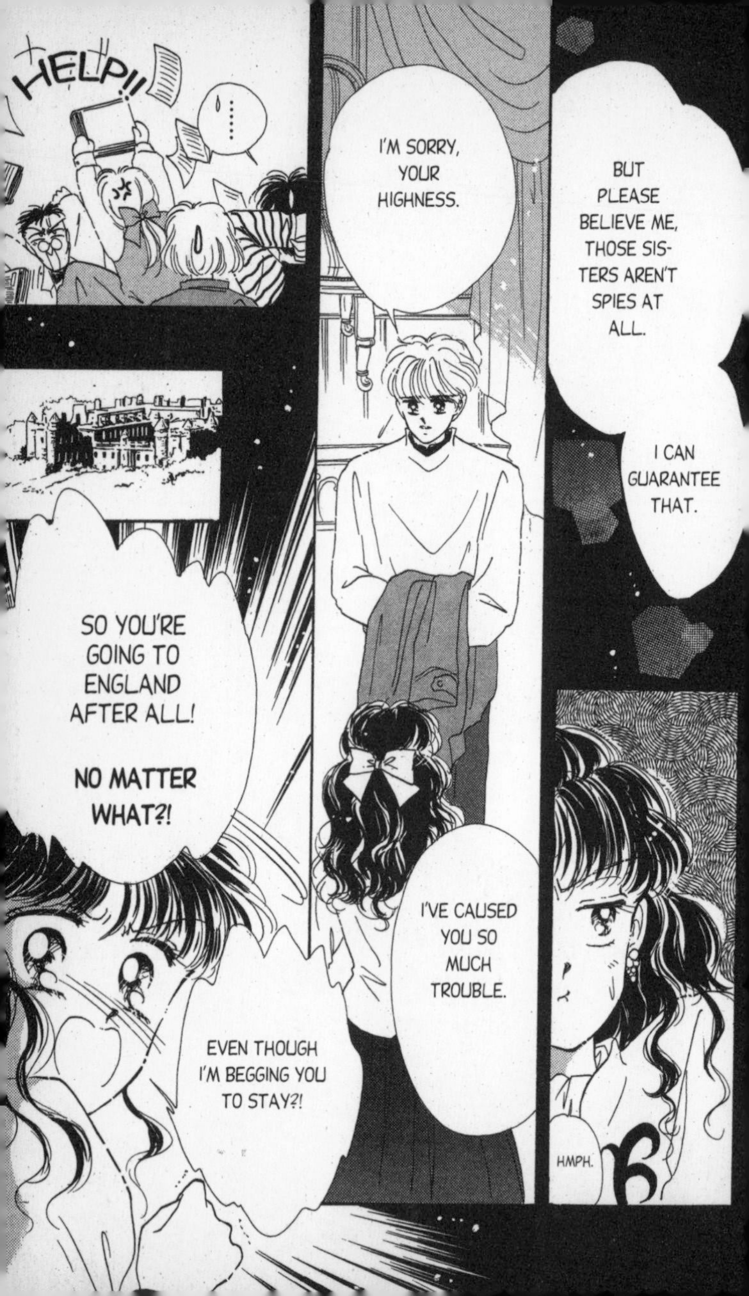
HELP!!
......
SO YOU'RE GOING TO ENGLAND AFTER ALL!
NO MATTER WHAT?!
EVEN THOUGH I'M BEGGING YOU TO STAY?!
I'M SORRY, YOUR HIGHNESS.
I'VE CAUSED YOU SO MUCH TROUBLE.
BUT PLEASE BELIEVE ME, THOSE SIS-TERS AREN'T SPIES AT ALL.
I CAN GUARANTEE THAT.
HMPH.

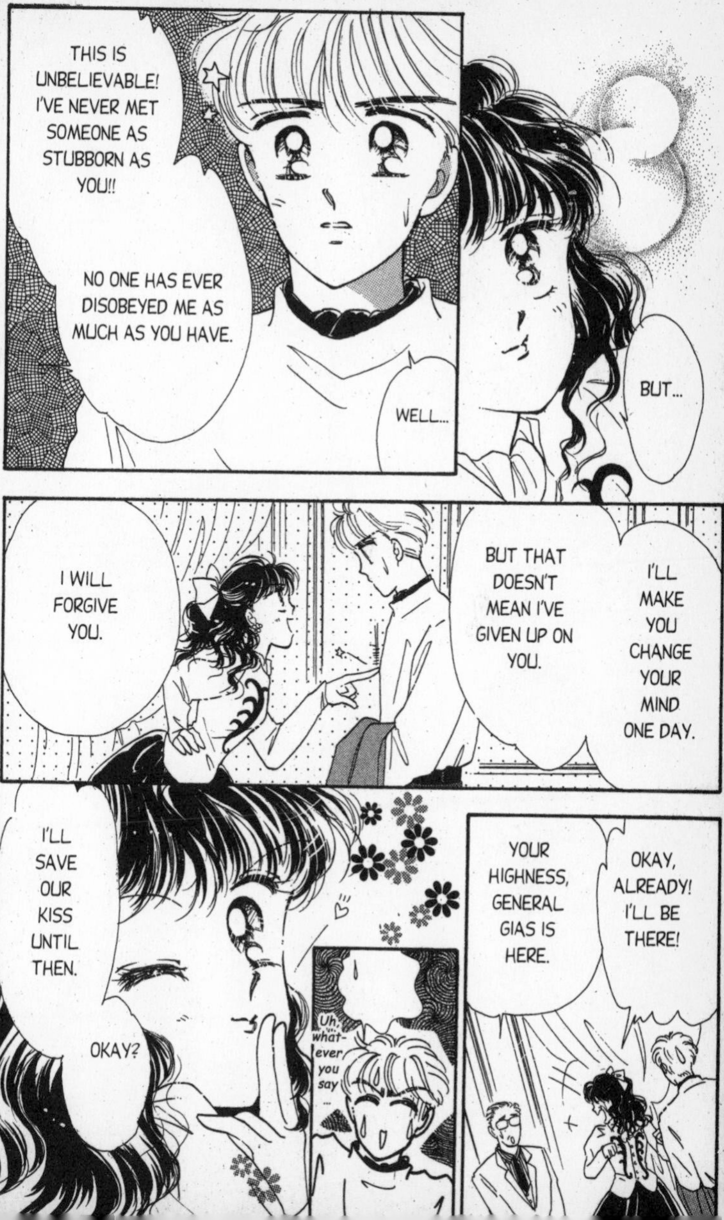

THIS IS UNBELIEVABLE! I'VE NEVER MET SOMEONE AS STUBBORN AS YOU!!
NO ONE HAS EVER DISOBEYED ME AS MUCH AS YOU HAVE.
WELL...
BUT...
I WILL FORGIVE YOU.
BUT THAT DOESN'T MEAN I'VE GIVEN UP ON YOU.
I'LL MAKE YOU CHANGE YOUR MIND ONE DAY.
I'LL SAVE OUR KISS UNTIL THEN.
OKAY?
Uh, whatever you say ...
YOUR HIGHNESS, GENERAL GIAS IS HERE.
OKAY, ALREADY! I'LL BE THERE!

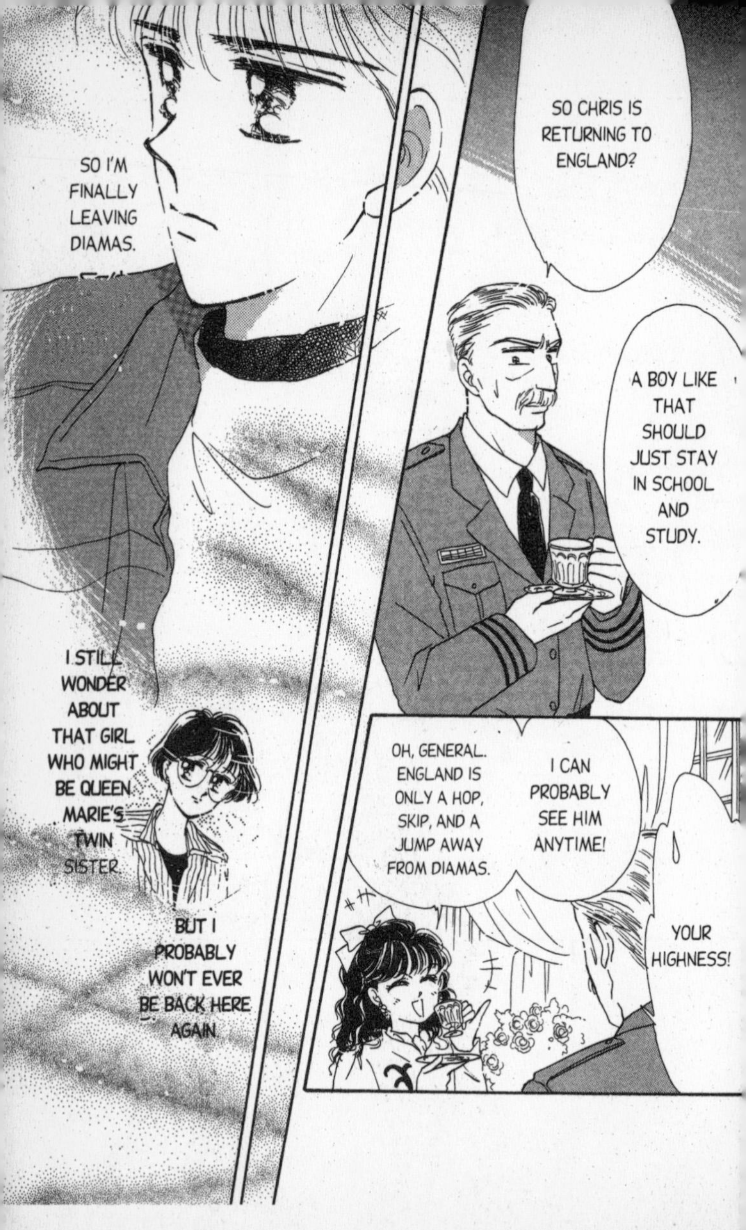
SO I'M FINALLY LEAVING DIAMAS.
I STILL WONDER ABOUT THAT GIRL WHO MIGHT BE QUEEN MARIE'S TWIN SISTER.
BUT I PROBABLY WON'T EVER BE BACK HERE AGAIN.
SO CHRIS IS RETURNING TO ENGLAND?
A BOY LIKE THAT SHOULD JUST STAY IN SCHOOL AND STUDY.
OH, GENERAL. ENGLAND IS ONLY A HOP, SKIP, AND A JUMP AWAY FROM DIAMAS.
I CAN PROBABLY SEE HIM ANYTIME!
YOUR HIGHNESS!

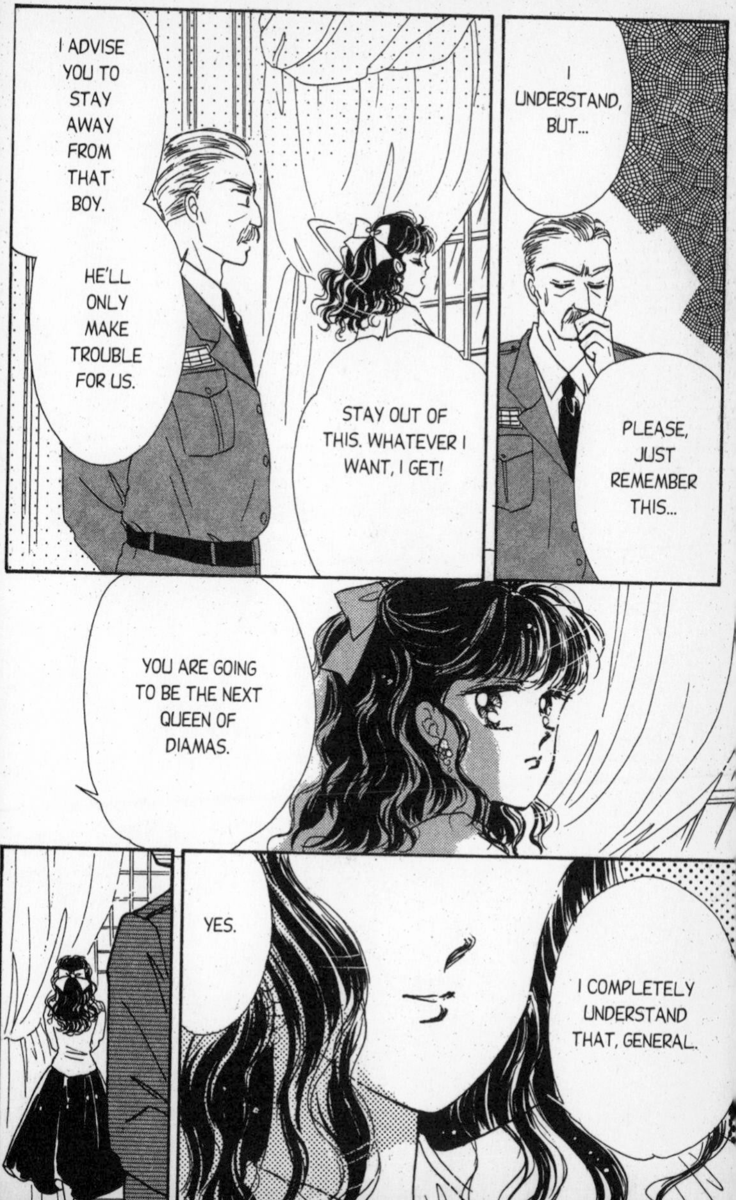
I ADVISE YOU TO STAY AWAY FROM THAT BOY.
HE'LL ONLY MAKE TROUBLE FOR US.
STAY OUT OF THIS. WHATEVER I WANT, I GET!
I UNDERSTAND, BUT...
PLEASE, JUST REMEMBER THIS...
YOU ARE GOING TO BE THE NEXT QUEEN OF DIAMAS.
YES.
I COMPLETELY UNDERSTAND THAT, GENERAL.

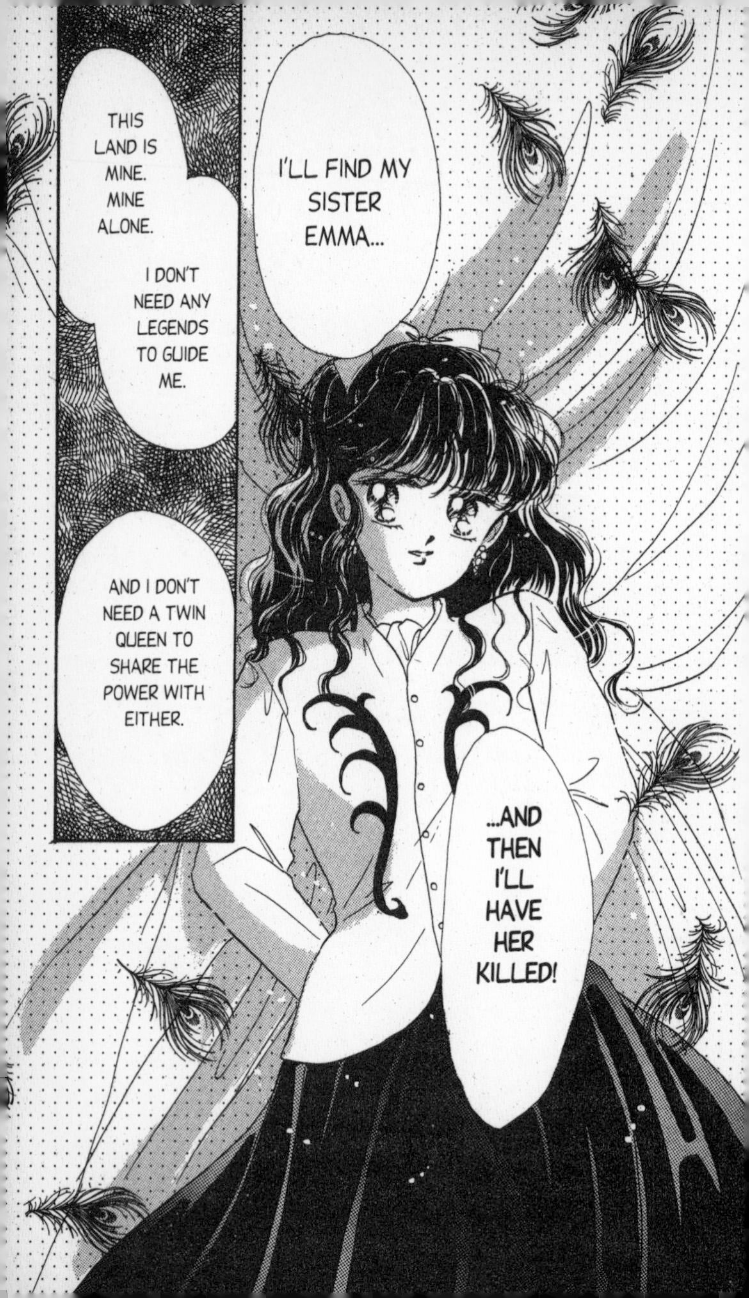
THIS LAND IS MINE. MINE ALONE.
I DON'T NEED ANY LEGENDS TO GUIDE ME.
AND I DON'T NEED A TWIN QUEEN TO SHARE THE POWER WITH EITHER.
I'LL FIND MY SISTER EMMA...
...AND THEN I'LL HAVE HER KILLED!

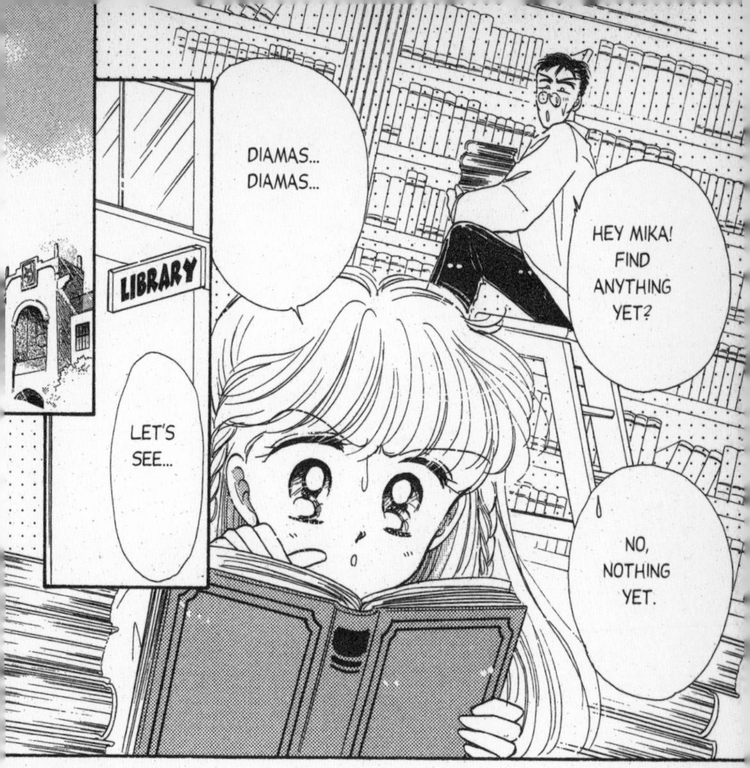
LIBRARY
LET'S SEE...
DIAMAS... DIAMAS...
HEY MIKA! FIND ANYTHING YET?
NO, NOTHING YET.

BONUS

I had always wanted to do a story about twins, and that's why I created Miracle Girls starring Toni and Mika. But at the time I began drawing, my editor said that it would be too confusing to have twins, so I should make just one of them the main character. So I chose Toni. I was worried that some of my fans may have been confused, thinking that the two of them would equally share the spotlight, but instead Toni was front and center. Once the story began though, no one complained about not being able to tell the two apart! So I guess the only ones who didn't get it were my editors! Silly old men! Heh heh...

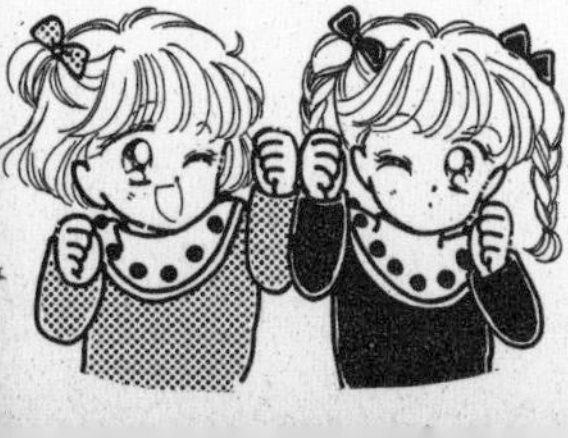

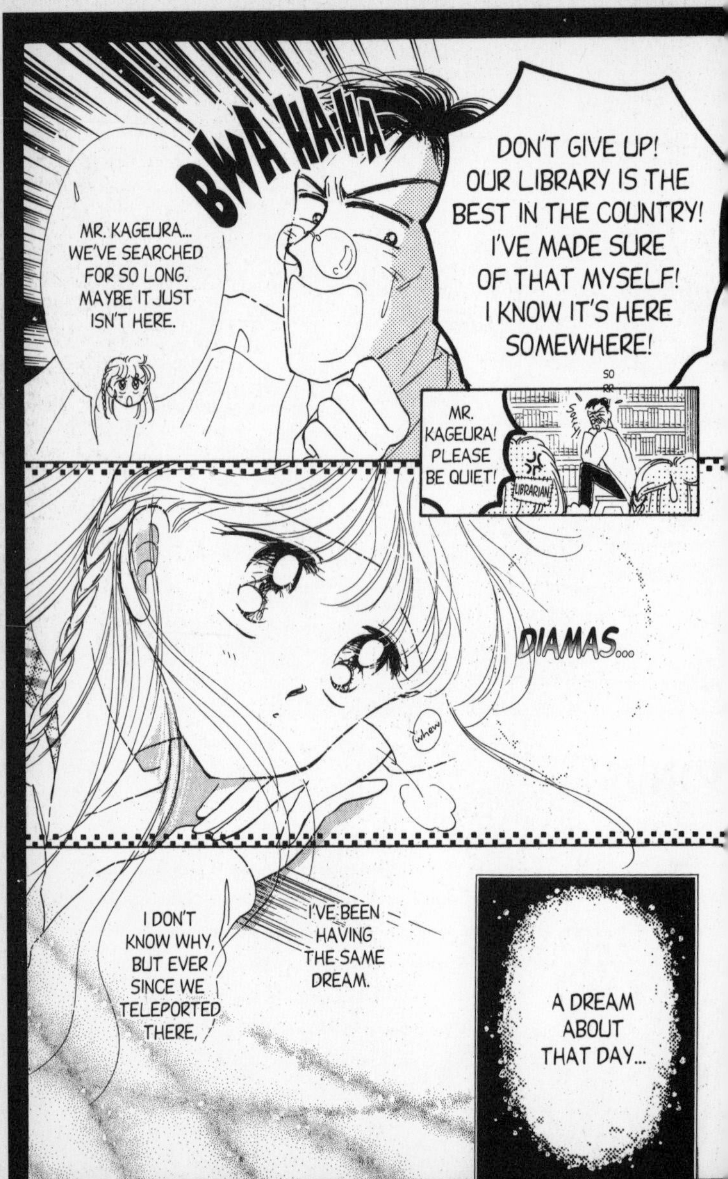

BWA HA HA HA
MR. KAGEURA... WE'VE SEARCHED FOR SO LONG. MAYBE IT JUST ISN'T HERE.
DON'T GIVE UP! OUR LIBRARY IS THE BEST IN THE COUNTRY! I'VE MADE SURE OF THAT MYSELF! I KNOW IT'S HERE SOMEWHERE!
MR. KAGEURA! PLEASE BE QUIET!
LIBRARIAN
DIAMAS...
whew
I DON'T KNOW WHY, BUT EVER SINCE WE TELEPORTED THERE,
I'VE BEEN HAVING THE SAME DREAM.
A DREAM ABOUT THAT DAY...

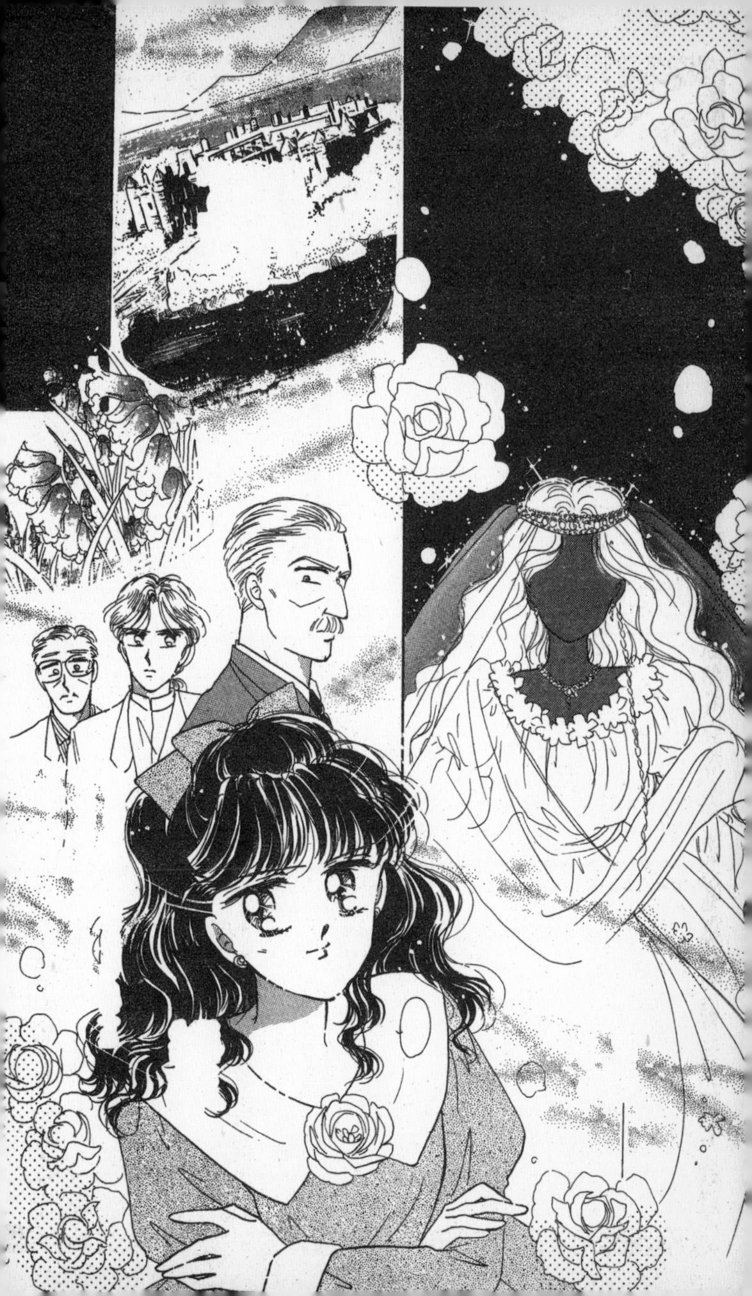

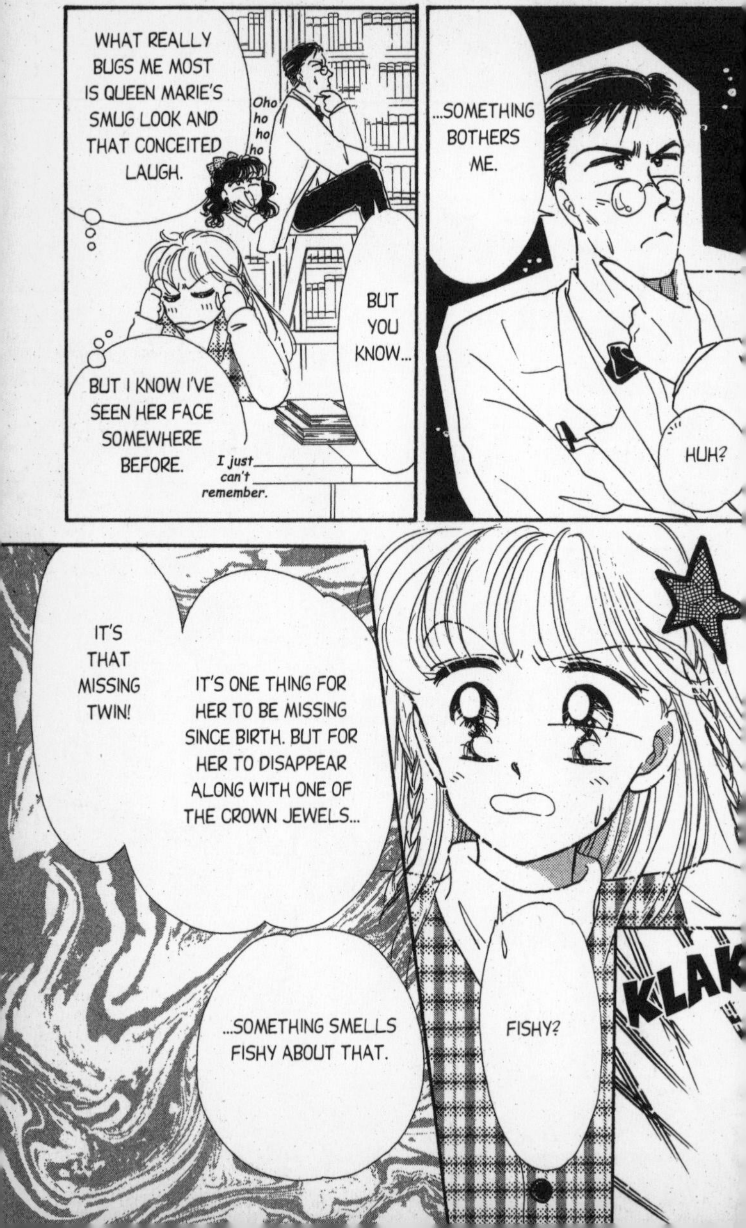
WHAT REALLY BUGS ME MOST IS QUEEN MARIE'S SMUG LOOK AND THAT CONCEITED LAUGH.
Oho ho ho ho
BUT I KNOW I'VE SEEN HER FACE SOMEWHERE BEFORE.
I just can't remember.
BUT YOU KNOW...
...SOMETHING BOTHERS ME.
HUH?
IT'S THAT MISSING TWIN!
IT'S ONE THING FOR HER TO BE MISSING SINCE BIRTH. BUT FOR HER TO DISAPPEAR ALONG WITH ONE OF THE CROWN JEWELS...
...SOMETHING SMELLS FISHY ABOUT THAT.
FISHY?
KLAK

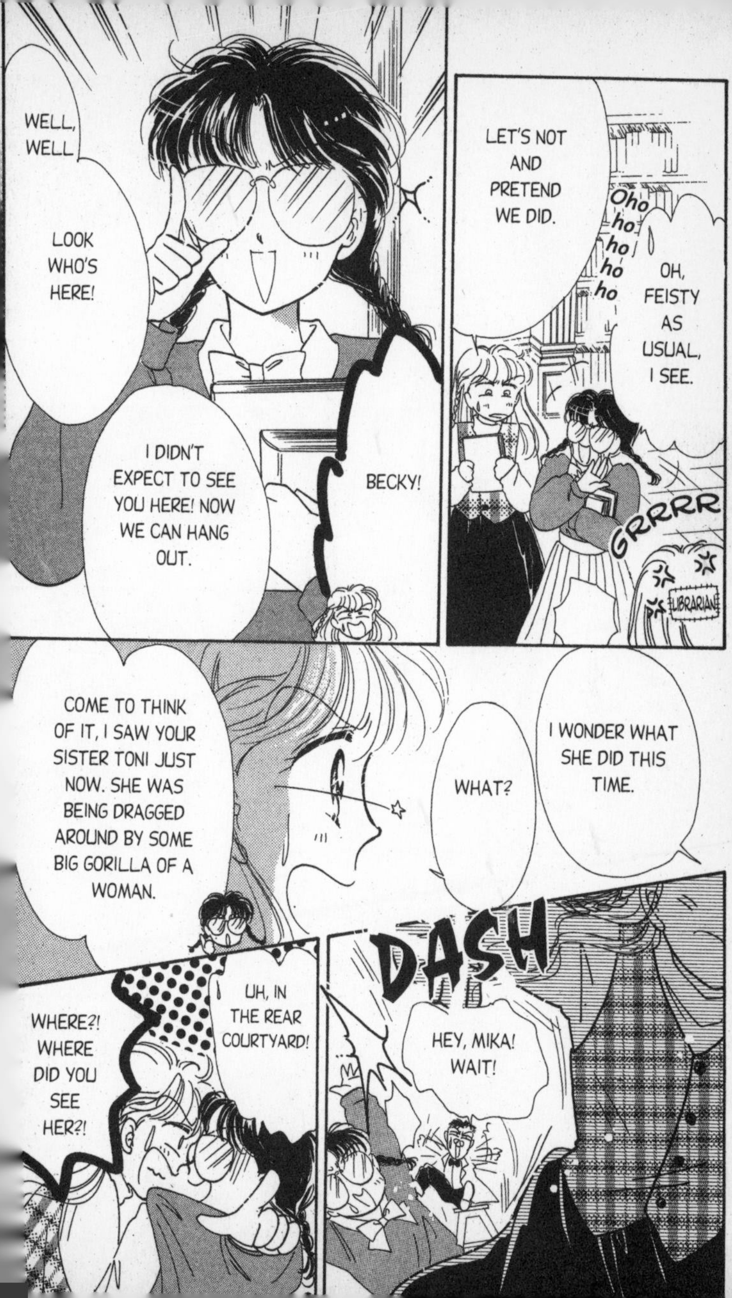
WELL, WELL
LOOK WHO'S HERE!
I DIDN'T EXPECT TO SEE YOU HERE! NOW WE CAN HANG OUT.
BECKY!
LET'S NOT AND PRETEND WE DID.
Oho ho ho ho ho
OH, FEISTY AS USUAL, I SEE.
GRRRR
LIBRARIAN
COME TO THINK OF IT, I SAW YOUR SISTER TONI JUST NOW. SHE WAS BEING DRAGGED AROUND BY SOME BIG GORILLA OF A WOMAN.
WHAT?
I WONDER WHAT SHE DID THIS TIME.
WHERE?! WHERE DID YOU SEE HER?!
UH, IN THE REAR COURTYARD!
DASH
HEY, MIKA! WAIT!

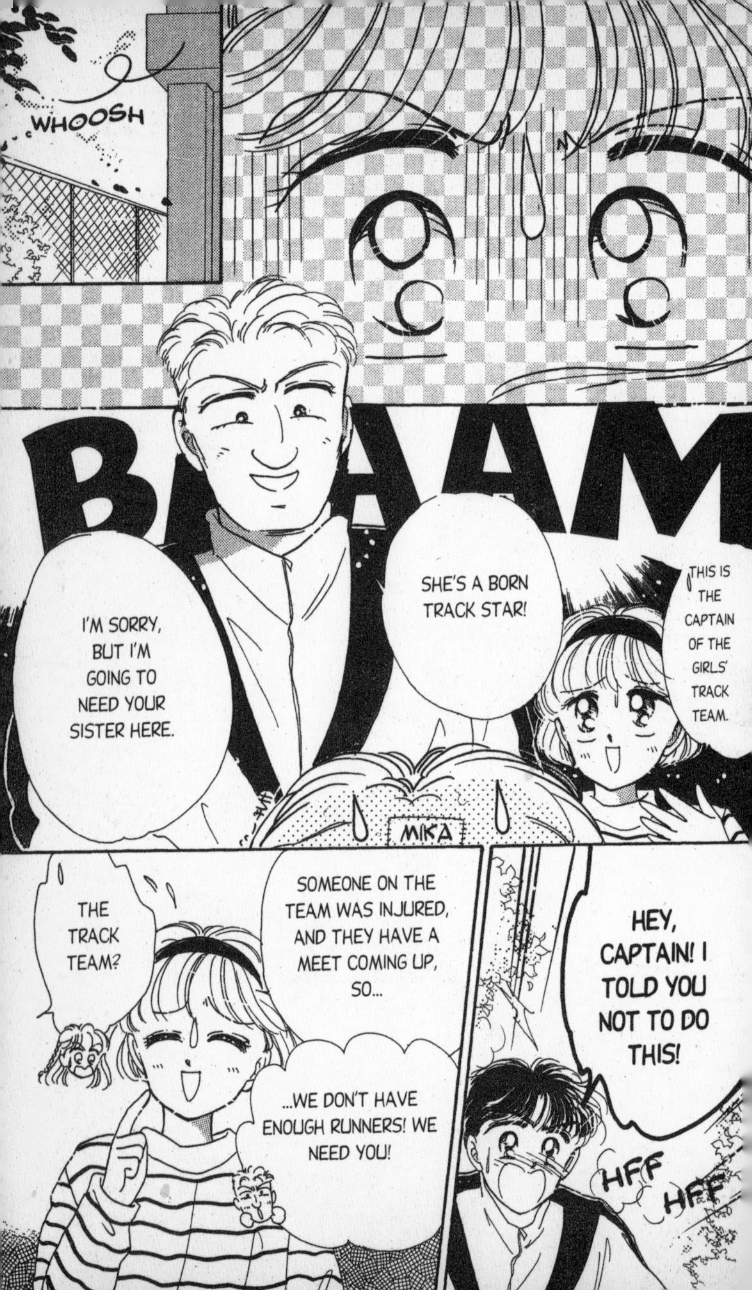
WHOOSH
BAAM
I'M SORRY, BUT I'M GOING TO NEED YOUR SISTER HERE.
SHE'S A BORN TRACK STAR!
THIS IS THE CAPTAIN OF THE GIRLS' TRACK TEAM.
MIKA
THE TRACK TEAM?
SOMEONE ON THE TEAM WAS INJURED, AND THEY HAVE A MEET COMING UP, SO...
...WE DON'T HAVE ENOUGH RUNNERS! WE NEED YOU!
HEY, CAPTAIN! I TOLD YOU NOT TO DO THIS!
HFF
HFF

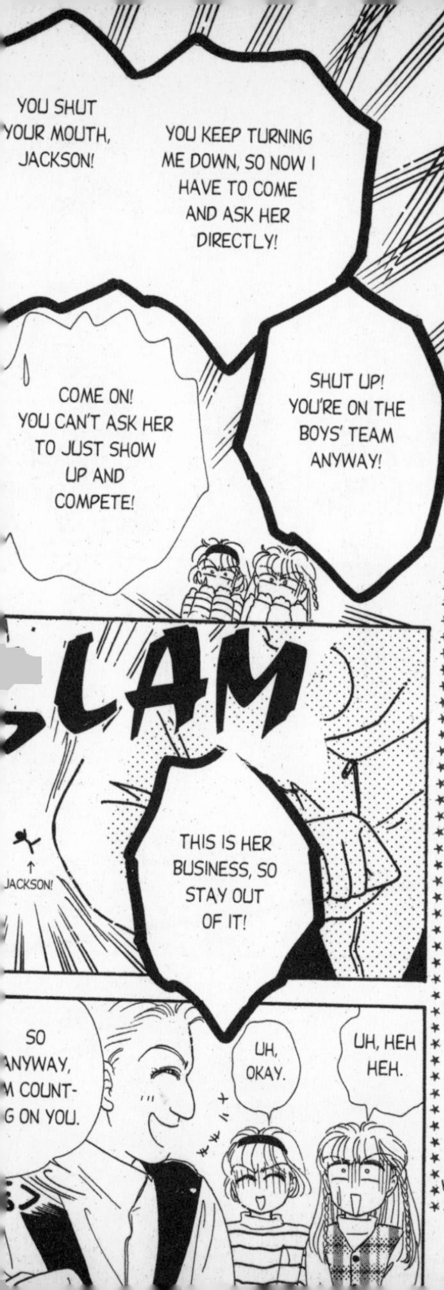
YOU SHUT YOUR MOUTH, JACKSON!
YOU KEEP TURNING ME DOWN, SO NOW I HAVE TO COME AND ASK HER DIRECTLY!
COME ON! YOU CAN'T ASK HER TO JUST SHOW UP AND COMPETE!
SHUT UP! YOU'RE ON THE BOYS' TEAM ANYWAY!
SLAM
JACKSON!
THIS IS HER BUSINESS, SO STAY OUT OF IT!
SO ANYWAY, M COUNT- G ON YOU.
UH, OKAY.
UH, HEH HEH.

BONUS

At first, I was going to draw Toni and Mika with the same hairstyle! But then no one would have been able to tell the difference, so I scrapped that idea. Then again, their tastes in clothes are so different I'd have to put them in matching outfits. Otherwise, no one would think they were twins!

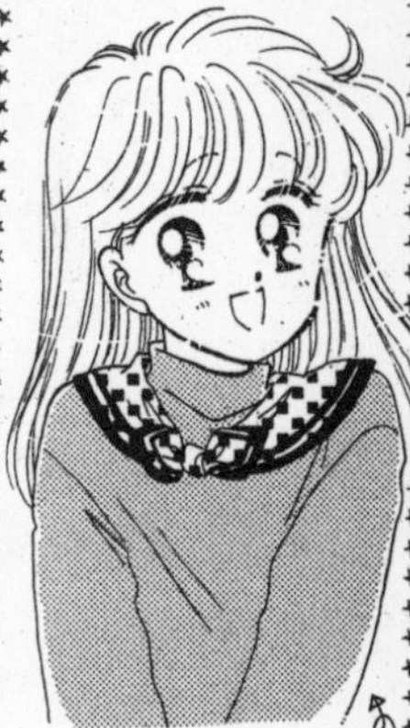

Toni with long hair. What do you think? Maybe she looks better with short hair.

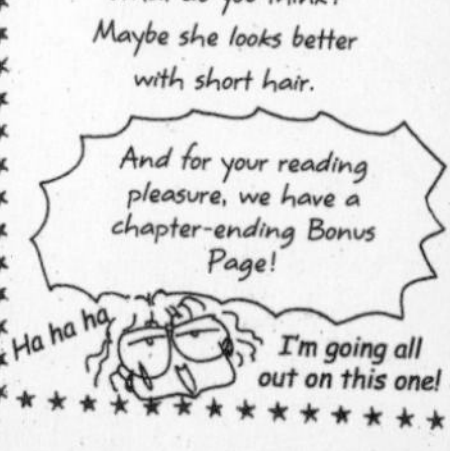
And for your reading pleasure, we have a chapter-ending Bonus Page!
Ha ha ha
I'm going all out on this one!

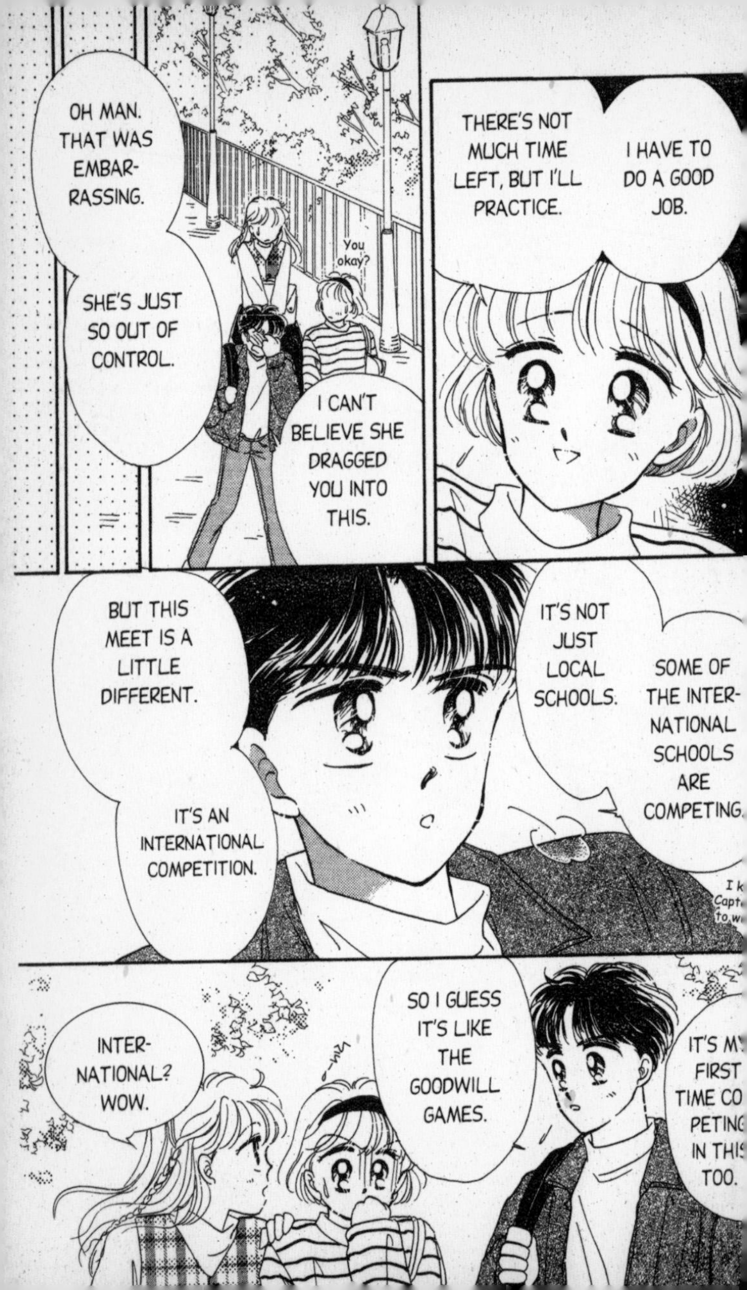
OH MAN. THAT WAS EMBAR-RASSING.
SHE'S JUST SO OUT OF CONTROL.
You okay?
I CAN'T BELIEVE SHE DRAGGED YOU INTO THIS.
THERE'S NOT MUCH TIME LEFT, BUT I'LL PRACTICE.
I HAVE TO DO A GOOD JOB.
BUT THIS MEET IS A LITTLE DIFFERENT.
IT'S AN INTERNATIONAL COMPETITION.
IT'S NOT JUST LOCAL SCHOOLS.
SOME OF THE INTER-NATIONAL SCHOOLS ARE COMPETING.
INTER-NATIONAL? WOW.
SO I GUESS IT'S LIKE THE GOODWILL GAMES.
IT'S MY FIRST TIME CO PETING IN THIS TOO.

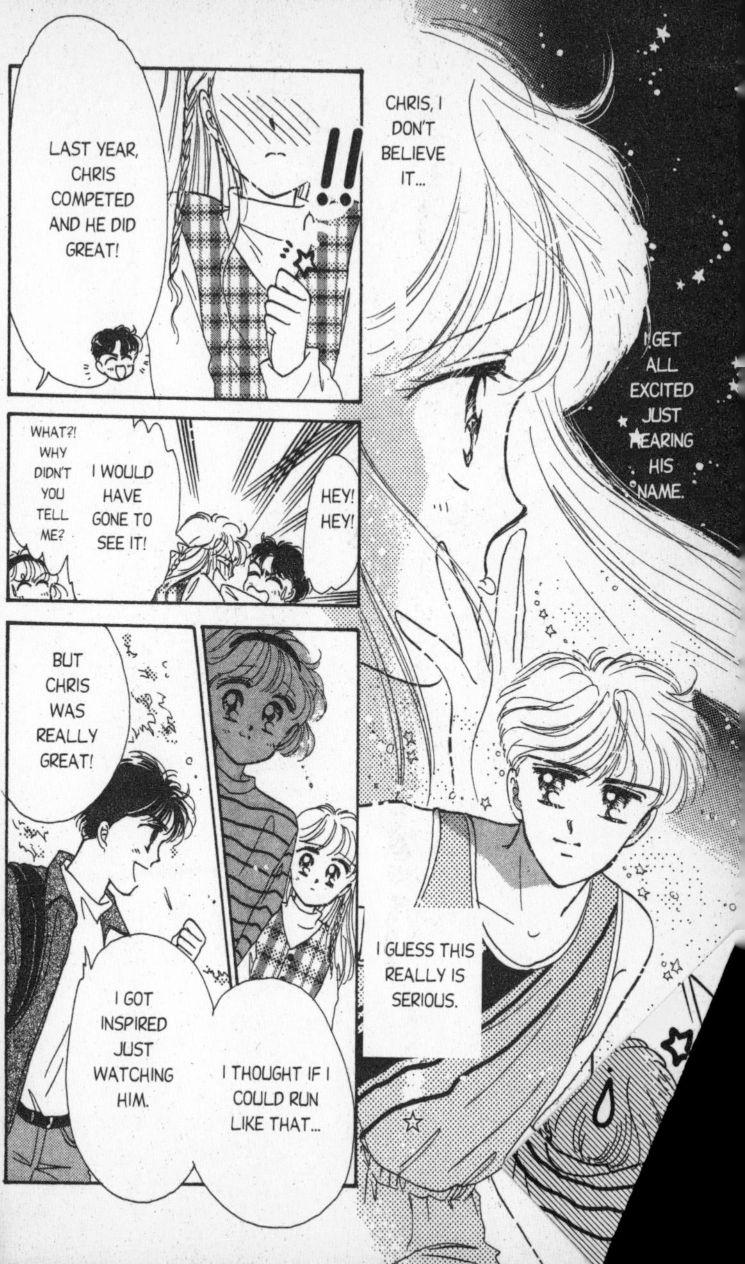
LAST YEAR, CHRIS COMPETED AND HE DID GREAT!
!!
WHAT?! WHY DIDN'T YOU TELL ME?
I WOULD HAVE GONE TO SEE IT!
HEY! HEY!
BUT CHRIS WAS REALLY GREAT!
I GOT INSPIRED JUST WATCHING HIM.
I THOUGHT IF I COULD RUN LIKE THAT...
CHRIS, I DON'T BELIEVE IT...
I GET ALL EXCITED JUST HEARING HIS NAME.
I GUESS THIS REALLY IS SERIOUS.

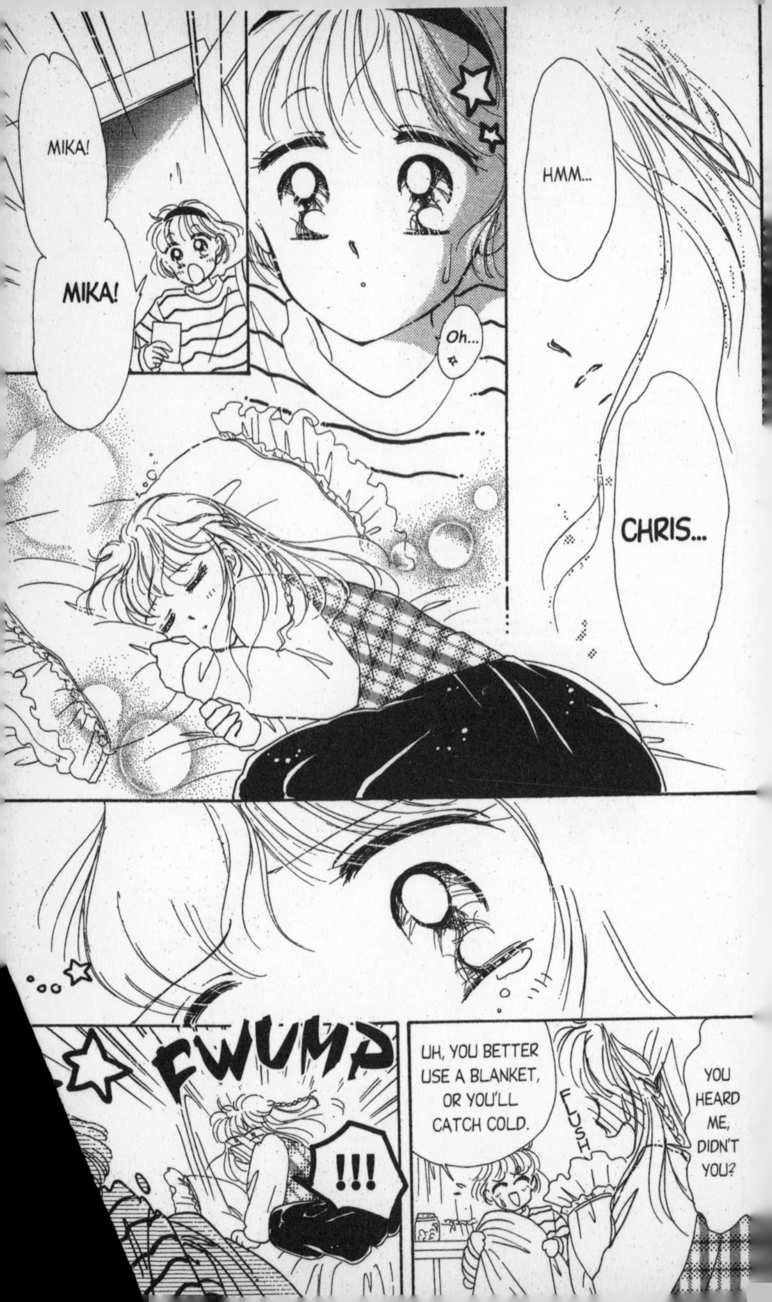
MIKA!
MIKA!
Oh...
HMM...
CHRIS...
FWUMP
!!!
UH, YOU BETTER USE A BLANKET, OR YOU'LL CATCH COLD.
FLUSH
YOU HEARD ME, DIDN'T YOU?

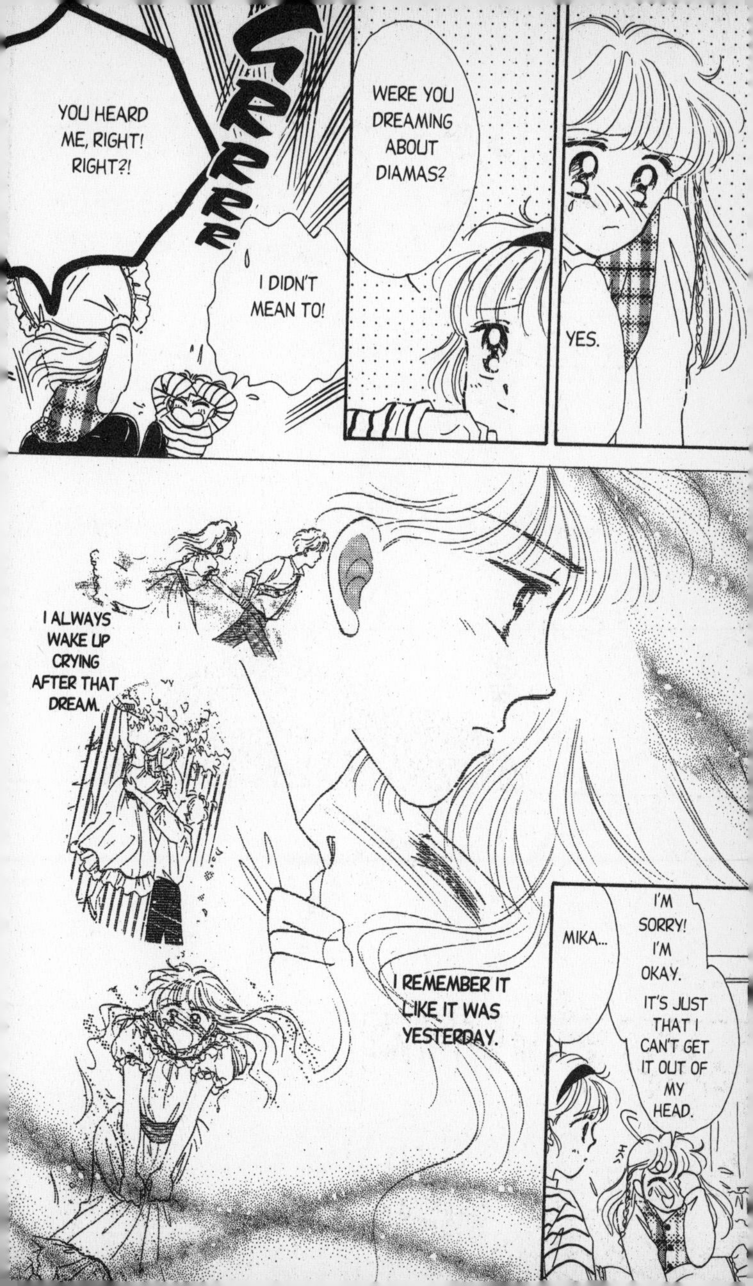
YOU HEARD ME, RIGHT! RIGHT?!
SRRRR
I DIDN'T MEAN TO!
WERE YOU DREAMING ABOUT DIAMAS?
YES.
I ALWAYS WAKE UP CRYING AFTER THAT DREAM.
I REMEMBER IT LIKE IT WAS YESTERDAY.
MIKA...
I'M SORRY! I'M OKAY.
IT'S JUST THAT I CAN'T GET IT OUT OF MY HEAD.

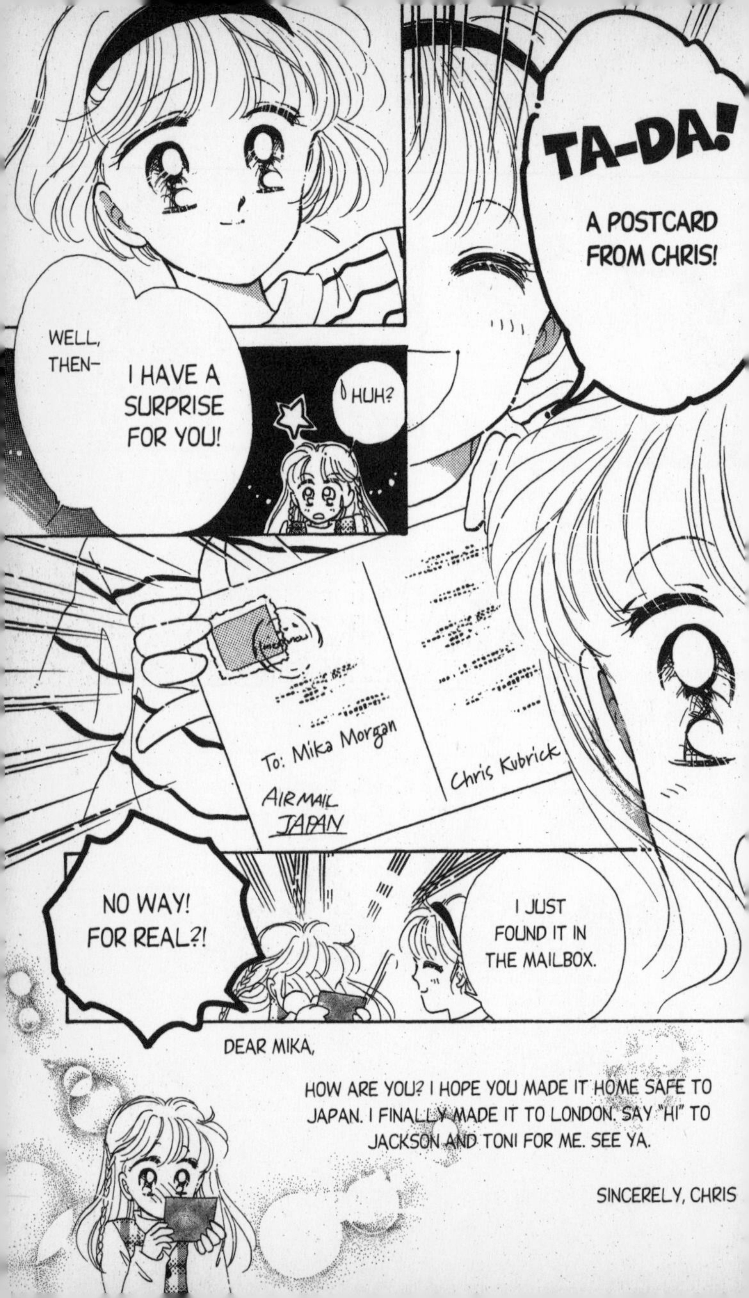
WELL, THEN–
I HAVE A SURPRISE FOR YOU!
HUH?
TA-DA!
A POSTCARD FROM CHRIS!
To: Mika Morgan
AIRMAIL
JAPAN
Chris Kubrick
NO WAY! FOR REAL?!
I JUST FOUND IT IN THE MAILBOX.
DEAR MIKA,
HOW ARE YOU? I HOPE YOU MADE IT HOME SAFE TO JAPAN. I FINALLY MADE IT TO LONDON. SAY "HI" TO JACKSON AND TONI FOR ME. SEE YA.
SINCERELY, CHRIS

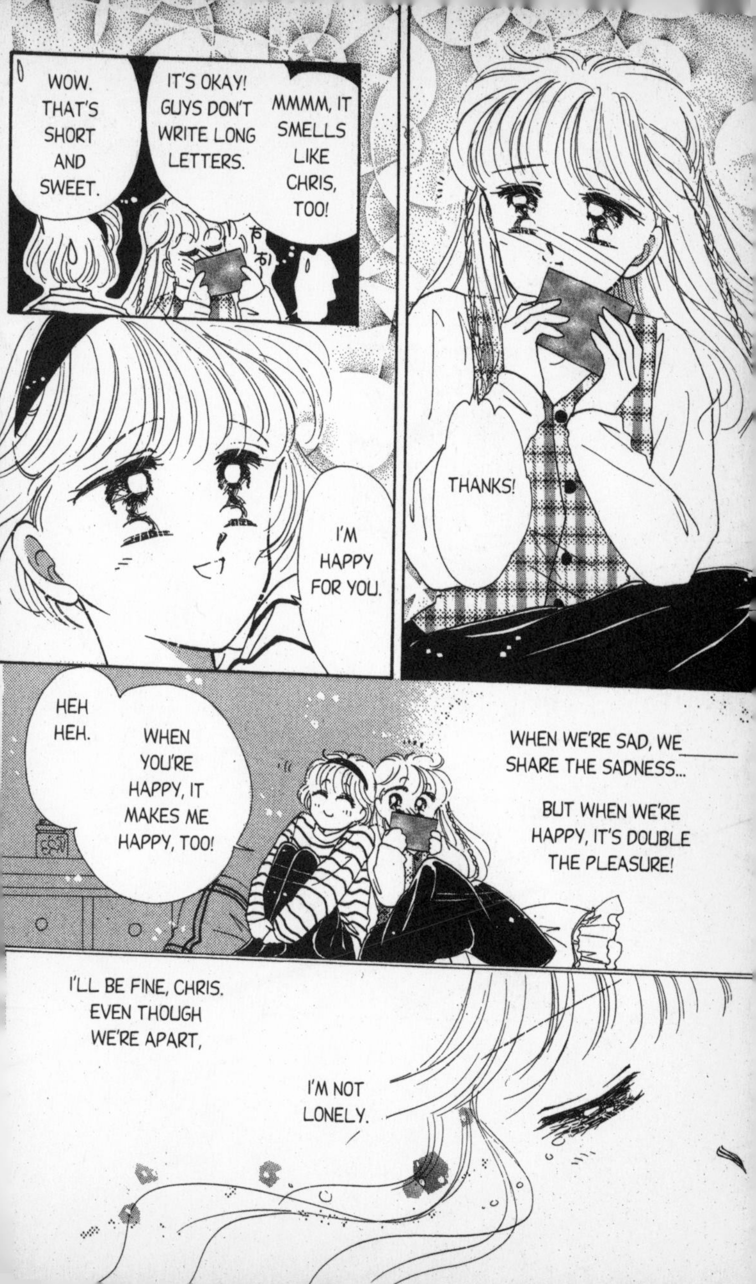
WOW. THAT'S SHORT AND SWEET.
IT'S OKAY! GUYS DON'T WRITE LONG LETTERS.
MMMM, IT SMELLS LIKE CHRIS, TOO!
I'M HAPPY FOR YOU.
THANKS!
HEH HEH.
WHEN YOU'RE HAPPY, IT MAKES ME HAPPY, TOO!
WHEN WE'RE SAD, WE SHARE THE SADNESS...
BUT WHEN WE'RE HAPPY, IT'S DOUBLE THE PLEASURE!
I'LL BE FINE, CHRIS. EVEN THOUGH WE'RE APART,
I'M NOT LONELY.

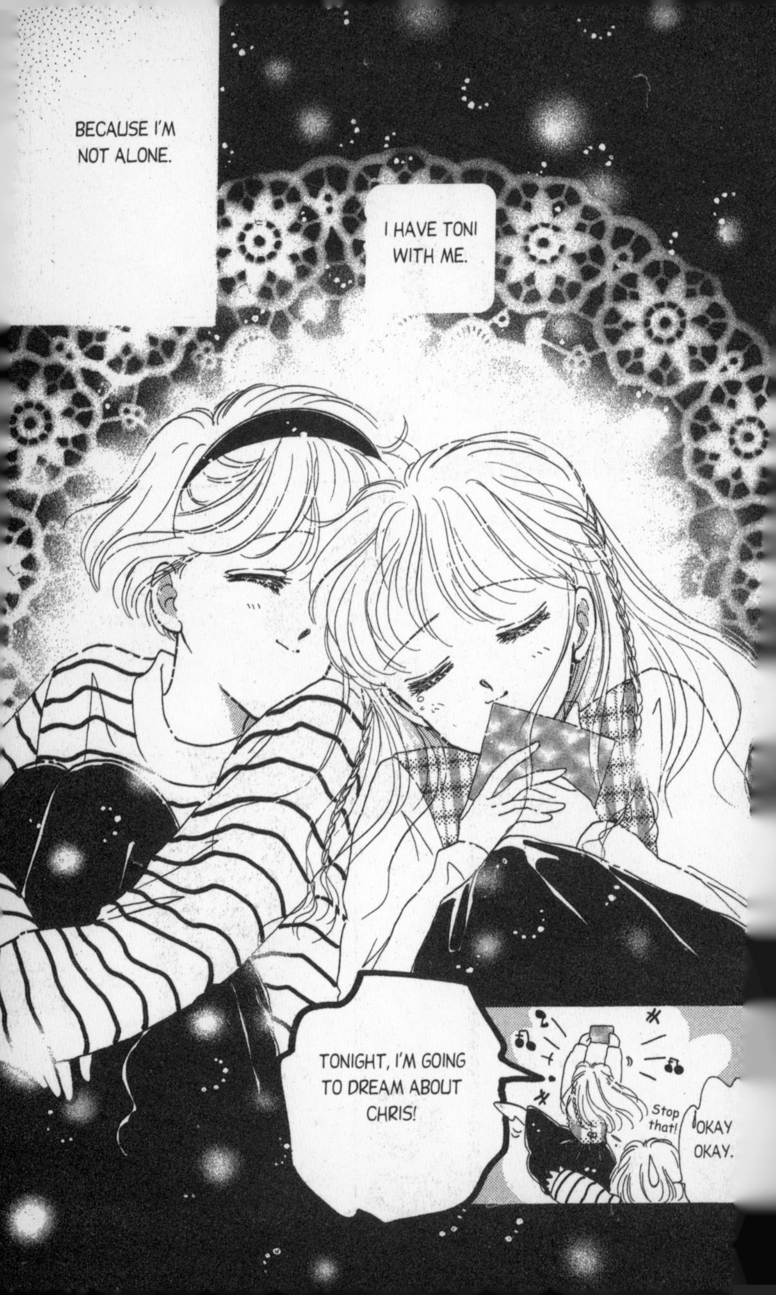
BECAUSE I'M NOT ALONE.
I HAVE TONI WITH ME.
TONIGHT, I'M GOING TO DREAM ABOUT CHRIS!
Stop that!
OKAY OKAY.

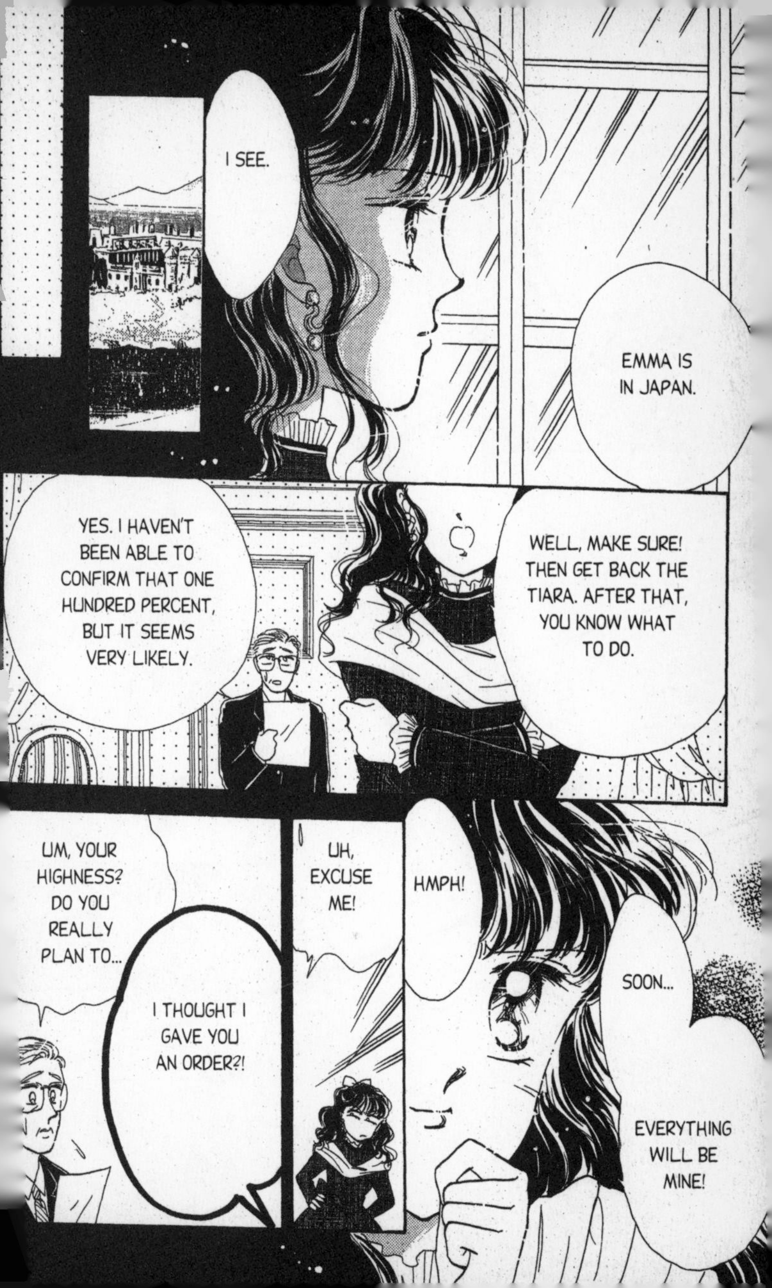
I SEE.
EMMA IS IN JAPAN.
YES. I HAVEN'T BEEN ABLE TO CONFIRM THAT ONE HUNDRED PERCENT, BUT IT SEEMS VERY LIKELY.
WELL, MAKE SURE! THEN GET BACK THE TIARA. AFTER THAT, YOU KNOW WHAT TO DO.
UM, YOUR HIGHNESS? DO YOU REALLY PLAN TO...
I THOUGHT I GAVE YOU AN ORDER?!
UH, EXCUSE ME!
HMPH!
SOON...
EVERYTHING WILL BE MINE!

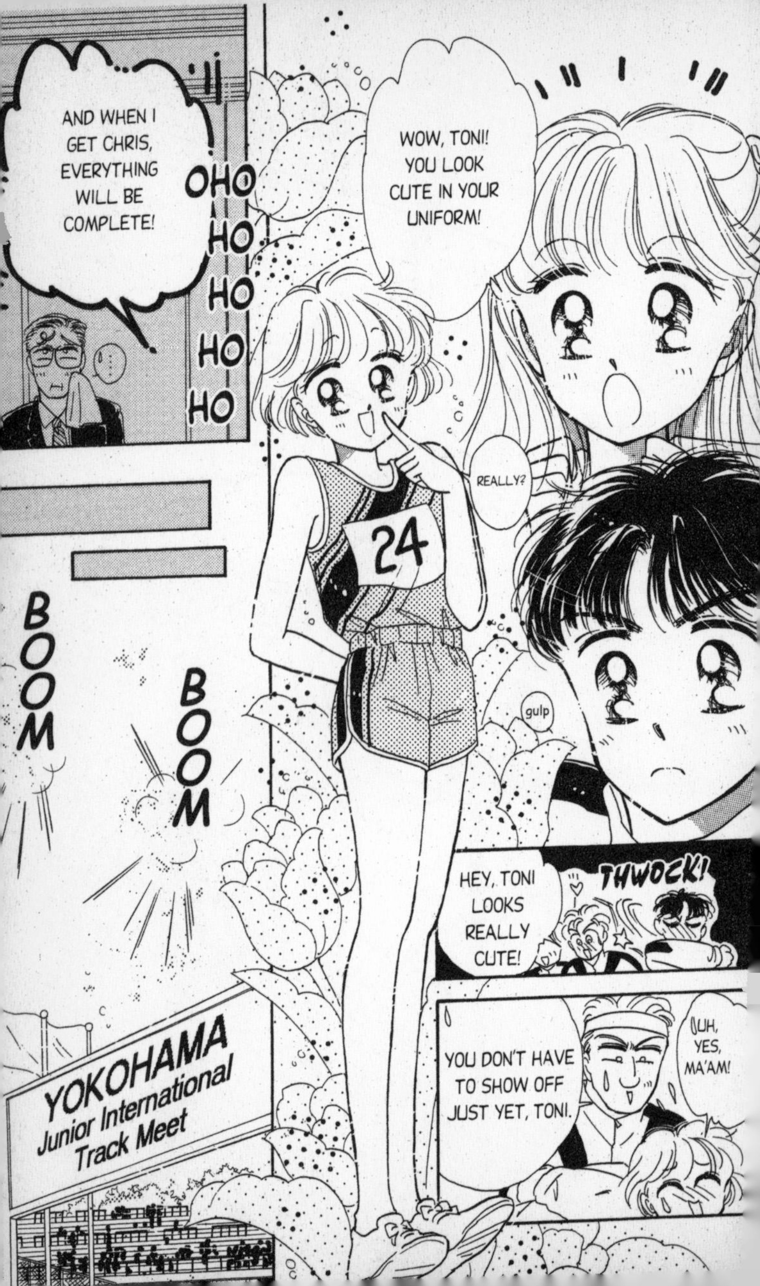

...AND WHEN I GET CHRIS, EVERYTHING WILL BE COMPLETE!
OHO HO HO HO HO
!!
BOOM
BOOM
YOKOHAMA Junior International Track Meet
WOW, TONI! YOU LOOK CUTE IN YOUR UNIFORM!
REALLY?
24
gulp
HEY, TONI LOOKS REALLY CUTE!
THWOCK!
YOU DON'T HAVE TO SHOW OFF JUST YET, TONI.
UH, YES, MA'AM!

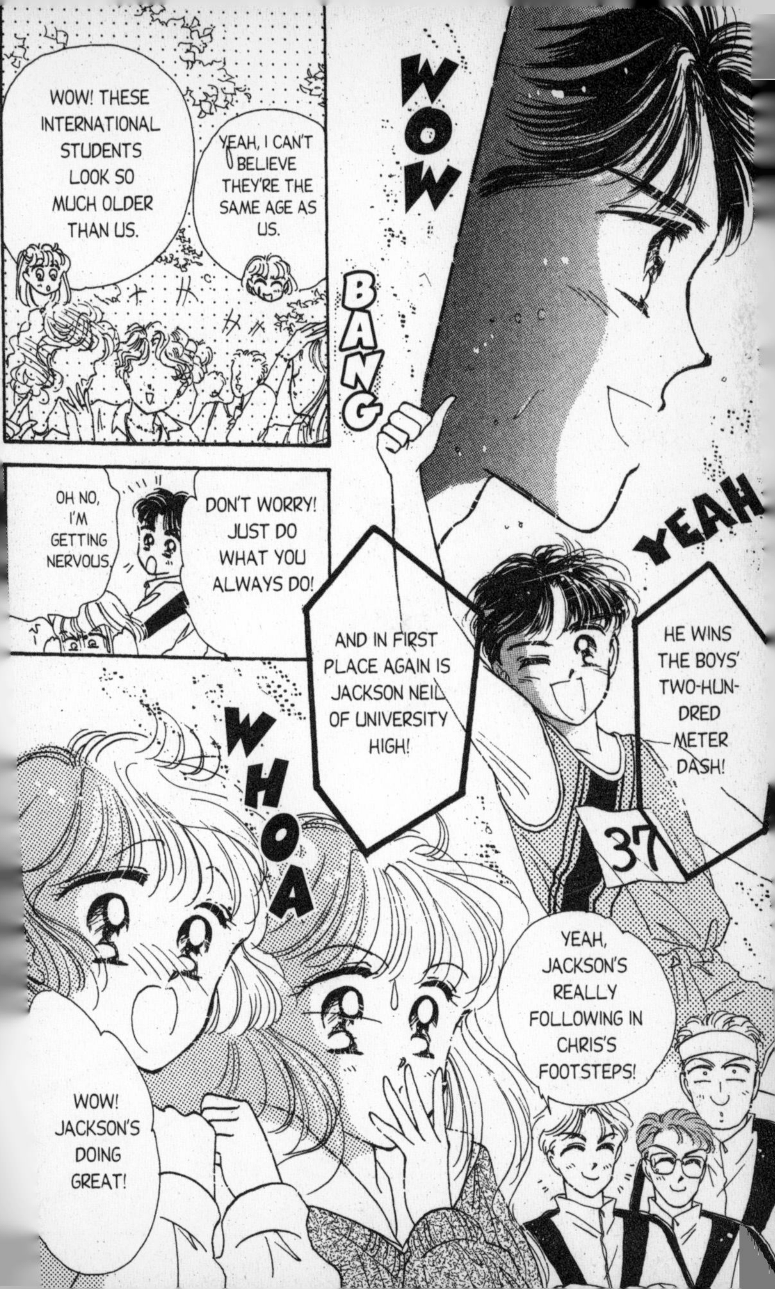
WOW! THESE INTERNATIONAL STUDENTS LOOK SO MUCH OLDER THAN US.
YEAH, I CAN'T BELIEVE THEY'RE THE SAME AGE AS US.
OH NO, I'M GETTING NERVOUS.
DON'T WORRY! JUST DO WHAT YOU ALWAYS DO!
WOW
BANG
YEAH
WHOA
AND IN FIRST PLACE AGAIN IS JACKSON NEIL OF UNIVERSITY HIGH!
HE WINS THE BOYS' TWO-HUN-DRED METER DASH!
37
WOW! JACKSON'S DOING GREAT!
YEAH, JACKSON'S REALLY FOLLOWING IN CHRIS'S FOOTSTEPS!

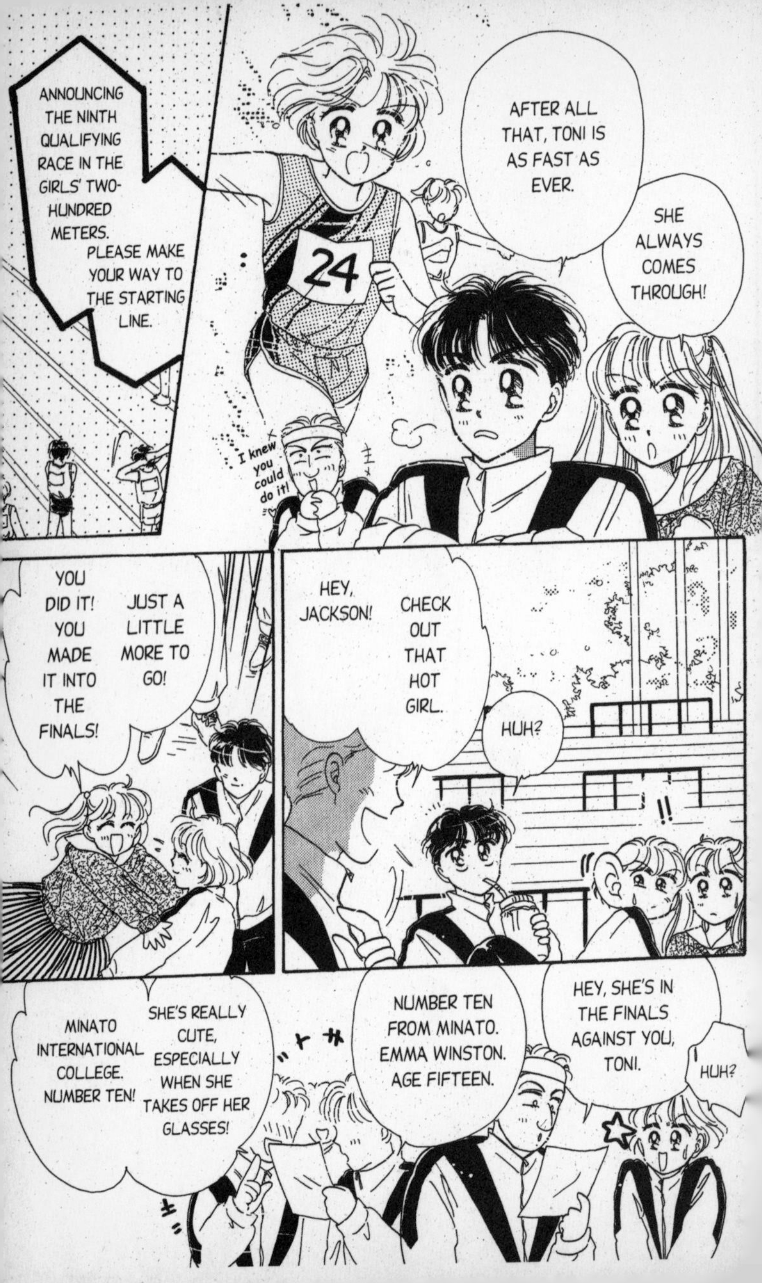
ANNOUNCING THE NINTH QUALIFYING RACE IN THE GIRLS' TWO-HUNDRED METERS. PLEASE MAKE YOUR WAY TO THE STARTING LINE.
24
AFTER ALL THAT, TONI IS AS FAST AS EVER.
SHE ALWAYS COMES THROUGH!
I knew you could do it!
YOU DID IT! YOU MADE IT INTO THE FINALS!
JUST A LITTLE MORE TO GO!
HEY, JACKSON!
CHECK OUT THAT HOT GIRL.
HUH?
!!
MINATO INTERNATIONAL COLLEGE. NUMBER TEN!
SHE'S REALLY CUTE, ESPECIALLY WHEN SHE TAKES OFF HER GLASSES!
NUMBER TEN FROM MINATO. EMMA WINSTON. AGE FIFTEEN.
HEY, SHE'S IN THE FINALS AGAINST YOU, TONI.
HUH?

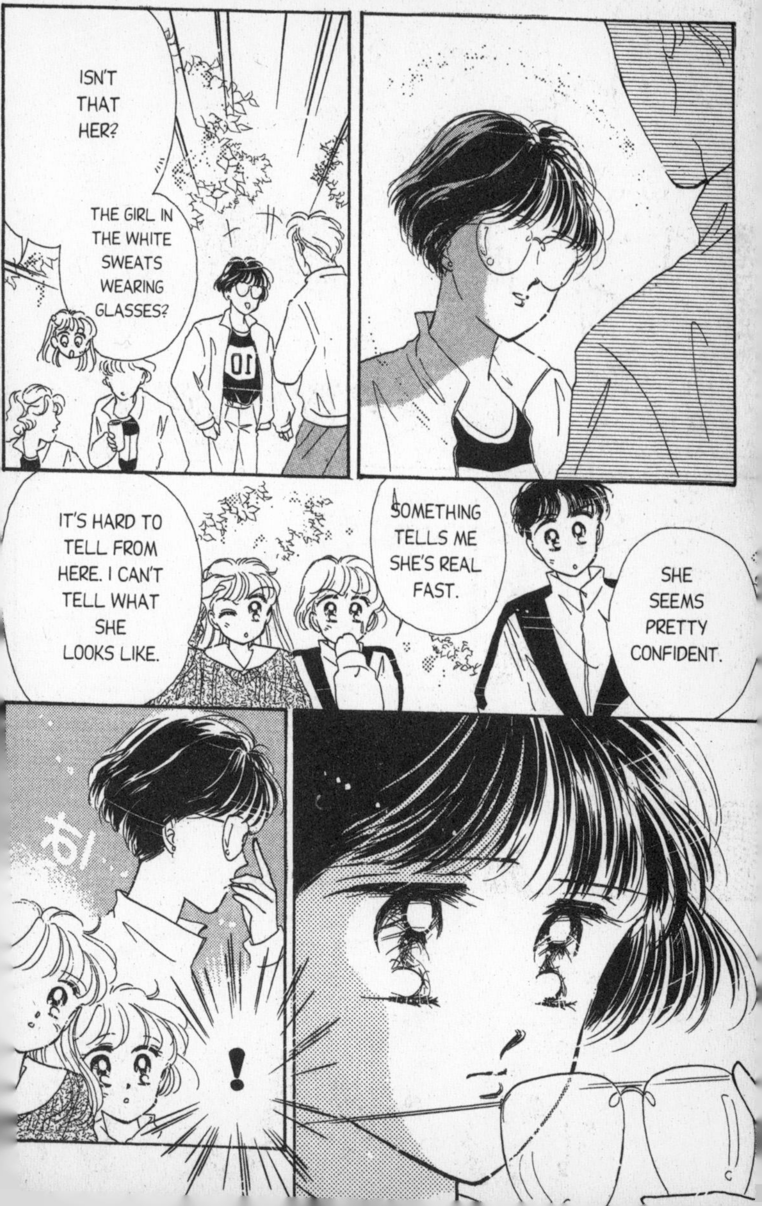
ISN'T THAT HER?
THE GIRL IN THE WHITE SWEATS WEARING GLASSES?
IT'S HARD TO TELL FROM HERE. I CAN'T TELL WHAT SHE LOOKS LIKE.
SOMETHING TELLS ME SHE'S REAL FAST.
SHE SEEMS PRETTY CONFIDENT.
お!
!

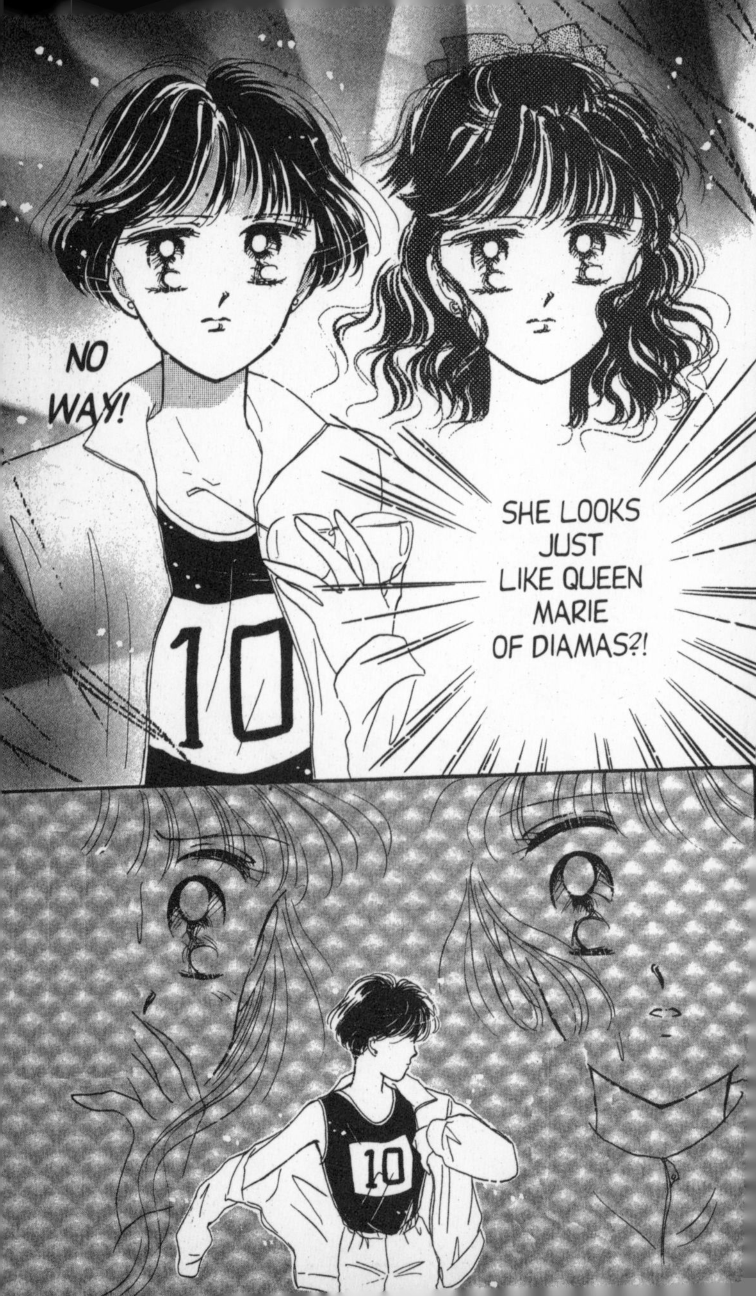
NO WAY!
SHE LOOKS JUST LIKE QUEEN MARIE OF DIAMAS?!

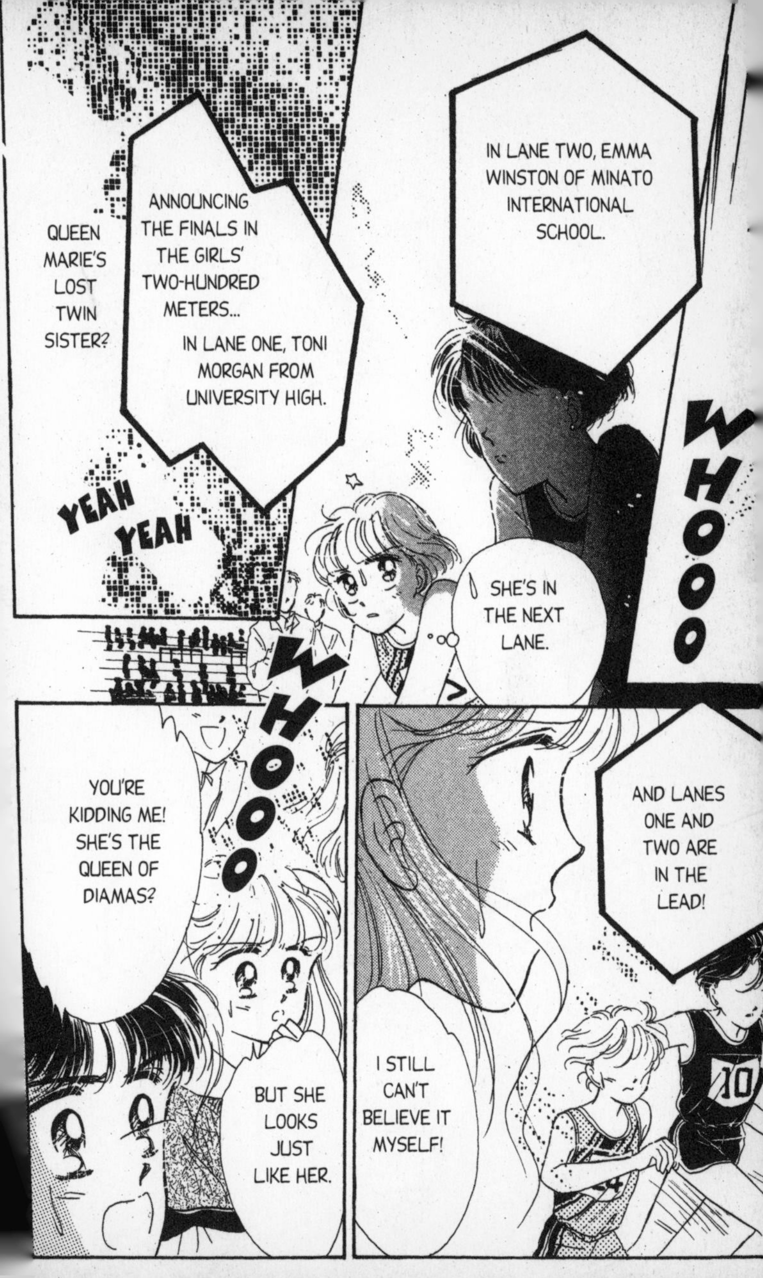
QUEEN MARIE'S LOST TWIN SISTER?
ANNOUNCING THE FINALS IN THE GIRLS' TWO-HUNDRED METERS...
IN LANE ONE, TONI MORGAN FROM UNIVERSITY HIGH.
YEAH YEAH
IN LANE TWO, EMMA WINSTON OF MINATO INTERNATIONAL SCHOOL.
SHE'S IN THE NEXT LANE.
WHOOOO
WHOOOO
YOU'RE KIDDING ME! SHE'S THE QUEEN OF DIAMAS?
BUT SHE LOOKS JUST LIKE HER.
AND LANES ONE AND TWO ARE IN THE LEAD!
I STILL CAN'T BELIEVE IT MYSELF!

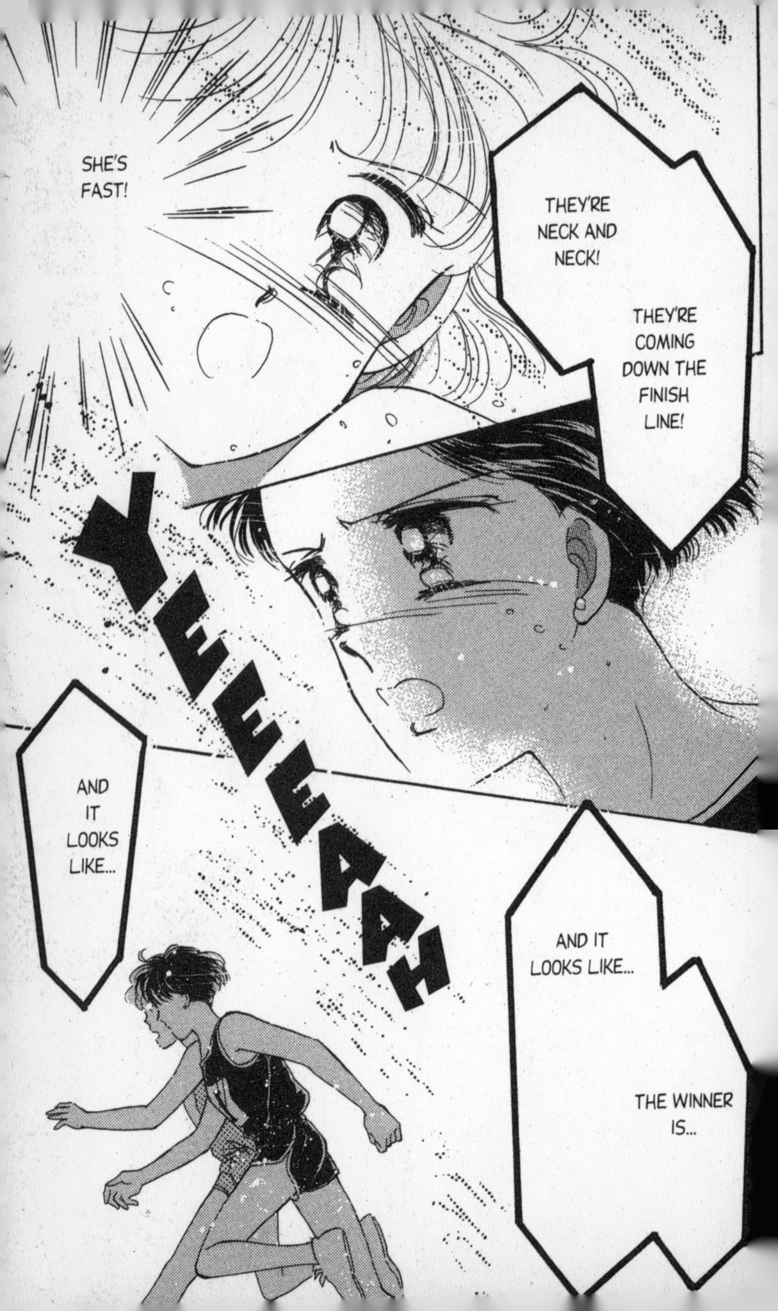
SHE'S FAST!
THEY'RE NECK AND NECK!
THEY'RE COMING DOWN THE FINISH LINE!
YEEEAAH
AND IT LOOKS LIKE...
AND IT LOOKS LIKE...
THE WINNER IS...

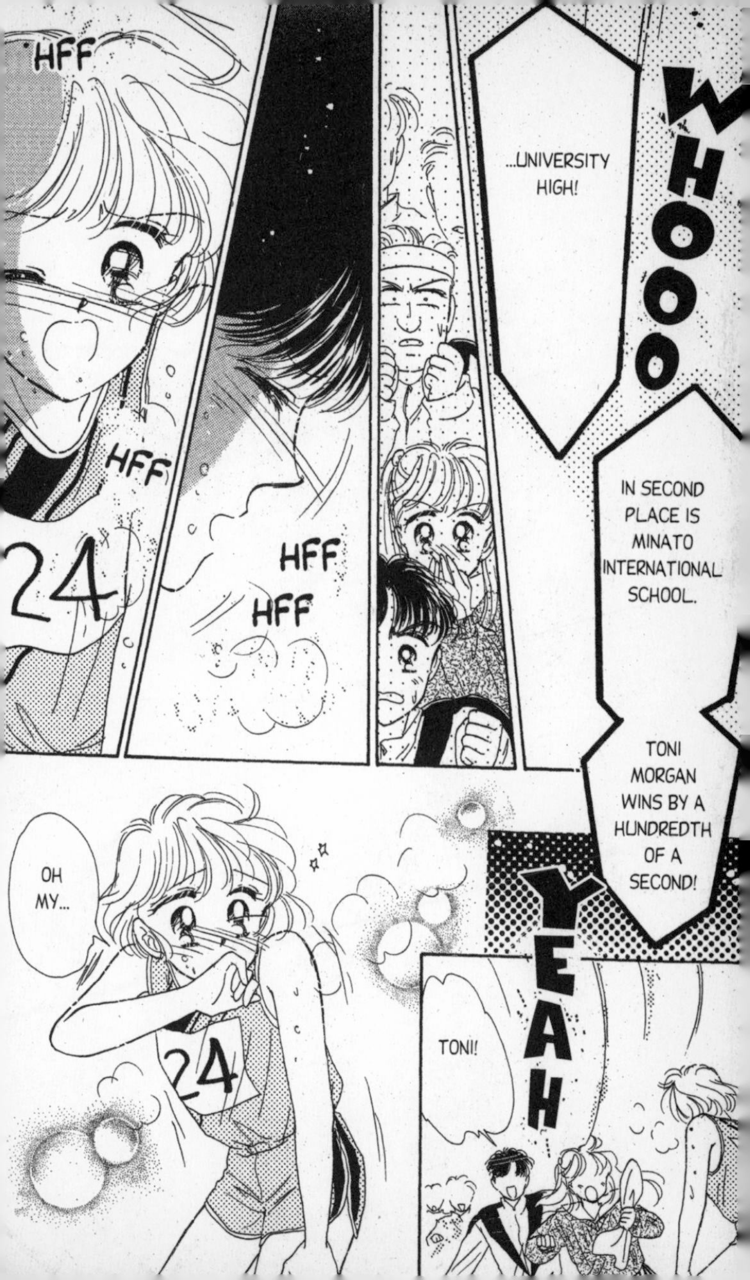
HFF
HFF
HFF
HFF
...UNIVERSITY HIGH!
WHOOO
IN SECOND PLACE IS MINATO INTERNATIONAL SCHOOL.
TONI MORGAN WINS BY A HUNDREDTH OF A SECOND!
OH MY...
YEAH
TONI!

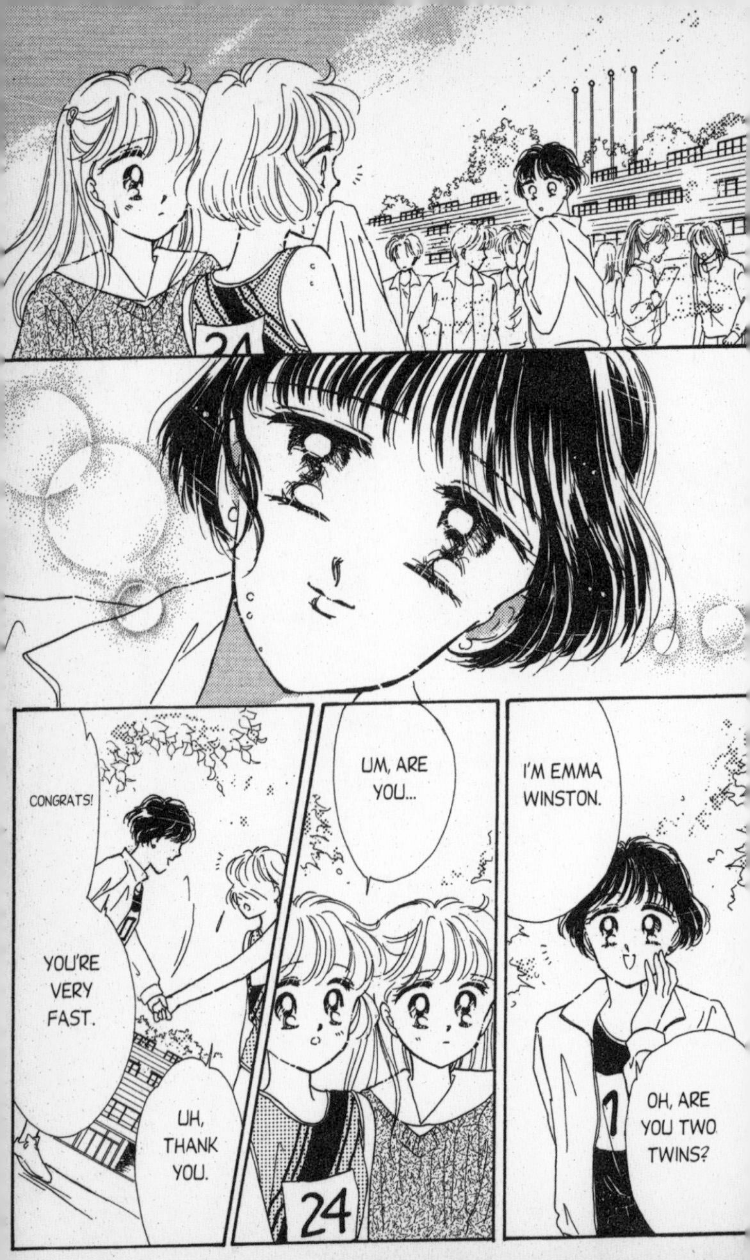
CONGRATS!
YOU'RE VERY FAST.
UH, THANK YOU.
24
UM, ARE YOU...
I'M EMMA WINSTON.
OH, ARE YOU TWO TWINS?

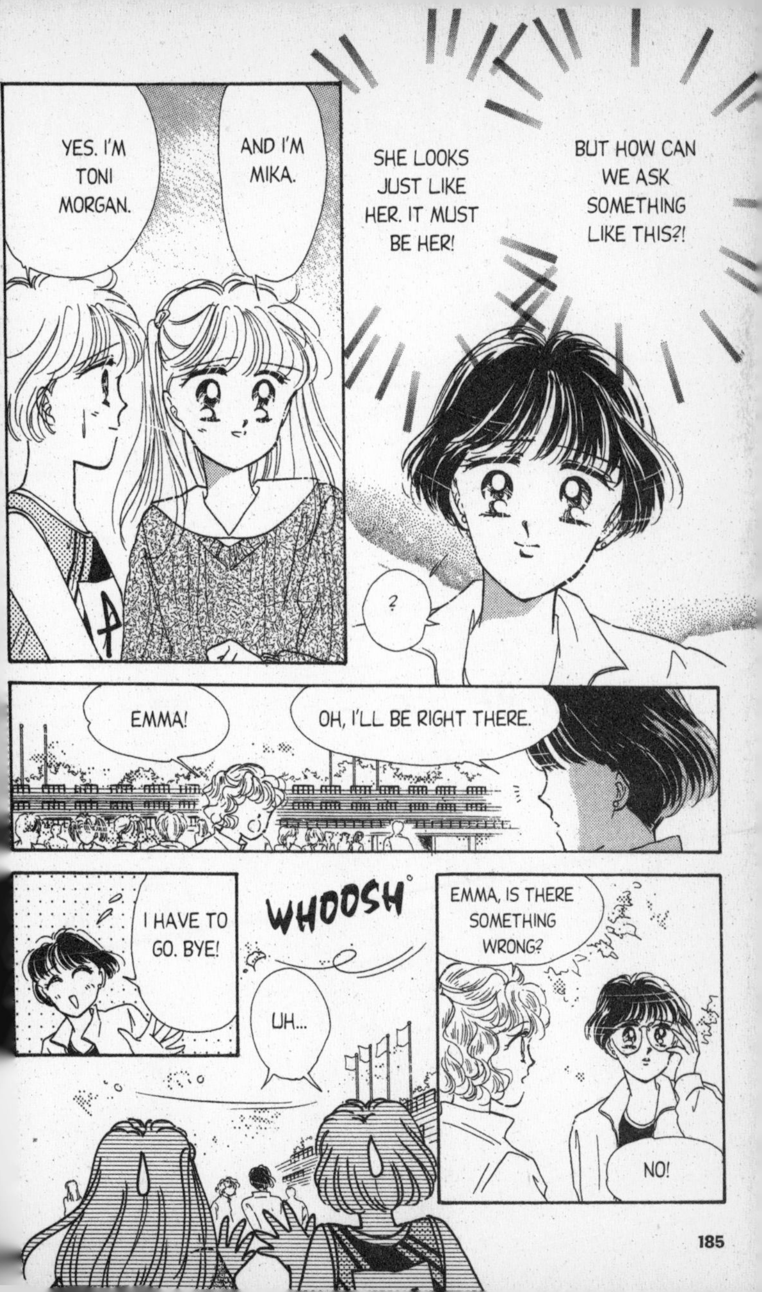
YES. I'M TONI MORGAN.
AND I'M MIKA.
SHE LOOKS JUST LIKE HER. IT MUST BE HER!
BUT HOW CAN WE ASK SOMETHING LIKE THIS?!
?
EMMA!
OH, I'LL BE RIGHT THERE.
I HAVE TO GO. BYE!
WHOOSH
UH...
EMMA, IS THERE SOMETHING WRONG?
NO!

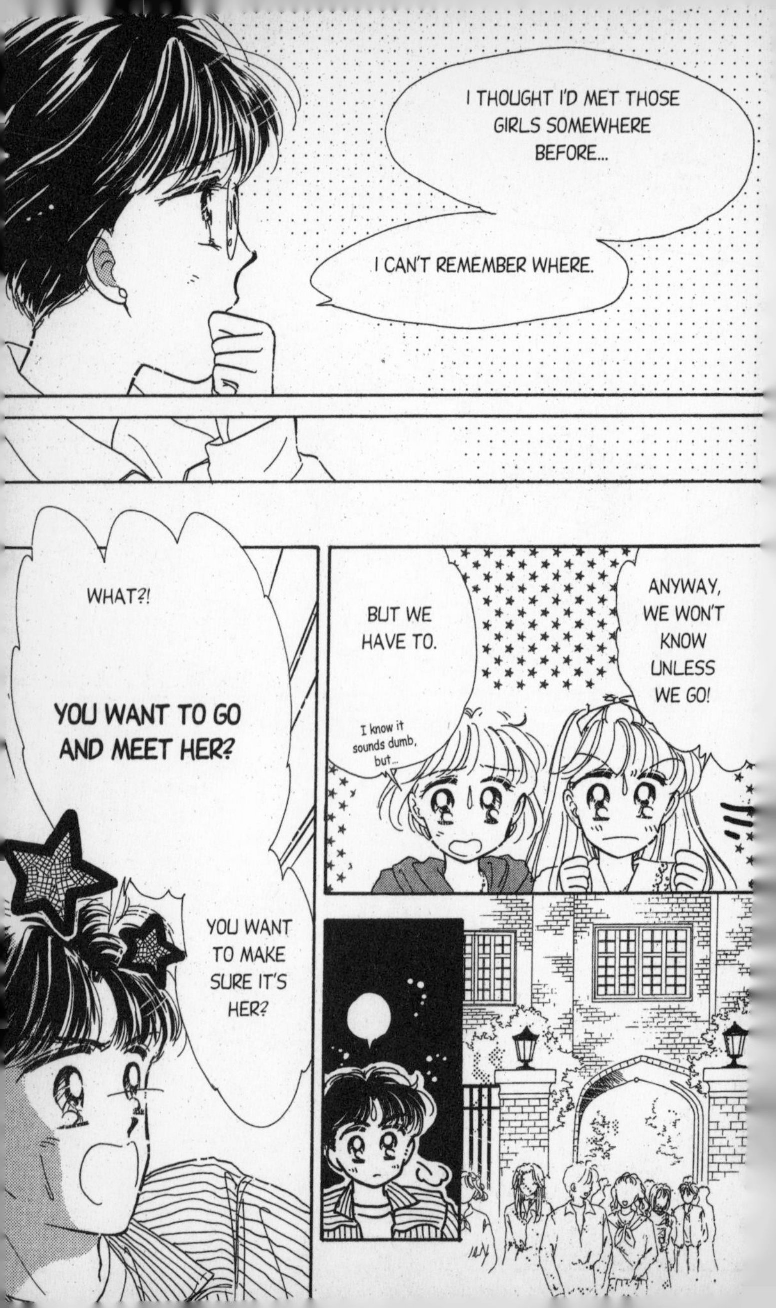
I THOUGHT I'D MET THOSE GIRLS SOMEWHERE BEFORE...
I CAN'T REMEMBER WHERE.
WHAT?!
YOU WANT TO GO AND MEET HER?
YOU WANT TO MAKE SURE IT'S HER?
BUT WE HAVE TO.
I know it sounds dumb, but...
ANYWAY, WE WON'T KNOW UNLESS WE GO!

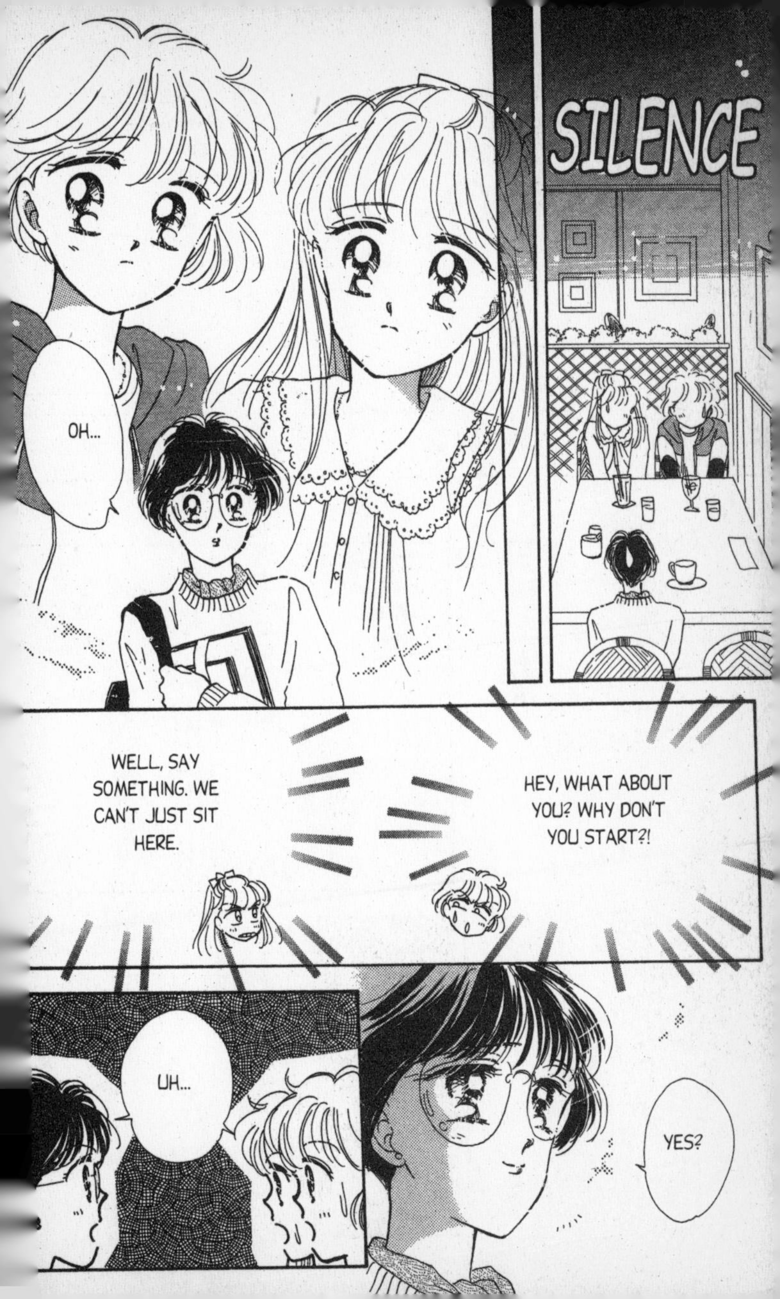
OH...
SILENCE
WELL, SAY SOMETHING. WE CAN'T JUST SIT HERE.
HEY, WHAT ABOUT YOU? WHY DON'T YOU START?!
UH...
YES?

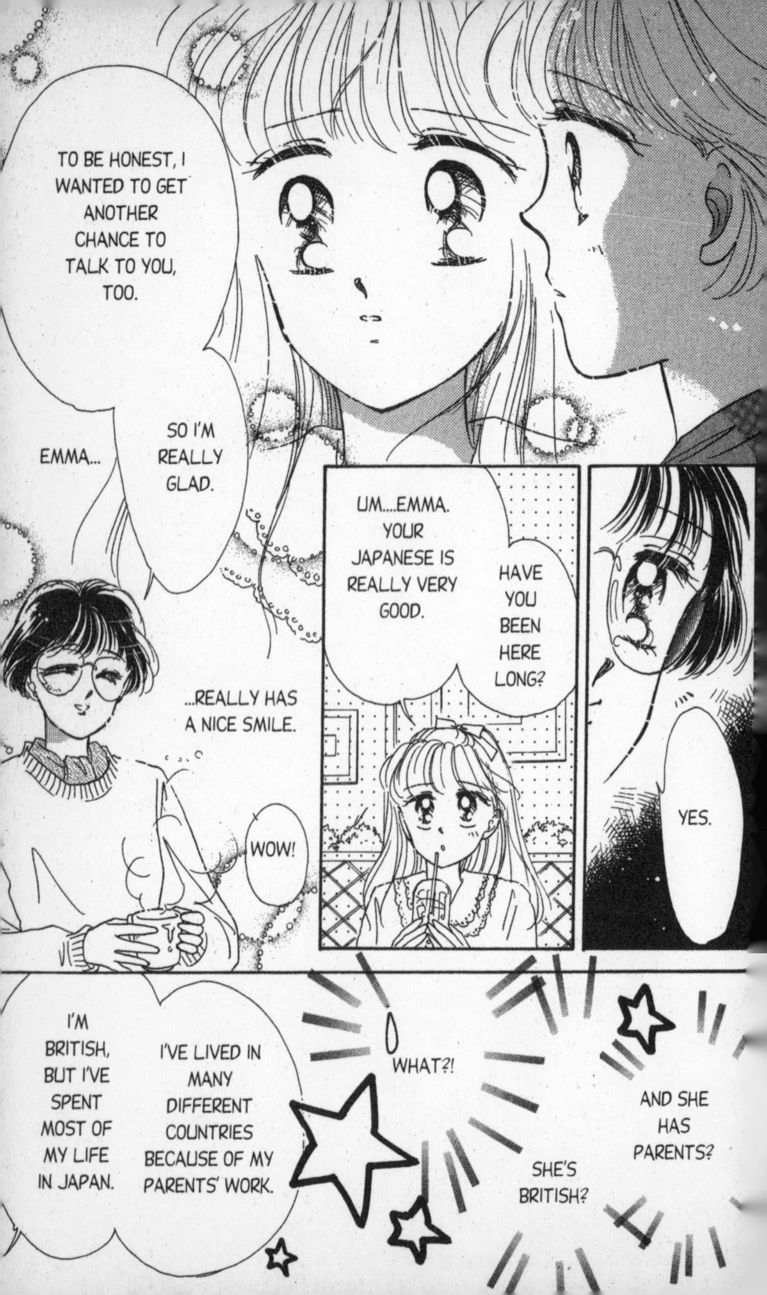
TO BE HONEST, I WANTED TO GET ANOTHER CHANCE TO TALK TO YOU, TOO.
SO I'M REALLY GLAD.
EMMA...
...REALLY HAS A NICE SMILE.
WOW!
UM....EMMA. YOUR JAPANESE IS REALLY VERY GOOD.
HAVE YOU BEEN HERE LONG?
YES.
I'M BRITISH, BUT I'VE SPENT MOST OF MY LIFE IN JAPAN.
I'VE LIVED IN MANY DIFFERENT COUNTRIES BECAUSE OF MY PARENTS' WORK.
WHAT?!
SHE'S BRITISH?
AND SHE HAS PARENTS?

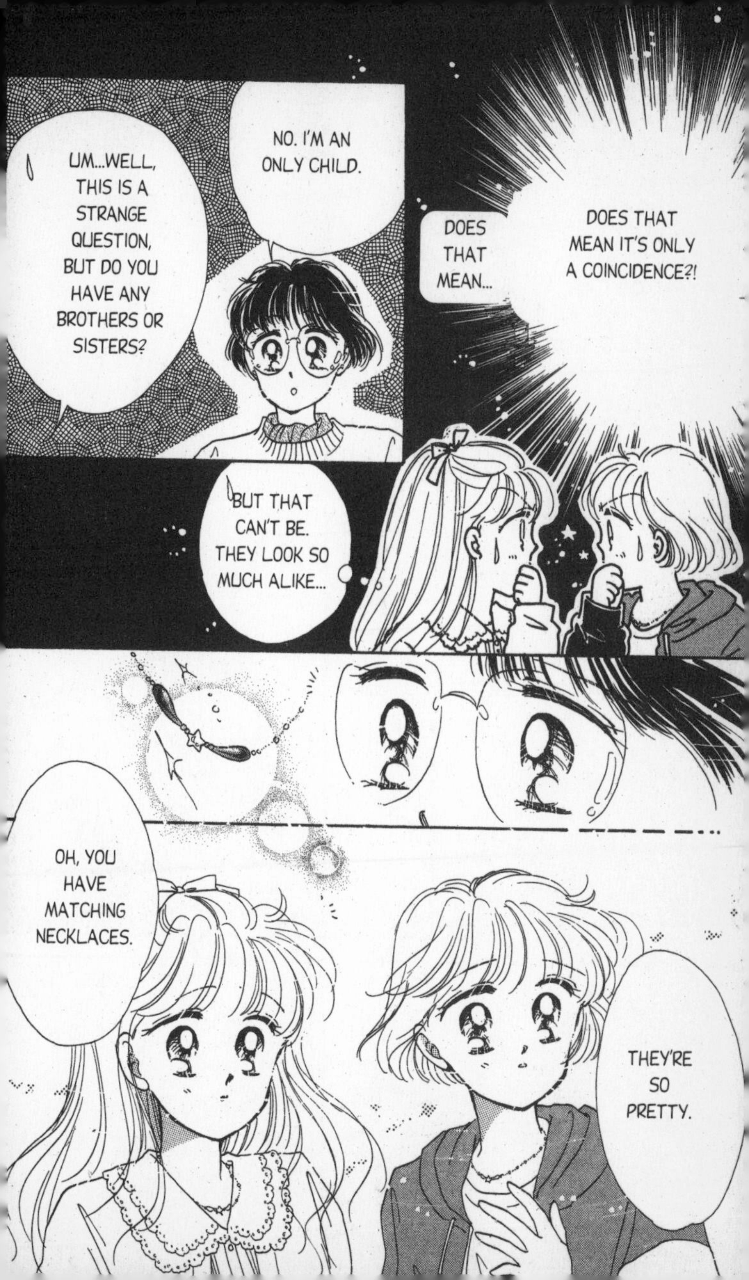
UM...WELL, THIS IS A STRANGE QUESTION, BUT DO YOU HAVE ANY BROTHERS OR SISTERS?
NO. I'M AN ONLY CHILD.
DOES THAT MEAN...
DOES THAT MEAN IT'S ONLY A COINCIDENCE?!
BUT THAT CAN'T BE. THEY LOOK SO MUCH ALIKE...
OH, YOU HAVE MATCHING NECKLACES.
THEY'RE SO PRETTY.

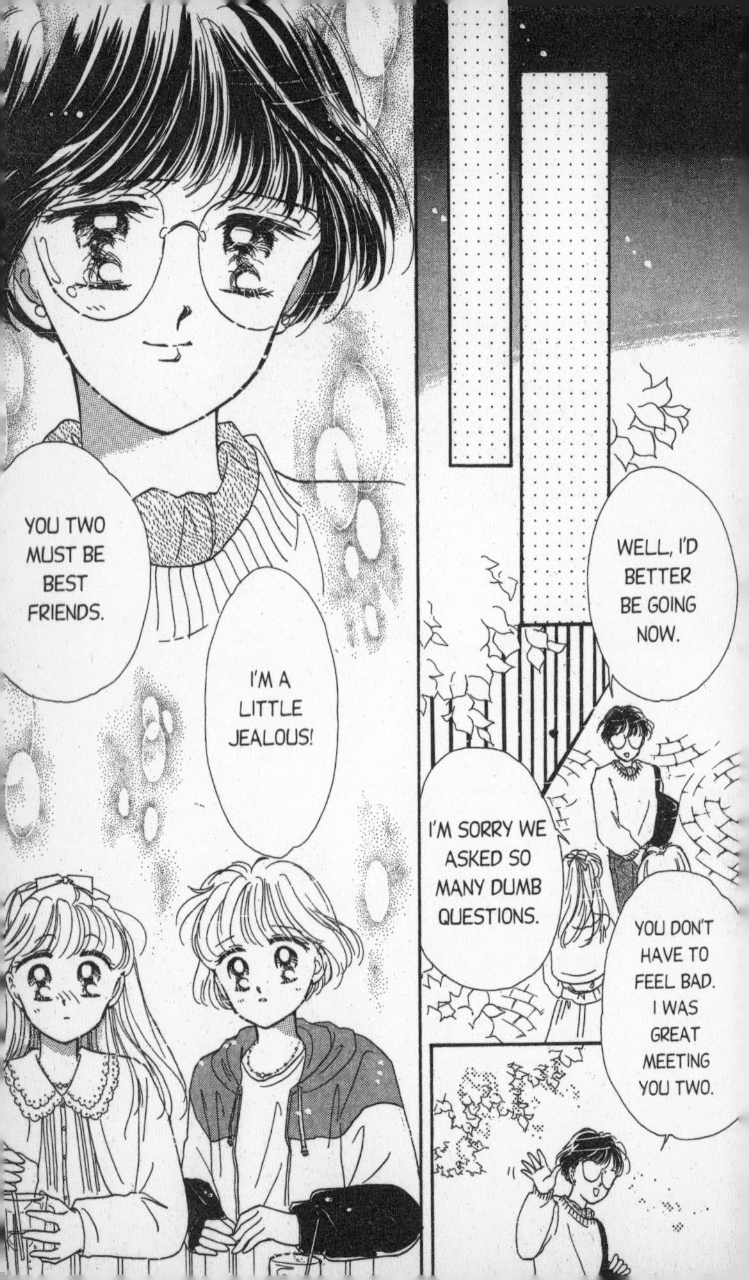
YOU TWO MUST BE BEST FRIENDS.
I'M A LITTLE JEALOUS!
WELL, I'D BETTER BE GOING NOW.
I'M SORRY WE ASKED SO MANY DUMB QUESTIONS.
YOU DON'T HAVE TO FEEL BAD. I WAS GREAT MEETING YOU TWO.

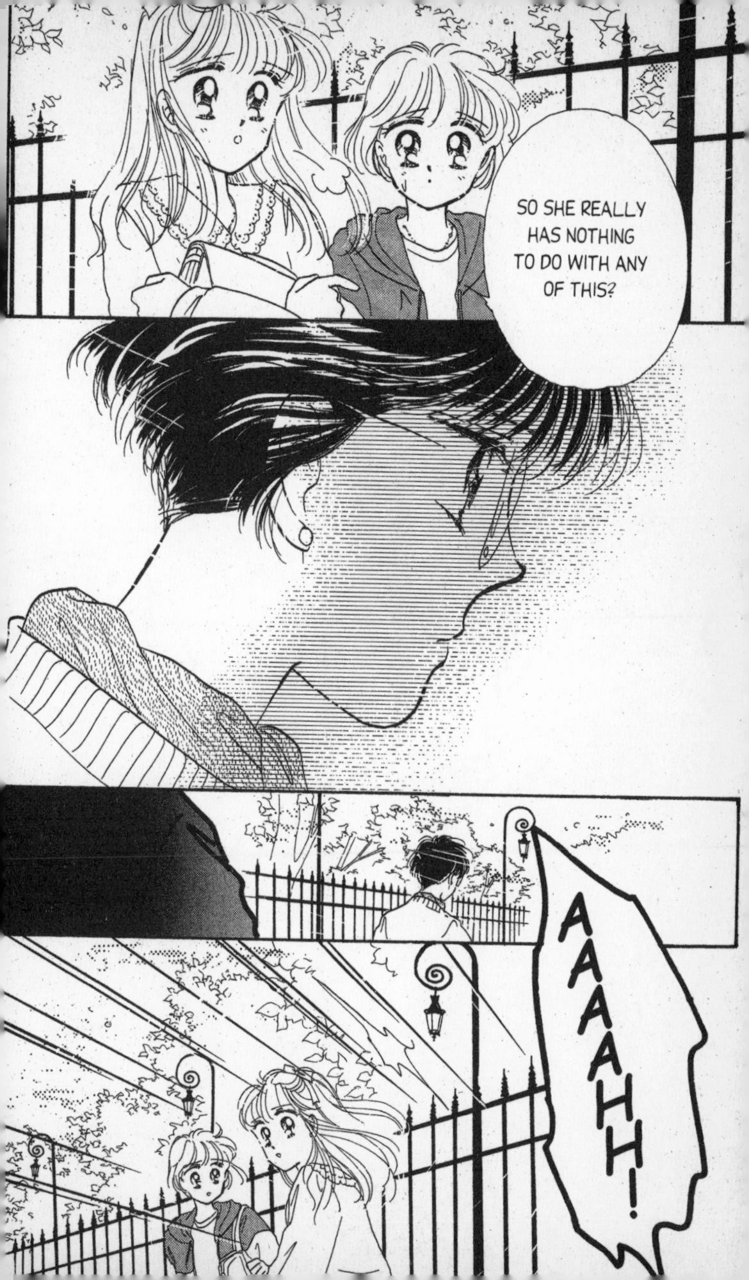
SO SHE REALLY HAS NOTHING TO DO WITH ANY OF THIS?
AAAAHH!

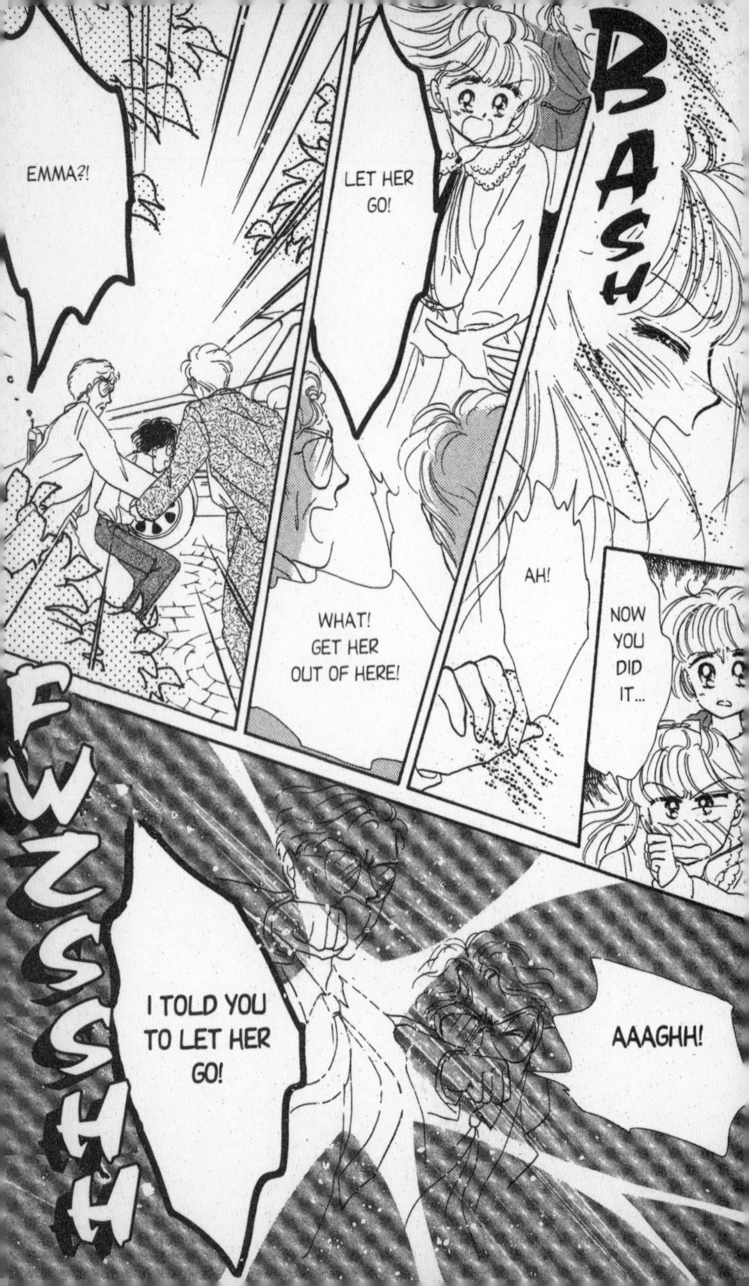

EMMA?!
LET HER GO!
WHAT! GET HER OUT OF HERE!
BASH
AH!
NOW YOU DID IT...
FWSSHH
I TOLD YOU TO LET HER GO!
AAAGHH!

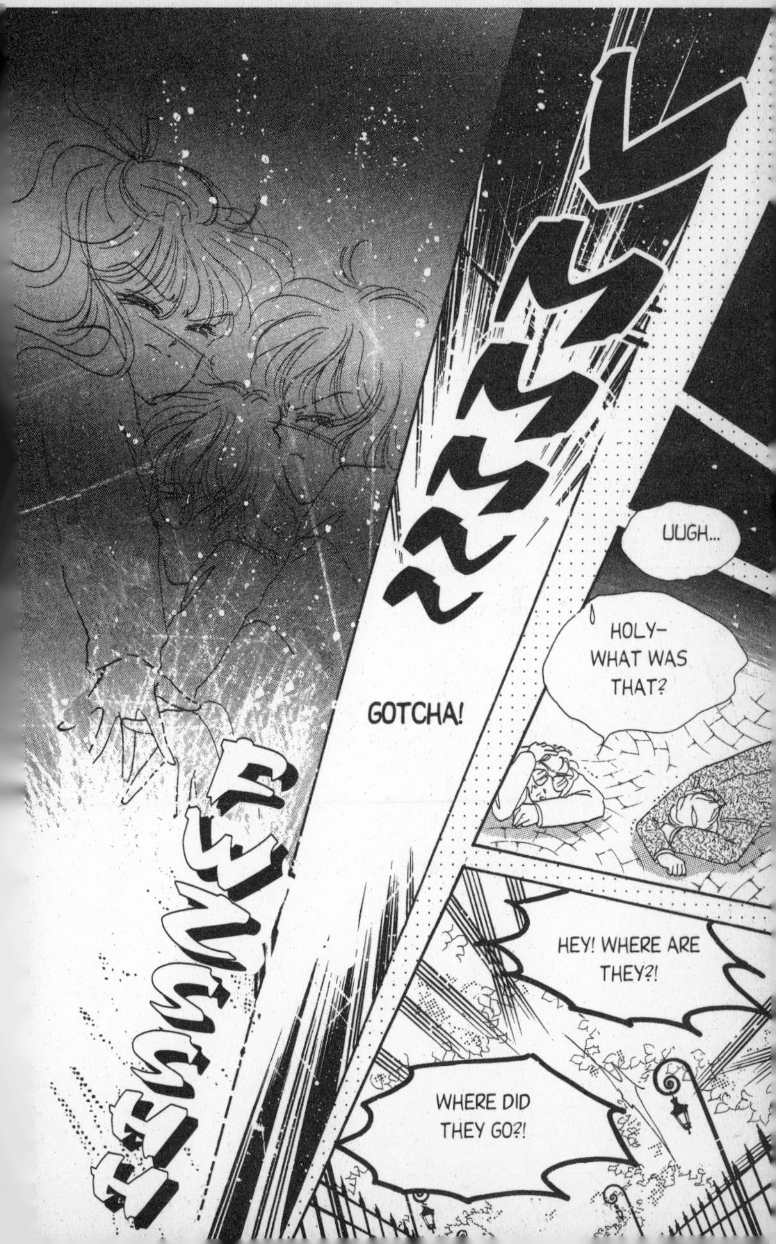
GOTCHA!
UUGH...
HOLY—
WHAT WAS
THAT?
HEY! WHERE ARE
THEY?!
WHERE DID
THEY GO?!

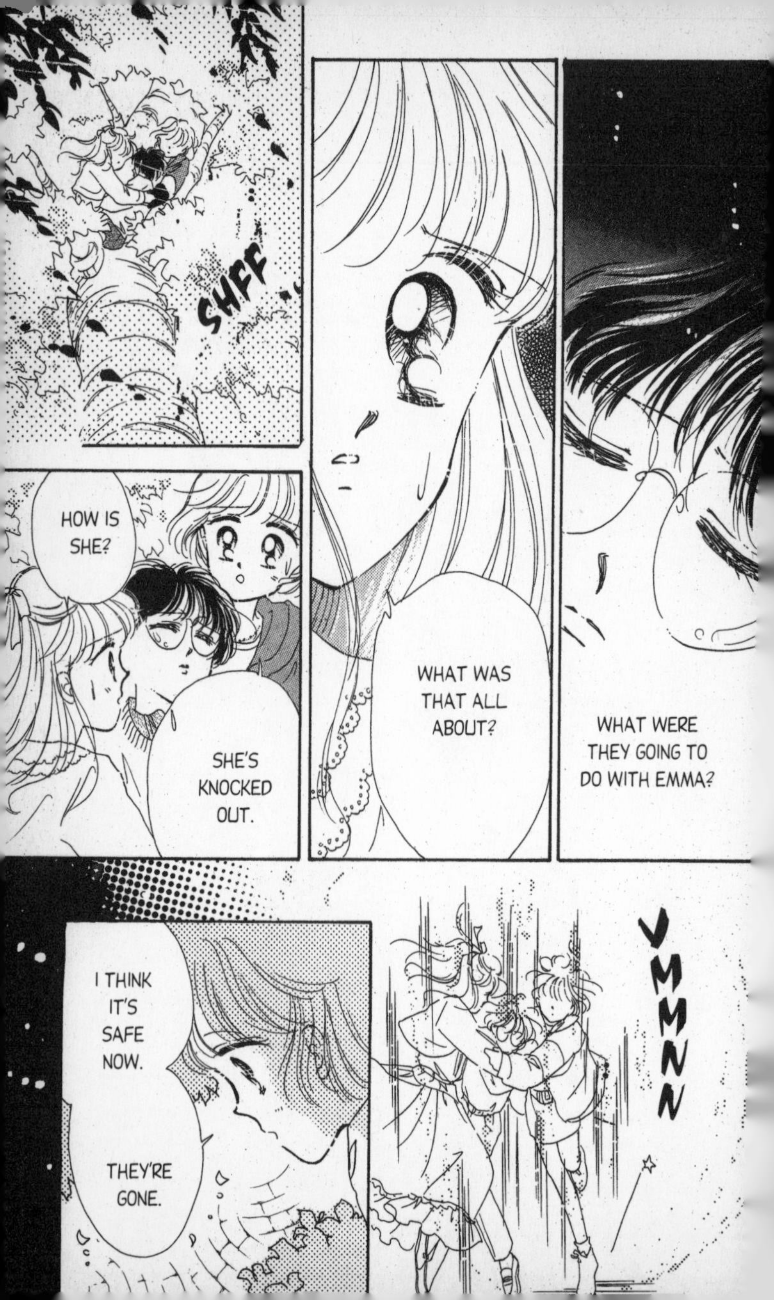
SHFF
HOW IS SHE?
SHE'S KNOCKED OUT.
WHAT WAS THAT ALL ABOUT?
WHAT WERE THEY GOING TO DO WITH EMMA?
I THINK IT'S SAFE NOW.
THEY'RE GONE.
VMMNN

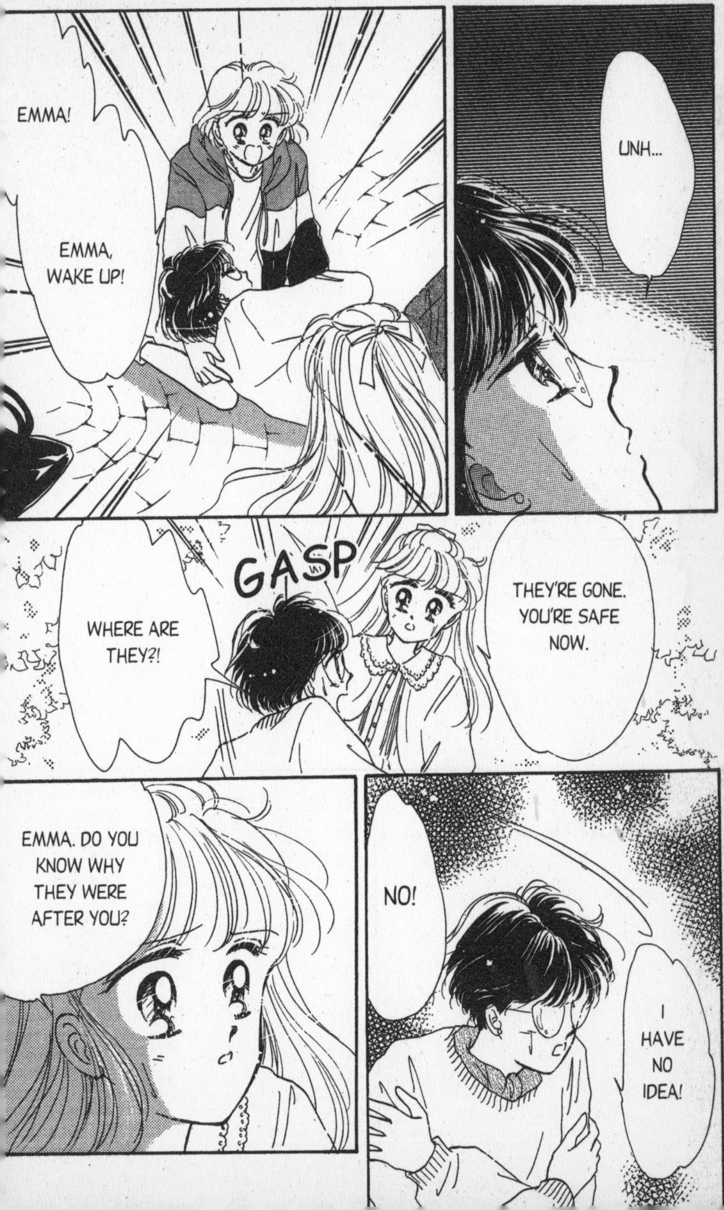
EMMA!
EMMA, WAKE UP!
UNH...
WHERE ARE THEY?!
GASP
THEY'RE GONE. YOU'RE SAFE NOW.
EMMA. DO YOU KNOW WHY THEY WERE AFTER YOU?
NO!
I HAVE NO IDEA!

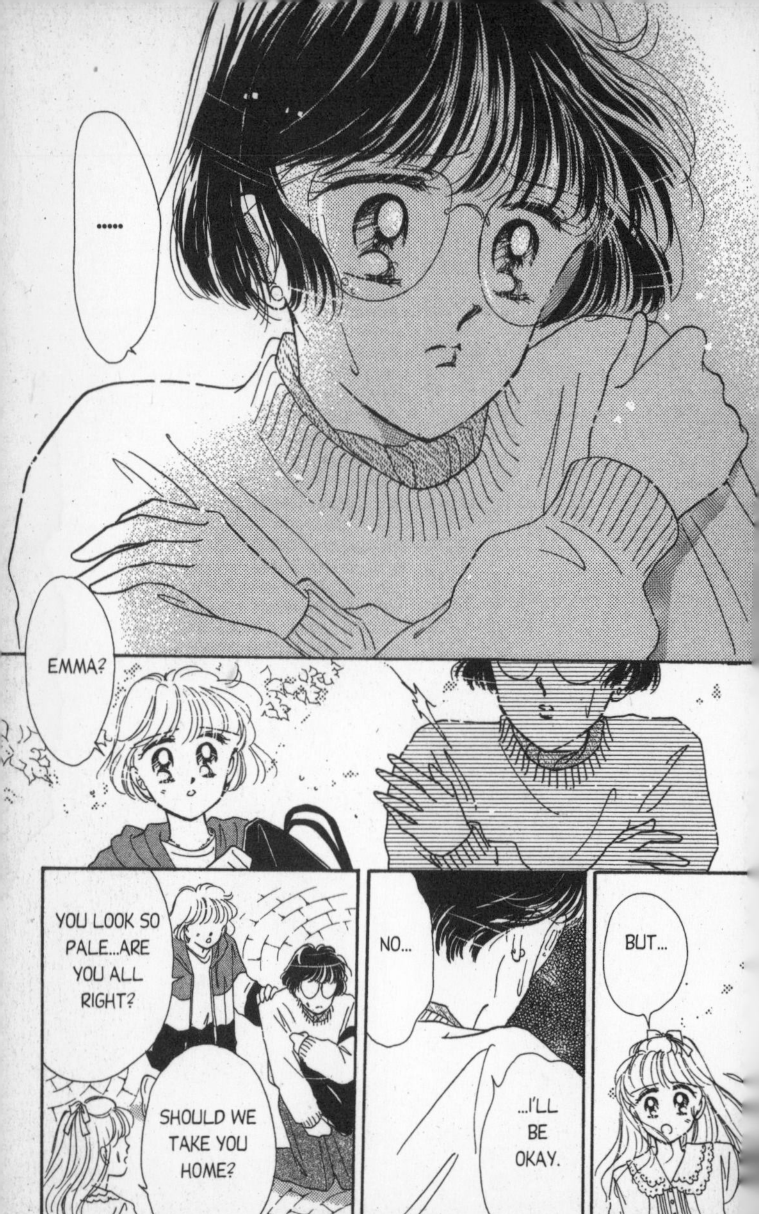
......
EMMA?
YOU LOOK SO PALE...ARE YOU ALL RIGHT?
SHOULD WE TAKE YOU HOME?
NO...
...I'LL BE OKAY.
BUT...

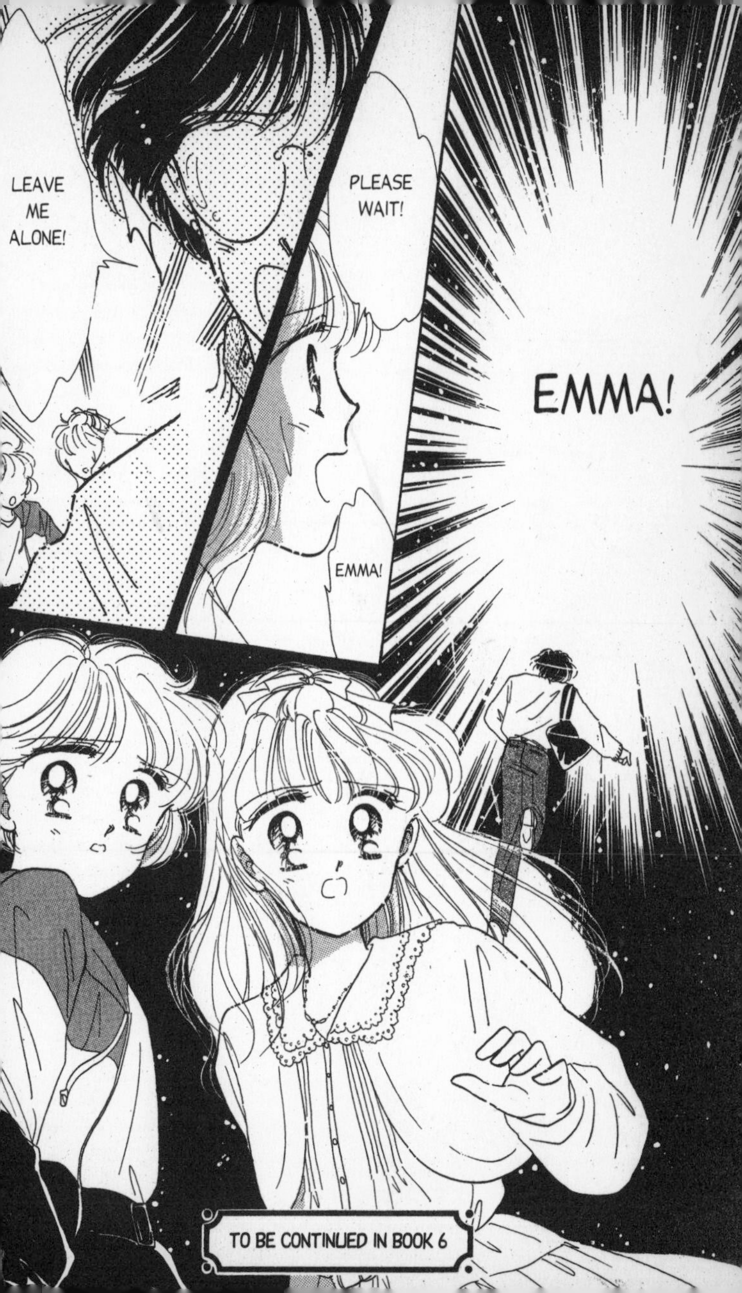
LEAVE ME ALONE!
PLEASE WAIT!
EMMA!
EMMA!
TO BE CONTINUED IN BOOK 6

IN COMMEMORATION OF BOOK 5: ANOTHER BONUS PAGE SPECIAL!

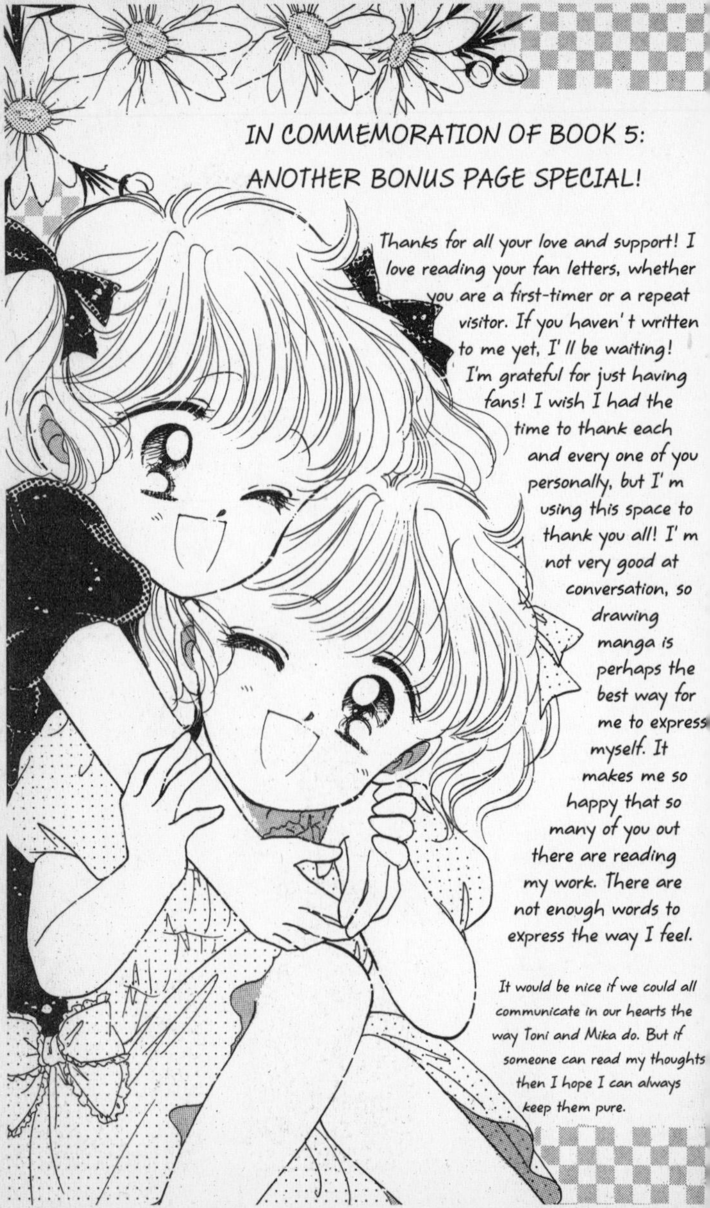

Thanks for all your love and support! I love reading your fan letters, whether you are a first-timer or a repeat visitor. If you haven't written to me yet, I'll be waiting! I'm grateful for just having fans! I wish I had the time to thank each and every one of you personally, but I'm using this space to thank you all! I'm not very good at conversation, so drawing manga is perhaps the best way for me to express myself. It makes me so happy that so many of you out there are reading my work. There are not enough words to express the way I feel.

It would be nice if we could all communicate in our hearts the way Toni and Mika do. But if someone can read my thoughts then I hope I can always keep them pure.

Well, then...I finally get to show you a little more of Toni and Mika's parents. Let's take a look...

YASUSHI MORGAN, AGE 43 ▶

Dad is such a warm person, but he's never home. His job? Well, let's see...he's a very successful stockbroker. In fact, he's a high-powered company man! You might not know if from looking at him, but he travels all over the world. (I wish I had a dad like this, heh heh.) I wonder why my manga always features old guys so often? Even among all my colleagues at "Nakayoshi," I'm probably number one when it comes to drawing old guys.

Typically, dads in comics are usually reading the paper (ha ha). But Toni and Mika's dad can read the English papers too. How about that?

The Daily Telegraph

TAKAE MORGAN (ON THE LEFT) AGE 40
NOE KANZAKI (ON THE RIGHT) AGE 40 ▶

Mom is a really strong person. She runs a beauty salon. Remember the wig Toni wore in Part 1? That's from Mom's store. And Mom has a twin sister, too! That's Auntie Noe. Noe is also married to a stockbroker. (But since she got married a bit late, they don't have any children yet.) They're currently living in London. Ah, it makes me jealous...

If you didn't already know, "Miracle Girls" is set in Yokohama. (Some of you may be thinking, "So what?") So why Yokohama? Because I grew up there. Hey, Yokohama is cool! I like it very much.

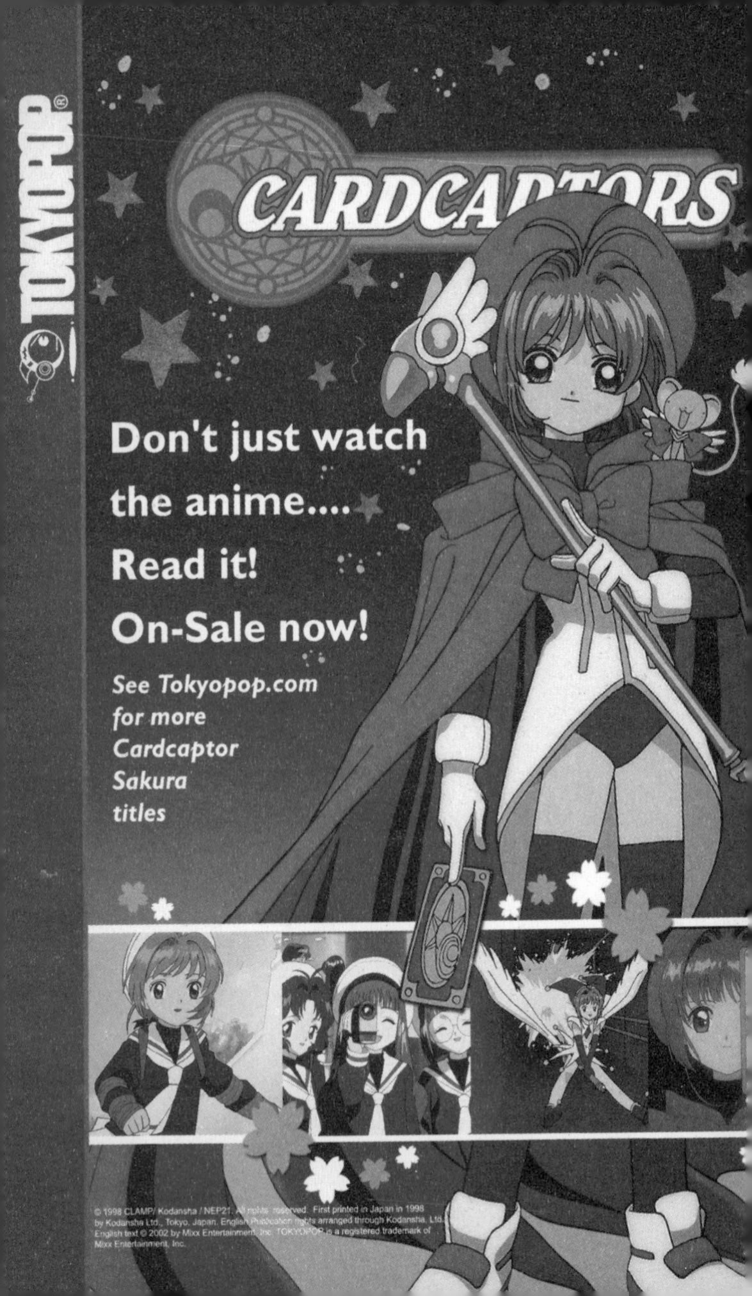
TOKYOPOP®
CARDCAPTORS
Don't just watch
the anime....
Read it!
On-Sale now!
See Tokyopop.com
for more
Cardcaptor
Sakura
titles
© 1998 CLAMP/ Kodansha / NEP21. All rights reserved. First printed in Japan in 1998
by Kodansha Ltd., Tokyo, Japan. English Publication rights arranged through Kodansha, Ltd.
English text © 2002 by Mixx Entertainment, Inc. TOKYOPOP is a registered trademark of
Mixx Entertainment, Inc.